CSET MSAT:
101
102
103
Multiple Subjects
Teacher Certification Exam

By: Sharon Wynne, M.S
Southern Connecticut State University

"And, while there's no reason yet to panic, I think it's only prudent that we make preparations to panic."

XAMonline, INC.
Boston

XAMonline, Inc.
21 Orient Ave.
Melrose, MA 02176
Toll Free 1-800-301-4647
Email: info@xamonline.com
Web www.xamonline.com
Fax: 1-781-662-9268

Library of Congress Cataloging-in-Publication Data

Wynne, Sharon A.
    MSAT: Multiple Subjects 101, 102, 103: Teacher Certification / Sharon A. Wynne. -2nd ed.
    ISBN 978-1-58197-803-2
        1. MSAT: Multiple Subjects 101, 102, 103   2. Study Guides.   3. CSET.
    4. Teachers' Certification & Licensure.   5. Careers

Disclaimer:

The opinions expressed in this publication are the sole works of XAMonline and were created independently from the National Education Association, Educational Testing Service, or any State Department of Education, National Evaluation Systems or other testing affiliates.

Between the time of publication and printing, state specific standards as well as testing formats and website information may change that is not included in part or in whole within this product. Sample test questions are developed by XAMonline and reflect similar content as on real tests; however, they are not former tests. XAMonline assembles content that aligns with state standards but makes no claims nor guarantees teacher candidates a passing score. Numerical scores are determined by testing companies such as NES or ETS and then are compared with individual state standards. A passing score varies from state to state.

Printed in the United States of America

CSET: MSAT Multiple Subjects 101, 102, 103
ISBN: 978-1-58197-803-2

TABLE OF CONTENTS

CONTENT AREA – SCIENCE

DOMAIN I – PHYSICAL SCIENCE

DOMAIN II – LIFE SCIENCE

COMPETENCY 35.0 STRUCTURE OF LIVING ORGANISMS AND THEIR FUNCTION

COMPETENCY 36.0 LIVING AND NON-LIVING COMPONENTS IN ENVIRONMENTS

CONTENT AREA – VISUAL AND PERFORMING ARTS

DOMAIN I – DANCE

DOMAIN III – INFLUENCE ON DEVELOPMENT FROM BIRTH THROUGH ADOLESCENCE

Great Study and Testing Tips!

What to study in order to prepare for the subject assessments is the focus of this study guide but equally important is *how* you study.

You can increase your chances of truly mastering the information by taking some simple, but effective steps.

Study Tips:

1. <u>Some foods aid the learning process</u>. Foods such as milk, nuts, seeds, rice, and oats help your study efforts by releasing natural memory enhancers called CCKs (*cholecystokinin*) composed of *tryptophan*, *choline*, and *phenylalanine*. All of these chemicals enhance the neurotransmitters associated with memory. Before studying, try a light, protein-rich meal of eggs, turkey, and fish. All of these foods release the memory enhancing chemicals. The better the connections, the more you comprehend.

Likewise, before you take a test, stick to a light snack of energy boosting and relaxing foods. A glass of milk, a piece of fruit, or some peanuts all release various memory-boosting chemicals and help you to relax and focus on the subject at hand.

2. <u>Learn to take great notes</u>. A by-product of our modern culture is that we have grown accustomed to getting our information in short doses (i.e. TV news sound bites or USA Today style newspaper articles.)

Consequently, we've subconsciously trained ourselves to assimilate information better in <u>neat little packages</u>. If your notes are scrawled all over the paper, it fragments the flow of the information. Strive for clarity. Newspapers use a standard format to achieve clarity. Your notes can be much clearer through use of proper formatting. A very effective format is called the *"Cornell Method."*

> Take a sheet of loose-leaf lined notebook paper and draw a line all the way down the paper about 1-2" from the left-hand edge.

> Draw another line across the width of the paper about 1-2" up from the bottom. Repeat this process on the reverse side of the page.

Look at the highly effective result. You have ample room for notes, a left hand margin for special emphasis items or inserting supplementary data from the textbook, a large area at the bottom for a brief summary, and a little rectangular space for just about anything you want.

3. Get the concept then the details. Too often we focus on the details and don't gather an understanding of the concept. However, if you simply memorize only dates, places, or names, you may well miss the whole point of the subject.

A key way to understand things is to put them in your own words. If you are working from a textbook, automatically summarize each paragraph in your mind. If you are outlining text, don't simply copy the author's words.

Rephrase them in your own words. You remember your own thoughts and words much better than someone else's, and subconsciously tend to associate the important details to the core concepts.

4. Ask Why? Pull apart written material paragraph by paragraph and don't forget the captions under the illustrations.

Example: If the heading is "Stream Erosion", flip it around to read "Why do streams erode?" Then answer the questions.

If you train your mind to think in a series of questions and answers, not only will you learn more, but it also helps to lessen the test anxiety because you are used to answering questions.

5. Read for reinforcement and future needs. Even if you only have 10 minutes, put your notes or a book in your hand. Your mind is similar to a computer; you have to input data in order to have it processed. *By reading, you are creating the neural connections for future retrieval.* The more times you read something, the more you reinforce the learning of ideas.

Even if you don't fully understand something on the first pass, *your mind stores much of the material for later recall.*

6. Relax to learn so go into exile. Our bodies respond to an inner clock called biorhythms. Burning the midnight oil works well for some people, but not everyone.

If possible, set aside a particular place to study that is free of distractions. Shut off the television, cell phone, and pager and exile your friends and family during your study period.

If you really are bothered by silence, try background music. Light classical music at a low volume has been shown to aid in concentration over other types. Music that evokes pleasant emotions without lyrics is highly suggested. Try just about anything by Mozart. It relaxes you.

7. <u>Use arrows not highlighters</u>. At best, it's difficult to read a page full of yellow, pink, blue, and green streaks. Try staring at a neon sign for a while and you'll soon see that the horde of colors obscure the message.

A quick note, a brief dash of color, an underline, and an arrow pointing to a particular passage is much clearer than a horde of highlighted words.

8. <u>Budget your study time</u>. Although you shouldn't ignore any of the material, *allocate your available study time in the same ratio that topics may appear on the test.*

Testing Tips:

1. <u>**Get smart, play dumb.**</u> **Don't read anything into the question.** Don't make an assumption that the test writer is looking for something else than what is asked. Stick to the question as written and don't read extra things into it.

2. <u>**Read the question and all the choices *twice* before answering the question.**</u> You may miss something by not carefully reading, and then re-reading both the question and the answers.

If you really don't have a clue as to the right answer, leave it blank on the first time through. Go on to the other questions, as they may provide a clue as to how to answer the skipped questions.

If later on, you still can't answer the skipped ones . . . *Guess.* The only penalty for guessing is that you *might* get it wrong. Only one thing is certain; if you don't put anything down, you will get it wrong!

3. <u>**Turn the question into a statement.**</u> Look at the way the questions are worded. The syntax of the question usually provides a clue. Does it seem more familiar as a statement rather than as a question? Does it sound strange?

By turning a question into a statement, you may be able to spot if an answer sounds right, and it may also trigger memories of material you have read.

4. <u>**Look for hidden clues.**</u> It's actually very difficult to compose multiple-foil (choice) questions without giving away part of the answer in the options presented.

In most multiple-choice questions you can often readily eliminate one or two of the potential answers. This leaves you with only two real possibilities and automatically your odds go to Fifty-Fifty for very little work.

5. <u>**Trust your instincts.**</u> For every fact that you have read, you subconsciously retain something of that knowledge. On questions that you aren't really certain about, go with your basic instincts. **Your first impression on how to answer a question is usually correct.**

6. <u>**Mark your answers directly on the test booklet.**</u> Don't bother trying to fill in the optical scan sheet on the first pass through the test.

Just be very careful not to miss-mark your answers when you eventually transcribe them to the scan sheet.

7. <u>**Watch the clock!**</u> You have a set amount of time to answer the questions. Don't get bogged down trying to answer a single question at the expense of 10 questions you can more readily answer.

CONTENT AREA – READING, LANGUAGE ARTS AND LITERATURE

DOMAIN I – LANGUAGE AND LINGUISTICS

COMPETENCY 1.0 LANGUAGE STRUCTURE AND LINGUISTICS

Skill 1.1   Identify and demonstrate an understanding of the fundamental components of human language, including phonology, morphology, syntax, and semantics, as well as the role of pragmatics in using language to communicate.

Phonics

As opposed to phonemic awareness, the study of phonics must be done with the eyes open. It's the connection between the sounds and letters on a page. In other words, students learning phonics might see the word "bad" and sound each letter out slowly until they recognize that they just said the word.

Phonological awareness means the ability of the reader to recognize the sound of spoken language. This recognition includes how these sounds can be blended together, segmented (divided up), and manipulated (switched around). This awareness then leads to phonics, a method for teaching children to read. It helps them "sound out words."

Development of phonological skills may begin during pre-K years. Indeed by the age of 5, a child who has been exposed to rhyme can recognize a rhyme. Such a child can demonstrate phonological awareness by filling in the missing rhyming word in a familiar rhyme or rhymed picture book.

You teach children phonological awareness when you teach them the sounds made by the letters, the sounds made by various combinations of letters and to recognize individual sounds in words.

Phonological awareness skills include:

I. Rhyming and syllabification
2. Blending sounds into words—such as pic-tur-bo-k
3. Identifying the beginning or starting sounds of words and the ending or closing sounds of words
4. Breaking words down into sounds-also called "segmenting" words
5. Recognizing other smaller words in the big word, by removing starting sounds, "hear" to ear

Phonemic Awareness
See Skill 1.2

Morphology, Syntax and Semantics

Morphology is the study of word structure. When readers develop morphemic skills, they are developing an understanding of patterns they see in words. For example, English speakers realize that cat, cats, and caterpillar share some similarities in structure. This understanding helps readers to recognize words at a faster and easier rate, since each word doesn't need individual decoding.

Syntax refers to the rules or patterned relationships that correctly create phrases and sentences from words. When readers develop an understanding of syntax, they begin to understand the structure of how sentences are built, and eventually the beginning of grammar.

> Example: "I am going to the movies"
> This statement is syntactically and grammatically correct
>
> Example: "They am going to the movies:
> This statement is syntactically correct since all the words are in their correct place, but it is grammatically incorrect with the use of the word "They" rather than "I."

Semantics refers to the meaning expressed when words are arranged in a specific way. This is where connotation and denotation of words eventually will have a role with readers.

All of these skill sets are important to eventually developing effective word recognition skills, which help emerging readers develop fluency.

Pragmatics

Pragmatics is concerned with the difference between the writer's meaning and the sentence meaning (the literal meaning of the sentence) based on social context. When someone is competent in pragmatics, he or she is able to understand the writer's intended meaning or what the writer is trying to convey. In a simpler sense, pragmatics can be considered the social rules of language.

For example, a child sitting beside her mother at a fancy restaurant after her great-grandmother's funeral looks over to the table next to them. She sees a very elderly woman eating her dessert. "Mom?" she asks, patiently waiting for response. When her mother addresses her, she states loudly, "That woman is old like Grandma. Is she going to die soon too?" Of course embarrassed, the mother hushes her child. However, this is a simple example of immature pragmatics. The child has the vocabulary, the patience to wait her turn, and some knowledge of conversational rules; however, she is not aware that certain topics are socially inappropriate and therefore adapt her language to the situation.

Skill 1.2 **Demonstrate knowledge of phonemic awareness and apply knowledge of similarities and differences among groups of phonemes that vary in their placement and manner of articulation.**

Phonemic awareness is the acknowledgement of sounds and word, for example, a child's realization that some words rhyme. Onset and rhyme, for example, are skills that might help students learn that the sound of the first letter "b" in the word "bad" can be changed with the sound "d" to make it "dad." The key in phonemic awareness is that when you teach it to children, it can be taught with the students' eyes closed. In other words, it's all about sounds, not about ascribing written letters to sounds.

To be phonemically aware, means that the reader and listener can recognize and manipulate specific sounds in spoken words. Phonemic awareness deals with sounds in words that are spoken. The majority of phonemic awareness tasks, activities, and exercises are ORAL.

Since the ability to distinguish between individual sounds, or phonemes, within words is a prerequisite to association of sounds with letters and manipulating sounds to blend words—a fancy way of saying "reading," the teaching of phonemic awareness is crucial to emergent literacy (early childhood K-2 reading instruction). Children need a strong background in phonemic awareness in order for phonics instruction (sound –spelling relationship-printed materials) to be effective.

Theorist Marilyn Jager Adams who researches early reading has outlined five basic types of phonemic awareness tasks.

Task 1- Ability to hear rhymes and alliteration.
For example, the children would listen to a poem, rhyming picture book or song and identify the rhyming words heard which the teacher might then record or list on an experiential chart.

Task 2- Ability to do oddity tasks (recognize the member of a set that is different [odd} among the group.
For example, the children would look at the pictures of a blade of grass, a garden and a rose—which starts with a different sound?

Task 3 –The ability to orally blend words and split syllables.
For example, the children can say the first sound of a word and then the rest of the word and put it together as a single word.

Task 4 –The ability to orally segment words.
For example, the ability to count sounds. The children would be asked as a group to count the sounds in "hamburger."

Task 5- The ability to do phonics manipulation tasks.
For example, replace the "r" sound in rose with a "p" sound.

The role of phonemic awareness in reading development

Children who have problems with phonics generally have not acquired or been exposed to phonemic awareness activities usually fostered at home and in preschool-2. This includes extensive songs, rhymes and read –alouds.

Instructional Methods

Since the ability to distinguish between individual sounds, or phonemes, within words is a prerequisite to association of sounds with letters and manipulating sounds to blend words—a fancy way of saying "reading," the teaching of phonemic awareness is crucial to emergent literacy (early childhood K-2 reading instruction). Children need a strong background in phonemic awareness in order for phonics instruction (sound –spelling relationship-printed materials) to be effective.

Instructional methods that may be effective for teaching phonemic awareness can include:
- Clapping syllables in words
- Distinguishing between a word and a sound
- Using visual cues and movements to help children understand when the speaker goes from one sound to another
- Incorporating oral segmentation activities which focus on easily distinguished syllables rather than sounds
- Singing familiar songs (e.g. Happy Birthday, Knick Knack Paddy Wack) and replacing key words in it with words with a different ending or middle sound (oral segmentation)
- Dealing children a deck of picture cards and having them sound out the words for the pictures on their cards or calling for a picture by asking for its first and second sound.

Knowledge of Phonemes

In everyday language, we attach affective meanings to words unconsciously; we exercise more conscious control of informative connotations. In the process of language development, the student must come not only to grasp the definitions of words but also to become more conscious of the affective connotations and how his listeners process these connotations. Gaining this conscious control over language makes it possible to use language appropriately in various situations and to evaluate its uses in literature and other forms of communication.

The manipulation of language for a variety of purposes is the goal of language instruction. Advertisers and satirists are especially conscious of the effect word choice has on their audiences. By evoking the proper responses from readers/listeners, we can prompt them to take action.

A phoneme is the smallest contrastive unit in a language system, and the representation of a sound. The phoneme has been described as the smallest meaningful psychological unit of sound. The phoneme is said to have mental, physiological, and physical substance: our brains process the sounds; the sounds are produced by the human speech organs; and the sounds are physical entities that can be recorded and measured. Consider the English words "pat" and "sat," which appear to differ only in their initial consonants. This difference, known as contrastiveness or opposition, is adequate to distinguish these words, and therefore the P and S sounds are said to be different phonemes in English. A pair of words, identical except for such a sound, is known as a minimal pair, and the two sounds are separate phonemes.

Where no minimal pair can exists to demonstrate that two sounds are distinct, it may be that they are allophones. Allophones are variant phones (sounds) that are not recognized as distinct by a speaker, and are not meaningfully different in the language, and so are perceived as being the same. An example of this would be the heavy sounding "L" when landed on at the end of a word like "wool," as opposed to the lighter sounding "L" when starting a word like "leaf." This demonstrates allophones of a single phoneme. While it may exist and be measurable, such a difference is unrecognizable and meaningless to the average English speaker. The real value is as a technique for teaching reading and pronunciation. Identifying phonemes for students and applying their use is a step in the process of developing language fluency.

EXAMPLES OF COMMON PHONEMES APPLIED

Phoneme	Uses
/A/	a (table), a_e (bake), ai (train), ay (say)
/a/	a (flat)
/b/	b (ball)
/k/	c (cake), k (Key), ck (back)
/d/	d (door)
/E/	e (me), ee (feet), ea (leap), y (baby)
/e/	e (pet), ea (head)
/f/	f (fix), ph (phone)
/g/	g (gas)
/h/	h (hot)
/I/	i (I), i_e (bite), igh (light), y (sky)
/i/	i (sit)
/j/	j (jet), dge (edge), g (gem)
/l/	l (lamp)
/m/	m (map)

/n/	n (no), kn (knock)
/O/	o (okay), o_e (bone), oa (soap), ow (low)
/o/	o (hot)
/p/	p (pie)
/kw/	qu (quick)
/r/	r (road), wr (wrong), er (her), ir (sir), ur (fur)
/s/	s (say), c (cent)
/t/	t (time)
/U/	u (future), u_e (use), ew (few)
/u/	u thumb, a (about)
/v/	v (voice)
/w/	w (wash)
/gz/	x (exam)
/ks/	x (box)
/y/	y (yes)
/z/	z (zoo), s (nose)
/OO/	oo (boot), u (truth), u_e (rude), ew (chew)
/oo/	oo (book), u (put)
/oi/	oi (soil), oy (toy)
/ou/	ou (out), ow (cow)
/aw/	aw (saw), au (caught), al (tall)
/ar/	ar (car)
/sh/	sh (ship), ti (nation), ci (special)
/hw/	wh (white)
/ch/	ch (chest), tch (catch)
/th/	th (thick)
/th̲/	th (this)
/ng/	ng (sing)
/zh/	s (measure)

Choice of the medium through which the message is delivered to the receiver is a significant factor in controlling language. Spoken language relies as much on the gestures, facial expression, and tone of voice of the speaker as on the words he speaks. Slapstick comics can evoke laughter without speaking a word. Young children use body language overtly and older children more subtly to convey messages. These refinings of body language are paralleled by an ability to recognize and apply the nuances of spoken language. To work strictly with the written work, the writer must use words to imply the body language.

By the time children begin to speak, they have begun to acquire the ability to use language to inform and manipulate. They have already used kinesthetic and verbal cues to attract attention when they seek some physical or emotional gratification. Children learn to apply names to objects and actions. They learn to use language to describe the persons and events in their lives and to express their feelings about the world around them.

Skill 1.3   Candidates know the differences between phoneme awareness and phonics.

Phonics is a widely used method for teaching students to read. This method includes studying the rules and patterns found in language. By age 5 or 6, children can typically begin to use phonics to begin to understand the connections between letters, their patterns, vowel sounds (i.e., short vowels, long vowels) and the collective sounds they all make.

Phonemic awareness is the ability to break down and hear separate and/or different sounds and distinguish between the sounds one hears. These terms are different, however they are interdependent. Phonemic awareness is required to begin studying phonics, where students will require the ability to break down words into the smalls units of sound, or phonemes, to later identify syllables, blends, and patterns.

For more information on these terms, see Skills 1.1 and 1.2.

Skill 1.4   Knowledge of the predictable patterns of sound-symbol and symbol-sound relationships in English (the Alphabetic Principle)

Alphabetic Principle

The Alphabetic Principle is sometimes called Graphophonemic Awareness. This multi-syllabic technical reading foundation term details the understanding that written words are composed of patterns of letters which represent the sounds of spoken words.

There are basically two parts to the alphabetic principle:
- An understanding that words are made up of letters and that each of these letters has a specific sound
- The correspondence between sounds and letters leads to phonological reading. This consists of reading regular and irregular words and doing advanced analysis of words.

Since the English language is dependant on the alphabet, being able to recognize and sound out letters is the first step for beginning readers. Relying simply on memorization for recognition of words is just not feasible as a way for children to learn to recognize words. Therefore decoding is essential. The most important goal of beginning reading teachers is to teach students to decode text so that they can read fluently and with understanding.

There are four basic features of the alphabetic principle:
1. Students need to be able to take spoken words apart and blend different sounds together to make new words
2. Students need to apply letter sounds to all their reading
3. Teachers need to use a systematic effective program in order to teach children to read
4. The teaching of the alphabetic principle usually begins in Kindergarten.

It is important to keep in mind that some children already know the letters and sounds before they come to school. Others may catch on to this quite quickly and still others need to have one-on-one instruction in order to learn to read.

Critical skills that students need to learn are:
- Letter sound correspondence
- How to sound out words
- How to decode text to make meaning

Skill 1.5 Identify examples of parts of speech, and their functions, as well as the morphology contributing to their classification

English grammar, in conventional use, classifies words based on the following eight parts of speech,

1) The VERB: essential to a sentence, a verb asserts something about the subject of the sentence and expresses action, event, or state of being. The verb is the critical element of the predicate of a sentence.
2) The NOUN: a word used to name/identify a person, animal, place, thing, or abstract idea. Within the structure of a sentence, a noun can function as a subject, a direct or indirect object, a subject or object complement, an appositive, and adjective, or an adverb.
3) The PRONOUN: can be substituted for a noun or another pronoun. Pronoun classifications include the personal pronoun, the demonstrative pronoun, the interrogative pronoun, the indefinite pronoun, the relative pronoun, the reflexive pronoun, and the intensive pronoun. The appropriate use of pronouns (e.g.,"he," "which," "none," "you") can make sentences less cumbersome and less repetitive-and, therefore, more readable.
4) The ADJECTIVE: modifies a noun or a pronoun by describing, identifying, or quantifying words. An adjective usually precedes the noun or the pronoun which it modifies.
5) The ADVERB: can modify a verb, an adjective, another adverb, a phrase, or a clause. An adverb indicates manner, time, place, cause, or degree and answers questions such as "how," "when," "where," "how much." While some adverbs can be identified by their characteristic "ly" suffix, most adverbs must be identified by analyzing the grammatical relationships within the sentence or clause as a whole. Unlike the adjective, the adverb can be found in various places within the sentence.

6) The <u>PREPOSITION</u>: links nouns, pronouns and phrases to other words in a sentence. The word or phrase that the preposition introduces is the <u>object</u> of the preposition. A preposition usually indicates the temporal, spatial or logical relationship of its object to the rest of the sentence (e.g., <u>on</u>, <u>beneath</u>, <u>against</u>, <u>beside</u>, <u>over</u>, <u>during</u>).

7) The <u>CONJUNTION</u>: is used to link words, phrases or clauses. For independent clauses, phrases and individual words, use <u>coordinating conjunctions</u> (e.g., <u>and</u>, <u>but</u>, <u>or</u>, <u>nor</u>, <u>for</u>, <u>so</u>, <u>yet</u>). To introduce a dependent clause and indicate the nature of a relationship between the independent clause and dependent clause, use a <u>subordinating conjunction</u> (e.g., <u>after</u>, <u>although</u>, <u>as</u>, <u>because</u>, <u>before</u>, <u>how</u>, <u>if</u>, <u>once</u>, <u>since</u>, <u>than</u>, <u>that</u>, <u>though</u>, <u>till</u>, <u>until</u>, <u>when</u>, <u>where</u>, <u>whether</u>, <u>while</u>). Equivalent sentence elements would be linked with <u>correlative conjunctions</u>, which always appear in pairs (e.g., <u>both...and</u>, <u>either...or</u>, <u>neither...nor</u>, <u>not only...but also</u>, <u>so...as</u>, <u>whether...or</u>). Strictly speaking, correlative conjunctions consist simply of a coordinating conjunction linked to an adjective or adverb.

8) The <u>INTERJECTION</u>: is a word added to a sentence to convey emotion, and usually compels the sentence to be closed with an exclamation mark. It is not grammatically related to any other part of the sentence. Some examples would be "ouch," "hey," "wow," "oh no."

It is important to remember that each <u>part of speech</u> explains <u>not what the word is</u>, but <u>how the word is used</u>. In some instances (for example), the same word can be used as a noun in one sentence and as a verb or adjective in the next.

Skill 1.6   They recognize and use syntactic components to understand and develop a variety of sentence types.

Clauses

Clauses are connected word groups that are composed of at least one subject and one verb. A subject is the doer of an action or the element that is being joined. A verb conveys either the action or the link.

<u>Students</u> are <u>waiting</u> for the start of the assembly.
subject   verb

At the end of the play, <u>students</u> <u>wait</u> for the curtain to come down.
                       subject   verb

Clauses can be independent or dependent. Independent clauses can stand alone or can be joined to other clauses. Dependent clauses, by definition, contain at least one subject and one verb. However, they cannot stand alone as a complete sentence. They are structurally dependent on the main clause.

Sentences

Sentences are made up of two parts: the subject and the predicate. The subject (like in the clause section above) is the doer of an action or the element that is being joined. In addition, any adjectives describing this doer or element are also part of the subject. The predicate is made up of the verb and any other adverbs, adjectives, pronouns or clauses that describe the action of the sentence.

A simple sentence contains one independent clause which contains one subject, one verb, and one predicate.

In the following examples, the subject is underlined once and the predicate is underlined twice.

> The dancer bowed.

> Nathan skied down the hill.

A compound sentence is made up of two independent clauses which are joined by a conjunction, a correlative conjunction (i.e., either-or, neither-nor) or a semicolon. Both of these independent clauses could stand on their own, but for sentence variety, authors will often combine two independent clauses.

In the following examples, the subjects of each independent clause are underlined once, and the predicates of each independent clause are underlined twice. The conjunction is in bold.

> Samantha ate the cookie, **and** she drank her milk.

> Mark is excellent with computers; he has worked with them for years.

> **Either** Terry runs the project **or** I will not participate.

A complex sentence is made up of one independent clause and at least one dependent clause. In the following examples, the subjects of each clause are underlined once, and the predicates are underlined twice. The independent clause is in plain text, and the dependent clause is in italics.

> When Jody saw how clean the house was, she was happy.

> Brian loves taking diving lessons, which he has done for years.

COMPETENCY 2.0 LANGAUGE DEVELOPMENT AND ACQUISITION

Skill 2.1 Apply knowledge of both the development of a first language and the acquisition of subsequent ones, as well as describe the principal observable milestones in each domain, and identify the major theories that attempt to explain the processes of development and acquisition.

One of the most important things to know about the differences between L1 (first language) and L2 (second language) acquisition is that people usually will master L1, but they will almost never be fully proficient in L2. However, if children can be trained in L2 before about the age of seven, their chances at full mastery will be much higher. Children learn language with so little effort, which is why they can be babbling one year and speaking with complete, complex ideas just a few years later. It is important to know that language is innate, meaning that our brains are ready to learn a language from birth. Yet a lot of language learning is behavioral, meaning that children imitate adults' speech.

Stages of Language Acquisition

There is wide agreement that there are generally five stages of second language development. The first stage is "pre-production." While these students may actually understand what someone says to them (for the most part), they have a much harder time talking back in the target language. Teachers must realize that if a student cannot "produce" the target language, it does not mean that they aren't learning. Most likely, they are. They are taking it in, and their brains are trying to figure out what to do with all the new language.

The second phase is early production. This is where the student can actually start to produce the target language. It is quite limited, and teachers most likely should not expect students to produce eloquent speeches during this time.

The third phase is emergent speech or speech emergence. Longer, more complex sentences are used, particularly in speech—and in social situations. But remember that students aren't fully fluent in this stage, and they cannot handle complex academic language tasks.

The fourth phase is intermediate fluency. This is where more complex language is produced. Grammatical errors are common.

The fifth stage is advanced fluency. While students may appear to be completely fluent, though, they will still need academic and language support from teachers.

Many people say that there are prescribed amounts of time by which students should reach each stage. However, keep in mind that it depends on the level at which students are exposed to the language. For example, students who get opportunities to practice with the target language outside of school may have greater ease in reaching the fifth stage quicker. In general, though, it does take years to reach the fifth stage, and students should never be expected to have complete mastery within one school year.

Theories of Language Acquisition

L2 acquisition is much harder for adults. Multiple theories of L2 acquisition have come about. Some of the more notable ones come from Jim Cummins. Cummins argues that there are two types of language that usually need to be acquired by students learning English as a second language: Basic Interpersonal Communication Skills (BICS) Cognitive Academic Language Proficiency (CALP). BICS is general, everyday language used to communicate simple thoughts, whereas CALP is the more complex, academic language used in school. It is harder for students to acquire CALP, and many teachers mistakenly assume that students can learn complex academic concepts in English if they have already mastered BICS. The truth is that CALP takes much longer to master, and in some cases, particularly with little exposure in certain subjects, it may never be mastered.

Another set of theories is based on Stephen Krashen's research in L2 acquisition. Most people understand his theories based on five principles:

1. The acquisition-learning hypothesis: This states that there is a difference between learning a language and acquiring it. Children "acquire" a first language easily—it's natural. But adults often have to "learn" a language through coursework, studying, and memorizing. One can acquire a second language, but often it requires more deliberate and natural interaction within that language.
2. The monitor hypothesis: This is when the learned language "monitors" the acquired language. In other words, this is when a person's "grammar check" kicks in and keeps awkward, incorrect language out of a person's L2 communication.
3. The natural order hypothesis: This suggests that the learning of grammatical structures is predictable and follows a "natural order."
4. The input hypothesis: Some people call this "comprehensible input." This means that a language learner will learn best when the instruction or conversation is just above the learner's ability. That way, the learner has the foundation to understand most of the language, but still will have to figure out, often in context, what that extra more difficult element means.
5. The affective filter hypothesis: This suggests that people will learn a second language when they are relaxed, have high levels of motivation, and have a decent level of self-confidence.

Skill 2.2   Demonstrate and understanding of the range of issues related to the interaction of first languages and other languages.

Teaching students who are learning English as a second language poses some unique challenges, particularly in a standards-based environment. The key is realizing that no matter how little English a student knows, the teacher should teach with the student's developmental level in mind. This means that instruction should not be "dumbed-down" for ESOL students. Different approaches should be used, however, to ensure that these students (a) get multiple opportunities to learn and practice English and (b) still learn content.

Many ESOL approaches are based on social learning methods. By being placed in mixed level groups or by being paired with a student of another ability level, students will get a chance to practice English in a natural, non-threatening environment. Students should not be pushed in these groups to use complex language or to experiment with words that are too difficult. They should simply get a chance to practice with simple words and phrases.

In teacher-directed instructional situations, visual aids, such as pictures, objects, and video are particularly effective at helping students make connections between words and items they are already familiar with

ESOL students may need additional accommodations with assessments, assignments, and projects. For example, teachers may find that written tests provide little to no information about a student's understanding of the content. Therefore, an oral test may be better suited for ESOL students. When students are somewhat comfortable and capable with written tests, a shortened test may actually be preferable; take note that they will need extra time to translate.

Skill 2.3   Recognize special features that may identify a pupil's language development as exceptional, distinguishing such features from inter-language effects.

The concept of readiness is generally regarded as a developmentally-based phenomenon. Various abilities, whether cognitive, affective, or psychomotor, are perceived to be dependent upon the mastery or development of certain prerequisite skills or abilities. Readiness, then, implies that the necessary prior knowledge, experience, and readiness prerequisites should not engage in the new task until first acquiring the necessary readiness foundation.

It should be noted, then, that a concept such as "readiness to learn" is too broad to be meaningful. Readiness needs to be considered in terms of readiness to "learn science" or, even more accurately, readiness to "learn photosynthesis." Since it is not feasible for the classroom teacher to assess each student's readiness for each lesson, mastery of one lesson is generally assumed to imply readiness for the next sequential lesson.

However, at each grade level, there exist readiness expectations and assumptions based on the previous year's instruction. Students who have not yet mastered those concepts are not ready to progress. Failure on the part of the teacher to address student deficiencies may lead to failure of the student to learn the new material.

Readiness for subject area learning is dependent not only on prior knowledge, but also on affective factors such as interest, motivation, and attitude. These factors are often more influential on student learning than the pre-existing cognitive base.

COMPETENCY 3.0 LITERACY

Skill 3.1   Understand and use the major descriptions of developing literacy.

In 2000, the National Reading Panel released its now well-known report on teaching children to read. In a way, this report slightly put to rest the debate between phonics and whole-language. It argued, essentially, that word-letter recognition was important, as was understanding what the text means. The report's "big 5" critical areas of reading instruction are as follows:

- Phonemic Awareness
- Phonics
- Fluency
- Comprehension
- Vocabulary

Methods used to teach these skills are often featured in a "balanced literacy" curriculum that focuses on the use of skills in various instructional contexts. For example, with independent reading, students independently choose and books that are at their reading levels; with guided reading, teachers work with small groups of students to help them with their particular reading problems; with whole group reading, the entire class will read the same text, and the teacher will incorporate activities to help students learn phonics, comprehension, fluency, and vocabulary. In addition to these components of balanced literacy, teachers incorporate writing so that students can learn the structures of communicating through text.

Phonemic Awareness
See Skill 1.2

Phonics

As opposed to phonemic awareness, the study of phonics must be done with the eyes open. It's the connection between the sounds and letters on a page. In other words, students learning phonics might see the word "bad" and sound each letter out slowly until they recognize that they just said the word.

Phonological awareness means the ability of the reader to recognize the sound of spoken language. This recognition includes how these sounds can be blended together, segmented (divided up), and manipulated (switched around). This awareness then leads to phonics, a method for teaching children to read. It helps them "sound out words."

Development of phonological skills may begin during pre-K years. Indeed by the age of 5, a child who has been exposed to rhyme can recognize a rhyme. Such a child can demonstrate phonological awareness by filling in the missing rhyming word in a familiar rhyme or rhymed picture book.

You teach children phonological awareness when you teach them the sounds made by the letters, the sounds made by various combinations of letters and to recognize individual sounds in words.

Phonological awareness skills include:
      I. Rhyming and syllabification
      2. Blending sounds into words—such as pic-tur-bo-k
      3. Identifying the beginning or starting sounds of words and the ending or closing sounds of words
      4. Breaking words down into sounds-also called "segmenting" words
      5. Recognizing other smaller words in the big word, by removing starting sounds, "hear" to ear

Fluency
      See Skill 8.2

Comprehension
      See Skill 3.2

Vocabulary
      See Skill 3.3

The typical variation in literacy backgrounds that children bring to reading can make teaching more difficult. Often a teacher has to choose between focusing on the learning needs of a few students at the expense of the group or focusing on the group at the risk of leaving some students behind academically. This situation is particularly critical for children with gaps in their literacy knowledge who may be at risk in subsequent grades for becoming "diverse learners."

Areas of Emerging Evidence

1. **Experiences with print (through reading and writing) help preschool children develop an understanding of the conventions, purpose, and functions of print.** Children learn about print from a variety of sources and in the process come to realize that print carries the story. They also learn how text is structured visually (i.e., text begins at the top of the page, moves from left to right, and carries over to the next page when it is turned). While knowledge about the conventions of print enables children to understand the physical structure of language, the conceptual knowledge that printed words convey a message also helps children bridge the gap between oral and written language.

2. **Phonological awareness and letter recognition** contribute to initial reading acquisition by helping children develop efficient word recognition strategies (e.g., detecting pronunciations and storing associations in memory.) Phonological awareness and knowledge of print-speech relations play an important role in facilitating reading acquisition. Therefore, phonological awareness instruction should be an integral component of early reading programs. Within the emergent literacy research, viewpoints diverged on whether acquisition of phonological awareness and letter recognition are preconditions of literacy acquisition or whether they develop interdependently with literacy activities such as story reading and writing.

3. **Storybook reading affects children's knowledge about, strategies for, and attitudes towards reading.** Of all the strategies intended to promote growth in literacy acquisition, none is as commonly practiced, nor as strongly supported across the emergent literacy literature as storybook reading. Children in different social and cultural groups have differing degrees of access to storybook reading. For example, it is not unusual for a teacher to have students who have experienced thousands of hours of story reading time, along with other students who have had little or no such exposure.

Design Principles in Emergent Literacy

Conspicuous Strategies

As an instructional priority, conspicuous strategies are a sequence of teaching events and teacher actions used to help students learn new literacy information and relate it to their existing knowledge. Conspicuous strategies can be incorporated in beginning reading instruction to ensure that all learners have basic literacy concepts. For example, during storybook reading teachers can show students how to recognize the fronts and backs of books, locate titles, or look at pictures and predict the story, rather than assume children will learn this through incidental exposure. Similarly, teachers can teach students a strategy for holding a pencil appropriately or checking the form of their letters against an alphabet sheet on their desks or the classroom wall.

Mediated Scaffolding

Mediated scaffolding can be accomplished in a number of ways to meet the needs of students with diverse literacy experiences. To link oral and written language, for example, teachers may use texts that simulate speech by incorporating oral language patterns or children's writing. Or teachers can use daily storybook reading to discuss book-handling skills and directionality-concepts that are particularly important for children who are unfamiliar with printed texts.

Teachers can also use repeated readings to give students multiple exposures to unfamiliar words or extended opportunities to look at books with predictable patterns, as well as provide support by modeling the behaviors associated with reading. Teachers can act as scaffolds during these storybook reading activities by adjusting their demands (e.g., asking increasingly complex questions or encouraging children to take on portions of the reading) or by reading more complex text as students gain knowledge of beginning literacy components.

Strategic Integration

Many children with diverse literacy experiences have difficulty making connections between old and new information. Strategic integration can be applied to help link old and new learning. For example, in the classroom, strategic integration can be accomplished by providing access to literacy materials in classroom writing centers and libraries. Students should also have opportunities to integrate and extend their literacy knowledge by reading aloud, listening to other students read aloud, and listening to tape recordings and videotapes in reading corners.

Primed Background Knowledge

All children bring some level of background knowledge (e.g., how to hold a book, awareness of directionality of print) to beginning reading. Teachers can utilize children's background knowledge to help children link their personal literacy experiences to beginning reading instruction, while also closing the gap between students with rich and students with impoverished literacy experiences. Activities that draw upon background knowledge include incorporating oral language activities (which discriminate between printed letters and words) into daily read-alouds, as well as frequent opportunities to retell stories, look at books with predictable patterns, write messages with invented spellings, and respond to literature through drawing.

Emergent Literacy

Emergent literacy research examines early literacy knowledge and the contexts and conditions that foster that knowledge. Despite differing viewpoints on the relation between emerging literacy skills and reading acquisition, strong support was found in the literature for the important contribution that early childhood exposure to oral and written language makes to the facility with which children learn to read.

Reading for comprehension of factual material - content area textbooks, reference books, and newspapers - is closely related to study strategies in the middle/junior high. Organized study models, such as the SQ3R method, a technique that makes it possible and feasible to learn the content of even large amounts of text (Survey, Question, Read, Recite, and Review Studying), teach students to locate main ideas and supporting details, recognize sequential order, distinguish fact from opinion, and to determine cause/ effect relationships.

Instructional Strategies

1. Teacher-guided activities that require students to organize and to summarize information based on the author's explicit intent are pertinent strategies in middle grades. Evaluation techniques include oral and written responses to standardized or teacher-made worksheets.

2. Reading of fiction introduces and reinforces skills in inferring meaning from narration and description. Teaching-guided activities in the process of reading for meaning should be followed by cooperative planning of the skills to be studied and of the selection of reading resources. Many printed reading for comprehension instruments as well as individualized computer software programs exist to monitor the progress of acquiring comprehension skills.

3. Older middle school students should be given opportunities for more student-centered activities - individual and collaborative selection of reading choices based on student interest, small group discussions of selected works, and greater written expression. Evaluation techniques include teacher monitoring and observation of discussions and written work samples.

4. Certain students may begin some fundamental critical interpretation - recognizing fallacious reasoning in news media, examining the accuracy of news reports and advertising, explaining their reasons for preferring one author's writing to another's. Development of these skills may require a more learning-centered approach in which the teacher identifies a number of objectives and suggested resources from which the student may choose his course of study. Self-evaluation through a reading diary should be stressed. Teacher and peer evaluation of creative projects resulting from such study is encouraged.

5. Reading aloud before the entire class as a formal means of teacher evaluation should be phased out in favor of one-to-one tutoring or peer-assisted reading. Occasional sharing of favored selections by both teacher and willing students is a good oral interpretation basic.

Skill 3.2 **In both English speakers and English learners, candidates can identify the progressive development of phonemic awareness, decoding, comprehension, word recognition, and spelling.**

There are many factors that impact someone's ability to pick up a second or third language. Age is one common factor. It is said that after a certain age (usually seven), learning a second language becomes dramatically harder. But there are also many social factors, such as anxiety, that influence language learning. Often, informal, social settings are more conducive to second language learning. Motivation is another factor, obviously. A final important factor, particularly for teachers, is the strategies one uses to learn a language. For example, memorizing words out of context is not as effective as using words strategically for a real-life purpose.

The most important concept to remember regarding the difference between learning a first language and a second one is that if the learner is approximately age seven or older, learning a second language will occur very differently in the learner's brain than it will had the learner been younger. The reason for this is that there is a language-learning function that exists in young children that appears to go away as they mature. Learning a language prior to age seven is almost guaranteed, with relatively little effort. The mind is like a sponge, and it soaks up language very readily. Some theorists, including the famous linguist Noam Chomsky, argue that the brain has a "universal grammar" and that only vocabulary and very particular grammatical structures, related to specific languages, need to be introduced in order for a child to learn a language. What this really means is that, in essence, there are slots into which language gets filled in a child's mind. This is definitely not the case with learning a second language after about seven years old.

Learning a second language as a pre-adolescent, adolescent or adult requires quite a bit of translation from the first language to the second. Vocabulary and grammar particulars are memorized, not necessarily internalized (at least, as readily as a first language). In fact, many (though not all) people who are immersed in a second language never fully function as fluent in the language. They may appear to be totally fluent, but often there will be small traits that are hard to pick up and internalize.

It is fairly clear that learning a second language successfully does require fluency in the first language. This is because, as stated above, the second language is translated from the first in the learner's mind. First language literacy is also a crucial factor in second language learning, particularly second language literacy.

When helping second language learners make the "cross-over" in language fluency or literacy from first language to second language, it is important to help them identify strategies they use in the first language and apply those to the second language. It is also important to note similarities and differences in phonetic principals in the two languages. Sometimes it is helpful to encourage students to translate; other times, it is helpful for them to practice production in the target language. In either case, teachers must realize that learning a second language is a slow and complicated process.

Comprehension

Comprehension simply means that the reader can ascribe meaning to text. Even though students may be good with phonics and even know what many words on a page mean, some of them are not good with comprehension because they do not know the strategies that would help them to comprehend. For example, students should know that stories often have structures (beginning, middle, and end). They should also know that when they are reading something and it does not make sense, they will need to employ "fix-up" strategies where they go back into the text they just read and look for clues. Teachers can use many strategies to teach comprehension, including questioning, asking students to paraphrase or summarize, utilizing graphic organizers, and focusing on mental images.

Decoding, Word Recognition, & Spelling

Word analysis (a.k.a. phonics or decoding) is the process readers use to figure out unfamiliar words based on written patterns. Word recognition is the process of automatically determining the pronunciation and some degree of the meaning of an unknown word. In other words, fluent readers recognize most written words easily and correctly, without consciously decoding or breaking them down. These elements of literacy below are skills readers need for word recognition.

To decode means to change communication signals into messages. Reading comprehension requires that the reader learn the code within which a message is written and be able to decode it to get the message. Encoding involves changing a message into symbols. For example to encode oral language into writing (spelling) or to encode an idea into words or to encode a mathematical or physical idea into appropriate mathematical symbols.

Although effective reading comprehension requires identifying words automatically (Adams, 1990, Perfetti, 1985), children do not have to be able to identify every single word or know the exact meaning of the every word in a text to understand it. Indeed, Nagy (1988) says that, children can read a work with a high level of comprehension even if they do not fully know as many as 15 percent of the words within a given text. Children develop the ability to decode and recognize words automatically.

They then can extend their ability to decode to multi-syllabic words.

Spelling instruction should include words misspelled in daily writing, generalizing spelling knowledge, and mastering objectives in progressive phases of development. Developmental stages of spelling:

1) **Pre-phonemic spelling**—Children know that letters stand for a message, but they do not know the relationship between spelling and pronunciation.

2) **Early phonemic spelling**—Children are beginning to understand spelling. They usually write the beginning letter correctly, with the rest consonants or long vowels.

3) **Letter-name spelling**—Some words are consistently spelled correctly. The student is developing a sight vocabulary and a stable understanding of letters as representing sounds. Long vowels are usually used accurately, but silent vowels are omitted. Unknown words are spelled by the child attempting to match the name of the letter to the sound.

4) **Transitional spelling**—This phase is typically entered in late elementary school. Short vowel sounds are mastered and some spelling rules known. They are developing a sense of which spellings are correct and which are not.

5) **Derivational spelling**—This is usually reached from high school to adulthood. This is the stage where spelling rules are being mastered.

For more information on **phonemic awareness**, see Skill 1.2

For more information on the **alphabet principle**, see Skill 1.4

For more information on **phonics**, see Skill 3.1

Skill 3.3 **Understand how these processes interact with the development of concepts, of vocabulary (including relationships among etymologies and both denotative and connotative word meanings), and of contextual analysis.**

The National Reading Panel has put forth the following conclusions about vocabulary instruction.

1. There is a need for direct instruction of vocabulary items required for a specific text.
2. Repetition and multiple exposures to vocabulary items are important. Students should be given items that will be likely to appear in many contexts.
3. Learning in rich contexts is valuable for vocabulary learning. Vocabulary words should be those that the learner will find useful in many contexts. When vocabulary items are derived from content learning materials, the learner will be better equipped to deal with specific reading matter in content areas.
4. Vocabulary tasks should be restructured as necessary. It is important to be certain that students fully understand what is asked of them in the context of reading rather than focusing only on the words to be learned.
5. Vocabulary learning is effective when it entails active engagement in learning tasks.
6. Computer technology can be used effectively to help teach vocabulary.
7. Vocabulary can be acquired through incidental learning. Much of a student's vocabulary will have to be learned in the course of doing things other than explicit vocabulary learning. Repetition, richness of context, and motivation may also add to the efficacy of incidental learning of vocabulary.
8. Dependence on a single vocabulary instruction method will not result in optimal learning. A variety of methods were used effectively with emphasis on multimedia aspects of learning, richness of context in which words are to be learned, and the number of exposures to words that learners receive.

The Panel found that a critical feature of effective classrooms is the instruction of specific words that includes lessons and activities where students apply their vocabulary knowledge and strategies to reading and writing. Included in the activities were discussions where teachers and students talked about words, their features, and strategies for understanding unfamiliar words.

There are many methods for directly and explicitly teaching words. In fact, the Panel found twenty-one methods that have been found effective in research projects. Many emphasize the underlying concept of a word and its connections to other words such as semantic mapping and diagrams that use graphics. The keyword method uses words and illustrations that highlight salient features of meaning. Visualizing or drawing a picture either by the student or by the teacher was found to be effective. Many words cannot be learned in this way, of course, so it should be used as only one method among others. Effective classrooms provide multiple ways for students to learn and interact with words. The Panel also found that computer-assisted activities can have a very positive role in the development of vocabulary.

COMPETENCY 4.0 ASSESSMENT

Skill 4.1 **Apply knowledge of the implications that language development and differences have for the processes of learning to read and reading to learn.**

If there were two words which can be synonymous with reading comprehension as far as the balanced literacy approach is concerned, they would be "Constructing Meaning."

Cooper, Taberski, Strickland, and other key theorists and classroom teachers, conceptualize the reader as designating a specific meaning to the text using both clues in the text and his/her own prior knowledge. Comprehension for the balanced literacy theorists is a strategic process.

The reader interacts with the text and brings his/her prior knowledge and experience to it or LACK of prior knowledge and experience to it. Writing is interlaced with reading and is a mutually integrative and supportive parallel process. Hence the division of literacy learning by the balanced literacy folks into reading workshop and writing workshop, with the same anchor "readings: or books being used for both.

Consider the sentence, "The test booklet was white with black print, but very scary looking."

According to the idea of constructing meaning as the reader read this sentence, the schemata (generic information stored in the mind) of tests he or she was personally activated by the author's ideas that tests are scary. Therefore the ultimate meaning that the reader derives from the page is from the reader's own responses and experiences with the ideas the author presents. The reader constructs a meaning that reflects the author's intent and also the reader's response to that intent.

It is also to be remembered that generally readings are fairly lengthy passages, comprised of paragraphs which in turn are comprised of more than one sentence. With each successive sentence, and every new paragraph, the reader refocuses. The schemata are reconsidered, and a new meaning is constructed.

Language development is definitively paralleled along the physiological development of the learner. The cognitive processes that occur during the physical development have been documented in the writings of Piaget and Kohlberg's cognitive learning theories.

Piaget's developmental intellectual stages projects that children possess schemas that include various concepts and intellectual stages. As children develop physically, their cognitive development incorporates the experiences of the environment and facilitates learning into specific schemas. Children acquire life experiences that they assimilate into projected behaviors. New information is accommodated into the assimilation of new experiences and cognitive development becomes more complex.

Applying Piaget's theories to the process of learning to read and reading to learn means that children are able to develop and assimilate environment and educational cues and learnings that develop reading skills as they get older. Once the cognitive development is able to accommodate even great amounts of learning, the child is able to reverse the experience to assimilate reading into a learning experience that then becomes foundational for the learner. The exposure of the child to learning experiences increases the assimilation of the experience into that child's cognitive development.

Skill 4.2   They know and apply a range of assessment methods and instruments to the respective and interrelated developing abilities in listening (for aural/oral languages), speaking, reading (decoding and comprehension), vocabulary, and spelling conventions

Assessment skills should be an integral part of teacher training where teachers are able to monitor student learning using pre and post assessments of content areas; analyze assessment data in terms of individualized support for students and instructional practice for teachers; and designing lesson plans that have measurable outcomes and definitive learning standards. Assessment information should be used to provide performance-based criteria and academic expectations for all students in evaluating whether students have learned the expected skills and content of the subject area.

Teachers can use assessment data to inform and impact instructional practices by making inferences on teaching methods and gathering clues for student performance. By analyzing the various types of assessments, teachers can gather more definitive information on projected student academic performance. Instructional strategies for teachers would provide learning targets for student behavior, cognitive thinking skills, and processing skills that can be employed to diversify student learning opportunities.

Assessment for learning is the main focus which teachers should employ. Instead of testing simply to find out what students have learned, teachers need to assess to find out what students need to learn. In this way assessment drives the instruction. By assessing students prior knowledge, keeping notes on what they can and cannot do, teachers are better able to help students that need extra instruction and allow those students that are succeeding to move on to higher order skills and challenges.

Some of the different methods that teachers can employ to assess for learning involve both formative and summative evaluation. Since formative assessment consists of testing, these do play a part. However, teachers can make summative assessment part of their daily routine by using such measures as:

- Anecdotal records
- Portfolios
- Listening to children read
- Oral presentations
- Checklists
- Running records
- Samples of work
- Self-evaluation

Information gathered from all of these sources provides the teacher with the material he/she needs to determine how much help students need to become independent readers and to communicate to parents about how their children are doing.

DOMAIN II – NON-WRITTEN AND WRITTEN COMMUNICATION

COMPETENCY 5.0 CONVENTIONS OF LANGUAGE

Skill 5.1 **Identify and use the conventions associated with what is called standard English.**

Conventions for language that appears in print have been developed over several centuries; they change somewhat from generation to generation but compared to the use of language in electronic media, they are fairly static. On the other hand, language use in radio and television has undergone rapid changes. Listening to a radio show from the thirties is a step back in time. The intonation had its own peculiar qualities. Even in its own time, it would not have been recognized as a conversation between two people. Listening to President Franklin Delano Roosevelt's "fireside chats" also takes us back in time, not only because of the content of the speeches but also by the way they were delivered. "Declamation" is a good term for the radio presentation style of that day and even the style of public speeches to some extent. It was notable for rhetorical effect or display. The same is true of television. Listening to early television news shows— Edward R. Murrow, for example—reminds us instantly of an earlier time. It followed in the style of the radio shows. It was declamatory in nature and sounded more like an announcement than a conversation.

Radio and television speech nowadays is much more conversational in tone. In fact, on many of the news shows, there are two or more news people who will carry on a conversation before, after, and between the news stories. This would have seemed peculiar to earlier listeners.

Candidate teachers should be cognizant of proper rules and conventions of punctuation, capitalization, and spelling. Competency exams will generally test the ability to apply the more advanced skills; thus, a limited number of more frustrating rules is presented here. Rules should be applied according to the American style of English, i.e. spelling theater instead of theatre and placing terminal marks of punctuation almost exclusively within other marks of punctuation. The most common conventions are discussed below:

Spelling

Concentration in this section will be on spelling plurals and possessives. The multiplicity and complexity of spelling rules based on phonics, letter doubling, and exceptions to rules - not mastered by adulthood - should be replaced by a good dictionary. As spelling mastery is also difficult for adolescents, our recommendation is the same. Learning the use of a dictionary and thesaurus will be a more rewarding use of time.

Most plurals of nouns that end in hard consonants or hard consonant sounds followed by a silent e are made by adding s. Some words ending in vowels only add s.

fingers, numerals, banks, bugs, riots, homes, gates, radios, bananas

Nouns that end in soft consonant sounds s, j, x, z, ch, and sh, add es. Some nouns ending in o add es.

dresses, waxes, churches, brushes, tomatoes, potatoes

Nouns ending in y preceded by a vowel just add s.

boys, alleys

Nouns ending in y preceded by a consonant change the y to i and add es.

babies, corollaries, frugalities, poppies

Some nouns plurals are formed irregularly or remain the same.

sheep, deer, children, leaves, oxen

Some nouns derived from foreign words, especially Latin, may make their plurals in two different ways - one of them Anglicized. Sometimes, the meanings are the same; other times, the two plurals are used in slightly different contexts. It is always wise to consult the dictionary.

appendices, appendixes   criterion, criteria
indexes, indices   crisis, crises

Make the plurals of closed (solid) compound words in the usual way except for words ending in ful which make their plurals on the root word.

timelines, hairpins, cupsful

Make the plurals of open or hyphenated compounds by adding the change in inflection to the word that changes in number.

fathers-in-law, courts-martial, masters of art, doctors of medicine

Make the plurals of letters, numbers, and abbreviations by adding s.

fives and tens, IBMs, 1990s, ps and qs (Note that letters are italicized.)

Sentence completeness

Avoid fragments and run-on sentences. Recognition of sentence elements necessary to make a complete thought, proper use of independent and dependent clauses, and proper punctuation will correct such errors.

Capitalization

Capitalize all proper names of persons (including specific organizations or agencies of government); places (countries, states, cities, parks, and specific geographical areas); and things (political parties, structures, historical and cultural terms, and calendar and time designations); and religious terms (any deity, revered person or group, sacred writings).

Percy Bysshe Shelley, Argentina, Mount Rainier National Park, Grand Canyon, League of Nations, the Sears Tower, Birmingham, Lyric Theater, Americans, Midwesterners, Democrats, Renaissance, Boy Scouts of America, Easter, God, Bible, Dead Sea Scrolls, Koran

Capitalize proper adjectives and titles used with proper names.

California gold rush, President John Adams, French fries, Homeric epic, Romanesque architecture, Senator John Glenn

Note: Some words that represent titles and offices are not capitalized unless used with a proper name.

Capitalized	Not Capitalized
Congressman McKay	the congressman from Florida
Commander Alger	commander of the Pacific Fleet
Queen Elizabeth	the queen of England

Capitalize all main words in titles of works of literature, art, and music. (See "Using Italics" in the Punctuation section.)

Punctuation

In a quoted statement that is either declarative or imperative, place the period inside the closing quotation marks.

"The airplane crashed on the runway during takeoff."

If the quotation is followed by other words in the sentence, place a comma inside the closing quotations marks and a period at the end of the sentence.

"The airplane crashed on the runway during takeoff," said the announcer.

In most instances in which a quoted title or expression occurs at the end of a sentence, the period is placed before either the single or double quotation marks.

"The middle school readers were unprepared to understand Bryant's poem 'Thanatopsis.'"

Early book-length adventure stories like Don Quixote and The Three Musketeers were known as "picaresque novels."

There is an instance in which the final quotation mark would precede the period - if the content of the sentence were about a speech or quote so that the understanding of the meaning would be confused by the placement of the period.

The first thing out of his mouth was "Hi, I'm home."
but
The first line of his speech began "I arrived home to an empty house".

In sentences that are interrogatory or exclamatory, the question mark or exclamation point should be positioned outside the closing quotation marks if the quote itself is a statement or command or cited title.

Who decided to lead us in the recitation of the "Pledge of Allegiance"?

Why was Tillie shaking as she began her recitation, "Once upon a midnight dreary..."?

I was embarrassed when Mrs. White said, "Your slip is showing"!

In sentences that are declarative but the quotation is a question or an exclamation, place the question mark or exclamation point inside the quotation marks.

The hall monitor yelled, "Fire! Fire!"

"Fire! Fire!" yelled the hall monitor.

Cory shrieked, "Is there a mouse in the room?" (In this instance, the question supersedes the exclamation.)

Commas

Separate two or more coordinate adjectives, modifying the same word and three or more nouns, phrases, or clauses in a list.

Maggie's hair was dull, dirty, and lice-ridden.

Dickens portrayed the Artful Dodger as skillful pickpocket, loyal follower of Fagin, and defendant of Oliver Twist.

Ellen daydreamed about getting out of the rain, taking a shower, and eating a hot dinner.

In Elizabethan England, Ben Johnson wrote comedy, Christopher Marlowe wrote tragedies, and William Shakespeare composed both.

Use commas to separate antithetical or complimentary expressions from the rest of the sentence.

The veterinarian, not his assistant, would perform the delicate surgery.

The more he knew about her, the less he wished he had known.

Randy hopes to, and probably will, get an appointment to the Naval Academy.

His thorough, though esoteric, scientific research could not easily be understood by high school students.

Using semicolons

Use semicolons to separate independent clauses when the second clause is introduced by a transitional adverb. (These clauses may also be written as separate sentences, preferably by placing the adverb within the second sentence.)

The Elizabethans modified the rhyme scheme of the sonnet; thus, it was called the English sonnet.
                              or
The Elizabethans modified the rhyme scheme of the sonnet. It thus was called the English sonnet.

Use semicolons to separate items in a series that are long and complex or have internal punctuation.

The Italian Renaissance produced masters in the fine arts: Dante

Alighieri, author of the Divine Comedy; Leonardo da Vinci, painter of The Last Supper; and Donatello, sculptor of the Quattro Coronati, the four saints.

The leading scorers in the WNBA were Haizhaw Zheng, averaging 23.9 points per game; Lisa Leslie, 22; and Cynthia Cooper, 19.5.

Using colons

Place a colon at the beginning of a list of items. (Note its use in the sentence about Renaissance Italians on the previous page.)

The teacher directed us to compare Faulkner's three symbolic novels: Absalom, Absalom; As I Lay Dying; and Light in August.

Do **not** use a comma if the list is preceded by a verb.

Three of Faulkner's symbolic novels are Absalom, Absalom; As I Lay Dying, and Light in August.

Subject-verb agreement

A verb agrees in number with its subject. Making them agree relies on the ability to properly identify the subject.

One of the boys was playing too rough.
No one in the class, not the teacher nor the students, was listening to the message from the intercom.
The candidates, including a grandmother and a teenager, are debating some controversial issues.

If two singular subjects are connected by and the verb must be

plural. A man and his dog were jogging on the beach.

If two singular subjects are connected by or or nor, a singular verb is required.

Neither Dot nor Joyce has missed a day of school this year. Either Fran or Paul is missing.

If one singular subject and one plural subject are connected by or or nor, the verb agrees with the subject nearest to the verb.

Neither the coach nor the players were able to sleep on the bus.

If the subject is a collective noun, its sense of number in the sentence determines the verb: singular if the noun represents a group or unit and plural if the noun represents individuals.

> The <u>House of Representatives</u> <u>has adjourned</u> for the holidays.

> The <u>House of Representatives</u> <u>have failed</u> to reach agreement on the subject of adjournment.

Use of verbs (tense)

Present tense is used to express that which is currently happening or is always true.

> Randy is playing the piano.

> Randy plays the piano like a pro.

Past tense is used to express action that occurred in a past time.

> Randy learned to play the piano when he was six years old.

Future tense is used to express action or a condition of future time.

> Randy will probably earn a music scholarship.

Present perfect tense is used to express action or a condition that started in the past and is continued to or completed in the present.

> Randy has practiced piano every day for the last ten years. Randy has never been bored with practice.

Past perfect tense expresses action or a condition that occurred as a precedent to some other action or condition.

> Randy had considered playing clarinet before he discovered the piano.

Future perfect tense expresses action that started in the past or the present and will conclude at some time in the future.

> By the time he goes to college, Randy will have been an accomplished pianist for more than half of his life.

Use of verbs (mood)

Indicative mood is used to make unconditional statements; subjunctive mood is used for conditional clauses or wish statements that pose conditions that are untrue. Verbs in subjunctive mood are plural with both singular and plural subjects.

> If I were a bird, I would fly.

> I wish I were as rich as Donald Trump.

Verb conjugation

The conjugation of verbs follows the patterns used in the discussion of tense above. However, the most frequent problems in verb use stem from the improper formation of past and past participial forms.

> Regular verb: believe, believed, (have) believed

> Irregular verbs: run, ran, run; sit, sat, sat; teach, taught, taught

Other problems stem from the use of verbs that are the same in some tense but have different forms and different meanings in other tenses.

> I lie on the ground. I lay on the ground yesterday. I have lain down.

> I lay the blanket on the bed. I laid the blanket there
> yesterday. I have laid the blanket every night.

> The sun rises. The sun rose. The sun has risen.

> He raises the flag. He raised the flag. He had raised the flag.
> I sit on the porch. I sat on the porch. I have sat in the porch swing.

> I set the plate on the table. I set the plate there yesterday. I
> had set the table before dinner.

Two other verb problems stem from misusing the preposition of for the verb auxiliary have and misusing the verb ought (now rare).

> Incorrect: I should of gone to bed.
> Correct: I should have gone to bed.

> Incorrect: He hadn't ought to get so angry.
> Correct: He ought not to get so angry.

Use of pronouns

A pronoun used as a subject of predicate nominative is in nominative case.

> She was the drum majorette. The lead trombonists were Joe and he. The band director accepted whoever could march in step.

A pronoun used as a direct object, indirect object or object of a preposition is in objective case.

> The teacher praised him. She gave him an A on the test. Her praise of him was appreciated. The students whom she did not praise will work harder next time.

Common pronoun errors occur from misuse of reflexive

> pronouns: Singular: myself, yourself, herself, himself,

> itself Plural: ourselves, yourselves, themselves.

> Incorrect: Jack cut hisself shaving.
> Correct: Jack cut himself shaving.

> Incorrect: They backed theirselves into a

> corner. Correct: They backed themselves

> into a corner.

Use of adjectives

An adjective should agree with its antecedent in number.

> Those apples are rotten. This one is ripe. These peaches are hard.

Comparative adjectives end in -er and superlatives in -est, with some exceptions like worse and worst. Some adjectives that cannot easily make comparative inflections are preceded by more and most.

> Mrs. Carmichael is the better of the two basketball

> coaches. That is the hastiest excuse you have ever

> contrived.

Avoid double comparisons.

Incorrect: This is the worstest headache I ever

had. Correct: This is the worst headache I

ever had.

When comparing one thing to others in a group, exclude the thing under comparison from the rest of the group.

Incorrect: Joey is larger than any baby I have ever seen. (Since you have
seen him, he cannot be larger than himself.)
Correct: Joey is larger than any other baby I have ever seen.

Include all necessary word to make a comparison clear in meaning.

I am as tall as my mother. I am as tall as she (is).
My cats are better behaved than those of my neighbor.

Skill 5.2   Recognize, understand, and use a range of conventions in both spoken and written English, including varieties of sentence structure, preferred usage and conventional forms of spelling, capitalization and punctuation in written English.

See Skill 5.1

COMPETENCY 6.0 WRITING STRATEGIES

Skill 6.1 Describe the stages of the writing process.

Writing is a recursive process. As students engage in the various stages of writing, they develop and improve not only their writing skills, but their thinking skills as well. Students must understand that writing is a process and typically involves many steps when writing quality work. No matter the level of writer, students should be experienced in the following stages of the writing process. The stages of the writing process are as follows:

Prewriting

Students gather ideas before writing. Prewriting may include clustering, listing, brainstorming, mapping, free writing, and charting. Providing many ways for a student to develop ideas on a topic will increase his/her chances for success. Remind students that as they prewrite they need to consider their audience.

Drafting

Students compose the first draft. Students should follow their notes/writing plan from the prewriting stage.

Revision and Editing

Revise comes from the Latin word revidere, meaning, "to see again." Revision is probably the most important step for the writer in the writing process. Here, students examine their work and make changes in wording, details and ideas. So many times, students write a draft and then feel they're done. On the contrary – students must be encouraged to develop, change, and enhance their writing as they go, as well as once they've completed a draft.

As you discuss revision, you begin with discussing the definition of revise. Also, state that all writing must be revised to improve it. After students have revised their writing, it is time for the final editing and proofreading.

Proofreading

Students proofread the draft for punctuation and mechanical errors. There are a few key points to remember when helping students learn to edit and proofread their work.

- It is crucial that students are not taught grammar in isolation, but in context of the writing process
- Ask students to read their writing and check for specific errors like using a subordinate clause as a sentence

- Provide students with a proofreading checklist to guide them as they edit their work

Publishing

Students may have their work displayed on a bulletin board, read aloud in class, or printed in a literary magazine or school anthology.

It is important to realize that these steps are recursive; as a student engages in each aspect of the writing process, he or she may begin with prewriting, write, revise, write, revise, edit, and publish. They do not engage in this process in a lockstep manner; it is more circular.

Skill 6.2   Understand the purpose and techniques of various prewriting strategies.

Prewriting strategies assist students in a variety of ways. Listed below are the most common prewriting strategies students can use to explore, plan and write on a topic. It is important to remember when teaching these strategies that not all prewriting must eventually produce a finished piece of writing. In fact, in the initial lesson of teaching prewriting strategies, it might be more effective to have students practice prewriting strategies without the pressure of having to write a finished product.

- Keep an idea book so that they can jot down ideas that come to mind
- Write in a daily journal
- Write down whatever comes to mind; this is called free writing. Students do not stop to make corrections or interrupt the flow of ideas.

A variation of this technique is focused free writing - writing on a specific topic - to prepare for an essay.

- Make a list of all ideas connected with their topic; this is called brainstorming
- Make sure students know that this technique works best when they let their mind work freely. After completing the list, students should analyze the list to see if a pattern or way to group the ideas
- Ask the questions Who? What? When? Where? When? and How? Help the writer approach a topic from several perspectives
- Create a visual map on paper to gather ideas. Cluster circles and lines to show connections between ideas. Students should try to identify the relationship that exists between their ideas. If they cannot see the relationships, have them pair up, exchange papers and have their partners look for some related ideas
- Observe details of sight, hearing, taste, touch, and taste

- Visualize by making mental images of something and write down the details in a list

After they have practiced with each of these prewriting strategies, ask them to pick out the ones they prefer and ask them to discuss how they might use the techniques to help them with future writing assignments. It is important to remember that they can use more than one prewriting strategy at a time. Also they may find that different writing situations may suggest certain techniques.

Most libraries will only allow the downloading and printing of 75 pages of information during any given month. The point is to provide the user with hardcopy of specific information in a limited and environmentally friendly manner. Libraries limit the number of pages that could be wasted during a singular download which limits the number of trees needed to conduct Internet research and subsequent printing. Once the information is collected and categorized according to the research design and outline, the user can begin to take notes on the gathered information to create a cut and paste format for the final report.

Being effective note takers require consistent technique whether the mode of note taking is on 5X7 note cards; lined notebook; or on a computer. Organizing all collected information according to a research outline will allow the user to take notes on each section and begin the writing process. If the computer is used, then the actual format of the report can be word-processed and information input to speed up the writing process of the final research report. Creating a title page and the bibliography page will allow each downloaded report to have its resources cited immediately in that section.

Note taking involves identification of specific resources that include the author's or organization's name, year of publication, title, publisher location and publisher. When taking notes, whether on the computer or using note cards, use the author's last name and page number on cited information. In citing information for major categories and subcategories on the computer, create a file for notes that includes summaries of information and direct quotes. When direct quotes are put into a word file, the cut and paste process for incorporation into the report is quick and easy.

In outline information, it is crucial to identify the headings and subheadings for the topic being researched. When researching information, it is easier to cut and paste information under the indicated headings in creating a visual flow of information for the report. In the actual drafting of the report, the writer is able to lift direct quotations and citations from the posted information to incorporate in the writing.

Skill 6.3   **Revise and edit writing, drawing upon their understanding of principles of organization, transitions, point-of-view, word-choices, and conventions.**

Both teachers and students should be aware of the difference between these two writing processes. Revising typically entails substantial changes to a written draft, and it is during this process that the look, idea and feel of a draft may be altered, sometimes significantly. Like revising, editing continues to make changes to a draft; however the chances made during the editing process do more to enhance the ideas in the draft, rather than change or alter them. Finally, proofreading is the stage where grammatical and technical errors are addressed.

Effective teachers realize that revision and editing go hand-in-hand and those students often move back and forth between these stages during the course of one written work. Also, these stages must be practiced in small groups, pairs and/or individually. Students must learn to analyze and improve their own work as well as the works of their peers. Some methods to use include:

1. Students, working in pairs, analyze sentences for variety.
2. Students work in pairs or groups to ask questions about unclear areas in the writing or to help students add details, information, etc.
3. Students perform final edit.

Many teachers introduce Writer's Workshop to their students to maximize learning about the writing process. Writer's Workshops vary across classrooms, but the main idea is for students to become comfortable with the writing process to produce written work. A basic Writer's Workshop will include a block of classroom time committed to writing various projects (i.e., narratives, memoirs, book summaries, fiction, book reports, etc). Students use this time to write, meet with others to review/edit writing, make comments on writing, revise their own work, proofread, meet with the teacher, and publish their work.

Teachers who facilitate effective Writer's Workshops are able to meet with students one at a time and can guide that student in their individual writing needs. This approach allows the teacher to differentiate instruction for each student's writing level.

Students need to be trained to become effective at proofreading, revising and editing strategies. Begin by training them using both desk-side and schedule conferences. Listed below are some strategies to use to guide students through the final stages of the writing process (and these can easily be incorporated into Writer's Workshop).

- Provide some guide sheets or forms for students to use during peer responses
- Allow students to work in pairs and limit the agenda

- Model the use of the guide sheet or form for the entire class
- Give students a time limit or number of written pieces to be completed in a specific amount of time
- Have the students read their partners' papers and ask at least three who, what, when, why, how questions. The students answer the questions and use them as a place to begin discussing the piece
- At this point in the writing process a mini-lesson that focuses on some of the problems your students are having would be appropriate

To help students revise, provide students with a series of questions that will assist them in revising their writing

- Do the details give a clear picture? Add details that appeal to more than just the sense of sight.
- How effectively are the details organized? Reorder the details if it is needed.
- Are the thoughts and feelings of the writer included? Add personal thoughts and feelings about the subject.

Gone are the days when students engage in skill practice with grammar worksheets. Grammar needs to be taught in the context of the students' own work. Listed below is a series of classroom practices that encourage meaningful context-based grammar instruction, combined with occasional mini-lessons and other language strategies that can be used on a daily basis.

* Connect grammar with the student's own writing while emphasizing grammar as a significant aspect of effective writing.

* Emphasize the importance of editing and proofreading as an essential part of classroom activities.

* Provide students with an opportunity to practice editing and proofreading cooperatively.

* Give instruction in the form of 15-20 minute mini-lessons.

* Emphasize the sound of punctuation by connecting it to pitch, stress, and pause.

* Involve students in all facets of language learning including reading, writing, listening, speaking and thinking. Good use of language comes from exploring all forms of it on a regular basis.

There are a number of approaches that involve grammar instruction in the context of the writing.

1.   Sentence Combining—try to use the student's own writing as much as possible. The theory behind combining ideas and the correct punctuation should be emphasized.

2.   Sentence and paragraph modeling—provide students with the opportunity to practice imitating the style and syntax of professional writers.

3.   Sentence transforming—give students an opportunity to change sentences from one form to another, i.e. from passive to active, inverting the sentence order, change forms of the words used.

4.   Daily Language Practice—introduce or clarify common errors using daily language activities. Use actual student examples whenever possible. Correct and discuss the problems with grammar and usage.

See Skill 7.1 for more information on writing with good transitions, vocabulary and overall content.

COMPETENCY 7.0 WRITING APPLICATIONS

Skill 7.1   Demonstrate their knowledge of principles of composition, such as paragraphing, transitional phrases, appropriate vocabulary, and context.

Reading an essay should not take extraordinary effort. Particularly if the concepts are not too complex, reading an essay should not require extensive re-reading. The ideas should be clear and straightforward. Anyone who has tried to write an essay knows that this sounds much easier than it really is! So, how do teachers actually help students to become proficient with writing multi-paragraph essays in ways that allow them to clearly communicate their ideas? The trick is to help them understand that various conventions of writing serve the purpose of making comprehension easier for their readers. Those conventions include good paragraphing, transitions between paragraphs, ideas, and sentences, topic sentences, concluding sentences, appropriate vocabulary, and sufficient context.

Good paragraphing entails dividing up ideas into bite-sized chunks. A good paragraph typically includes a topic sentence that explains the content of the paragraph. A good paragraph also includes sufficient explanation of that topic sentence. So, for example, if a topic sentence suggests that the paragraph will be about the causes of the Civil War, the rest of the paragraph should actually explain specific causes of the Civil War.

As writers transition from one paragraph to another—or sentence to another—they will usually provide transitional phrases that give sign-posts to readers about what is coming next. Words like "however," "furthermore," "although," "likewise," etc., are good ways of communicating intention to readers. When ideas are thrown together on a page, it is hard to tell what the writer is actually doing with those ideas. Therefore, students need to become familiar with using transitional phrases.

Concluding sentences can often be unnecessary, but when done right, they provide a nice "farewell" or closing to a piece of writing. Students do not always need to use concluding sentences in paragraphs; however, they should be alerted to their potential benefits.

When writers use appropriate vocabulary, they are sensitive to the audience and purpose of what they are writing. For example, if I am writing an essay on a scientific concept to a group of non-scientists, I will not use specialized vocabulary to explain concepts. However, if I were writing for a group of scientists, not using that vocabulary may not look so good. It depends on what the writer intends with the piece of writing. Therefore, students need to learn early on that all writing has purpose and that because of that purpose, good writers will make conscious decisions about how to arrange their texts, which words to use, and which examples and metaphors to include.

Finally, when writers provide sufficient context, they ensure that readers do not have to extensively question the text to figure out what is going on. Again, this has a lot to do with knowing the audience. Using the scientific concept example from above, I would need to provide more context if my audience was a group of non-scientists than I would if my audience were scientists. In other words, I would have to provide more background so that the non-scientists could understand the concepts.

Skill 7.2   **Compose and/or analyze writing according to conventions in different genres, including narrative, interpretive, descriptive, persuasive and expository writing, as well as summaries, letters, and research reports.**

Discourse, whether in speaking or writing, falls naturally into four different forms: narrative, descriptive, expository, and persuasive. The first question to be asked when reading a written piece, listening to a presentation, or writing is "What's the point?" This is usually called the thesis. If you are reading an essay, when you've finished, you want to be able to say, "The point of this piece is that the foster-care system in America is a disaster." If it's a play, you should also be able to say, "The point of that play is that good overcomes evil." The same is true of any written document or performance. If it doesn't make a point, the reader/listener/viewer is confused or feels that it's not worth the effort. Knowing this is very helpful when you are sitting down to write your own document, be it essay, poem, or speech. What point do you want to make? We make these points in the forms that have been the structure of western thinking since the Greek Rhetoricians.

Persuasion is a piece of writing, a poem, a play, a speech whose purpose is to change the minds of the audience members or to get them to do something. This is achieved in many ways: (1) The credibility of the writer/speaker might lead the listeners/readers to a change of mind or a recommended action. (2) Reasoning is important in persuasive discourse. No one wants to believe that he accepts a new viewpoint or goes out and takes action just because he likes and trusts the person who recommended it. Logic comes into play in reasoning that is persuasive. (3) The third and most powerful force that leads to acceptance or action is emotional appeal. Even if a person has been persuaded logically, reasonably, that he should believe in a different way, he is unlikely to act on it unless he is moved emotionally. A man with resources might be convinced that people suffered in New Orleans after Katrina, but he will not be likely to do anything about it until he is moved emotionally, until he can see dead bodies floating in the dirty water or elderly people stranded on houses. Sermons are good examples of persuasive discourse.

Exposition is discourse whose only purpose is to inform. Expository writing is not interested in changing anyone's mind or getting anyone to take a certain action. It exists to give information. Some examples are driving directions to a particular place or the directions for putting together a toy that arrives unassembled. The writer doesn't care whether you do or don't follow the directions. She only wants to be sure you have the information in case you do decide to use them.

Narration is discourse that is arranged chronologically—something happened, and then something else happened, and then something else happened. It is also called a story. News reports are often narrative in nature as are records of trips, etc.

Description is discourse whose purpose is to make an experience available through one of the five senses—seeing, smelling, hearing, feeling (as with the fingers), and tasting. Descriptive words are used to make it possible for the reader to "see" with her own mind's eye, hear through her own mind's ear, smell through her own mind's nose, taste with her mind's tongue, and feel with her mind's fingers. This is how language moves people. Only by experiencing an event can the emotions become involved. Poets are experts in descriptive language.

Persuasive writing often uses all forms of discourse. The introduction may be a history or background of the idea being presented—exposition. Details supporting some of the points may be stories—narrations. Descriptive writing will be used to make sure the point is established emotionally.

Paraphrase is the rewording of a piece of writing. The result will not necessarily be shorter than the original. It will use different vocabulary and possibly different arrangement of details. Paraphrases are sometimes written to clarify a complex piece of writing. Sometimes, material is paraphrased because it cannot be borrowed as is for purposes of copyright restraints.

Summary is a distilling of the elements of a piece of writing or speech. It will be much shorter than the original. To write a good summary, the writer must determine what the "bones" of the original piece are. What is its structure? What is the thesis and what are the subpoints? A summary does not make judgments about the original; it simply reports the original in condensed form.

Letters are often expository in nature—their purpose is to give information. However, letters are also often persuasive—the writer wants to persuade or get the recipient to do something. They are also sometimes descriptive or narrative— the writer will share an experience or tell about an event.

Research reports are a special kind of expository writing. A topic is researched—explored by some appropriate means such as searching literature, interviewing experts, or even conducting experiments, and the findings will be written up in such a way that a particular audience may know what was discovered. They can be very simple such as delving into the history of an event or very complex such as a report on a scientific phenomenon that requires complicated testing and reasoning to explain. A research reports often reports possible conclusions but puts forth one as the best answer to the question that inspired the research in the first place, which will become the thesis of the report.

Skill 7.3 Understand and are able to use bibliographic citations in a standard format.

Preparing the bibliographic citations requires an understanding of the various formats for specific citations. The reference listings should be double-spaced and each entry should be alphabetized by last name of author and first name initial or organization name with the second line indented five spaces. For example a book entry would look like the following in APA style:

Casey, B. (2004). Creating resiliency in educational practices. New York: McGraw Hill.

There are two major styles of citations that are used in most reports and research projects: APA and MLA style.

APA style: American Psychological Association

In an in-text citation, APA style would use the following conventions: last name of author and year in parentheses with the page number in parentheses located at the end of the quote or citation. APA style requires an abstract summarizing the thesis of report.

Smith (2006) understands the "role of educational reform and school communication in promoting student achievement" (p. 6).

MLA style: Modern Language Association

In an in-text citation, MLA style would incorporate the following conventions in a research paper: last name and first name of author or organization; title all capital letters underlined; edition number if applicable; state of publication; and year published.

Jones, Mark. How Life Began. 2ⁿᵈ ed. New York: Barron Press, 2006.

Bibliographic Citations: References

Below are sample bibliographic citations that are used in either APA or MLA citation style. It is important the writer use the designated style of writing and citation defined by the institution or agency requesting the report or research project.

Periodicals: journal or magazine articles use the following format.

- Author(s)
- Article title
- Periodical name
- Volume number
- Issue number (if indicated)
- Publication date
- Page numbers

Example: Johnson, Samuel. Examination of Educational Reform. Education Review 45(12). May 2006. 162-189.

Internet Sources-
- Author/Editor
- Title
- Printed version include publication information and date
- Electronic site include title of site; date of posting; and organization hosting website
- URL (Uniform Resource Locator) in brackets
- Don't include page numbers in citation

Example: Article/Nonprint version:
"Weather Safety." National Weather Bureau. N.d. 12 Nov. 2005
http://www.nwb.dot.gov/weather/safety/ .

COMPETENCY 8.0 NON-WRITTEN COMMUNICATION

Skill 8.1 **Demonstrate knowledge of non-written genres and traditions, and their characteristics including narratives, persuasive pieces, research presentations, poetry recitations, and responses to literature.**

The skills needed in order to write an essay always come in handy when trying to prepare a presentation, participate in a discussion on literature, or orally re-tell a story. Non-written genres and traditions that include literary elements contain very systematic organizational structures. Such genres and traditions include, but are not limited to, oral narratives, persuasive rhetoric, research presentations, poetry recitations, and responses to literature.

Narratives are stories, and when orally presented, they often take on a unique flavor and characteristic of the content. For example, slave narratives are often told in the "voice" and persona of 19th Century slaves. Organizationally, narratives are chronological; however, various disruptions in time-sequence can occur—sometimes very suddenly. Occasionally, narratives get side-tracked based on the specific content.

Persuasive pieces are heard in speeches, on television, at political rallies, and in many other places. When a speaker works to persuade an audience of a particular issue, he or she will often present many scenarios or examples that demonstrate why the speaker's opinion is correct. Usually, such pieces will cover up disagreements, and they will often emphasize examples and stories over explaining the actual issue in full detail. The method ensures that people are emotionally and logically persuaded without overtly making it sound as if the issue is being pounded down peoples' throats.

Research presentations are structured similarly to essays. They often present a thesis or over-arching claim/argument. Then, they explicate—or explain—the thesis or argument with examples and details. The point of a research presentation is to provide an audience with enough details so that they will (a) remember the presentation and (b) believe the argument, but not so many that they will become bored with the presentation.

Poetry recitation is different from all other genres listed here as it does not (always) involve the creation of new material. Often, people will recite poetry written by others. However, many poets do enjoy reciting their own poetry in many cases. The point is, though, that poetry recitation involves the reading aloud of written poetry. It stands out in that it requires a careful understanding of the poetry before reading it, as the meaning often will change the way it is read out loud. That is because good poetry recitation involves drama, persona, and charisma.

Finally, responding to literature, particularly in discussions, involves making claims about the literature and then defending those claims with specific details from the text or from personal, real-life experiences. Good responses to literature will make claims about a character's intent, for example, or the importance of the setting in a story. And plenty of details are provided to ensure that fellow discussers will accept such a claim. Often, though, a good piece of literature will provoke many different viewpoints, so while not everyone must agree on a claim, everyone involved in a conversation on the literature should at least be able to see how the claim was arrived at.

Skill 8.2   Apply understandings of language development stages, from pre-production (beginning) to intermediate fluency, to children's developing abilities in such areas.

Learning approach

Early theories of language development were formulated from learning theory research. The assumption was that language development evolved from learning the rules of language structures and applying them through imitation and reinforcement. This approach also assumed that language, cognitive, and social developments were independent of each other. Thus, children were expected to learn language from patterning after adults who spoke and wrote Standard English. No allowance was made for communication through child jargon, idiomatic expressions, or grammatical and mechanical errors resulting from too strict adherence to the rules of inflection (childs instead of children) or conjugation (runned instead of ran). No association was made between physical and operational development and language mastery.

Linguistic approach

Studies spearheaded by Noam Chomsky in the 1950s formulated the theory that language ability is innate and develops through natural human maturation as environmental stimuli trigger acquisition of syntactical structures appropriate to each exposure level. The assumption of a hierarchy of syntax downplayed the significance of semantics. Because of the complexity of syntax and the relative speed with which children acquire language, linguists attributed language development to biological rather than cognitive or social influences.

Cognitive approach

Researchers in the 1970s proposed that language knowledge derives from both syntactic and semantic structures. Drawing on the studies of Piaget and other cognitive learning theorists, supporters of the cognitive approach maintained that children acquire knowledge of linguistic structures after they have acquired the cognitive structures necessary to process language. For example, joining words for specific meaning necessitates sensory motor intelligence. The child must be able to coordinate movement and recognize objects before she can identify words to name the objects or word groups to describe the actions performed with those objects. Children must have developed the mental abilities for organizing concepts as well as concrete operations, predicting outcomes, and theorizing before they can assimilate and verbalize complex sentence structures, choose vocabulary for particular nuances of meaning, and examine semantic structures for tone and manipulative effect.

Socio-cognitive approach

Other theorists in the 1970s proposed that language development results from sociolinguistic competence. Language, cognitive, and social knowledges are interactive elements of total human development. Emphasis on verbal communication as the medium for language expression resulted in the inclusion of speech activities in most language arts curricula.

Unlike previous approaches, the socio-cognitive allowed that determining the appropriateness of language in given situations for specific listeners is as important as understanding semantic and syntactic structures. By engaging in conversation, children at all stages of development have opportunities to test their language skills, receive feedback, and make modifications. As a social activity, conversation is as structured by social order as grammar is structured by the rules of syntax. Conversation satisfies the learner's need to be heard and understood and to influence others. Thus, his choices of vocabulary, tone, and content are dictated by his ability to assess the language knowledge of his listeners. He is constantly applying his cognitive skills to using language in a social interaction. If the capacity to acquire language is inborn, without an environment in which to practice language, a child would not pass beyond grunts and gestures as did primitive man.

Of course, the varying degrees of environmental stimuli to which children are exposed at all age levels creates a slower or faster development of language. Some children are prepared to articulate concepts and recognize symbolism by the time they enter fifth grade because they have been exposed to challenging reading and conversations with well-spoken adults at home or in their social groups. Others are still trying to master the sight recognition skills and are not yet ready to combine words in complex patterns.

When students practice fluency, they practice reading connected pieces of text. In other words, instead of looking at a word as just a word, they might read a sentence straight through. The point of this is that in order for the student to comprehend what she is reading, she would need to be able to "fluently" piece words in a sentence together quickly. If a student is NOT fluent in reading, he or she would sound each letter or word out slowly and pay more attention to the phonics of each word. A fluent reader, on the other hand, might read a sentence out loud using appropriate intonations. The best way to test for fluency, in fact, is to have a student read something out loud, preferably a few sentences in a row— or more. Sure, most students just learning to read will probably not be very fluent right away; but with practice, they will increase their fluency. Even though fluency is not the same as comprehension, it is said that fluency is a good predictor of comprehension. Think about it: If you're focusing too much on sounding out each word, you're not going to be paying attention to the meaning.

During the preschool years, children acquire cognitive skills in oral language that they apply later on to reading comprehension. Reading aloud to young children is one of the most important things that an adult can do because they are teaching children how to monitor, question, predict, and confirm what they hear in the stories. (Reid 1988, p. 165) described four metalinguistic abilities that young children acquire through early involvement in reading activities:

1. Word consciousness. Children who have access to books first can tell the story through the pictures. Gradually they begin to realize the connection between the spoken words and the printed words. The beginning of letter and word discrimination begins in the early years.

2. Language and conventions of print. During this stage children learn the way to hold a book, where to begin to read, the left to right motion, and how to continue from one line to another.

3. Functions of print. Children discover that print can be used for a variety of purposes and functions, including entertainment and information.

4. Fluency. Through listening to adult models, children learn to read in phrases and use intonation.

Mercer and Mercer divide the reading experience into two basic processes: word recognition and word and idea comprehension. Reading programs may differ in how and when these skills are presented.

WORD RECOGNITION	WORD AND IDEA COMPREHENSION
Configuration	Vocabulary Development
Content Analysis	Literal Comprehension
Sight Words	Inferential Comprehension
Phonics Analysis	Evaluation or Critical Reading
Syllabication	Appreciation
Structural Analysis	
Dictionary Analysis	

Skill 8.3   Analyze speech in terms of presentation components, pronunciation fluency, and identify the integration of nonverbal components with verbal elements.

Analyzing the speech of others is a very good technique for helping students improve their own public speaking abilities. Because in most circumstances, students cannot view themselves as they give speeches and presentations, when they get the opportunity to critique, question, and analyze others' speeches, they begin to learn what works and what doesn't work in effective public speaking. However, a very important word of warning: DO NOT have students critique each others' public speaking skills. It could be very damaging to a student to have his or her peers point out what did not work in a speech. Instead, video is a great tool teachers can use. Any appropriate source of public speaking can be used in the classroom for students to analyze and critique.

Some of the things students can pay attention to include the following:

- Volume: A speaker should use an appropriate volume—not too loud to be annoying, but not too soft to be inaudible.
- Pace: The rate at which words are spoken should be appropriate—not too fast to make the speech non-understandable, but not too slow so as to put listeners to sleep.
- Pronunciation: A speaker should make sure words are spoken clearly. Listeners do not have a text to go back and re-read things they didn't catch.
- Body language: While animated body language can help a speech, too much of it can be distracting. Body language should help convey the message, not detract from it.
- Word choice: The words speakers choose should be consistent with their intended purpose and the audience.

- Visual aids: Visual aids, like body language, should enhance a message. Many visual aids can be distracting, and that detracts from the message.

Overall, instead of telling students to keep these above factors in mind when presenting information orally, having them view speakers who these things well and poorly will help them know and remember the next time they give a speech.

Skill 8.4   **Demonstrate knowledge of dialects, idiolects, and changes in what is considered standard oral English usage and their effects on perceptions of speaker performance, with attention to the dangers of stereotyping and bias.**

Although an entire group of Americans may all speak English, they may each have a very unique style of speaking English. Some styles are classified as dialects, which are regional variations in language. For example, words such as "pop" and "soda" are used to describe the same thing in different parts of the country; likewise, in various parts of the country, speech is slow and circular, while in other parts of the country, speech is direct and fast. These are examples of dialectical differences.

Idiolects are individual differences in language. Have you ever heard someone say that a phrase or message sounds like someone you know? For example, you may recognize that your friend speaks in very choppy sentences and uses big words. Or you may notice that your neighbor explains simple ideas through very complex stories. These are all examples of idiolects: they are very specific distinctive features of language in specific people.

Both idiolects and dialects are noticed in words, narrative fashions, sentence structures, and many other facets of language. Often, people consider idiolects and dialects to be non-standard versions of the English language. Truthfully, however, oral English is anything but standard. Due to the large number of speakers in this country, as well as the diversity of geography, ethnicity, and race, variation in oral language is pretty much expected. However, regardless, people still make assumptions about dialect and idiolect. In general, the farther a dialect or idiolect gets away from standard written English language, the more people assume that the individual is uneducated.

While students should not be discouraged to use their own dialects (as dialect can be a very personal and identifying factor for people, often related to their home culture), all students do need to know how to write and speak in standard English. Many successful Americans retain a very strong dialect or idiolect, while being able to also communicate entirely in standard English, both in writing and in oral speech. Helping students understand when to use standard English and when they can use their individualistic languages is a central task that all teachers must pursue on a regular basis.

Skill 8.5   Demonstrate an understanding of the potential impact on non-written presentations of images, sound, and other features from electronic media.

Non-standard forms of English, including regional dialects and personal idiolects, impact non-written presentations of images, sound, and other features of electronic media in a few ways. Most notably, the reputation of the media is negatively affected when standard forms of English are not used in textual and auditory versions of language. Yet, images and sounds that are devoid of language still communicate a significant amount to viewers and listeners, and those elements still carry considerable weight about the values, levels of education, and levels of "normalcy" inherent in the producers of such media.

Let's put this in classroom terminology. While images that are associated with gangs and drugs are indeed pervasive in youth culture, teachers can help students understand that certain values are communicated when those images are used in multi-media presentations, for example. Teachers should help students understand that while personal expression is fine in certain circumstances, a professional presentation, devoid of elements that are generally considered to be deviant, is best.

Another way to understand this is strictly in terms of more individualized and/or regional methods of presentation of material in electronic, visual, or auditory form. While individual and cultural differences SHOULD indeed be highlighted, students also need to understand basic elements of professional (standard) visual representation and audio in multi-media presentation. For example, a PowerPoint done for artistic or personal expression purposes can include regional and individualist variations. However, a PowerPoint proposal to a government group, for example, should be very standard and professional.

COMPETENCY 9.0 RESEARCH STRATEGIES

Skill 9.1   Use a variety of research sources, both print and electronic.

Locating information for research projects and compiling research sources using both print and electronic resources is vital in the construct of written documents. The resources that are available in today's school communities include a large database of Internet resources and World Wide Web access that provides individual navigation for print and electronic information. Research sources include looking at traditional commercial databases and using The Electronic Library to print and cite a diversity of informational resources.

The vital aspect of the research process includes learning to analyze the applicability and validity of the massive amounts of accessible information in cyberspace. Verifying and evaluating electronic resources are part of the process of sorting through the downloaded hardcopies or scrolling through the electronic databases. In using a diversity of research sources, the user must be able to discern authentic sources of information from the mass collections of websites and information databases.

In primary research, selecting a topic and setting up an outline for research information precedes using the secondary research of both print and electronic resources. Using conceptual Venn diagrams to center the topic and brainstorm the peripheral information pertaining to the topic clarifies the purpose of the research. There are two aspects of the secondary research: 1. using print sources and 2. using electronic research tools.

Print sources provide guides on locations for specific or general information resources. Libraries have floors or designated areas dedicated to the collection of encyclopedias, specific resource manuals, card catalogs, and periodical indexes that will provide information on the projected topic. Electronic research tools includes a listing of the latest and most effective search engines like Goggle, Microsoft, AOL, Infotrac and Yahoo to find the topic of research, along with peripheral support information. Electronic databases that contain extensive resources will provide the user with selecting resources, choosing effective keywords, and constructing search strategies. The world of electronic research opens up a global library of resources for both print and electronic information.

The major online services such as Microsoft, Prodigy, and CompuServe provide users with assess information of specialized information that is either free or one that has a minimal charge assessed for that specific service or website. Online resources teach effective ways to bookmark sites of interest and how to cut and paste relevant information onto word documents for citation and reference.

Bookmarking favorite Internet searches that contain correct sources for reference can save a lot of research time. On AOL, book marking is known as favorites and with one click of the mouse, a user can type in the email address on the browser's location bar and create instant access to that location. Netscape uses the terminology of "bookmarks" to save browser locations for future research.

Online search engines and web portals create avenues of navigating the World Wide Web. Web portals provide linkages to other websites and are typically subdivided into other categories for searching. Portals are also specific to certain audience interests that index parts of the web. Search engines can provide additional strategic site searches.

Skill 9.2   Interpret such research, putting to use their findings and interpretations to construct their own reports and narratives.

Evaluating copious collections of print and electronic resource information requires a strategic game plan. Judging the credibility of the Internet sources will increase the validity of the research reports. In evaluating the sources, the user should consider the following information:

- Author, Organization, Origination of the report
- Source, Date of Source, Reputable research
- Audience, Point of View, Targeted Readers
- Arguments, Thesis, Point of Reference
- Evidence, Supportive Themes, Facts vs. Fiction
- Verification of Sources

Reports and narratives require reliable and verifiable sources that use Internet and hardcopy print resources to construct and validate meaning. When choosing the most reliable resources for reports, the writer must be careful that the printed word used is verifiable. The sources must be authentic and validated. Some writers will download and print copious amounts of Internet sources and Xerox larger amounts of hardcopy sources to list pages of bibliographic resources that contribute minimally to the reports or narratives. The quality of bibliographic citations should be the objective instead of the quantity of the citations.

Sources for Research

- Books-using books written by well known authors who are recognizable in their field of study can add validity and authenticity to reports
- Encyclopedia-the information is designed to be brief in summarizing well-known persons, places, and events. Research must go beyond this resource to more specific and further developed for interpretation into reports.
- Journals, magazines-the targeted audience for articles and stories written in these specific resources are sometimes highly defined and elitist. For example, the New Yorker, Time, Atlantic Monthly, Scientific Review and Harper's Bazaar are intellectual magazines that have targeted audiences and require a superior quality of writing which are used as credible resources for reports.
- Internet, Websites-the worldwide web provides thousands of websites and millions of data bits of information that could provide credibility to a research project. The objective is to find the valid information among the postings. Oftentimes, when a subject is posted on a Search engine, the websites that respond are homepages to advertisements that link to other commercial sites. It might take an investment of time to find the real gems of credible information that would provide qualitative and quantitative data to a report or narrative.

Skill 9.3   Understand the importance of citing research sources, using recognizable and accepted conventions for doing so.

See Skill 7.3

DOMAIN III - TEXTS

COMPETENCY 10.0 CONCEPTS AND CONVENTIONS

Skill 10.1   Analyze narrative and expository texts, with special attention to children's literature, from a range of cultures, for both literary elements and structural features.

Some basic principles apply to the analysis of any text whether magazine articles, newspaper articles, or even children's literature. The steps of analysis follow:

Structure:

- Where does the thesis—the point—of the document or speech occur?
    a. At the beginning
    b. In the middle
    c. At the end
    d. Unstated
- Is the reasoning deductive (general to specific) or inductive (specific to general)?
- Is the outline chronological or spatial?
- Figures of speech
    a) Metaphor
    b) Allegory
    c) Simile

Content:

- Thesis—the point the document or speech makes.
- Support—the points or examples the writer/speaker uses to establish the thesis.
- Purpose—persuasive, descriptive, expository, or narrative.
- Fallacies:
    (a) Ad hominem
    (b) Slippery slope
    (c) False dilemma
    (d) Begging the question
    (e) Post hoc ergo propter hoc (false cause)
    (f) Red herring
    (g) Hasty conclusion
- Coherence—the supporting points move in a logical sequence from first to last and have transitions that establish the relationship to the preceding point.
- Bias—does the background or belief system of the speaker/writer affect the position taken?

- Value—is the information useful or relevant?
- Ethics
  a) Respect for sensitivities of diverse audience/readership.
  b) Honesty, transparency.

Prior to twentieth century research on child development and child/adolescent literature's relationship to that development, books for adolescents were primarily didactic. They were designed to be instructive of history, manners, and morals.

See also Skill 11.1 for more detailed information on children's literature.

Skill 10.2 Identify themes derived from cultural patterns and symbols found in rituals, mythologies, and traditions.

It seems that in every generation, there is one writer or one book that tends to dominate children's literature—the most recent one being the Harry Potter books. There is always a lot of discussion about what is appropriate for children and at what age. The criticism about the themes in the Harry Potter books is that it revolves around witchery and witchcraft, which is upsetting enough in some communities that the books have been abolished in the curricula and libraries of the schools.

Another theme that is extremely controversial is violence. Some parents go so far as to condemn the traditional and time-tested fairy tales because of the amount of violence in them. Themes that are adult in nature have also been the source of controversy. For example, And Tango Makes Three, a book based on a true story of two obviously homosexual male penguins in New York City's Central Park Zoo who adopted a fertilized egg and raised the chick as their own stirred up a controversy when it began to appear on elementary school library shelves. Many parents felt that their children were not ready for such an adult theme.

What actually constitutes "children's literature"? It is usually defined as literature that is selected and read by children rather than those that the powers-that-be such as teachers, reviewers, parents, etc., deem appropriate. However, sometimes it is defined as literature written especially for children, but that definition tends to fall by the wayside when we look at some of the major books that are read primarily by children such as Mark Twain's The Prince and the Pauper and Huckleberry Finn that were written specifically for adults. There is great ambiguity in the publishing world as to whether a book will be categorized and marketed as children's literature or adult literature or even young adult literature, and many books cross the line in all directions.

Of course, much of what has been traditionally regarded as children's literature has multiple levels of meaning and adults who read Alice in

Wonderland, for example, as a child, will read it again as an adult and will derive meanings they did not see and could not understand as a child.

Following are some authors who have are making significant contributions to children's literature and some examples of their works:

Enid Blyton, British author, The Famous Five, The Secret Seven series.

J.K. Rowling, British author, Harry Potter series.

Jacqueline Wilson, British author, Tracy Beaker series.

Jane Yolen, American author, Owl Moon, Devil's Arithmetic.

Betsy Byars, American author, Summer of the Swans.

Skill 10.3   Identify and analyze evidence of an author's or narrator's perspective in both fiction and non-fiction.

Students need to be able to distinguish between fiction and non-fiction in order to determine the author's or narrator's perspective. Generally fiction is divided into three main areas:
- Story
- Novel
- Novella

These usually have a main character, setting, plot, climax and resolution. Non-fiction on the other hand is usually intended to inform the reader. Common types of non-fiction include:
- Essays
- Documentaries
- Biographies
- Autobiographies
- Informational books

The meaning of the message portrayed by each author or narrator comes through in the words of the text. Abstract themes of love, hatred, friendship, honor, good, justice and power become real through the words and actions of the character in works of fiction. In order to teach students to find the perspective used by the author or narrator, the teacher has to help them analyze the work. This means that through discussion and direct teaching the students can look at the characters, actions, problems and the dialogue in order to discern how they are related to or help develop the theme.

Some of the ways the theme can be determined in fiction are:

- Finding the main idea expressed through the text and speech of the characters
- The actual statements that the character makes
- Narrators tell readers how they feel about a topic by inserting their own ideas in the text.
- The actions and words of characters who may be in conflict with each other.
- The use of figurative language

Figurative language is present in both fiction and non-fiction. This is one element of reading that students often have problems with. Therefore, the teacher has to help them find the symbolism in the text. In literature, a symbol can be an idea, an object or a person that the writer is using to make a point, develop the theme or create a mood. They can be underlying tenets of a culture or even biblical or mythological in nature. Once students decide on the symbolism used in a text, they need to judge its importance in the work.

There are also fiction texts that teach a lesson, such as fables and parables. These are short stories that the teacher can read to the class and have them decide on what lesson the story is teaching. Modeling and practice is the key here. Students should not be expected to read a fable and guess its meaning if they have not been previously exposed to this type of writing. The classroom should also contain multiple texts that the students can read on their own.

The author's or narrator's perspective is easier to discern in non-fiction. This is because the meaning comes from the writer's thesis, which is often found in the very first paragraph. However, it is not always directly stated and may be implied. Students have to read between the lines of the text to find out exactly what the author's feelings toward the topic are.

There are four main types of writing in the non-fiction category:
- Expository – explains a topic or how to do something
- Persuasive – tries to persuade the reader to adopt the author's or narrator's point of view
- Descriptive – transmits description and images through words. In other words, descriptive writing excites the senses.
- Narrative – instructing by telling a story. This form of non-fiction usually presents a series of actions to let the reader know what has happened at some point in time.

Teachers should model questioning for the students when identifying the author's or narrator's perspective in both fiction and non-fiction. This includes such questions as:

- Is the text fiction or non-fiction? How do you know?
- Why do you think the author wrote this work?
- What feelings did the text evoke in you?
- What is the author's main idea?
- How do the setting, characters, actions and problem help bring out the meaning or the author's point of view in the text?

Students should be encourage to make personal responses to the texts they read (e.g. how it made them feel, if it reminded them of anything in their own lives, which part they liked best or what they learned from the reading) Depending on the grade level, students can use a variety of ways in responding, such as through drawings, retellings, talking, painting.

Skill 10.4   Identify and evaluate structural devices in prose and poetry and they examine the connections among organizational structures, the writer's view point, and the goals of reading.

People read poetry for many reasons, and they are often the very same reasons poets would give for writing it. Just the feel and sounds of the words that are turned by the artistic hands and mind of a poet into a satisfying and sometimes delightful experience is a good reason to read a poem. Good poetry constantly surprises.

However, the major purpose a writer of poetry has for creating his works of art is the sharing of an experience, a feeling, an emotion, and that is also the reason a reader turns to poetry rather than prose in his search for variety, joy, and satisfaction.

There is another important reason why poets create and readers are drawn to their poems: they are interpreters of life. Poets feel deeply the things that others feel or even things that may be overlooked by others, and they have the skill and inspiration to recreate those feelings and interpret them in such a way that understanding and insight may come from the experience. They often bring understanding to life's big (or even not-so-big) questions.

Children can respond to poetry at very early stages. Elementary students are still at the stage where the sounds of unusual words intrigue them and entertain them. They are also very open to emotional meanings of passages. Teaching poetry to 5th graders can be an important introduction to seeking for meaning in literature. If a 5th grader enjoys reading poetry both silently and aloud, a habit may be formed that will last a lifetime.

When we speak of structure with regard to poetry, we usually mean one of three things:

1. The pattern of the sound and rhythm

It helps to know the history of this peculiarity of poetry. History was passed down in oral form almost exclusively until the invention of the printing press and was often set to music. A rhymed story is much easier to commit to memory. Adding a tune makes it even easier to remember, so it's not a surprise that much of the earliest literature—epics, odes, etc., are rhymed and were probably sung. When we speak of the pattern of sound and rhythm, we are referring to two things: verse form and stanza form.

The verse form is the rhythmic pattern of a single verse. An example would be any meter: blank verse, for instance, is iambic pentameter. A stanza is a group of a certain number of verses (lines), having a rhyme scheme. If the poem is written, there is usually white space between the verses although a short poem may be only one stanza. If the poem is spoken, there will be a pause between stanzas.

2. The visible shape it takes

In the seventeenth century, some poets shaped their poems to reflect the theme. A good example is George Herbert's Easter Wings. Since that time, poets have occasionally played with this device; it is, however, generally viewed as nothing more than a demonstration of ingenuity. The rhythm, effect, and meaning are often sacrificed to the forcing of the shape.

3. Rhyme and free verse

Poets also use devices to establish form that will underscore the meanings of their poems. A very common one is alliteration. When the poem is read (which poetry is usually intended to be), the repetition of a sound may not only underscore the meaning, it may also add pleasure to the reading. Following a strict rhyming pattern can add intensity to the meaning of the poem in the hands of a skilled and creative poet. On the other hand, the meaning can be drowned out by the steady beat-beat-beat of it. Shakespeare very skillfully used the regularity of rhyme in his poetry, breaking the rhythm at certain points to very effectively underscore a point. For example, in Sonnet #130, "My mistress' eyes are nothing like the sun," the rhythm is primarily iambic pentameter. It lulls the reader (or listener) to accept that this poet is following the standard conventions for love poetry, which in that day reliably used rhyme and more often than not iambic pentameter to express feelings of romantic love along conventional lines. However, in Sonnet #130, the last two lines sharply break from the monotonous pattern, forcing reader or speaker to pause:

> And yet, by heaven, I think my love as rare
> As any she belied with false compare

Shakespeare's purpose is clear: he is not writing a conventional love poem; the object of his love is not the red-and-white conventional woman written about in other poems of the period. This is a good example where a poet uses form to underscore meaning.

Poets eventually began to feel constricted by the rhyming conventions and began to break away and make new rules for poetry. When poetry was only rhymed, it was easy to define it. When free verse, or poetry written in a flexible form, came upon the scene in France in the 1880s, it quickly began to influence English-language poets such as T. S. Eliot, whose memorable poem, The Wasteland, had an alarming but desolate message for the modern world. It's impossible to imagine that it could have been written in the soothing, lulling rhymed verse of previous periods. Those who first began writing in free verse in English were responding to the influence of the French vers libre. However, it should be noted that it could be loosely applied to the poetry of Walt Whitman, writing in the mid-nineteenth century, as can be seen in the first stanza of Son of Myself:

> I celebrate myself, and sing myself,
> And what I assume you shall assume,
> For every atom belonging to me as good belongs to you.

When poetry was no longer defined as a piece of writing arranged in verses that had a rhyme-scheme of some sort, distinguishing poetry from prose became a point of discussion. Merriam Webster's Encyclopedia of Literature defines poetry as follows: "Writing that formulates a concentrated imaginative awareness of experience in language chosen and arranged to create a specific emotional response through its meaning, sound and rhythm."

A poet chooses the form of his poetry deliberately, based upon the emotional response he hopes to evoke and the meaning he wishes to convey. Robert Frost, a twentieth-century poet who chose to use conventional rhyming verse to make his point is a memorable and often-quoted modern poet. Who can forget his closing lines in "Stopping by Woods"?

> And miles to go before I sleep,
> And miles to go before I sleep.

Would they be as memorable if the poem had been written in free verse?

Slant Rhyme: Occurs when the final consonant sounds are the same, but the vowels are different. Occurs frequently in Irish, Welsh, and Icelandic verse. Examples include: green and gone, that and hit, ill and shell.

Alliteration: Alliteration occurs when the initial sounds of a word, beginning either with a consonant or a vowel, are repeated in close succession. Examples include: Athena and Apollo, Nate never knows, People who pen poetry.

Note that the words only have to be close to one another: Alliteration that repeats and attempts to connect a number of words is little more than a tongue-twister.

The function of alliteration, like rhyme, might be to accentuate the beauty of language in a given context, or to unite words or concepts through a kind of repetition. Alliteration, like rhyme, can follow specific patterns. Sometimes the consonants aren't always the initial ones, but they are generally the stressed syllables. Alliteration is less common than rhyme; but because it is less common, it can call our attention to a word or line in a poem that might not have the same emphasis otherwise.

Assonance: If alliteration occurs at the beginning of a word and rhyme at the end, assonance takes the middle territory. Assonance occurs when the vowel sound within a word matches the same sound in a nearby word, but the surrounding consonant sounds are different. "Tune" and "June" are rhymes; "tune" and "food" are assonant. The function of assonance is frequently the same as end rhyme or alliteration; all serve to give a sense of continuity or fluidity to the verse. Assonance might be especially effective when rhyme is absent: It gives the poet more flexibility, and it is not typically used as part of a predetermined pattern. Like alliteration, it does not so much determine the structure or form of a poem; rather, it is more ornamental.

Onomatopoeia: Word used to evoke the sound in its meaning. The early Batman series used pow, zap, whop, zonk and eek in an onomatopoetic way.

Rhythm in poetry refers to the recurrence of stresses at equal intervals. A stress (accent) is a greater amount of force given to one syllable in speaking than is given to another. For example, we put the stress on the first syllable of such words as father, mother, daughter, and children. The unstressed or unaccented syllable is sometimes called a slack syllable. All English words carry at least one stress except articles and some prepositions such as by, from, at, etc. Indicating where stresses occur is to scan; doing this is called scansion. Very little is gained in understanding a poem or making a statement about it by merely scanning it. The pattern of the rhythm—the meter—should be analyzed in terms of its overall relationship to the message and impression of the poem.

Slack syllables, when they recur in pairs cause rhythmic trippings and bouncings; on the other hand, recurrent pairs of stresses will create a heavier rocking effect. The rhythm is dependent on words to convey meaning. Alone, they communicate nothing. When examining the rhythm and meaning of a poem, a good question to ask is whether the rhythm is appropriate to the theme. A bouncing rhythm, for example, might be dissonant in a solemn elegy.

Stops are those places in a poem where the punctuation requires a pause. An end-stopped line is one that ends in a pause whereas one that has no punctuation at its end and is, therefore, read with only a slight pause after it is said to be run-on and the running on of its thought into the next line is called enjambment. These are used by a poet to underscore, intensify, communicate meaning.

Rhythm, then, is a pattern of recurrence and in poetry is made up of stressed and relatively unstressed syllables. The poet can manipulate the rhythm by making the intervals between his stresses regular or varied, by making his lines short or long, by end-stopping his lines or running them over, by choosing words that are easier or less easy to say, by choosing polysyllabic words or monosyllables. The most important thing to remember about rhythm is that it conveys meaning.

The basic unit of rhythm is called a foot and is usually one stressed syllable with one or two unstressed ones or two stressed syllables with one unstressed one. A foot made up of one unstressed syllable and one stressed one is called an iamb. If a line is made of five iambs, it is iambic pentameter. A rhymed poem typically establishes a pattern such as iambic pentameter, and even though there will be syllables that don't fit the pattern, the poem, nevertheless, will be said to be in iambic pentameter. In fact, a poem may be considered weak if the rhythm is too monotonous.

The most common kinds of feet in English poetry:

iamb: -'
anapest: --'
trochee: '-
dactyl: '--
Monosyllabic: '
Spondee: "
Pyrrhic foot: --

Iambic and anapestic are said to be rising because the movement is from slack to stressed syllables. Trochaic and dactylic are said to be falling.

Meters are named as follows:
Monometer: a line of one foot
Dimeter: a line of two feet
Trimeter: a line of three feet
Tetrameter: a line of four feet
Pentameter: a line of five feet
Hexameter: a line of six feet
Heptameter: a line of seven feet
Octameter: a line of eight feet

Longer lines are possible, but a reader will tend to break it up into shorter lengths.

A caesura is a definite pause within a line, in scansion indicated by a double line: ||

A stanza is a group of a certain number of lines with a rhyme scheme or a particular rhythm or both, typically set off by white space.

Some typical patterns of English poetry:
- Blank verse: unrhymed iambic pentameter.
- Couplet: two-line stanza usually rhymed and typically not separated by white space.
- Heroic couplet or closed couplet: two rhymed lines of iambic pentameter, the first ending in a light pause, the second more heavily end-stopped.
- Tercet: a three-line stanza, which, if rhymed, usually keeps to one rhyme sound.
- Terza rima: the middle line of the tercet rhymes with the first and third lines of the next tercet.
- The quatrain: four-line stanza, the most popular in English.
- The ballad stanza: four iambic feet in lines 1 and 3, three in lines 2 and 4. Rhyming is abcb.
- The refrain: a line or lines repeated in a ballad as a chorus.
- Terminal refrain: follows a stanza in a ballad.
- Five-line stanzas occur, but not frequently.
- Six-line stanzas, more frequent than five-line ones.
- The sestina: six six-line stanzas and a tercet. Repeats in each stanza the same six end-words in a different order.
- Rime royal: seven-line stanza in iambic pentameter with rhyme ababbcc.
- Ottava rima: eight-line stanza of iambic pentameter rhyming abababcc.
- Spenserian stanza: nine lines, rhyming ababbcbcc for eight lines then concludes with an Alexandrine.
- The Alexandrine: a line of iambic hexameter.
- Free verse: no conventional patterns of rhyme, stanza, or meter.
- Sonnet: a fourteen-line poem in iambic pentameter.
  1) English sonnet: sometimes called a Shakespearean sonnet. Rhymes cohere in four clusters: abab cdcd efef gg
  2) Italian or Petrarchan sonnet: first eight lines (the octave), abbaabba; then the sestet, the last six lines add new rhyme sounds in almost any variation; does not end in a couplet.

COMPETENCY 11.0 GENRES

Skill 11.1   **Analyze texts in different literary genres (novels, short stories, folk and fairy tales, and poetry of various types, for example), as they are represented in different cultures, according to their structure, organization, and purpose.**

The major literary genres include allegory, ballad, drama, epic, epistle, essay, fable, novel, poem, romance, and the short story.

Allegory: A story in verse or prose with characters representing virtues and vices. There are two meanings, symbolic and literal. John Bunyan's The Pilgrim's Progress is the most renowned of this genre.

Ballad: An in medias res story told or sung, usually in verse and accompanied by music. Literary devices found in ballads include the refrain, or repeated section, and incremental repetition, or anaphora, for effect. Earliest forms were anonymous folk ballads. Later forms include Coleridge's Romantic masterpiece, "The Rime of the Ancient Mariner."

Drama: Plays – comedy, modern, or tragedy - typically in five acts. Traditionalists and neoclassicists adhere to Aristotle's unities of time, place and action. Plot development is advanced via dialogue. Literary devices include asides, soliloquies and the chorus representing public opinion. Greatest of all dramatists/playwrights is William Shakespeare. Other dramaturges include Ibsen, Williams, Miller, Shaw, Stoppard, Racine, Moliére, Sophocles, Aeschylus, Euripides, and Aristophanes.

Epic: Long poem usually of book length reflecting values inherent in the generative society. Epic devices include an invocation to a Muse for inspiration, purpose for writing, universal setting, protagonist and antagonist who possess supernatural strength and acumen, and interventions of a God or the gods. Understandably, there are very few epics: Homer's Iliad and Odyssey, Virgil's Aeneid, Milton's Paradise Lost, Spenser's The Fairie Queene, Barrett Browning's Aurora Leigh, and Pope's mock-epic, The Rape of the Lock.

Epistle: A letter that is not always originally intended for public distribution, but due to the fame of the sender and/or recipient, becomes public domain. Paul wrote epistles that were later placed in the Bible.

Essay: Typically a limited length prose work focusing on a topic and propounding a definite point of view and authoritative tone. Great essayists include Carlyle, Lamb, DeQuincy, Emerson and Montaigne, who is credited with defining this genre.

Fable: Terse tale offering up a moral or exemplum. Chaucer's "The Nun's Priest's Tale" is a fine example of a bete fabliau or beast fable in which animals speak and act characteristically human, illustrating human foibles.

Legend: A traditional narrative or collection of related narratives, popularly regarded as historically factual but actually a mixture of fact and fiction.

Myth: Stories that are more or less universally shared within a culture to explain its history and traditions.

Novel: The longest form of fictional prose containing a variety of characterizations, settings, local color and regionalism. Most have complex plots, expanded description, and attention to detail. Some of the great novelists include Austin, the Brontes, Twain, Tolstoy, Hugo, Hardy, Dickens, Hawthorne, Forster, and Flaubert.

Poem: The only requirement is rhythm. Sub-genres include fixed types of literature such as the sonnet, elegy, ode, pastoral, and villanelle. Unfixed types of literature include blank verse and dramatic monologue.

Romance: A highly imaginative tale set in a fantastical realm dealing with the conflicts between heroes, villains and/or monsters. "The Knight's Tale" from Chaucer's Canterbury Tales, Sir Gawain and the Green Knight and Keats' "The Eve of St. Agnes" are prime representatives.

Short Story: Typically a terse narrative, with less developmental background about characters. May include description, author's point of view, and tone. Poe emphasized that a successful short story should create one focused impact. Considered to be great short story writers are Hemingway, Faulkner, Twain, Joyce, Shirley Jackson, Flannery O'Connor, de Maupasssant, Saki, Edgar Allen Poe, and Pushkin.

Children's literature is a genre of its own and emerged as a distinct and independent form in the second half of the 18th century. The Visible World in Pictures by John Amos Comenius, a Czech educator, was one of the first printed works and the first picture book. For the first time, educators acknowledged that children are different from adults in many respects. Modern educators acknowledge that introducing elementary students to a wide range of reading experiences plays an important role in their mental/social/psychological development. Some of the most common forms of literature specifically for children follow:

- **Traditional Literature:** Traditional literature opens up a world where right wins out over wrong, where hard work and perseverance are rewarded, and where helpless victims find vindication—all worthwhile values that children identify with even as early as kindergarten. In traditional literature, children will be introduced to fanciful beings, humans with exaggerated powers, talking animals, and heroes that will inspire them. For younger elementary children, these stories in Big Book format are ideal for providing predictable and repetitive elements that can be grasped by these children.

- **Folktales/Fairy Tales:** Some examples: The Three Bears, Little Red Riding Hood, Snow White, Sleeping Beauty, Puss-in-Boots, Rapunzel and Rumpelstiltskin. Adventures of animals or humans and the supernatural characterize these stories. The hero is usually on a quest and is aided by other-worldly helpers. More often than not, the story focuses on good and evil and reward and punishment.

- **Fables:** Animals that act like humans are featured in these stories and usually reveal human foibles or sometimes teach a lesson. Example: Aesop's Fables.

- **Myths:** These stories about events from the earliest times, such as the origin of the world, are considered true in their own societies.

- **Legends:** These are similar to myths except that they tend to deal with events that happened more recently. Example: Arthurian legends.

- **Tall tales:** Examples: Paul Bunyan, John Henry, and Pecos Bill. These are purposely exaggerated accounts of individuals with superhuman strength.

- **Modern Fantasy:** Many of the themes found in these stories are similar to those in traditional literature. The stories start out based in reality, which makes it easier for the reader to suspend disbelief and enter worlds of unreality. Little people live in the walls in The Borrowers and time travel is possible in The Trolley to Yesterday. Including some fantasy tales in the curriculum helps elementary-grade children develop their senses of imagination. These often appeal to ideals of justice and issues having to do with good and evil; and because children tend to identify with the characters, the message is more likely to be retained.

- **Science Fiction:** Robots, spacecraft, mystery, and civilizations from other ages often appear in these stories. Most presume advances in science on other planets or in a future time. Most children like these stories because of their interest in space and the "what if" aspect of the stories. Examples: Outer Space and All That Junk and A Wrinkle in Time.

- **Modern Realistic Fiction:** These stories are about real problems that real children face. By finding that their hopes and fears are shared by others, young children can find insight into their own problems. Young readers also tend to experience a broadening of interests as the result of this kind of reading. It's good for them to know that a child can be brave and intelligent and can solve difficult problems.

- **Historical Fiction:** Rifles for Watie is an example of this kind of story. Presented in a historically-accurate setting, it's about a young boy (16 years) who serves in the Union army. He experiences great hardship but discovers that his enemy is an admirable human being. It provides a good opportunity to introduce younger children to history in a beneficial way.
- **Biography:** Reading about inventors, explorers, scientists, political and religious leaders, social reformers, artists, sports figures, doctors, teachers, writers, and war heroes help children to see that one person can make a difference. They also open new vistas for children to think about when they choose an occupation to fantasize about.
- **Informational Books:** These are ways to learn more about something you are interested in or something that you know nothing about. Encyclopedias are good resources, of course, but a book like Polar Wildlife by Kamini Khanduri shows pictures and facts that will capture the imaginations of young children.

Skill 11.2   Demonstrate an understanding of structural features and their applications in various types of expository and narrative materials, including popular media such as magazines and newspapers.

See Skill 10.1

Skill 11.3   Understand and evaluate the use of elements of persuasive argument in print, speech, videos, and in other media.

More money is spent each year on advertising towards children than educating them. Thus, the media's strategies are considerably well thought out and effective. They employ large, clear letters, bold colors, simple line drawings, and popular symbols to announce upcoming events, push ideas and advertise products. By using attractive photographs, brightly colored cartoon characters or instructive messages, they increase sales, win votes or stimulate learning. The graphics are designed to communicate messages clearly, precisely, and efficiently. Some even target subconscious yearnings for sex and status.

Because so much effort is being spent on influencing students through media tactics, just as much effort should be devoted to educating those students about media awareness. A teacher should explain that artists and the aspect they choose to portray, as well as the ways in which they portray them, reflect their attitude and understanding of those aspects. The artistic choices they make are not entirely based on creative license—they also reflect an imbedded meaning the artist wants to represent. Colors, shapes, and positions are meant to arouse basic instincts for food, sex, and status, and are often used to sell cars, clothing, or liquor.

To stimulate analysis of media strategies, ask students such questions as:

- Where/when do you think this picture was taken/film was shot/piece was written?
- Would you like to have lived at this time in history, or in this place?
- What objects are present?
- What do the people presented look like? Are they happy or sad?
- Who is being targeted?
- What can you learn from this piece of media?
- Is it telling you something is good or bad?
- What message is being broadcasted?

Freedom of the press is essential to democracy. In this form of government, representatives are elected by the people, are responsible to them, and they are entitled to know what those representatives are doing. The only way that can happen is if the press is free to report the news in an unbiased manner. If the mayor of a city has a conflict of interest that is profiting him, the people need to know. If an elected representative is arrested for driving under the influence, that representative's constituency has a right to know. It's the only way unbiased management of the public interest can occur. For these reasons, news media have an obligation to keep themselves unencumbered and unbiased. Most news people pride themselves on their objectivity.

News stories are always assumed to be unbiased. It can be argued, of course, that no one can be entirely unbiased and that it's the nature of the written word that those biases may creep into the reporting of news. Even so, the professional reporter and/or editor will exercise the strength necessary to keep his or her own biases out of the reporting as much as possible.

Editorializing is an entirely different thing. Most newspapers, for instance, have an editorial position, which will often correspond to political parties. A newspaper may, for instance, declare itself to be Republican. This does not mean that the newspaper will favor the party of choice in news reporting. It does, however, mean that editorial materials will probably be slanted in that direction. In a time of election, a newspaper will often come out for one candidate over another and try to influence its readership to follow suit. A newspaper will often take a side when an issue is on the docket at time of election or even at other times. An editorial will frequently state an opinion about a matter that concerns the newspaper's readership.

COMPETENCY 12.0 INTERPREATION OF TEXTS

Skill 12.1 **Analyze both implicit and explicit themes and interpret both literal and figurative meanings in texts, from a range of cultures and genres, using textual support for inferences, conclusions, and generalizations they draw from any work.**

In looking at any piece of writing regardless of genre, it's important to think about what was going on in the writer's world at the time the piece was being written. This includes the political milieu, societal mores, the social level of the writer, and cultural influences. "A writer can only write what he knows" is a statement often heard in discussions about literature. However, Tom Wolfe, a contemporary writer (*Bonfire of the Vanities*) disputes that. He insists that a writer can use exploration and research to write effectively and successfully about topics that he hasn't experienced first-hand. Even so, it's important to think about the influence that what was going on at the time of the writing of a piece of literature had on the writer and on the ultimate published work.

A good example is John Steinbeck and his popular novel, *The Grapes of Wrath*. It would certainly be possible to read this book and be moved by it, even to understand the point Steinbeck intended to make without knowing that it was written during America's Great Depression of the nineteen thirties, but it is much better understood when viewed through that context.

This writer didn't suffer the tribulations that many did during the Depression; his own family was little affected by it. Once he decided that he wanted to write about the people who were being displaced by the political, cultural, and social crisis, he went to Oklahoma and lived with a family that had lost its farm not only because of the economic disaster but also because of the dust bowl effect in that part of the country. In other words, he obtained the information and experience he needed in order to be sure that he wrote "what he knew" by exploration and research. The result is a family that Steinbeck named the Joads, who illustrate and demonstrate in clear, moving, and understandable terms what the Great Depression meant in human lives.

He doesn't just stop there, however. He also interposes chapters that fill in the cultural, political, and social situation that make certain his readers understand clearly where the life of the Joads fits in those environments. He tells what is going on in the churches where the common approach was to pretend either that the suffering was the fault of the victims themselves or that the drastic effects were not happening at all. The social situation that most accounted for a lack of concern for these suffering fellow-Americans was that the economic well-being of the wealthy landowners in California was dependent on these migrants, and the landowners were more often than not deacons and elders in the churches. They had a vested interest in the status quo.

Politically, President Hoover, who had devoted his life to providing food for hungry people all over the world, found himself in a dilemma: he couldn't meet the needs of his own people. He had a congress that opposed his efforts to make organizational changes to avoid such things as the crisis of the migrants that Steinbeck wrote about. Hoover got much of the blame for the situation although there were many forces beyond his control that accounted for it.

Another important aspect of a piece of writing that is directly related to political, cultural, and social influences is the writer's purpose for writing it in the first place. In Steinbeck's case, his purpose was to bring about change. His book is considered a novel of protest, a social document.

It's important to note that *Grapes of Wrath* is an extreme example of a novel that was strongly influenced by the political, cultural, and social background of the times in which it was written. Even so, most works whether written or presented via some other medium, reflect the times and the cultural, social, and political atmosphere of the time in which they are written.

Skill 12.2   Evaluate the structure, purpose, and potential uses of visual text features, such as graphics, illustrations, and maps.

While the teaching of writing undoubtedly involves an enormous of work on the composition of text, it also involves the general idea of ideas conveyed in the best possible manner. In other words, I could explain the results of a survey in words, but it might be easier to understand in a graph or chart. If that is the case, why would we want to present it in words. The important point is for the information to be conveyed.

So, as students write reports and respond to ideas in writing, they can learn how to incorporate multiple representations of information, including various graphic representations, into written text. While this is seemingly fairly easy to do considering the word processing technology we have available to us, students struggle with knowing how to appropriately and successfully do this. They can learn to do this in three primary ways: explanation, observation/modeling, and practice.

First, students need to have clear explanations from teachers on appropriate forms of graphical representations in text, as well as the methods in which to include those representations. They need to see plenty of examples of how it is done.

Second, they need to be able to see teacher-modeled examples where text has been replaced or enhanced by graphical representations. The more they see of examples, the clearer the concepts will be to them.

Finally, students need to get a chance to practice incorporating graphical representations in their writing. This, of course, will require technology and plenty of feedback.

Students will most likely appreciate the ability to utilize graphical representations in place of text, but they will soon realize that deciding which type of representation to use and how to actually use it will be very challenging. Generally, graphical representations should be used only if they can convey information better than written text can. This is an important principal that students will need to learn through constant practice.

Skill 12.3   Recognize and analyze instances of bias and stereotyping in a text.

See Skill 8.4

CONTENT AREA II – SOCIAL SCIENCE

DOMAIN I – WORLD HISTORY

COMPETENCY 13.0 ANCIENT CIVILIZATIONS

Skill 13.1   Trace the impact of physical geography on the development of ancient civilizations.

The earliest known civilizations developed in the Tigris-Euphrates valley of **Mesopotamia** (modern Iraq) and the Nile valley of Egypt between 4000 BCE and 3000 BCE. Because these civilizations arose in river valleys, they are known as fluvial civilizations. Geography and the physical environment played a critical role in the rise and the survival of both of these civilizations. The Fertile Crescent was bounded on the West by the Mediterranean, on the South by the Arabian Desert, on the north by the Taurus Mountains, and on the east by the Zagros Mountains. It included Mesopotamia, Syria and Palestine. This region was marked by almost constant invasions and migrations. These invaders and migrants seemed to have destroyed the culture and civilization that existed. Upon taking a longer view, however, it becomes apparent that they actually absorbed and supplemented the civilization that existed before their arrival. This is one of the reasons the civilization developed so quickly and created so such an advanced culture.

First, the **rivers** provided a source of water that would sustain life, including animal life. The hunters of the society had ample access to a variety of animals, initially for hunting to provide food, as well as hides, bones, antlers, etc. from which clothing, tools and art could be made. Second the proximity to water provided a natural attraction to animals which could be herded and husbanded to provide a stable supply of food and animal products. Third, the rivers of these regions overflowed their banks each year, leaving behind a deposit of very rich soil. As these early people began to experiment with growing crops rather than gathering food, the soil was fertile and water was readily available to produce sizeable harvests. In time, the people developed systems of irrigation that channeled water to the crops without significant human effort on a continuing basis.

Ancient civilizations were able to thrive and flourish because human communities subsisted initially as gatherers – gathering berries, leaves, etc. With the invention of tools it became possible to dig for roots, hunt small animals, and catch fish from **rivers** and **oceans**. Humans observed their environments and soon learned to plant seeds and harvest crops. As people migrated to areas in which game and fertile soil were abundant, communities began to develop. When people had the knowledge to grow crops and the skills to hunt game, they began to understand division of labor. Some of the people in the community tended to agricultural needs while others hunted game.

As habitats attracted larger numbers of people, environments became crowded and there was competition. The concept of division of labor and sharing of food soon came, in more heavily populated areas, to be managed. Camps soon became villages. Villages became year-round settlements. Animals were domesticated and gathered into herds that met the needs of the village. With the settled life it was no longer necessary to "travel light." Pottery was developed for storing and cooking food.

By 8000 BCE, culture was beginning to evolve in these villages. Agriculture was developed for the production of grain crops, which led to a decreased reliance on wild plants. Domesticating animals for various purposes decreased the need to hunt wild game. Life became more settled. It was then possible to turn attention to such matters as managing water supplies, producing tools, making cloth, etc. There was both the social interaction and the opportunity to reflect upon existence. Mythologies arose and various kinds of belief systems. Rituals arose that re-enacted the mythologies that gave meaning to life. As farming and animal husbandry skills increased, the dependence upon wild game and food gathering declined. With this change came the realization that a larger number of people could be supported on the produce of farming and animal husbandry.

Two things seem to have come together to produce cultures and civilizations: a society and culture based on agriculture and the development of centers of the community with literate social and religious structures. The members of these hierarchies then managed water supply and irrigation, ritual and religious life, and exerted their own right to use a portion of the goods produced by the community for their own subsistence in return for their management.

As **trade routes** developed and travel between cities became easier, trade led to specialization. Trade enables a people to obtain the goods they desire in exchange for the goods they are able to produce. This, in turn, leads to increased attention to refinements of technique and the sharing of ideas. The knowledge of a new discovery or invention provides knowledge and technology that increases the ability to produce goods for trade.

Mountains and **rivers** still formed formidable boundaries for countries and civilizations. This was the case everywhere around the world, except, of course, in the sands of sub-Saharan Africa, where struggles took the form of wars of attrition, the victors being those who weathered the sandstorms and lack of water the best. The Middle East, with its flat lands interrupted by only a few hills, rivers, and isolated mountains, saw more than its fair share of combat, as was the case in the early history and continues to be the case today.

Skill 13.2   Identify the intellectual contributions, artistic forms, and traditions of these civilizations.

When Egypt came under the domination of the Hyksos, Kush reached its greatest power and cultural energy (1700-1500 BCE). When the Hyksos were eventually expelled from Egypt, the New Kingdom brought Kush back under Egyptian colonial control. The collapse of the New Kingdom in Egypt (ca. 1000 BCE), provided the second opportunity for Kush to develop independently of Egyptian control and to conquer the entire Nubian region. **Egypt** made numerous significant contributions including construction of the great pyramids; development of hieroglyphic writing; preservation of bodies after death; making paper from papyrus; contributing to developments in arithmetic and geometry; the invention of the method of counting in groups of 1-10 (the decimal system); completion of a solar calendar; and the foundation for science and astronomy.

The ancient civilization of the **Sumerians** invented the wheel; developed irrigation through use of canals, dikes, and devices for raising water; devised the system of cuneiform writing; learned to divide time; and built large boats for trade. The Babylonians devised the famous **Code of Hammurabi**, a code of laws.

The ancient **Assyrians** were warlike and aggressive due to a highly organized military and used horse drawn chariots. The **Hebrews**, also known as the ancient Israelites instituted "monotheism," which is the worship of one God, Yahweh, and combined the 66 books of the Hebrew and Christian Greek scriptures into the Bible we have today. The **Minoans** had a system of writing using symbols to represent syllables in words. They built palaces with multiple levels containing many rooms, water and sewage systems with flush toilets, bathtubs, hot and cold running water, and bright paintings on the walls.

The **Mycenaeans** changed the Minoan writing system to aid their own language and used symbols to represent syllables. The **Phoenicians** were sea traders well known for their manufacturing skills in glass and metals and the development of their famous purple dye. They became so very proficient in the skill of navigation that they were able to sail by the stars at night. Further, they devised an alphabet using symbols to represent single sounds, which was an improved extension of the Egyptian principle and writing system.

In **India**, the caste system was developed, the principle of zero in mathematics was discovered, and the major religion of Hinduism was begun. In **India**, Hinduism was a continuing influence along with the rise of Buddhism. Industry and commerce developed along with extensive trading with the Near East. Outstanding advances in the fields of science and medicine were made along with being one of the first to be active in navigation and maritime enterprises during this time.

China is considered by some historians to be the oldest, uninterrupted civilization in the world and was in existence around the same time as the ancient civilizations founded in Egypt, Mesopotamia, and the Indus Valley. The Chinese studied nature and weather; stressed the importance of education, family, and a strong central government; followed the religions of Buddhism, Confucianism, and Taoism; and invented such things as gunpowder, paper, printing, and the magnetic compass. **China** began building the Great Wall; practiced crop rotation and terrace farming; increased the importance of the silk industry, and developed caravan routes across Central Asia for extensive trade. Also, they increased proficiency in rice cultivation and developed a written language based on drawings or pictographs (no alphabet symbolizing sounds as each word or character had a form different from all others).

The ancient **Persians** developed an alphabet; contributed the philosophies of **Zoroastrianism**, **Mithraism**, and **Gnosticism**; and allowed conquered peoples to retain their own customs, laws, and religions.

The classical civilization of **Greece** reached the highest levels in man's achievements based on the foundations already laid by such ancient groups as the Egyptians, Phoenicians, Minoans, and Mycenaeans. Among the more important contributions of Greece were the Greek alphabet derived from the Phoenician letters which formed the basis for the Roman alphabet and our present-day alphabet. Extensive trading and colonization resulted in the spread of the Greek civilization. The love of sports, with emphasis on a sound body, led to the tradition of the Olympic Games. Greece was responsible for the rise of independent, strong city-states. Other important areas that the Greeks are credited with influencing include drama, epic and lyric poetry, fables, myths centered on the many gods and goddesses, science, astronomy, medicine, mathematics, philosophy, art, architecture, and recording historical events. The conquests of Alexander the Great spread Greek ideas to the areas he conquered and brought to the Greek world many ideas from Asia and the value of ideas, wisdom, curiosity, and the desire to learn as much about the world as possible.

The civilization in **Japan** appeared during this time having borrowed much of their culture from China. It was the last of these classical civilizations to develop. Although they used, accepted, and copied Chinese art, law, architecture, dress, and writing, the Japanese refined these into their own unique way of life, including incorporating the religion of Buddhism into their culture.

The civilizations in **Africa** south of the Sahara were developing the refining and use of iron, especially for farm implements and later for weapons. Trading was overland using camels and at important seaports. The Arab influence was extremely important, as was their later contact with Indians, Christian Nubians, and Persians. Their trading activities were the most important factor in the spread of and assimilation of different ideas and stimulation of cultural growth.

In other parts of the world were the **Byzantine** and **Saracen** (or Islamic) civilizations, both dominated by religion. The major contributions of the Saracens were in the areas of science and philosophy. Included were accomplishments in astronomy, mathematics, physics, chemistry, medicine, literature, art, trade and manufacturing, agriculture, and a marked influence on the Renaissance period of history. The **Byzantines** (Christians) made important contributions in art and the preservation of Greek and Roman achievements including architecture (especially in Eastern Europe and Russia), the Code of Justinian and Roman law.

The ancient civilization of **Rome** lasted approximately 1,000 years including the periods of republic and empire, although its lasting influence on Europe and its history was for a much longer period. There was a very sharp contrast between the curious, imaginative, inquisitive Greeks and the practical, simple, down-to-earth, no-nonsense Romans, who spread and preserved the ideas of ancient Greece and other culture groups. The contributions and accomplishments of the Romans are numerous but their greatest included language, engineering, building, law, government, roads, trade, and the "**Pax Romana**". Pax Romana was the long period of peace enabling free travel and trade, spreading people, cultures, goods, and ideas all over a vast area of the known world.

The ancient empire of **Ghana** occupied an area that is now known as Northern Senegal and Southern Mauritania. There is no absolute certainty regarding the origin of this empire. Oral history dates the rise of the empire to the seventh century BCE. Most believe, however, that the date should be placed much later. Many believe the nomads who were herding animals in the fringes of the desert posed a threat to the early Soninke people, who were an agricultural community. In times of drought, it is believed the nomads raided the agricultural villages for water and places to pasture their herds. To protect their selves it is believed that these farming communities formed a loose confederation that eventually became the empire of ancient Ghana.

Skill 13.3 Recognize patterns of trade and commerce that influenced these civilizations.

Refer to Skill 13.1 and Skill 13.2.

COMPETENCY 14.0 MEDIEVAL AND EARLY MODERN TIMES

Skill 14.1   Describe the influence of physical geography on the development of medieval and early modern civilizations.

The official end of the **Roman Empire** came when Germanic tribes took over and controlled most of Europe. The five major tribes were the Visigoths, Ostrogoths, Vandals, Saxons, and the Franks. In later years, the Franks successfully stopped the invasion of southern Europe by Muslims by defeating them under the leadership of Charles Martel at the Battle of Tours in 732 AD. Thirty-six years later in 768 AD, the grandson of Charles Martel became King of the Franks and is known throughout history as Charlemagne.   Charlemagne was a man of war but was unique in his respect for and encouragement of learning.

The system of **feudalism** became the dominant feature of society. It was a system of loyalty and protection. The strong protected the weak that returned the service with farm labor, military service, and loyalty. Life was lived out on a vast estate, owned by a nobleman and his family, called a "manor." It was a complete village supporting a few hundred people, mostly peasants. Improved tools and farming methods made life more bearable although most never left the manor or traveled from their village during their lifetime.

The Andean Highlands of **Peru** offer additional insights into the civilizations of early humans and their adaptations to the environment. This region of Peru reaches heights of up to 6,768 meters, with hundreds of towering, snowcapped peaks, some of which are permanently ice-covered. The Pacific side of the Andes is very sparsely populated. Tropical forests cover the eastern side. Between these two extreme areas, there is a higher-population region made up of several zones. The intermontane valleys, the higher uplands, and the grassy puna or plateaus are home to about one third of the Peruvian people today. It was in this region that evidence of human habitation has been found which appears to date back some 12,000 years.

Skill 14.2   Trace the decline of the Western Roman Empire and the development of feudalism as a social and economic system in Europe and Japan.

The primary factors that led to the overthrow of the last king and the establishment of the Roman Republic appear to be: (1) a desire to be free of the Etruscans, (2) a desire to put an end to the tyranny of the last king, and (3) the kind of political evolution that occurred elsewhere as the noble classes wanted to establish an aristocratic form of government. The next 275 years were occupied with expansion. This involved numerous wars of conquest. By 100 BC Rome controlled most of the Hellenistic world. This rapid conquest was one of the factors in the decline of the Republic.

The republic did not have the infrastructure to absorb the conquered people. In addition, there was political decay, vast economic and social change, and military failure. In politics, the Senate refused to grant rights to the mass of the populace. A civil war erupted between rival factions. And, lacking adequate infrastructure, Rome was not able to provide good government to conquered territories.

Heavy taxation of these territories, oppression by the government, and corrupt resident government officials led to decay. Critical social and economic changes included: the ruin of small farmers by importing slaves from conquered areas, a vast migration of the poor to the city of Rome, a failure to encourage and invest in industry and trade, the dissatisfaction of the new business class, and a general decline in morale among all classes of citizens. At the same time, the republic experienced a vast slave uprising in Southern Italy and faced the first attacks from Germanic invaders.

The reasons for the decline of the Roman Empire are still a matter of debate.

1. **Political**: a period of anarchy and military emperors led to war and destruction;

2. **Economic**: the rise of large villas owned and controlled by landlords who settled poor people on the land as hereditary tenants who lived under conditions of partial servitude; use of wasteful agricultural methods; a decline of commerce; skilled workers were bound to jobs and were forced to accept government wages and prices; corruption, lack of productivity and inadequate investment of capital; the draining of gold from the western part of the empire through unfavorable trade balances with the East.

3. **Biological, ecological and social**: deforestation, bad agricultural methods, diseases (particularly malaria), earthquakes, immorality, brutalization of the masses in the cities, demoralization of the upper classes. This was accompanied by the decay of pagan beliefs and Roman ideals with the rise of Christianity.

The beginning of the barbarian infiltrations and invasions further weakened the sense of Roman identity. All of these factors contributed to an empire that was ill equipped to contend with invaders.

With the increase in trade and travel, cities sprang up and began to grow. Craft workers in the cities developed their skills to a high degree, eventually organizing guilds to protect the quality of the work and to regulate the buying and selling of their products. City government developed and flourished centered on strong town councils. The end of the feudal manorial system was sealed by the outbreak and spread of the infamous **Black Death**, which killed over one third of the total population of Europe. Those who survived and were skilled in any job or occupation were in demand and many serfs or peasants found freedom and, for that time, a decidedly improved standard of living. Strong **nation-states** became powerful and people developed a renewed interest in life and learning.

Skill 14.3   Identify the art, architecture, and science of Pre-Columbian America.

One of the best known of the North American tribes was the Pueblo, who lived in what is now the American Southwest. They are perhaps best known for the challenging vista-based villages that they constructed from the sheer faces of cliffs and rocks and for their **adobes**, mud-brick buildings that housed their living and meeting quarters. The Pueblos chose their own chiefs. This was perhaps one of the oldest representative governments in the world.

Known also for their organized government were the Iroquois, who lived in the American Northeast. The famous Five Nations of the Iroquois made treaties among themselves and shared leadership of their peoples. Religion was a personal affair for nearly all of these tribes, with beliefs in higher powers extending to Spirits in the sky and elsewhere in Nature. Native Americans had none of the one-god-only mentality that developed in Europe and the Middle East, nor did they have the wars associated with the conflict that those monotheistic religions had with one another.

Those people who lived in North America had large concentrations of people and houses, but they didn't have the kind of large civilization centers like the cities of elsewhere in the world. These people didn't have an exact system of writing, either. These were two technological advances that were found in many other places in the world, including, to varying degrees, South America.

Skill 14.4   Describe the role of Christianity in medieval and early modern Europe, its expansion beyond Europe, and the role of Islam and its impact on Arabia, Africa, Europe and Asia.

Christianity: Christianity grew out of Judaism and its belief that God would send a Messiah ("anointed one") who would establish the Kingdom of God on earth. Jesus of Nazareth appeared in the early years of the first century CE, preaching repentance in preparation for the arrival of the Kingdom of God. His brief (about three years) ministry of teaching, preaching, healing and miracles gathered followers from among the common and the despised of his day, as well as non-Jews and the wealthy. This ministry was confined to the areas of Galilee and northwest Palestine. According to Christian writings, Jesus eschewed the separatism of Judaism and reached out to the poor, the sick, and the social outcasts. He preached a Kingdom of God not of this world, which ran contrary to Jewish expectation of a political Messiah who would establish an earthly kingdom. As the movement grew, the teachings of Jesus were perceived as a danger to the political order by both the Jews and the Roman government. Jesus was handed over to the authorities by one of his closest followers, arrested, tried, and crucified. According to Christian belief, Jesus rose from the dead on the third day, appeared to his disciples and then ascended to heaven.

Christian scripture (**the Bible**) consists of two major parts: the Old Testament, which is an adoption of the Hebrew Scripture, and the New Testament, which consists of 27 books. Fundamental beliefs of Christianity are: (1) there is one God who is the creator and redeemer of humankind; God is all-knowing, all-powerful, and all-present; (2) Jesus Christ is the unique Son of God who is the savior of humankind. The doctrine of the Trinity teaches that the one God has three natures through/by which God is active in the world: God the Father, the creator and governor of creation, is the judge of humankind, God the Son (Jesus) is God in the flesh, who came among humankind to save them from sin, and God the Holy Spirit is the invisible presence of God. Christian ethics are based on the **Ten Commandments** of the Old Testament and the teachings of Jesus, which include the "Golden Rule" (Do unto others as you would have them do unto you") and a broadening of the application of the commandments.

In about 610, Mohammed came to some prominence. He called his new religion **Islam** (submission [to the will of God]) and his followers were called Moslems – those who had surrendered themselves. Islam slowly gained ground, and the persecutions became more severe around Mecca. In 622, Mohammed and his close followers fled the city and found refuge in Medina to the North. His flight is called the **Hegira**. This event marks the beginning of the Moslem calendar. Mohammed took advantage of the ongoing feuds between Jews and Arabs in the city and became the ruler of Medina, making it the capital of a rapidly growing state.

The **Koran** contains Mohammed's teachings on moral and theological questions, his legislation on political matters, and his comments on current events. Islam has five basic principles:
1. The oneness and omnipotence of God – Allah
   - Mohammed is the prophet of Allah to whom all truth has been revealed by God
   - To each of the previous prophets (Adam, Noah, Abraham, Moses and Jesus) a part of the truth was revealed
2. One should pray five times a day at prescribed intervals, facing Mecca
3. Charity – for the welfare of the community
4. Fasting from sunrise to sunset every day during the holy month of Ramadan to cleanse the spirit
5. Pilgrimage to Mecca should be made if possible and if no one suffers thereby

The converts to Islam, who brought their cultural traditions, probably contributed more to this emerging synthetic civilization than the Arabs. This blending of cultures, facilitated by a common language, a common religion, and a strong economy, created learning, literature, science, technology and art that surpassed anything found in the Western Christian world during the Early Middle Ages. Interestingly, the most brilliant period of Moslem culture was from the eighth century through the eleventh, coinciding with the West's darkest cultural period.

Skill 14.5   Trace the development of the Renaissance and the Scientific Revolution in Europe.

The word **Renaissance** literally means "rebirth", and signaled the rekindling of interest in the glory of ancient classical Greek and Roman civilizations. It was the period in human history marking the start of many ideas and innovations leading to our modern age. The Renaissance began in Italy with many of its ideas starting in Florence, controlled by the infamous Medici family. Education, especially for some of the merchants, required reading, writing, and math, the study of law, and the writings of classical Greek and Roman writers. Contributions of the Italian Renaissance period were in: **art, political philosophy, literature, science and medicine.**

In **Germany**, Gutenberg's invention of the **printing press** with movable type facilitated the rapid spread of Renaissance ideas, writings and innovations, thus ensuring the enlightenment of most of Western Europe. Contributions were also made by Durer and Holbein in art and by Paracelsus in science and medicine. The effects of the Renaissance in the **Low Countries** can be seen in the literature and philosophy of Erasmus and the art of van Eyck and Breughel the Elder. Rabelais and de Montaigne in France also contributed to literature and philosophy. In **Spain**, the art of El Greco and de Morales flourished, as did the writings of Cervantes and De Vega. In **England**, Sir Thomas More and Sir Francis Bacon wrote and taught philosophy and inspired by Vesalius. William Harvey made important contributions in medicine. The greatest talent was found in literature and drama and given to mankind by Chaucer, Spenser, Marlowe, Jonson, and the incomparable Shakespeare.

The Renaissance ushered in a time of curiosity, learning, and incredible energy sparking the desire for trade to procure these new, exotic products and to find better, faster, cheaper trade routes to get to them. The work of geographers, astronomers and mapmakers made important contributions and many studied and applied the work of such men as Hipparchus of Greece, Ptolemy of Egypt, Tycho Brahe of Denmark, and Fra Mauro of Italy.

The **Scientific Revolution** was characterized by a shift in scientific approach and ideas. Near the end of the sixteenth century Galileo Galilei introduced a radical approach to the study of motion. He moved from attempts to explain why objects move the way they do and began to use experiments to describe precisely how they move. He also used experimentation to describe how forces affect non-moving objects. Other scientists continued in the same approach. Outstanding scientists of the period included Johannes Kepler, Evangelista Torricelli, Blaise Pascal, Isaac Newton and Leibniz. This was the period when experiments dominated scientific study. This method was particularly applied to the study of physics.

Skill 14.6   Define the development of early modern capitalism and its global consequences.

Capitalism is an economic system characterized by privately-owned means of production, the investment of capital in the production, distribution and trade of goods and services and by sale and distribution for profit in a competitive free market. Capitalism developed in Europe in the sixteenth through nineteenth centuries. It has become the dominant economic system of the West since the death of feudalism. From Europe, capitalism spread throughout the world along with the effects of the Industrial Revolution.

Between the fifteenth and eighteenth centuries the idea of private property emerged and achieved legal recognition. Locke, in particular, argued that the right to hold private property is a natural right of humans. The earliest stage in the development of capitalism was mercantilism, which was a system of trade for profit. Key elements of mercantilism were the belief in the importance of accumulating precious metals, an emphasis on state power and overseas conquest. The theory stated that if a state could not produce the raw materials it needed, it should acquire colonies that could provide those raw materials.

The second stage in the development of capitalism occurred in the middle of the eighteenth century. Industrial capitalism was marked by the birth of the factory system of manufacturing. The Industrial Revolution streamlined the manual tasks of labor, as well as producing more consistent products faster. The industrialist quickly replaced the merchant. By the late nineteenth century, financiers began to control production, marking the beginning of Finance Capitalism. The ability of these financiers to band together to form cartels fostered the development of monopolies.

Skill 14.7   Describe the evolution of the idea of representative democracy from the Magna Carta through the Enlightenment.

The Magna Carta - This charter has been considered the basis of English constitution liberties. It was granted to a representative group of English barons and nobles on **June 15, 1215** by the British King John, after they had forced it on him. The Magna Carta is considered to be the first modern document that sought to try to limit the powers of the given state authority. It guaranteed feudal rights, regulated the justice system, and abolished many abuses of the King's power to tax and regulates trade. It said that the king could not raise new taxes without first consulting a Great Council, made up of nobles, barons, and Church people. The rights won by the nobles were given to other English people. The Great Council grew into a representative assembly called the Parliament. By the 1600s, Parliament was divided into the House of Lords, made up of nobles and the House of Commons. Members of the House of Commons were elected to office. In the beginning, only a few wealthy men could vote.

The Petition of Right - In English history, it was the title of a petition that was addressed to the King of England **Charles I,** by the British parliament in **1628**. The Parliament demanded that the king stop proclaiming new taxes without its' consent. Parliament demanded that he cease housing soldiers and sailors in the homes of private citizens, proclaiming martial law in times of peace, and that no subject should be imprisoned without a good cause being shown. They later had an important effect on the demands of the revolutionary colonists, as these were some of the rights that as Englishmen, they felt were being denied. The Petition of Right was also the basis of specific protections that the designers of the Constitution made a point of inserting in the document.

The **Enlightenment** was a period of intense self-study that focused on ethics and logic. More so than at any time before, scientists and philosophers questioned cherished truths, widely held beliefs, and their own sanity in an attempt to discover why the world worked—from within. "I think, therefore I am" was one of the famous sayings of that or any day, uttered by **Rene Descartes**, a French scientist-philosopher whose dedication to logic and the rigid rules of observation were a blueprint for the thinkers who came after him.

During the Enlightenment, the idea of the "**social contract**" confirmed the belief that government existed because people wanted it to, that the people had an agreement with the government that they would submit to it as long as it protected them and didn't encroach on their basic human rights. This idea was first made famous by the Frenchman Jean-Jacques Rousseau but was also adopted by England's John Locke and America's Thomas Jefferson.

Thomas Hobbes (1588-1679) author of the book *Leviathan* (1651) which was actually written as a reaction to the disorders caused by the English civil wars which had culminated with the execution of King Charles I.

John Locke (1632-1704) was an important thinker on the nature of democracy. Locke also believed that all men are born good, independent and equal and that it is their actions that will determine their fate. Locke's views in *Two Treatises of Civil Government* (1690) attacked the theory of the divine right of kings and the nature of the state as conceived by Thomas Hobbes.

Jean-Jacques Rousseau (1712-1778) was one of the most famous and influential political theorists before the French Revolution. His most important and most studied work is **The Social Contract** (1762). He was concerned with what should be the proper form of society and government. Rousseau's most direct influence was upon the **French Revolution** (1789-1815). In the **Declaration of the Rights of Man and The Citizen** (1789), it explicitly recognized the sovereignty of the general will as expressed in the law.

DOMAIN II – UNITED STATES HISTORY

COMPETENCY 15.0 EARLY EXPLORATION, COLONIAL ERA, AND THE WAR FOR INDEPENDENCE

Skill 15.1   Identify and describe European exploration and settlement, and the struggle for control of North America during the Colonial Era, including cooperation and conflict among American Indians and new settlers.

Portugal made the start under the encouragement, support, and financing of Prince Henry the Navigator. The better known explorers who sailed under the flag of Portugal included Cabral, Diaz, and Vasco da Gama, who successfully sailed all the way from Portugal, around the southern tip of Africa, to Calcutta, India.

Christopher Columbus, sailing for **Spain**, is credited with the discovery of America although he never set foot on its soil. Magellan is credited with the first circumnavigation of the earth. Other Spanish explorers made their marks in parts of what are now the United States, Mexico, and South America.

For **France**, claims to various parts of North America were the result of the efforts of such men as Verrazano, Champlain, Cartier, LaSalle, Father Marquette and Joliet. Dutch claims were based on the work of one Henry Hudson. John Cabot gave England its stake in North America along with John Hawkins, Sir Francis Drake, and the half-brothers Sir Walter Raleigh and Sir Humphrey Gilbert.

Actually the first Europeans in the New World were **Norsemen** led by Eric the Red and later, his son Leif the Lucky. However, before any of these, the ancestors of today's Native Americans and Latin American Indians crossed the Bering Strait from Asia to Alaska, eventually settling in all parts of the Americas.

Many of the Native Americans perished as a result of contracting diseases for which they no immunity from the European and African immigrants, such as smallpox, measles, shingles, cholera, influenza, etc. As successive Spanish expeditions established landfalls in Florida, the Gulf Coast, Mesoamerica and other locations, a similar pattern of the search for gold, the taking of native populations for slaves and the introduction of new diseases spelled disaster for the Native Americans in their early contacts with Europeans.

Skill 15.2   Identify the founders and discuss their religious, economic and political reasons for colonization of North America.

The part of North America claimed by France was called New France and consisted of the land west of the Appalachian Mountains. This area of claims and settlement included the St. Lawrence Valley, the Great Lakes, the Mississippi Valley, and the entire region of land westward to the Rocky Mountains. They established the permanent settlements of Montreal and New Orleans, thus giving them control of the two major gateways into the heart of North America. Most of the French settlements were in Canada along the St. Lawrence River. Only scattered forts and trading posts were found in the upper Mississippi Valley and Great Lakes region. The rulers of France originally intended New France to have vast estates owned by nobles and worked by peasants who would live on the estates in compact farming villages--the New World version of the Old World's medieval system of feudalism. The French fur traders made friends with the friendly tribes of Indians, spending the winters with them getting the furs needed for trade. Manufacturers and workmen back in France, ship-owners and merchants, as well as the fur traders and their Indian allies all benefited.

Spanish settlement had its beginnings in the Caribbean with the establishment of colonies on Hispaniola (at Santo Domingo which became the capital of the West Indies), Puerto Rico, and Cuba. The Spanish settlements in North America were not commercial enterprises but were for protection and defense of the trading and wealth from their colonies in Mexico and South America. The Russians hunting seals came down the Pacific coast, the English moved into Florida and west into and beyond the Appalachians, and the French traders and trappers were making their way from Louisiana and other parts of New France into Spanish territory.

The first permanent settlement in what is now the United States was in 1565 at St. Augustine, Florida. A later permanent settlement in the southwestern United States was in 1609 at Santa Fe, New Mexico. At the peak of Spanish power, the area in the United States claimed, settled, and controlled by Spain included Florida and all land west of the Mississippi River. Of course, France and England also lay claim to the same areas. Spain's control over her New World colonies lasted more than 300 years, longer than England or France. To this day, Spanish influence remains in names of places, art, architecture, music, literature, law, and cuisine.

The English colonies, with only a few exceptions, were considered commercial ventures to make a profit for the crown or the company or whoever financed its beginnings. One was strictly a philanthropic enterprise and three others were primarily for religious reasons but the other nine were started for economic reasons. Settlers in these unique colonies came for different reasons: religious freedom, political freedom, economic prosperity or land ownership.

Skill 15.3   Describe European colonial rule and its relationship with American Indian societies.

Perhaps the most famous of the Native American tribes is the **Algonquians**. We know so much about this tribe because they were one of the first to interact with the newly arrived English settlers in Plymouth, Massachusetts and elsewhere. Beginning with a brave man named Squanto, they shared this agricultural knowledge with the English settlers, including how to plant and cultivate corn, pumpkins, and squash.

Another group of tribes who lived in the Northeast were the **Iroquois**, who were fierce fighters but also forward thinkers. They lived in long houses and wore clothes made of buckskin. They, too, were expert farmers, growing the "Three Sisters" (corn, squash, and beans). Five of the Iroquois tribes formed a Confederacy that was a shared form of government. The Iroquois also formed the False Face Society, a group of medicine men who shared their medical knowledge with others but kept their identities secret while doing so. These masks are one of the enduring symbols of the Native American era. Much of the homeland of the Iroquois was ceded to New York land speculators through various treaties after the Revolutionary War. What made them unique was a sophisticated political system, with a system of checks, balances and supreme law. The central authority of the League was very limited. This left each tribe the autonomy to pursue its own interests. They were also quite skilled in diplomacy. There is great discussion about the influence the Iroquois government exerted upon the Framers of the Articles of Confederation and the U.S. Constitution.

Living in the Southeast were the **Seminoles** and **Creeks**, a huge collection of people who lived in chickees (open, bark-covered houses) and wore clothes made from plant fibers. They were expert planters and hunters and were proficient at paddling dugout canoes, which they made. The bead necklaces they created were some of the most beautiful on the continent. They are best known, however, for their struggle against Spanish and English settlers, especially led by the great Osceola. The **Cherokee** also lived in the Southeast. They were one of the most advanced tribes, living in domed houses and wearing deerskin and rabbit fur. Accomplished hunters, farmers, and fishermen, the Cherokee were known the continent over for their intricate and beautiful basketry and clay pottery. They also played a game called lacrosse, which survives to this day in countries around the world.

The Dutch were the primary trading partners of the Iroquois peoples. They traded beaver and other furs for various European goods. Roger Williams, founder of Providence and Rhode Island, had objected to the Massachusetts colonial seizure of Indian lands and settlements and the relationship between these seizures and the Church of England. Williams was banished from Massachusetts and purposely set up Rhode Island as the first colony with a true separation of church and state.

Skill 15.4   Development and institutionalization of African slavery in the western hemisphere and its consequences in Sub-Saharan Africa.

Several African nations on the Western coast of the continent quickly discovered a demand for African slaves. The people of these nations used slave labor, themselves. Peoples defeated and/or captured in war were placed in slavery. As these African people discovered the demand for more and more slaves, they moved into the interior of the continent, taking captives for sale to European traders. The transatlantic slave trade refers to the purchase and transportation of people from West and Central Africa to the New World for slavery and other forms of bondage. The slaves were the middle element of a very prosperous three-part trade cycle referred as **triangular trade**. The trade in slaves began in response to a labor shortage in the New World. There was a great need for cheap labor in mining and in agriculture. Particularly in the predominantly agricultural South, harvesting of many of the major cash crops - sugar, rice, tobacco, cotton was labor-intensive. Seventy percent of the slaves brought to the U.S. were used in the production of sugar, the most labor-intensive crop.

Agricultural economies developing in North and South America maintained a level of demand that enriched these slave-trading African nations. The slave trade became so lucrative that it became a critical point in the trade triangle that moved finished products from Europe to Africa, slaves from Africa to North and South America, and raw materials from North and South America to Europe. Many of the agricultural, mining, and related "industries" of the Americas depended heavily on a steady supply of cheap labor and upon the ability to force the labor force to work under any and all conditions. Although some religious leaders decried slavery from the beginning, most supported the slave trade by church teaching and by introducing the idea of the black man's and the white man's separate roles. Some taught that blacks should labor in exchange for the blessings of European civilization, including Christianity.

Skill 15.5   Describe the causes of the War for Independence, elements of political and military leadership, the impact of the war on Americans, the role of France, and the key ideas embodied within the Declaration of Independence.

The establishment of overseas colonies was first, and foremost, a commercial enterprise, not a political one. The political aspect was secondary and assumed. The British took it for granted that Parliament was supreme, was recognized so by the colonists, and were very resentful of the colonial challenge to Parliament's authority. They were contemptuously indifferent to politics in America and had no wish to exert any control over it.

The British had been extremely lax and totally inconsistent in enforcement of the mercantile or trade laws passed in the years before 1754. The government itself was not particularly stable so actions against the colonies occurred in anger and their attitude was one of a moral superiority, that they knew how to manage America better than the Americans did themselves. This of course points to a lack of sufficient knowledge of conditions and opinions in America. The colonists had been left on their own for nearly 150 years and by the time the Revolutionary War began, they were quite adept at self-government and adequately handling the affairs of their daily lives. The Americans equated ownership of land or property with the right to vote. Property was considered the foundation of life and liberty and, in the colonial mind and tradition, these went together.

These colonists also had their own tradition of publishing the views and sentiments of individuals regarding issues of parochial interest and matters of concern which crossed colonial boundaries. In print—via newspapers and pamphlets—dialogue and debate over matters quite trivial or quite significant became common public practice in the American colonies. As strains with the mother country began to develop and increase—especially after the French and Indian War—the resulting issues became increasingly focused in print throughout the colonies. No doubt the discussions and debates published carried their sentiments over to the homes, taverns and other places where the people met to discuss events of the day. An important result of this was a growing "Americanism" in the sentiments of those writers published, and a sense of connection among American people that transcended colonial boundaries.

From the initial **Stamp Act** in 1765, through the "Boston Massacre" in 1770, to the time of the Tea Act in 1773 (which resulted in the "Boston Tea Party") and beyond, colonial presses were rife with discussion and debate about what they considered to be an unacceptable situation. Parliament intended to assert its right to tax and legislatively control the colonies of Great Britain in whatever manner it saw as prudent and appropriate. Most American colonists, believing their selves to be full British subjects, would deny Parliaments assertions so long as they were not provided with full and equal representation within Parliament.

One of the most notable spokesmen for the American cause was, in fact, an Englishman. **Thomas Paine** (1737-1809) was born in England and came to America in November 1774. He was immediately taken up by the social issues and politics in the American colonies and insinuated himself into the dialogue of current issues, which was ongoing in the colonies—conducted via newspapers and pamphlets. But his topic at the time was an unusual public stand about African slavery. He is best remembered for "**Common Sense**."

Therefore when an indirect tax on tea was made, the British felt that since it wasn't a direct tax, there should be no objection to it. The colonists viewed any tax, direct or indirect, as an attack on their property. They felt that as a representative body, the British Parliament should protect British citizens, including the colonists, from arbitrary taxation. Since they felt they were not represented, Parliament, in their eyes, gave them no protection. So, war began. August 23, 1775, George III declared that the colonies were in rebellion and warned them to stop or else.

By 1776, the colonists and their representatives in the Second Continental Congress realized that things were past the point of no return. The **Declaration of Independence** was drafted and declared July 4, 1776. George Washington labored against tremendous odds to wage a victorious war. The turning point in the Americans' favor occurred in 1777 with the American victory at **Saratoga**. This victory decided for the French to align themselves with the Americans against the British. With the aid of **Admiral de Grasse** and French warships blocking the entrance to Chesapeake Bay, British General Cornwallis trapped at Yorktown, Virginia, surrendered in 1781 and the war was over. The **Treaty of Paris** officially ending the war was signed in 1783.

Other authors, other printers and publishers, and other factions, were also quite active in promoting the new American attitude toward independence. Of significant note, was the **Virginia Declaration of Rights**, drafted by George Mason in May 1776 and amended by Thomas Ludwell Lee and the Virginia Convention. Thomas Jefferson was influenced by it when he drafted the Declaration of Independence only a month later. This document would also influence James Madison when drawing up the **Bill of Rights** (1789) and also the Marquis de Lafayette when drafting the **French Declaration of the Rights of Man** (1789).

The Declaration's text can be divided into three main parts:

1. Statements of the general state of humanity and the natural rights inherent in all civil societies.

2. An enumeration of specific and detailed grievances, which point out why the current sovereign has lost the right to govern. It also lists how the king even subverted English Common Law and legal traditions dating back to antiquity.

3. The last part of the text states that the colonists had exhausted all civil and legal means of having their grievances addressed by British government, and now had the right and duty to break with the crown and be a free and independent nation.

The final section of the Declaration contains the signatures of the representatives of the colonies to the Continental Congress in Philadelphia. Realizing that they had committed an act of treason, punishable by death by hanging, Benjamin Franklin counseled unity, lest they all hang separately. It should also be noted that at that moment, open hostilities between British and Colonists had already been underway for over a year. **George Washington** had taken command of the Continental Army, organized on June 14, 1775 at Harvard Yard, and in the same year, the Continental Navy and the Marine Corps had been organized.

During the war, and after independence was declared, the former colonies now found themselves independent states. The Second Continental Congress was conducting a war with representation by delegates from thirteen separate states. The Congress had no power to act for the states or to require them to accept and follow its wishes. A permanent united government was desperately needed. On November 15, 1777, the **Articles of Confederation** were adopted, creating a league of free and independent states.

COMPETENCY 16.0 THE DEVELOPMENT OF THE CONSTITUTION AND THE EARLY REPUBLIC

Skill 16.1 Describe the political system of the United States and the ways that citizens participate in it through executive, legislative and judicial processes.

In the United States, the three branches of the federal government: the **Executive**, the **Legislative**, and the **Judicial** divide their powers thus:

Legislative - Article I of the Constitution established the legislative or law-making branch of the government called the Congress. It is made up of two houses, the House of Representatives and the Senate. Voters in all states elect the members who serve in each respective house of Congress. The Legislative branch is responsible for making laws, raising and printing money, regulating trade, establishing the postal service and federal courts, approving the President's appointments, declaring war and supporting the armed forces. The Congress also has the power to change the Constitution itself and to impeach (bring charges against) the President. Charges for impeachment are brought by the House of Representatives and are tried in the Senate.

Executive – Article II of the Constitution created the Executive branch of the government, headed by the President, who leads the country, recommends new laws, and can veto bills passed by the Legislative branch. As the chief of state, the President is responsible for carrying out the laws of the country and the treaties and declarations of war passed by the Legislative branch. The President also appoints federal judges and is Commander in Chief of the military when it is called into service. Other members of the Executive branch include the Vice-President, also elected. Various cabinet members as he might appoint, ambassadors, presidential advisers, members of the armed forces, and other appointed and civil servants of government agencies, departments and bureaus. Though the President appoints them, they then must be approved by the legislative branch.

Judicial - Article III of the Constitution established the Judicial branch of government headed by the Supreme Court. The Supreme Court has the power to rule that a law passed by the Legislature, or an act of the Executive branch is illegal and unconstitutional. In an appeal capacity, citizens, businesses, and government officials can also ask the Supreme Court to review a decision made in a lower court if someone believes that the ruling by a judge is unconstitutional. The Judicial branch also includes lower federal courts known as federal district courts that have been established by the Congress. The courts try lawbreakers and review cases refereed from other courts.

Skill 16.2   Define the Articles of Confederation and the factors leading to the development of the U.S. Constitution and the Bill of Rights.

Articles of Confederation - This was the first political system under which the newly independent colonies tried to organize themselves. It was drafted after the Declaration of Independence in 1776, was passed by the Continental Congress on November 15, 1777, ratified by the thirteen states, and took effect on March 1, 1781. The Articles gave Congress the power to declare war, appoint military officers, and coin money. The Articles of Confederation limited the powers of Congress by giving the states final authority. Although Congress could pass laws, at least nine of the thirteen states had to approve a law before it went into effect. To get money, Congress had to ask each state for it, no state could be forced to pay. Thus, the Articles created a loose alliance among the thirteen states. The national government was weak, in part, because it didn't have a strong chief executive to carry out laws passed by the legislature. Many different disputes arose and there was no way of settling them. Thus, the delegates went to meet again to try to fix the Articles; instead they ended up scrapping them and created a new **Constitution** that learned from these earlier mistakes.

The central government of the new United States of America consisted of a Congress of two to seven delegates from each state with each state having just one vote. Some of its powers included: borrowing and coining money, directing foreign affairs, declaring war and making peace, building and equipping a navy, regulating weights and measures, asking the states to supply men and money for an army. The delegates to Congress had no real authority as each state carefully and jealously guarded its own interests and limited powers under the Articles. Also, the delegates to Congress were paid by their states and had to vote as directed by their state legislatures.

The serious weaknesses were the lack of power: to regulate finances, over interstate trade, over foreign trade, to enforce treaties, and military power. Something better and more efficient was needed. In May of 1787, delegates from all states except Rhode Island began meeting in Philadelphia. At first, they met to revise the Articles of Confederation as instructed by Congress; but they soon realized that much more was needed. Abandoning the instructions, they set out to write a new Constitution, the foundation of all government in the United States and a model for representative government throughout the world.

All these ideas found their final expression in the United States Constitution's first ten amendments, known as the **Bill of Rights.** In 1789, the first Congress passed these first amendments and by December 1791, three-fourths of the states at that time had ratified them. The Bill of Rights protects certain liberties and basic rights. James Madison who wrote the amendments said that the Bill of Rights does not give Americans these rights.

Bill Of Rights - The first ten amendments to the United States Constitution dealing with civil liberties and civil rights. James Madison was credited with writing a majority of them. They are in brief:

1.   **Freedom of Religion.**
2.   **Right To Bear Arms.**
3.   **Security from the quartering of troops in homes.**
4.   **Right against unreasonable search and seizures.**
5.   **Right against self-incrimination.**
6.   **Right to trial by jury, right to legal council.**
7.   **Right to jury trial for civil actions.**
8.   **No cruel or unusual punishment allowed.**
9.   **These rights shall not deny other rights the people enjoy.**
10.   **Powers not mentioned in the Constitution shall be retained by the states or the people.**

Skill 16.3   Explain the major principles of government and political philosophy contained within the Constitution, especially separation of powers and federalism.

Article III of the US Constitution created a **Supreme Court** and authorized Congress to create other federal courts as it deemed necessary. In 1789, Congress passed the **Judiciary Act**, which set the number of Supreme Court justices at six, with one Chief Justice and five associates. The Judiciary Act also created 13 judicial districts, each with one district judge who was authorized to hear maritime cases and other types of cases. In 1793, Congress changed the circuit court to one Supreme Court justice and the local district judge.

Checks and Balances - System set up by the Constitution in which each branch of the federal government has the power to check, or limit the actions of other branches. **Separation of Powers** - System of American government in which each branch of government has its own specifically designated powers and can not interfere with the powers of another.

Federalism in colonial America meant belief in a strong central government. The Articles of Confederation provided for a weak central government, and lawmakers and citizens alike saw the unlikelihood of such an idea. One of the debates that shaped the ratification of the Constitution was the idea that the national government would be superior in status to state and local governments. Indeed, the national government is often called the federal government as well. In this historical political debate, those who favored a strong federal debate were called Federalists and those opposed styled themselves anti-Federalists.

Beginning with opinions written by Chief Justice John Marshall (including Gibbons v. Ogden and McCulloch v. Maryland), a series of Supreme Court decisions affirmed the supremacy of the federal government over that of the states. After all, if a state could tax the federal government, as was argued in McCulloch, then the federal government could theoretically yield its authority to that state, giving it supremacy over every other state; and that would undermine the authority of the federal government, not only in the minds of the judges of the federal and state courts but also in the hearts and minds of the people, of both the United States and other countries. This tradition has continued to the present day, with states being unable to sue the federal government, disputes between states being settled by federal courts, and foreign threats being answered by a national defense force. In today's political discussions, the idea of states' superseding the federal government seems foreign indeed.

Skill 16.4   Trace the evolution of political parties, describe their differing visions for the country, and analyze their impact on economic development policies.

The two parties that developed through the early 1790s were led by Jefferson as the Secretary of State and Alexander Hamilton as the Secretary of the Treasury. Jefferson and Hamilton were different in many ways. Hamilton wanted the federal government to be stronger than the state governments. Jefferson believed that the state governments should be stronger. Hamilton supported the creation of the first **Bank of the United States**; Jefferson opposed it because he felt that it gave too much power to wealthy investors who would help run it. Jefferson interpreted the Constitution strictly; he argued that nowhere did the Constitution give the federal government the power to create a national bank. Hamilton interpreted the Constitution much more loosely. He pointed out that the Constitution gave Congress the power to make all laws "necessary and proper" to carry out its duties. He reasoned that since Congress had the right to collect taxes, then Congress had the right to create the bank. Hamilton wanted the government to encourage economic growth. He favored the growth of trade, manufacturing, and the rise of cities as the necessary parts of economic growth. He favored the business leaders and mistrusted the common people. Jefferson believed that the common people, especially the farmers, were the backbone of the nation. He thought that the rise of big cities and manufacturing would corrupt American life.

The political party system in the U.S. has five main objects or lines of action:
> (1) to influence government policy
> (2) to form or shape public opinion
> (3) to win elections
> (4) to choose between candidates for office
> (5) to procure salaried posts for party leaders and workers

Skill 16.5   Identify historical, cultural, economic and geographic factors that led to the formation of distinct regional identities.

When the United States declared independence from England, the founding fathers created a political point of view that created a national unity while respecting the uniqueness and individual rights of each of the thirteen colonies or states. As the young nation grew, territories came to be defined as states. The states began to acquire their own particular **cultures** and **identities**. In time regional interests and cultures also began to take shape. Religious interests, economic life, and geography began to be understood as definitive of particular regions. The northeast tended toward industrial development. The south tended to rely upon agriculture. The west was an area of untamed open spaces where people settled and practiced agriculture and animal husbandry.

Each of these regions came to be defined, at least to some extent, on the basis of the way people made their living and the economic and social institutions that supported them. In the industrialized north, the factory system tended to create a division between the tycoons of business and industry and the poor industrial workers. The conditions in which the labor force worked were far from ideal – the hours were long, the conditions bad, and the pay was small. The South was characterized by cities that were centers of social and commercial life. The agriculture that supported the region was practiced on "plantations" that were owned by the wealthy and worked by slaves or indentured servants.   The west was a vast expanse to be explored and tamed. Life on a western ranch was distinctly different from either life in the industrial north or the agricultural south.

The regional differences between North and South came to a head over the issue of slavery. The rise of the abolitionist movement in the North, the publication of Uncle Tom's Cabin, and issues of trade and efforts by the national government to control trade for the regions coalesced around the issue of slavery in a nation that was founded on the principle of the inalienable right of every person to be free. As the South defended its lifestyle and its economy and the right of the states to be self-determining, the North became stronger in its criticism of slavery. The result was a growing **sectionalism**.

The **New England colonies** consisted of Massachusetts, Rhode Island, Connecticut, and New Hampshire. Life in these colonies was centered on the towns. What farming was done was by each family on its own plot of land but a short summer growing season and limited amount of good soil gave rise to other economic activities such as manufacturing, fishing, shipbuilding, and trade. The vast majority of the settlers shared similar origins, coming from England and Scotland. Towns were carefully planned and laid out the same way. The form of government was the town meeting where all adult males met to make the laws. The legislative body, the General Court, consisted of an Upper and Lower House.

The **Middle or Middle Atlantic colonies** included New York, New Jersey, Pennsylvania, Delaware, and Maryland. New York and New Jersey were at one time the Dutch colony of New Netherlands and Delaware at one time was New Sweden. These five colonies, from their beginnings were considered "melting pots" with settlers from many different nations and backgrounds. The main economic activity was farming with the settlers scattered over the countryside cultivating rather large farms. The Indians were not as much of a threat as in New England so they did not have to settle in small farming villages. The soil was very fertile, the land was gently rolling, and a milder climate provided a longer growing season.

These farms produced a large surplus of food, not only for the colonists themselves but also for sale. This colonial region became known as the "breadbasket" of the New World and the New York and Philadelphia seaports were constantly filled with ships being loaded with meat, flour, and other foodstuffs for the West Indies and England. There were other economic activities such as shipbuilding, iron mines, and factories producing paper, glass, and textiles. The legislative body in Pennsylvania was unicameral or consisted of one house. In the other four colonies, the legislative body had two houses. Also units of local government were in counties and towns.

The **Southern colonies** were Virginia, North and South Carolina, and Georgia. Virginia was the first permanent successful English colony and Georgia was the last. The year 1619 was a very important year in the history of Virginia and the United States with three very significant events. First, sixty women were sent to Virginia to marry and establish families, Second, twenty Africans, the first of thousands, arrived, Third, most importantly, the Virginia colonists were granted the right to self-government and they began by electing their own representatives to the House of Burgesses, their own legislative body. The major economic activity in this region was farming. Here the soil was very fertile and the climate was very mild with an even longer growing season. The large plantations eventually requiring large numbers of slaves were found in the coastal or tidewater areas. Although the wealthy slave-owning planters set the pattern of life in this region, most of the people lived inland away from coastal areas. They were small farmers and very few, it any, owned slaves.

The settlers in these four colonies came from diverse backgrounds and cultures. Virginia was colonized mostly by people from England while Georgia was started as a haven for debtors from English prisons. Pioneers from Virginia settled in North Carolina while South Carolina welcomed people from England and Scotland, French Protestants, Germans, and emigrants from islands in the West Indies. Products from farms and plantations included rice, tobacco, indigo, cotton, some corn and wheat. Other economic activities included lumber and naval stores (tar, pitch, rosin, and turpentine) from the pine forests and fur trade on the frontier. Cities such as Savannah and Charleston were important seaports and trading centers.

Skill 16.6   Describe the westward movement, expansion of U.S. borders and government policies toward American Indians and foreign nations during the Early Republic.

In 1800, Napoleon Bonaparte of France secured the **Louisiana Territory** from Spain, who had held it since 1792. The vast area stretched westward from the Mississippi River to the Rocky Mountains as well as northward to Canada. An effort was made to keep the transaction a secret but the news reached the U.S. State Department.

In President Monroe's message to Congress on December 2, 1823, he delivered what we have always called the **Monroe Doctrine**. The United States was informing the powers of the Old World that the American continents were no longer open to European colonization, and that any effort to extend European political influence into the New World would be considered by the United States "as dangerous to our peace and safety." The United States would not interfere in European wars or internal affairs, and expected Europe to stay out of American affairs.

By the terms of the **Treaty of Paris** which ended the Revolutionary War a large amount of land occupied and claimed by American Indians was ceded to the United States. The British, however, did not inform the Native People of the change. The government of the new nation first tried to treat the tribes who had fought with the British as conquered people and claimed their land. This policy was later abandoned because it could not be enforced. The next phase of the government's policy toward the American Indians was to purchase their land in treaties in order to continue national expansion. This created tension with the states and with settlers. This expansion and settlement of new territory forced the Native Americans to continue to move farther west. The Native Americans were gradually giving up their homelands, their sacred sites, and the burial grounds of their ancestors. Some of the American Indians chose to move west. Many, however, were relocated by force.

The **Indian Removal Act** of 1830 authorized the government to negotiate treaties with Native Americans to provide land west of the Mississippi River in exchange for lands east of the river. This policy resulted in the relocation of more than 100,000 Native Americans. Theoretically, the treaties were expected to result in voluntary relocation of the native people. In fact, however, many of the native chiefs were forced to sign the treaties.

One of the worst examples of "Removal" was the Treaty of New Echota. This treaty was signed by a faction of the Cherokees rather than the actual leaders of the tribe. When the leaders attempted to remain on their ancestral lands, the treaty was enforced by President Martin Van Buren. The removal of the Cherokees came to be known as "**The Trail of Tears**" and resulted in the deaths of more than 4000 Cherokees, mostly due to disease.

Skill 16.7   Identify the roles of Blacks (both slave and free), American Indians, the Irish and other immigrants, women and children in the political, cultural and economic life of the new country.

Immigration continues and increases during this period, especially as new territories open for exploration and settlement. Most of the new arrivals came from the same Western European countries as the original colonists; but there is soon a greater mix of non English residents than ever before—and an increasing membership in religious faiths other than the traditional Protestant denominations, including Roman Catholics and Jews. The major exception to the ethnicity of most immigrants to the United States, through much of this period, continued to be African slaves, imported against their will to provide a chattel labor force.

Due to compromises made by the federal government with certain states, Congress was unable to act against the importation trade until January 1, 1808. At that time, a bill was unanimously passed forbidding the importation of slaves. However, since smuggling slaves was lucrative and difficult for the government to control, the illicit trade continued for over a decade more. During this time, tens of thousands of additional African slaves were brought into the United States. Finally, in 1819 Congress declared this practice to be piracy. There is no record that any of the practitioners were ever condemned as pirates, but the effort by the federal government seemed to have the desired effect. Of course, the internal trade and sale of slaves continued to flourish up until the Civil War, becoming far more lucrative when importation ceased.

While most women were excluded from the franchise (they were not allowed to vote), many men were excluded as well. Slaves of either sex could not vote. Freedmen were often prevented from voting. And in various jurisdictions—federal, state, county, municipal elections, etc., a man could be prohibited from voting due to poverty, lack of property ownership, inability to write or any one of many restrictions intended to limit the franchise.

Some women during this period did have the right to vote and participated in the election process. These women were usually residents of a new territory, which did not adhere to the restrictions of the various states. When these territories eventually became states, however, these women were excluded from the franchise. There was one state in which women enjoyed the right to vote. This right was granted to women in the adoption of the constitution of New Jersey in 1776. And this right to vote was revoked for women in New Jersey in 1807.

COMPETENCY 17.0 CIVIL WAR AND RECONSTRUCTION

Skill 17.1   **Recognize the origin and the evolution of the anti-slavery movement, including the roles of free Blacks and women, and the response of those who defended slavery.**

Slavery in the English colonies began in 1619 when 20 Africans arrived in the colony of Virginia at Jamestown. From then on, slavery had a foothold, especially in the agricultural South, where a large amount of slave labor was needed for the extensive plantations.

The first serious clash between North and South occurred during 1819-1820 when James Monroe was in office as President and it was concerning admitting Missouri as a state. In 1819, the U.S. consisted of 21 states: 11 free states and 10 slave states. The Missouri Territory allowed slavery and if admitted would cause an imbalance in the number of U.S. Senators. Alabama had already been admitted as a slave state and that had balanced the Senate with the North and South each having 22 senators. The first Missouri Compromise resolved the conflict by approving the admission of Maine as a free state along with Missouri as a slave state. The balance of power in the Senate continued with the same number of free and slave states.

The Supreme Court in 1857 handed down a decision guaranteed to cause explosions throughout the country. **Dred Scott** was a slave whose owner had taken him from slave state Missouri, then to free state Illinois, into Minnesota Territory, free under the provisions of the Missouri Compromise, then finally back to slave state Missouri. Abolitionists pursued the dilemma by presenting a court case, stating that since Scott had lived in a free state and free territory, he was in actuality a free man. Two lower courts had ruled before the Supreme Court became involved, one ruling in favor and one against. The Supreme Court decided that residing in a free state and free territory did not make Scott a free man because Scott (and all other slaves) was not an U.S. citizen or a state citizen of Missouri. Therefore, he did not have the right to sue in state or federal courts. The Court went a step further and ruled that the old Missouri Compromise was now unconstitutional because Congress did not have the power to prohibit slavery in the Territories.

In 1859, abolitionist John Brown and his followers seized the federal arsenal at Harper's Ferry in what is now West Virginia. His purpose was to take the guns stored in the arsenal, give them to slaves nearby, and lead them in a widespread rebellion. He and his men were captured by Colonel Robert E. Lee of the United States Army and after a trial with a guilty verdict, he was hanged. This merely served to widen the gap between the two sections.

Refer to Skill 17.2 for further discussion.

Skill 17.2 **Describe evidence for the economic, social and political causes of the Civil War, including the constitutional debates over the doctrine of nullification and secession.**

This period of U.S. history was a period of compromises, breakdowns of the compromises, desperate attempts to restore and retain harmony among the three sections, short-lived intervals of the uneasy balance of interests, and ever-increasing conflict.

At the Constitutional Convention, one of the slavery compromises concerned counting slaves for deciding the number of representatives for the House and the amount of taxes to be paid. Southerners pushed for counting the slaves for representation but not for taxes. The Northerners pushed for the opposite. The resulting compromise, sometimes referred to as the **three-fifths compromise**, was that both groups agreed that three-fifths of the slaves would be counted for both taxes and representation.

The other compromise over slavery was part of the disputes over how much regulation the central government would control over commercial activities such as trade with other nations and the slave trade. It was agreed that Congress would regulate commerce with other nations including taxing imports. Southerners were worried about **taxing slaves** coming into the country and the possibility of Congress prohibiting the slave trade altogether. The agreement reached allowed the states to continue importation of slaves for the next 20 years until 1808, at which time Congress would make the decision as to the future of the slave trade.   During the 20-year period, no more than $10 per person could be levied on slaves coming into the country.

These two slavery compromises were a necessary concession to have Southern support and approval for the new document and new government. Many Americans felt that the system of slavery would eventually die out in the U.S., but by 1808, cotton was becoming increasingly important in the primarily agricultural South and the institution of slavery had become firmly entrenched in Southern culture. It is also evident that as early as the Constitutional Convention, active anti-slavery feelings and opinions were very strong, leading to extremely active groups and societies.

The first serious clash between North and South occurred during 1819-1820 when James Monroe was in office as President and it was concerning admitting Missouri as a state. Alabama had already been admitted as a slave state and that had balanced the Senate with the North and South each having 22 senators. The first **Missouri Compromise** resolved the conflict by approving admission of Maine as a free state along with Missouri as a slave state, thus continuing to keep a balance of power in the Senate with the same number of free and slave states.

An additional provision of this compromise was that with the admission of Missouri, slavery would not be allowed in the rest of the Louisiana Purchase territory north of latitude 36 degrees 30'. This was acceptable to the Southern Congressmen since it was not profitable to grow cotton on land north of this latitude line anyway. It was thought that the crisis had been resolved but in the next year, it was discovered that in its state constitution, Missouri discriminated against the free blacks. Anti-slavery supporters in Congress went into an uproar, determined to exclude Missouri from the Union. Henry Clay, known as the Great Compromiser, then proposed a **second Missouri Compromise** which was acceptable to everyone. His proposal stated that the Constitution of the United States guaranteed protections and privileges to citizens of states and Missouri's proposed constitution could not deny these to any of its citizens. The acceptance in 1820 of this second compromise opened the way for Missouri's statehood--a temporary reprieve only.

To protect and encourage its own industries and their products, Congress passed the Tariff of 1816, which required high duties to be levied on manufactured goods coming into the United States. Southern leaders, such as John C. Calhoun of South Carolina, supported the tariff with the assumption that the South would develop its own industries. In 1824, a higher tariff was passed by Congress, favoring the financial interests of the manufacturers in New England and the Middle Atlantic States. In addition, the 1824 tariff was closely tied to the presidential election of that year. Before becoming law, Calhoun had proposed the very high tariffs in an effort to get Eastern business interests to vote with the agricultural interests in the South (who were against it) with supporters of candidate Andrew Jackson siding with whichever side served their best interests. Jackson himself would not be involved in any of this scheming.

The doctrine of nullification states that the states have the right to "nullify" – declare invalid – any act of Congress they believed to be unjust or unconstitutional. The **nullification crisis** climaxed over a new tariff on imported manufactured goods that was enacted by the Congress in 1828. While this tariff protected the manufacturing and industrial interests of the North, it placed an additional burden of cost on the South, which was only affected by the tariff as consumers of manufactured goods. The north had become increasingly economically dependent on industry and manufacturing, while the south had become increasingly agricultural. Despite the fact that the tariff was primarily intended to protect Northern manufacturing interests in the face of imports from other countries, the effect on the south was to simply raise the prices of needed goods. This issue of disagreement reached its climax when John C. Calhoun, Jackson's vice president, led South Carolina to adopt the Ordinance of Nullification which declared the tariff null and void within state borders. Although this issue came to the brink of military action, it was resolved by the enactment of a new tariff in 1832.

In 1833, Congress lowered the tariffs again, this time at a level acceptable to South Carolina. Although President Jackson believed in states' rights, he also firmly believed in and determined to keep the preservation of the Union. A constitutional crisis had been averted but sectional divisions were getting deeper and more pronounced. The **abolition movement** was growing rapidly, becoming an important issue in the North.

The slavery issue was at the root of every problem, crisis, event, decision, and struggle from then on. The next crisis involved the issue concerning Texas. By 1836, Texas was an independent republic with its own constitution. During its fight for independence, Americans were sympathetic to and supportive of the Texans and some recruited volunteers who crossed into **Texas** to help the struggle.

Problems arose when the state petitioned Congress for statehood. Texas wanted to allow slavery but Northerners in Congress opposed admission to the Union because it would disrupt the balance between free and slave states and give Southerners in Congress increased influence. There were others who believed that granting statehood to Texas would lead to a war with Mexico, which had refused to recognize Texas independence. For the time being, statehood was put on hold.

The result was the **Compromise of 1850**, a series of laws designed as a final solution to the issue. Concessions made to the North included the admission of California as a free state and the abolition of slave trading in Washington, D.C. The laws also provided for the creation of the New Mexico and Utah territories. As a concession to Southerners, the residents there would decide whether to permit slavery when these two territories became states. In addition, Congress authorized implementation of stricter measures to capture runaway slaves.

A few years later, Congress took up consideration of new territories between Missouri and present-day Idaho. Again, heated debate over permitting slavery in these areas flared up. Those opposed to slavery used the Missouri Compromise to prove their point showing that the land being considered for territories was part of the area the Compromise had designated as banned to slavery. But on May 25, 1854, Congress passed the infamous **Kansas-Nebraska Act** which nullified this provision, created the territories of Kansas and Nebraska, and provided for the people of these two territories to decide for themselves whether or not to permit slavery to exist there. Feelings were so deep and divided that any further attempts to compromise would meet with little, if any, success. Political and social turmoil swirled everywhere. Kansas was called "Bleeding Kansas" because of the extreme violence and bloodshed throughout the territory because two governments existed there, one pro-slavery and the other anti-slavery.

The Supreme Court in 1857 handed down a decision guaranteed to cause explosions throughout the country. **Dred Scott** was a slave whose owner had taken him from slave state Missouri, then to free state Illinois, into Minnesota Territory, free under the provisions of the Missouri Compromise, then finally back to slave state Missouri. Abolitionists pursued the dilemma by presenting a court case, stating that since Scott had lived in a free state and free territory, he was in actuality a free man. Two lower courts had ruled before the Supreme Court became involved, one ruling in favor and one against. The Supreme Court decided that residing in a free state and free territory did not make Scott a free man because Scott (and all other slaves) was not U.S. citizens or state citizens of Missouri. Therefore, he did not have the right to sue in state or federal courts. The Court went a step further and ruled that the old Missouri Compromise was now unconstitutional because Congress did not have the power to prohibit slavery in the Territories.

In 1858, **Abraham Lincoln** and Stephen A. Douglas were running for the office of U.S. Senator from Illinois and participated in a series of debates, which directly affected the outcome of the 1860 Presidential Election. Douglas, a Democrat, was up for re-election and knew that if he won this race, he had a good chance of becoming President in 1860. Lincoln, a Republican, was not an abolitionist but he believed that slavery was wrong morally and he firmly believed in and supported the Republican Party principle that slavery must not be allowed to extend any further.

Douglas, on the other hand, originated the doctrine of "popular sovereignty" and was responsible for supporting and getting through Congress the inflammatory Kansas-Nebraska Act. In the course of the debates, Lincoln challenged Douglas to show that popular sovereignty reconciled with the Dred Scott decision. Either way he answered Lincoln, Douglas would lose crucial support from one group or the other. If he supported the Dred Scott decision, Southerners would support him but he would lose Northern support. If he stayed with popular sovereignty, Northern support would be his but Southern support would be lost. His reply to Lincoln, stating that Territorial legislatures could exclude slavery by refusing to pass laws supporting it, gave him enough support and approval to be re-elected to the Senate. But it cost him the Democratic nomination for President in 1860.

The final straw came with the election of Lincoln to the Presidency the next year. Due to a split in the Democratic Party, there were four candidates from four political parties. With Lincoln receiving a minority of the popular vote and a majority of electoral votes, the Southern states, one by one, voted to **secede** from the Union as they had promised they would do if Lincoln and the Republicans were victorious. The die was cast.

As 1860 began, the nation had extended its borders north, south, and west. Industry and agriculture were flourishing. Although the U.S. did not involve itself actively in European affairs, the relationship with Great Britain was much improved and it and other nations that dealt with the young nation accorded it more respect and admiration. Nevertheless, war was on the horizon. The country was deeply divided along political lines concerning slavery and the election of Abraham Lincoln. Although the colonies won independence, wrote a Constitution forming a union of those states under a central government, fought wars and signed treaties, purchased and explored vast areas of land, developed industry and agriculture, improved transportation, saw population expansion westward, and increased the number of states admitted to the Union annually, the issue of human slavery had to be settled once and for all. One historian has stated that before 1865, the nation referred to itself as "the United States are ... ," but after 1865, "the United States is ..." It took the Civil War to finally, completely unify all states into one Union.

Skill 17.3   Identify the major battles of the Civil War and the comparative strengths and weaknesses of the Union and the Confederacy.

The Southern states numbered eleven and included South Carolina, Georgia, Florida, Alabama, Mississippi, Louisiana, Texas, Virginia, North Carolina, Tennessee, and Arkansas, making up the Confederacy. Although outnumbered in population, the South was completely confident of victory. They knew that all they had to do was fight a defensive war, protecting their own territory until the North, who had to invade and defeat an area almost the size of Western Europe, tired of the struggle and gave up. Another advantage of the South was that a number of its best officers had graduated from the U.S. Military Academy at West Point and had had long years of army experience, some even exercising varying degrees of command in the Indian wars and the war with Mexico. Men from the South were conditioned to living outdoors and were more familiar with horses and firearms than many men from northeastern cities. Since cotton was such an important crop, Southerners felt that British and French textile mills were so dependent on raw cotton that they would be forced to help the Confederacy in the war.

The South had specific reasons and goals for fighting the war, more so than the North. The major aim of the Confederacy never wavered: to win independence, the right to govern themselves as they wished, and to preserve slavery. The Northerners were not as clear in their reasons for conducting war. At the beginning, most believed, along with Lincoln, that preservation of the Union was paramount. Only a few extremely fanatical abolitionists looked on the war as a way to end slavery. However, by war's end, more and more northerners had come to believe that freeing the slaves was just as important as restoring the Union.

The war strategies for both sides were relatively clear and simple. The South planned a defensive war, wearing down the North until it agreed to peace on Southern terms. The exception was to gain control of Washington, D.C., go North through the Shenandoah Valley into Maryland and Pennsylvania in order to drive a wedge between the Northeast and mid-West, interrupt the lines of communication, and end the war quickly. The North had three basic strategies: blockade the Confederate coastline in order to cripple the South; seize control of the Mississippi River and interior railroad lines to split the Confederacy in two; and seize the Confederate capital of Richmond, Virginia, driving southward joining up with Union forces coming east from the Mississippi Valley.

The South won decisively until the Battle of Gettysburg, July 1 - 3, 1863. Until Gettysburg, Lincoln's commanders, **McDowell and McClellan**, were less than desirable, **Burnside and Hooker**, not what was needed. **Lee**, on the other hand, had many able officers, **Jackson and Stuart** depended on heavily by him. Jackson died at Chancellorsville and was replaced by Longstreet. Lee decided to invade the North and depended on **J.E.B. Stuart** and his cavalry to keep him informed of the location of Union troops and their strengths. Four things worked against Lee at Gettysburg:

1) The Union troops gained the best positions and the best ground first, making it easier to make a stand there.

2) Lee's move into Northern territory put him and his army a long way from food and supply lines. They were more or less on their own.

3) Lee thought that his Army of Northern Virginia was invincible and could fight and win under any conditions or circumstances.

4) Stuart and his men did not arrive at Gettysburg until the end of the second day of fighting and by then, it was too little too late. He and the men had had to detour around Union soldiers and he was delayed getting the information Lee needed.

Consequently, Lee made the mistake of failing to listen to Longstreet and following the strategy of regrouping back into Southern territory to the supply lines. Lee felt that regrouping was retreating and almost an admission of defeat. He was convinced the army would be victorious. **Longstreet** was concerned about the Union troops occupying the best positions and felt that regrouping to a better position would be an advantage.

It was not the intention of either side to fight there but the fighting began when a Confederate brigade stumbled into a unit of Union cavalry while looking for shoes. The third and last day Lee launched the final attempt to break Union lines. **General George Pickett** sent his division of three brigades under Generals Garnet, Kemper, and Armistead against Union troops on Cemetery Ridge under command of General Winfield Scott Hancock. Union lines held and Lee and the defeated Army of Northern Virginia made their way back to Virginia.

Although Lincoln's commander George Meade successfully turned back a Confederate charge, he and the Union troops failed to pursue Lee and the Confederates. This battle was the turning point for the North. After this, Lee never again had the troop strength to launch a major offensive.

The day after Gettysburg, on July 4, Vicksburg, Mississippi surrendered to Union **General Ulysses Grant**, thus severing the western Confederacy from the eastern part. In September 1863, the Confederacy won its last important victory at Chickamauga. In November, the Union victory at Chattanooga made it possible for Union troops to go into Alabama and Georgia, splitting the eastern Confederacy in two. Lincoln gave Grant command of all Northern armies in March of 1864. Grant led his armies into battles in Virginia while Phil Sheridan and his cavalry did as much damage as possible. In a skirmish at a place called Yellow Tavern, Virginia, Sheridan's and Stuart's forces met, with Stuart being fatally wounded. The Union won the Battle of Mobile Bay and in May 1864, William Tecumseh Sherman began his march to successfully demolish Atlanta, then on to Savannah. He and his troops turned northward through the Carolinas to Grant in Virginia. On April 9, 1865, Lee formally surrendered to Grant at Appamattox Courthouse, Virginia.

The Civil War took more American lives than any other war in history, the South losing one-third of its soldiers in battle compared to about one-sixth for the North. More than half of the total deaths were caused by disease and the horrendous conditions of field hospitals. Both sections paid a tremendous economic price but the South suffered more severely from direct damages. Destruction was pervasive with towns, farms, trade, industry, lives and homes of men, women, children all destroyed and an entire Southern way of life was lost. The deep resentment, bitterness, and hatred that remained for generations gradually lessened as the years went by but legacies of it surface and remain to this day. The South had no voice in the political, social, and cultural affairs of the nation, lessening to a great degree the influence of the more traditional Southern ideals. The Northern Yankee Protestant ideals of hard work, education, and economic freedom became the standard of the United States and helped influence the development of the nation into a modem, industrial power.

The effects of the Civil War were tremendous. Civil War soldiers were the first to fight in trenches, first to fight under a unified command, first to wage a defense called "major cordon defense", a strategy of advance on all fronts. They were also the first to use repeating and breech loading weapons. Observation balloons were first used during the war along with submarines, ironclad ships, and mines. Telegraphy and railroads were put to use first in the Civil War. It was considered a modern war because of the vast destruction and was "total war", involving the use of all resources of the opposing sides. There was probably no way it could have ended other than total defeat and unconditional surrender of one side or the other.

Skill 17.4   Describe the character of Reconstruction, factors leading to its abandonment, and the rise of Jim Crow practices.

By executive proclamation and constitutional amendment, slavery was officially and finally ended, although there remained deep prejudice and racism, still raising its ugly head today. Also, the Union was preserved and the states were finally truly united. **Sectionalism**, especially in the area of politics, remained strong for another 100 years but not to the degree and with the violence as existed before 1861.

The victory of the North established that no state has the right to end or leave the Union. Because of unity, the U.S. became a major global power. Lincoln never proposed to punish the South. He was most concerned with restoring the South to the Union in a program that was flexible and practical rather than rigid and unbending. In fact he never really felt that the states had succeeded in leaving the Union but that they had left the 'family circle" for a short time.

All Southerners taking an oath of allegiance to the Union promising to accept all federal laws and proclamations dealing with slavery would receive a full pardon, excluding men who had resigned from civil and military positions in the federal government to serve in the Confederacy, those who were part of the Confederate government, those in the Confederate army above the rank of lieutenant, and Confederates who were guilty of mistreating prisoners of war and blacks. A state would be able to write a new constitution, elect new officials, and return to the Union fully equal to all other states on certain conditions: a minimum number of persons must take an oath of allegiance.

The economic and social chaos in the South after the war was unbelievable with starvation and disease rampant, especially in the cities. The U.S. Army provided some relief of food and clothing for both white and blacks but the major responsibility fell to the **Freedmen's Bureau**. They were to assist the freedmen to become self-supporting and protect them from being taken advantage of by others. As a result, as southern leaders began to be able to restore life as it had once been, they adopted a set of laws known as "black codes", containing many of the provisions of the prewar "slave codes." There were certain improvements in the lives of freedmen, but the codes denied the freedmen their basic civil rights.

Radicals in Congress pointed out these illegal actions by white Southerners as evidence that they were unwilling to recognize, accept, and support the complete freedom of black Americans and could not be trusted. Therefore, Congress drafted its own program of Reconstruction, including laws that would protect and further the rights of blacks. Three amendments were added to the Constitution: the **13th Amendment** of 1865 outlawed slavery throughout the entire United States. The **14th Amendment** of 1868 made blacks American citizens. The **15th Amendment** of 1870 gave black Americans the right to vote and made it illegal to deny anyone the right to vote based on race.

COMPETENCY 18.0 THE RISE OF INDUSTRIAL AMERICA

Skill 18.1 **Recognize the pattern of urban growth in the United States, the impact of successive waves of immigration in the nineteenth century, and the response of renewed nativism.**

During the period before and after 1900 a large number of people migrated to the cities of America. Throughout the nineteenth century city populations grew faster than rural populations. The new immigrants were not farmers. Polish immigrants became steelworkers in Pittsburgh; Serbian immigrants became meatpackers in Chicago; Russian Jewish immigrants became tailors in New York City; Slovaks assembled cars in Detroit; Italians worked in the factories of Baltimore.

Several factors promoted urbanization during the decade of the 1920s.
1. The decline of agriculture, the drop in prices for grain and produce, and the end of financial support for farming after WWI caused many farmers to go under during the 1920s. Many sold or lost their farms and migrated to cities to find work.
2. Continuing industrialization drew increasing numbers of workers to the areas near or surrounding industrial or manufacturing centers.
3. Cities were becoming the locus of political, cultural, financial and economic life.
4. Transportation to the place of work or of shopping for necessities facilitates the growth of cities

As the population grew in cities, the demographic composition of those areas began to change. Workers flocked to the cities to be closer to the factories that employed them. As the populations of poorer workers increased, the wealthy moved from the city into the suburbs. The availability of automobiles and the extension of public transportation beyond the city limits enabled the middle and upper classes to leave city centers.

Urbanization brings certain needs in its wake, including:
- Adequate water supply
- Management of sewage and garbage
- Need for public services, such as fire and police
- Road construction and maintenance
- Building of bridges to connect parts of cities
- Taller buildings were needed. This led to the invention of steel-framed buildings and of the elevator
- Electricity and telephone lines
- The growth of department stores and supermarkets
- The need for additional schools

But with the large migration and low wages came overcrowding, often in old buildings. Slums began to appear. Soon public health issues began to arise.

In 1870 citizenship was granted to blacks. Asian immigrants were permitted to live within the borders of the nation, but not permitted to become citizens. At the state level, in California, non-citizen Asians were not permitted to own land. Between 1870 and 1890 more than 123,000 Chinese immigrated to the U.S. More than 105,000 had immigrated during the two previous decades. In 1882 Congress passed the **Chinese Exclusion Act** to limit further Chinese immigration. Most of these immigrants were men who had been admitted on work contracts. This action reversed the Burlingame Treaty that had encouraged immigration. Although this was intended as a temporary action, it was regularly extended and became permanent in 1904. The law did, however, permit the immigration of a limited number of Chinese, mostly women, until the 1930s. This law reflected years of conflict between Chinese and white American for jobs. It was not repealed until 1943.

Congress had restricted immigration on the basis of health or lack of education, barring carriers of infectious diseases. A literacy requirement was enacted in the Immigration Act of 1971.

In 1921 the **Emergency Quota Act** was passed by the U.S. Congress. This law set quotas on immigration based on the nationality of applicants for admission. These quotas were based on the number of foreign-born residents according to the 1910 census. This was followed in 1924 by the Immigration Act of 1924, which changed the reference census to the 1890 census. In 1932, immigration was essentially shut down during the Great Depression.

America was a nation of immigrants. Industrialization, the introduction of mechanized farming techniques, and the rise of Labor Unions, changed the industrial, agricultural and the general economic landscape. Immigrants who would work for low wages were highly desirable when the railroad was being built and when people were needed for dangerous work. The Gold Rush, the opportunities offered by Westward expansion, and the need for cheap labor had encouraged high levels of immigration. As the needs of the nation began to change, prejudice and job competition increased the friction between whites and immigrants. The rise of cities led to certain frictions with regard to the population of neighborhoods. The preferred immigrants were those of Europe, who spoke the same language, shared most of the same values, and were more completely assimilated. In essence, immigration policy during the 1920s was a tightening of restrictions on immigration until the Great Depression created a need to put a complete stop to all immigration.

Between 1870 and 1916, more than 25 million immigrants came into the United States adding to the phenomenal population growth taking place. This tremendous growth aided business and industry in two ways: (1) the number of consumers increased creating a greater demand for products thus enlarging the markets for the products. And (2) with increased production and expanding business, more workers were available for newly created jobs.

Skill 18.2   Understand the impact of major inventions of the Industrial Revolution and the quality of life.

Innovations in new industrial processes and technology grew at a pace unmatched at any other time in American history. Thomas Edison was the most prolific inventor of that time, using a systematic and efficient method to invent and improve on current technology in a profitable manner. The abundance of resources, together with growth of industry and the pace of capital investments led to the growth of cities. Populations were shifting from rural agricultural areas to urban industrial areas and by the early 1900s a third of the nation's population lived in cities. Industry needed workers in its factories, mills and plants and rural workers were being displaced by advances in farm machinery and their increasing use and other forms of automation. The dramatic growth of population in cities was fueled by growing industries, more efficient transportation of goods and resources, and the people who migrated to those new industrial jobs, either from rural areas of the United States or immigrants from foreign lands. Increased urban populations, often packed into dense tenements, often without adequate sanitation or clean water, led to public health challenges that required cities to establish sanitation, water and public health departments to cope with and prevent epidemics. Political organizations also saw the advantage of mobilizing the new industrial working class and created vast patronage programs that sometimes became notorious for corruption in big-city machine politics, like Tammany Hall in New York.

The first phase of the **Industrial Revolution** (1750-1830) saw the mechanization of the textile industry, vast improvements in mining, with the invention of the steam engine, and numerous improvements in transportation, with the development and improvement of turnpikes, canals, and the invention of the railroad.

The second phase (1830-1910) resulted in vast improvements in a number of industries that had already been mechanized through such inventions as the Bessemer steel process and the invention of steam ships. New industries arose as a result of the new technological advances, such as photography, electricity, and chemical processes. New sources of power were harnessed and applied, including petroleum and hydroelectric power. Precision instruments were developed and engineering was launched. It was during this second phase that the industrial revolution spread to other European countries, to Japan, and to the United States.

The direct results of the industrial revolution, particularly as they affected industry, commerce, and agriculture, included:
- Enormous increase in productivity
- Huge increase in world trade
- Specialization and division of labor
- Standardization of parts and mass production

- Growth of giant business conglomerates and monopolies
- A new revolution in agriculture facilitated by the steam engine, machinery, chemical fertilizers, processing, canning, and refrigeration

The political results included:
- Growth of complex government by technical experts
- Centralization of government, including regulatory administrative agencies
- Advantages to democratic development, including extension of franchise to the middle class, and later to all elements of the population, mass education to meet the needs of an industrial society, the development of media of public communication, including radio, television, and cheap newspapers
- Dangers to democracy included the risk of manipulation of the media of mass communication, facilitation of dictatorial centralization and totalitarian control, subordination of the legislative function to administrative directives, efforts to achieve uniformity and conformity, and social impersonalization.

The economic results were numerous:
- The conflict between free trade and low tariffs and protectionism
- The issue of free enterprise against government regulation
- Struggles between labor and capital, including the trade-union movement
- The Rise of socialism
- The Rise of the utopian socialists
- The rise of Marxian or scientific socialism

The social results of the Industrial Revolution include:
- Increase of population, especially in industrial centers
- Advances in science applied to agriculture, sanitation and medicine
- Growth of great cities
- Disappearance of the difference between city dwellers and farmers
- Faster tempo of life and increased stress from the monotony of the work routine
- The emancipation of women
- The decline of religion
- Rise of scientific materialism
- Darwin's theory of evolution

Increase mobility produced a rapid diffusion of knowledge and ideas. Increased mobility also resulted in wide-scale immigration to industrialized countries. Cultures clashed and cultures melded. Although the British patent for the **radio** was awarded in 1896, it was not until WWI that the equipment and capability of the use of radio was recognized. The first radio new program was broadcast August 31, 1920. Another innovation of the 1920s was the introduction of **mass production**.

DOMAIN III – CALIFORNIA HISTORY

COMPETENCY 19.0 PRE-COLUMBIAN PERIOD THROUGH THE GOLD RUSH

Skill 19.1   Identify the impact of California's physical geography on its history.

Geographically California can be understood in terms of four primary sections: the coast, the mountains, the central valley, and the deserts. California offers a wide variety of habitats and many species of plants and animals, as well as climates. As a result, there was great cultural diversity among the early people of California. These differences included housing, dress, kinship systems, political organizations, and religious beliefs and practices.

The native peoples of California believe that they were created in their homelands and have lived there forever. Each culture has its own story of creation. But most anthropologists believe that the early native population is descended from ancient people who crossed the land bridge that once connected Asia and North America. There is no certainty about when the first people reached California, but there is widespread belief that Native Americans were living in this region for 15,000 years before the first European explorers visited the California coast.

Most California Native Americans subsisted by hunting and gathering. But they also managed the natural resources. Some groups pruned plants and trees, culled animal populations, and periodically burned groundcover to enrich the earth. The **Cahuilla** dug wells in the deserts. They created pools by building up the sand around the wells. They cultivated melons, squash, beans and corn. The **Yumas,** who lived around the lower Colorado River, planted corn, pumpkins and beans in the mud after the annual floods of the river. The primary food for most tribes was the acorn. Hunters had access to deer, antelope, elk, sheep and bears. Fish were plentiful in the lakes, rivers, streams and in the ocean. It is believed (though it cannot be proven with certainty) that the population of California before the arrival of Europeans was about 300,000.

The number of tribes, cultures and languages of the early Native Californians was vast. The languages have been classified into seven groups: Penutian, Hokan, Utian, Yukian, Algic, Uto-Aztecan, and Na-Dene. Anthropologists have defined a "tribe" in California as "a body of people who occupied a distinct territory and shared a similar culture." [source: www.californiahistory.net] Based on this definition, over 100 tribes have been identified. The tribes, however, were further subdivided into "tribelets" or groups of villages. It is believed that there were as many as 500 of these communities.

Skill 19.2   Describe the geography, economic activities, folklore and religion of California's American Indian peoples.

Due to the great diversity of the native communities, the state is generally divided into six culture areas.

The Southern Culture Area was home to some of the most populous tribes. Some of these communities had as many as 2,000 residents. The Kumeyaay migrated each year as plants in their territory ripened. The Cahuilla hunted with bows and arrows, nets, traps, or by throwing sticks at small animals. The Tongva tribe had a structured society that was divided into distinct classes. The villages of the Chumash sometimes included as many as 2,000 people. The villages generally included a storehouse, sweathouse, cemetery, ceremonial enclosure and playing field. They were skilled fishermen and navigators. They made canoes of planks caulked with asphaltum. They harpooned seals, sea otters, and porpoises and traveled between the coast and the many islands off shore. They also produced spectacular colorful rock paintings.

The Central Culture Area included about 60% of all of the Native people of California. Tools and weapons made by these tribes were not very sophisticated, but basketry was quite advanced. These groups were organized into tribelets and small villages. The people of the villages were quite territorial and did not tolerate trespassing. The Yokuts were hunters and gatherers, as well as fishermen. They are notable for the development of hunting strategies such as wearing animal disguises and for building traps for quail. The Pomo were particularly known for their basketry.

The Northwestern Culture Area was notable for tribes that valued material wealth. The Yurok lived along the Klamath River in permanent villages of distinctive dwellings built of split planks. Their proximity to the redwood forests provided for wood which was made into numerous household items and dugout canoes. The Hupa lived near the Trinity River. Wealth determined social rank.. Their religion included the "world-renewal rituals" of the White Deerskin and Jumping Dances. The Shasta lived in the mountain area of northwestern California. They settled in river valleys or at the mouths of rivers. In these villages, individual families owned hunting and fishing grounds, tobacco plots and oak trees. They practiced trade with their neighbors.

The Northeastern Culture Area was sparsely settled and occupied rich lands. Other tribes, however, lived in more desolate areas and subsisted on small game and gathered seeds and roots. The Achumawi lived along the Pit River. These people dug pits to trap deer and other animals. They used the deer skins to make caps, capes, belts, moccasins, leggings, skirts and quivers. They had elaborate puberty rituals for girls, extensive mourning rites, and respected their Shamans. About half of their shamans were women.

The Atsugewi lived in rugged valleys and barren plains. Hard work was highly valued and respected. They fished with baskets and nets. Small game was hunted in groups; large game was usually hunted by individuals and was shared by the community. They set aside every sixth day for rest, and held an annual celebration to which they invited people of neighboring villages.

The Great Basic Culture Area included the areas along the current eastern border and the eastern deserts of the southern part of the state. This is an area in which food and water are scarce. The Tubatulabal lived in the southern foothills of the Sierra Nevada. They were divided into three groups, each speaking a different dialect of the language. They subsisted by hunting, fishing and gathering. The Owens Valley Paiute lived in an area that received very little rainfall and, hence, had little vegetation. The small groups tended to migrate frequently seeking food and water. The men hunted and the women gathered. This group was notable for its development of a system of agriculture that utilized communal labor. They built dams and ditches to irrigate wild plants.

The Colorado River Culture Area, on the western edge of the Southwest Culture Area. These Native Americans also hunted and gathered and grew beans, corn, and pumpkins. They considered themselves more unified than the tribes that divided themselves into tribelets. They traveled extensively outside their own regions. The people of this area include the Quechan (Yuma), the Halchidhoma, and the Mohave.

Skill 19.3   Discuss the impact of Spanish exploration and colonization, including the mission system and its influence on the development of the agricultural economy of early California.

The first explorers visited California in search of riches and a route to Asia. Cortes led an expedition north from Acapulco to the Baja peninsula in 1535. He established a colonial outpost on the coast of the Bay of La Paz, but it was abandoned in 1536. The coastal areas of California were first explored by Europeans in 1542 by the Portuguese explorer Juan Rodriguez Cabrillo, who was working for the Spaniard, Hernan Cortes. This expedition resulted in the discovery of Alta California. But Francis Drake, an Englishman, was the first to explore the entire coast and claim possession of the territory.

The strategy of the Spanish empire in California was to exploit, transform and include the native people of the Americas in the new settlements called **missions**.   The founding of missions was the key to transplanting the empire and converting the native people to Roman Catholicism. Beginning in 1769, California missions were established along the coast by Spanish Catholic Missionaries in a program called "the Sacred Expedition." The Spanish also founded four small towns called **presidios**.

The Franciscan order founded the first mission at San Diego. Others followed until there were 21 by 1823. Missions were generally established within a day's walk between them. The Franciscan leader of this mission was Father Junipero Serra.

After Serra's death, Fermin Francisco de Lasuen became the leader of the missionary effort. Once the native people were brought into the missions, they were given religious instruction and they were taught various practical skills. The secondary goal of the missions was to thoroughly transition the native people to the life of the Spanish empire. This included language, work habits, social organization, attire, etc. The missions were surrounded by orange groves, grape plantations and cattle ranches.

The impact of the missions on the native people of California is a matter of considerable debate. Some believe they had a destructive effect on the native people. Others believe the native people benefited from the missions. It is clear that the change in lifestyle, the compression of the people in a small area, and the introduction of new diseases resulted in an exceptionally high death rate. The life of the native people at the missions, while occasionally good, was generally described as very severe.

To ensure an adequate food supply for the soldiers, civilian towns were also founded. These were called **pueblos**. Settlers were attracted to these settlements with offers of free land, farming equipment, livestock, and an annual stipend. In return, they were required to sell their surplus agricultural products to the presidios.

For the next twenty-five years, California was considered a Mexican province. Cattle and horses were introduced in the late eighteenth century. These doubled in number about every five years, giving rise to cattle ranches (**ranchos**). These ranches quickly became the primary expressions of the lifestyle of Mexican California. The families that owned and operated these ranches were the elite of Mexican California. These ranches, however, used native labor, in return for which the natives received only food, clothing and shelter. This resulted in a society that closely resembled European feudalism.

Skill 19.4   Describe Mexican rule in California.

Mexican rule in California lasted between 1821, when Mexico gained independence from Spain, and 1846, when California was annexed to the United States following the Mexican American War. At that time, the territory known as Alta California extended over modern day California, Nevada, Utah and portions of Arizona and Wyoming. California was never admitted as a Mexican state, but remained a territory under the administration of an appointed governor, who was given the power to grant land to individuals. Monterey was the territorial capital. The first governor under Mexican rule was Luis Antonio Arguello.

Politics in Mexican California were unstable, and governors changed frequently. During one five-year period between 1831 and 1836, eleven different administrations were appointed. Native-born Californios sometimes became restless under Mexican administration and various movements for independence or autonomy from Mexico were undertaken, with little success. In 1836, Juan Bautista Alvarado led a successful takeover of the capital at Monterey and declared California an independent state. Mexico responded by offering Alvaredo the governorship, which he accepted.

One of the most significant changes under Mexican rule was the decline of the missions. The Spanish-built missions had been the centers of religious, political and economic activity when they were built, but under Mexican rule their influence began to weaken. In 1833, the Mexican Congress officially secularized the California missions, causing most of the Catholic Franciscan friars to abandon them within a year. The buildings themselves were often looted.

The large tracts of agricultural land that had supported the missions were granted to various wealthy families by the territorial governor, creating a landed elite that controlled these large ranchos. Over 800 such land grants were made under Mexican rule. Native Americans provided the labor to work the ranchos, just as they had worked for the missions.

Skill 19.5   State the causes of the war between Mexico and the United States and its consequences for California.

The immediate cause of the Mexican-American War was the annexation of Texas by the United States in 1845. In 1836, Texas had revolted from Mexico and established an independent republic. The Republic of Texas was recognized by the U.S. in 1837. Despite the fact that several European countries had recognized The Republic of Texas, Mexico never acknowledged its independence. In the face of constant friction between Texas and Mexico, the U.S. had been warned that Mexico would consider an attempt to annex Texas to the American Union a declaration of war. President Polk did not try diplomatic negotiation, but ordered General Zachary Taylor and his troops to the Rio Grande. This was met by a counter-advance by the Mexican army. On April 25, 1846 the war began. On May 13, Congress declared war.

In California Lt. John C. Fremont (an officer with the Army Corps of Topographical Engineers) and a troop of about 60 armed men arrived in California. All of the men were expert marksmen. Mexican officials ordered them out of California. After initially refusing to leave, Fremont relented and started moving north toward Oregon. He later returned to California and helped instigate what came to be called the **Bear Flag Revolt**.

Fremont joined forces with a group of Anglo-American settlers in northern California who had seized Colonel Mariano Guadalupe Vallejo and other Mexicans in Sonoma on June 14, 1846. The combined force (called the California Battalion) declared California an independent republic. When the settlers declared independence, they raised a flag that showed a crude drawing of a bear, a single star, and the words "California Republic." From this flag, the event came to be known as the **Bear Flag Revolt**. The Revolt had the main result of creating tension and bitterness between the Anglo-Americans and the Spanish-speaking Californios. U.S. naval forces landed on the coast of California in July 1846 and proclaimed California part of the United States. Mexico responded with military force that included the Californios. Fighting in California ended on January 13, 1847 when Andres Pico surrendered to John C. Fremont. Fighting continued elsewhere for another year.

The Mexican-American War officially ended with the signing of the **Treaty of Guadalupe Hidalgo** on February 2, 1848. The U.S. agreed to pay Mexico $15 million and to assume unpaid claims against Mexico. Mexico agreed to transfer to the United States more than 525,000 square miles of land. This area is now the states of California, Nevada and Utah, most of Arizona and New Mexico, and parts of Colorado and Wyoming. Mexico lost half of its land, and the American people believed they had achieved their Manifest Destiny. A small strip of land north of the Rio Grande remained in Mexican control. This was later purchased by the U.S. in the **Gadsden Purchase**. Slavery was prohibited in this area.

The major results of the Mexican-American War were:

- The addition of more than 525,000 square miles of territory to the United States
- The reorganization of the political parties along the lines of anti-slavery and pro-slavery.

The indirect results were:

- The prestige of the United States was increased with the acquisition of an extended coastline on the Pacific.
- The development of California facilitated by the discovery of gold in California, and the various additions to the nation's resources.
- The introduction of the doctrine of squatter sovereignty, which became one of the underlying causes of the Civil War.
- The military training obtained in the war by officers who would assume a major role in the Civil War.

Skill 19.6 **Describe the discovery of gold and its cultural, social, political and economic effects in California, including its impact on American Indians and Mexican nationals.**

On January 24, 1848, James Marshall, an employee of Captain John A. Sutter, observed the glitter of gold in sands he had picked up in a mill race at Sutter's Coloma sawmill. By August, word of the discovery of gold had reached the East. In December, more than 300 ounces of pure gold reached Washington, D.C. Gold fever swept the nation. Men left farms, businesses and families to become part of the **Gold Rush**. The population of California rose from 14,000 to over 100,000 within a year and to more than 220,000 by 1852. Mark Twain and Bret Harte later wrote of the Gold Rush. They wrote of the roughness, the sentiment and the unexpected heroism of the **forty-niners.**

People came from all over the world. Most came from the East by "prairie schooner," proclaiming the motto "California or bust". They made their way over mountains, through mountain passes and through canyons no one believed a wagon could cross. Many made the journey in ships, enduring the dangers of rounding Cape Horn. Expectedly, most of the people who came were men without families. Widespread disorder was the result of this influx of men who experienced the sudden rise to wealth or the dark despair of failure. The land had just been ceded from Mexico and had no established government and no laws. What law there was varied from camp to camp. Nugget stealing and horse stealing were considered worse than murder and was punished accordingly.

The successful miners were building the famous palaces along the crest of Nob Hill in San Francisco. The unsuccessful were drifting down into the valley and filling it with wheat fields and orchards, and beginning the remarkable agricultural development that would define California well into the future. To a large extent, California's economic and social character can be traced to both the successful and unsuccessful miners of the Gold Rush.

The largest boom towns were in the central part of the state: Sacramento and Stockton, which was the supply center for the southern mines. San Francisco, however, was the greatest of the boom towns, being the port through which those who traveled to California by sea entered the state and as the center of banking and manufacturing.

A second group that amassed great wealth was the people who provided supplies and services for the miners. The earliest mining methods (panning, rockers, and "long tom") were essentially innocuous in environmental terms. But as the supply of readily available gold was exhausted, miners turned to more destructive methods of finding and extracting gold from the earth. Some dug deep shafts or tunnels into the earth. Most destructive was **hydraulicking**. This method used high-pressure water to erode banks and hills. This uniquely California innovation was the predominant type of mining for about 30 years.

COMPETENCY 20.0 ECONOMIC, POLITICAL AND CULTURAL DEVELOPMENT SINCE THE 1850'S

Skill 20.1 **Identify key principles of the California Constitution, including the Progressive-era reforms of initiative, referendum and recall, and recognize similarities and differences between it and the U. S. Constitution.**

Between the end of the Mexican American War and California's admission to the Union in 1850, the political situation was quite unstable and confused. The U.S. Congress was consumed with the issue of slavery in the areas ceded to the U.S. by the treaty that ended the war. For this reason, no formal government was established for California until 1850. Recognizing the need for some form of government, forty-eight prominent men met in September of 1849 to draft a constitution for the new state. The most pressing issue was whether to petition for admission as a state. The second major issue facing the delegates was the question of slavery. Admission to the Union was requested as a free (non-slaveholding) state. The constitution also included a provision that permitted married women to own property independently of their husbands. Any property owned by a woman prior to marriage or during marriage would remain her personal property. This was the first such provision in the nation.

This pre-statehood constitution was superseded by the current California Constitution which was ratified in 1879. Unlike most constitutions, it is very long – 110 pages. It has been amended more than 425 times. Its length is generally attributed to a lack of faith in elected officials and to the fact that many of its provisions and initiatives are in the form of constitutional amendments.

Executive power is vested in a governor, lieutenant-governor, secretary of state, controller, treasurer, attorney-general and surveyor-general, each elected for a four-year term. The legislature is bi-cameral. The senate is made up of a representative of each county, elected for four years, and an assembly made up of representatives of districts of equal population elected for two years. The judiciary consists of a supreme court (a chief justice and six associates) elected for a twelve-year term, a superior court for each county, and inferior courts established by the legislature.

There are several notable provisions:

- Lobbying is a felony.
- In civil cases, a finding can be established by agreement of three-fourths of the jury.
- Trial by jury may be waived in minor criminal cases.

Comparison of the Constitution of the State of California with the U.S. Constitution:

1. Both documents establish three branches of government: executive, legislative and judicial.
2. Both documents establish a bi-cameral legislature.
3. In California, representation in both houses of the legislature is based on population. In the US. Government, the composition of the House of Representatives is based on population, the Senate consists of two Senators from each state.
4. California Senators are elected for a four-year term with a two-term limit. U.S. Senators are elected for a six-year term with no term limits.
5. In both the California Assembly and the U.S. House of Representatives, terms are two years. California limits members of the Assembly to two terms; members of the U.S. House of Representatives have no term limits.
6. While the U.S. President and Vice President are elected together, in California the Governor and Lieutenant Governor are elected separately.
7. The California Attorney General, Controller, Secretary of State, Superintendent of Public Instruction, and Treasurer are elected by the voters. The equivalent functions in the Federal Government are presidential appointments.
8. In California, Judges of the Supreme Court are elected at large to 12-year terms. Judges of the U.S. Supreme Court are nominated by the President and approved by the Senate. Judges of the Courts of Appeal are elected in their districts for twelve year terms. Federal Judges are nominated by the President and approved by the Senate. All Federal Justices serve for life.
9. Both documents establish a system of checks and balances between the branches of government.
10. The President of the United States can utilize a pocket veto. The Governor of California can utilize a line-item veto.
11. California added the initiative, referendum, and recall to its constitution during the era of Progressive Reforms at the turn of the twentieth century.
12. Many of the individual rights clauses in the California Constitution have been understood and interpreted to provide broader individual rights than the Bill of Rights in the U.S. Constitution.

Several very important amendments to the constitution were championed by the **Progressive Party** shortly after the turn of the twentieth century. In 1911, the Progressives introduced three measures intended to guarantee that government truly expressed the will of the people. **The initiative** allowed voters to directly create laws or constitutional amendments. **The referendum** allowed voters to veto acts of the legislature. **The recall** permitted voters to remove from office any elected official.

Skill 20.2 Identify patterns of immigration to California, including the Dust Bowl migration, and discuss their impact on the cultural, economic, social and political development of the state.

The discrimination practiced by the Anglo-American settlers had far-reaching effects on an increasingly and uniquely diverse and predominantly immigrant society. The lure of gold attracted people from all parts of America, from Mexico, Chile, Peru, and other South and Central American countries, from various European countries, and from China and the Pacific islands. In fact, the region became notorious for frequent ethnic conflicts.

Within four years of the beginning of the gold rush, the Native American population declined from about 150,000 to 30,000. Much of this was due to malnutrition and disease introduced by the white men (for which the native people had no immunity). Thousands of Native people died in campaigns of extermination carried out by the whites. Miners and ranchers joined forces, with the support of local sentiment, to carry out raids on native villages. Some frontier communities even paid bounties for Indian scalps and heads.

African Americans accounted for about one percent of the non-Indian population during the gold rush. These were both escaped slaves and free persons. The free blacks came to mine for themselves. Slaves were brought by their southern owners, despite the fact that California was a free state (no slavery). They were also victims of discrimination. The state constitution restricted voting rights to "free white males." Membership in the state militia was also restricted to whites. The state enacted a harsh fugitive slave law. And the state passed a law that made it illegal for "blacks, negroes, mulattoes" and Indians from testifying either for or against a "white man."

Latin American immigrants made up the largest group of foreign miners. There was great hostility between the Latino miners and the Anglo miners. Some of this hostility was a residual effect of the recent war. But a large part of the animosity was due to economic competition. Most of the Latino miners were more experienced and more knowledgeable in mining.

In 1853 one newspaper estimated that there were 32,000 French gold miners in the state. The French also suffered discrimination by U.S. citizens. Natives of the Hawaiian Islands (called Kanakas) began to immigrate to California fifty years earlier to hunt sea otter and work in other coastal areas. Hundreds more came to work in the gold mines. They were treated no better.

Thousands of Chinese came during the gold rush. At least one estimate indicates that one-fourth of the miners in the state in 1870 were Chinese. Anglo-American miners feared that they, too, would take too much of the gold. Others hated them because they were willing to work for very low wages. But, in general, their "foreignness" was considered dangerous to the state. The state legislature enacted another Foreign Miners License Tax of $3 per month in 1852 that was particularly directed against the Chinese. For 18 years this tax generated almost 25% of the state's annual revenue. It was not until 1870 that it was declared unconstitutional.

The completion of the transcontinental railroad in 1869 ended the problem of California's isolation from the rest of the country. The first ten years after the completion of the railroad were disappointing. The expected new prosperity did not arrive. In fact, what followed was ten years of depression. The immediate benefit of the completion of the railroad and the invention of the refrigerated car was that the cars could not only deliver California produce to the east quickly, but the produce could be kept ripe and cool during shipment. A second railroad line (the Atchison, Topeka, and Santa Fe) reached Los Angeles in the middle of the decade. A rate war between the two railroads ensued. Over 200,000 new residents came to California in 1887 alone. New towns were built and over half a million home sites were designated.

When construction of the railroad began, the investors recruited the Chinese laborers, even in China, because they were willing to work for low wages (usually a dollar a day) and to do dangerous work. More than 10,000 Chinese laborers, as well as many Irish immigrants, built the railroad. But when construction was complete and the Chinese returned to California, the resulting depression was blamed on them. Anti-Chinese activities included riots, looting and burning of Chinese settlements and the like. Several cities passed laws that were intended to drive out the Chinese. Unemployed whites frequently destroyed Chinese businesses. In 1877, unemployed white men of San Francisco formed a new political party called **The Workingmen's Party**. They demanded that "the Chinese must go."

California voters adopted a new state constitution in 1878, during the height of anti-Chinese hostility. The new constitution was approved by voters a year later. The new constitution included several anti-Chinese provisions.

- "No Chinese shall be employed on any state, county, municipal, or other public work, except in punishment for crime."
- The cities and towns were instructed by the legislature to either confine Chinese residents to certain parts of the city or town or to force them to live outside city or town limits.
- Chinese immigrants were determined to be ineligible for U.S. citizenship because of race.
- The state was instructed to discourage further immigration by Chinese by any means necessary.

Skill 20.3   Identify the effects of federal and state law on the legal status of immigrants.

The **Chinese Exclusion Act**, approved by the U.S. Congress in 1882 was the ultimate expression of anti-Chinese feeling. It prohibited Chinese immigration for ten years. In 1892, it was extended for another ten years. In 1902, it became permanent. It was not repealed until China and the U.S. became allies against the Japanese during World War II. This law also produced further difficulties for the Chinese, including boycotts of Chinese-produced goods.

A series of actions were taken against the Japanese immigrants:

- Labor leaders in San Francisco formed an "Asiatic Exclusion League" in 1905 and demanded public policies against the Japanese. They pressured the city into requiring that Japanese children attend only segregated schools with other Asian children. Protests from Japan led to intervention by President Theodore Roosevelt. The city agreed to suspend the segregation act in exchange for a law that would limit Japanese immigration. Japan agreed in 1907 to prohibit its workers from coming to the U.S.

- The Japanese immigrants were capable farmers. White farmers tried to eliminate the competition. In 1913 the state legislature passed a law prohibiting anyone who was not eligible for citizenship from owning land in the state. Asians were ineligible for naturalization (under federal law).

In 1924, U.S. Congress passed the "National Origins Quota Act". This law prohibited all further immigration from Japan.

From the turn of the twentieth century, there was tension between Caucasians and Japanese in California. A series of laws had been passed discouraging Japanese immigration and prohibiting land ownership by Japanese. The Alien Registration Act of 1940 (the Smith Act) required the fingerprinting and registration of all aliens over the age of 14. Aliens were also required to report any change of address within 5 days. Almost 5 million aliens registered under the provisions of this act. The Japanese attack on Pearl Harbor (December 7, 1941) raised suspicion that Japan was planning a full-scale attack on the West Coast. Many believed that American citizenship did not necessarily imply loyalty. Some authorities feared sabotage of both civilian and military facilities within the country. By February 1942, Presidential Executive Orders had authorized the arrest of all aliens suspected of subversive activities and the creation of exclusion zones where people could be isolated from the remainder of the population and kept where they could not damage national infrastructure. These War Relocation Camps were used to isolate about 120,000 Japanese and Japanese Americans (62% were citizens) during World War II.

The first to be subjected to the hostility of the natives were the **Filipinos**. White workers complained that the recent immigrants posed an economic threat to native-born workers. Numerous riots broke out. Congress passed the "Filipino Repatriation Act" in 1935. The government offered to pay transportation expenses for any Filipinos who wished to return home. Then **Mexican** immigrants became the targets. The federal government created a program of repatriation. Some left voluntarily, others were forced to leave. Up to 100,000 deportees left California and returned to Mexico.

But another occurrence in the 1930s created yet another, less desirable influx of people to California. **Dust Bowl refugees** came by the hundreds of thousands in search of a better life in California. The situation in California was not what they expected, and they were unwelcome to many Californians. But these refugees held on to the culture of the Southwest, and created their own subculture in California. They were called "Okies" because many came from Oklahoma, although they came from several states.

Skill 20.4 Describe historical and contemporary perspectives on cultural diversity in the United States and in California.

The Spanish colonists who established missions in California beginning in the late eighteenth century had as their primary goal the conversion of the native population to Catholicism and Spanish culture. The attitudes of the day were not inclusive and respectful of the native cultures, but considered them to be inferior. The Spanish had economic reasons for converting the natives to their own culture, as well. By teaching them European agricultural methods and bringing them to work at the missions, the Spanish hoped to establish a self-supporting colony that could be controlled through their cultural influence.

The result was that many natives of different tribes were brought together into the missions and were forced to abandon their former traditions. Not all natives went to the missions, but their tribes began to dwindle. The Mexican constitution granted equality to all Mexicans and there was a liberal faction in the government that believed the essential slave conditions of the missions were unconstitutional.

The **Gold Rush of 1849** brought a new wave of Americans to California. It also brought a wave of Chinese and other Eastern peoples brought to the U.S. to provide labor in mines and in the construction of railroads. These people were looked upon largely as simply workers and were not expected to assimilate or adopt American culture. As a result, their cultures were able to survive to an extent within the expanding American culture.

In the rest of the United States during California's early history, many diverse cultures were coming together in a steady stream of immigration to the new world. These cultures were mainly Western European and the immigrants that came to the U.S.

Skill 20.5   Understand the development and identify the locations of California's major economic activities mining, large-scale agriculture, entertainment, recreation, aerospace, electronics and international trade.

Despite discrimination and hostility, California's development resulted to a great extent from the labor and struggle of these immigrants. The Chinese, in particular, working in the mines, and with their superior knowledge of explosives, and working on the railroads, were the major source of labor that built the mechanisms of wealth and communication upon which the state has been built.

The climate of the central valley area made it perfect for growing wheat. This agricultural industry fostered the development of new approaches to agriculture and the development of new farming technology. The first was the "Stockton gang plow" which was made up of a beam to which was attached several plowshares, was mounted on wheels and pulled by a team of horses or mules. New machines were also developed for planting seeds and for cutting and threshing grain. Steam-powered "combined harvests" were invented, as well as the first steam-powered tractor. Luther Burbank, who came to California from Massachusetts in the latter part of the nineteenth century, was a horticulturist who created hundreds of new varieties of plants, including new types of plums, lilies, berries, apples, rhubarb, and quince. In 1870, John Wesley North began planting the orange trees into sandy soil of riverbanks and irrigating the groves with water from the river.

The discovery of extensive **oil deposits** in the late nineteenth century, created the California petroleum industry. The deposits were located in the San Joaquin Valley, the Los Angeles basin, and Santa Barbara County. Petroleum refining became the state's major manufacturing industry and the Los Angeles harbor became the leading oil-exporting port in the world. At about the same time as the discovery of oil in California the **automobile** was becoming more popular in California than anywhere else in the nation. The suburbs grew, connected to the cities by networks of new roads. The suburbs began to experience the rise of shopping centers, supermarkets and single-family homes. And tourism became a major industry for California, which in turn gave rise to motels, auto camps, tourist cabins, and even drive-ins.

Soon after this the **motion picture industry** made its home in southern California. But in 1913, Samuel Goldfish and Archibald Selwyn formed the feature motion picture company Goldwyn. They then partnered with Louis B. Mayer to form Metro-Goldwyn Mayer, the leading studio in Hollywood for more than a quarter of a century.

In the midst of the horrific Depression, Californians continued to build the state. Honoring a decade-old agreement to host the **Olympics in 1932**, in addition to a new coliseum, the city built a 250-acre Olympic village. And during the same decade a dream held since the days of the gold rush was fulfilled with the construction of the **San Francisco-Oakland Bay Bridge**.

Skill 20.6 Identify factors leading to the development of California's water delivery system, and describe its relationship to California geography.

Environmental issues have been part of the history of California since the beginning of its civilization. Long before the arrival of Europeans and Mexicans the native tribes in parts of the state subsisted by moving around constantly in search of water and food.

One of the major controversies in California history centered upon the very destructive mining practice called "**hydraulicking**." From 1850 to the 1880s this was the predominant approach to mining in California. High-pressure hoses were used to wash away the hills and banks in the search for gold. This "unnatural erosion" damaged more than the hills and banks that were being mined. The runoff deposited tons of mud, gravel, rock and sand into the rivers, burying farms, depositing silt in the rivers, and causing more frequent flooding. It became impossible to navigate several rivers. Farmers banded together to create the "**Anti-Debris Association**," which wanted the government to outlaw the dumping of mining debris into rivers. The U.S. Circuit Court agreed with the farmers and passed the law. But many miners continued this practice. The final act that protected the rivers and farmlands was the creation of the "California Debris Commission," a federal regulatory agency, to enforce the law.

John Muir was responsible for the establishment of **Yosemite National Park** in 1890. A few years later he founded the **Sierra Club**. Muir was not, however, able to stop the construction of the **Hetch Hetchy Dam** that provides water to San Francisco.

As Los Angeles grew, its water supply proved to be inadequate. The decision was made to divert the water of melting snows in the Sierra Nevada that flowed into the Owens River to provide water for Los Angeles with an aqueduct. This project was completed in 1913, but it deprived a farming community in the Owens Valley of much-needed water.

The construction of the **Hoover Dam** in the 1930s was an attempt to provide water for San Francisco, as well as hydroelectric power for the region. But the most aggressive approach to moving water in California was the Central Valley Project.

The water issue in California is that the majority of the precipitation in the state occurs in the northern third of the state while 80% of the need for water is in the southern two-thirds of the state. Moving water is a critical need. Construction of the **Central Valley Project** began in 1937. The original phase of the plan called for the construction of three dams, five canals, and two power transmission lines. This program provides flood control and water for agriculture throughout the Central Valley.

COMPETENCY 21.0 SKILLS AND ABILITIES

Skill 21.1   Utilize chronological and spatial thinking.

The practice of dividing time into a number of discrete periods or blocks of time is called "periodization." Because history is continuous, all systems of periodization are arbitrary to a greater or lesser extent. However, dividing time into segments facilitates understanding of changes that occur over time and identifying similarities of events, knowledge, and experience within the defined period. Some divisions of time into periods apply only under specific circumstances.

Divisions of time may be determined by date, by cultural advances or changes, by historical events, by the influence of particular individuals or groups, or by geography. Speaking of the World War II era defines a particular period of time in which key historical, political, social and economic events occurred. Speaking of the Jacksonian Era, however, has meaning only in terms of American history. Defining the "Romantic period" makes sense only in England, Europe and countries under their direct influence. Many of the divisions of time that are commonly used are open to some controversy and discussion. The use of BC and AD dating, for example, has clear reference only in societies that account time according to the Christian calendar. Similarly, speaking of "the year of the pig" has greatest meaning in China.

Spatial organization is a description of how things are grouped in a given space. In geographical terms, this can describe people, places, and environments anywhere and everywhere on Earth. The most basic form of spatial organization for people is where they live. The vast majority of people live near other people, in villages and towns and cities and settlements. These people live near others in order to take advantage of the goods and services that naturally arise from cooperation. These villages and towns and cities and settlements are, to varying degrees, near bodies of water. Water is a staple of survival for every person on the planet and is also a good source of energy for factories and other industries, as well as a form of transportation for people and goods.

Skill 21.2   Construct and interpret timelines, tables, graphs, maps and charts.

We use **illustrations** of various sorts because it is often easier to demonstrate a given idea visually instead of orally. Sometimes it is even easier to do so with an illustration than a description. This is especially true in the areas of education and research because humans are visually stimulated. It is a fact that any idea presented visually in some manner is always easier to understand and to comprehend than simply getting an idea across verbally, by hearing it or reading it. Among the more common illustrations used are various types of **maps, graphs and charts**.

Photographs and **globes** are useful as well, but as they are limited in what kind of information that they can show, they are rarely used. Unless, as in the case of a photograph, it is of a particular political figure or a time that one wishes to visualize. Although maps have advantages over globes and photographs, they do have a major disadvantage. This problem must be considered as well. The major problem of all maps comes about because most maps are flat and the Earth is a sphere. It is impossible to reproduce exactly on a flat surface an object shaped like a sphere. In order to put the earth's features onto a map they must be stretched in some way. This stretching is called **distortion.**

The process of putting the features of the Earth onto a flat surface is called **projection**. All maps are really map projections. There are many different types. Each one deals in a different way with the problem of distortion. Map projections are made in a number of ways. Some are done using complicated mathematics. However, the basic ideas behind map projections can be understood by looking at the three most common types: (1) **Cylindrical Projections,** (2) **Conical Projections** and (3) **Flat-Plane Projections.**

To properly analyze a given map one must be familiar with the various parts and symbols that most modern maps use. For the most part, this is standardized, with different maps using similar parts and symbols, these can include:

The Title - All maps should have a title, just like all books should. The title tells you what information is to be found on the map.

The Legend - Most maps have a legend. A legend tells the reader about the various symbols that are used on that particular map and what the symbols represent, (also called a **map key**).

The Grid - A grid is a series of lines that are used to find exact places and locations on the map. There are several different kinds of grid systems in use; however, most maps do use the longitude and latitude system, known as the **Geographic Grid System**.

Directions - Most maps have some directional system to show which way the map is being presented. Often on a map, a small compass will be present, with arrows showing the four basic directions, north, south, east, and west.

The Scale - This is used to show the relationship between a unit of measurement on the map versus the real world measure on the Earth. Maps are drawn to many different scales. For instance the scale might be something like 1 inch = 10 miles for a small area or for a map showing the whole world it might have a scale in which 1 inch = 1,000 miles. The point is that one must look at the map key in order to see what units of measurements the map is using.

Equal areas - One property which maps can have is that of equal areas, In an equal area map, the meridians and parallels are drawn so that the areas shown have the same proportions as they do on the Earth. For example, Greenland is about 118th the size of South America, thus it will be show as 118th the size on an equal area map. The **Mercator projection** is an example of a map that does not have equal areas. In it, Greenland appears to be about the same size of South America. This is because the distortion is very bad at the poles and Greenland lies near the North Pole.

Conformal - A second map property is conformal, or correct shapes. There are no maps which can show very large areas of the earth in their exact shapes. Only globes can really do that, however Conformal Maps are as close as possible to true shapes. The United States is often shown by a Lambert Conformal Conic Projection Map.

Consistent Scales - Many maps attempt to use the same scale on all parts of the map. Generally, this is easier when maps show a relatively small part of the earth's surface. For example, a map of Florida might be a Consistent Scale Map. Generally maps showing large areas are not consistent-scale maps. This is so because of distortion. Often such maps will have two scales noted in the key. One scale, for example, might be accurate to measure distances between points along the Equator. Another might be then used to measure distances between the North Pole and the South Pole.

Maps showing physical features often try to show information about the elevation or **relief** of the land. **Elevation** is the distance above or below the sea level. The elevation is usually shown with colors, for instance, all areas on a map which are at a certain level will be shown in the same color.

Relief Maps - Show the shape of the land surface, flat, rugged, or steep. Relief maps usually give more detail than simply showing the overall elevation of the land's surface. Relief is also sometimes shown with colors, but another way to show relief is by using **contour lines**. These lines connect all points of a land surface which are the same height surrounding the particular area of land.

Thematic Maps - These are used to show more specific information, often on a single **theme**, or topic. Thematic maps show the distribution or amount of something over a certain given area. Things such as population density, climate, economic information, cultural, political information, etc...

Information can be gained looking at a map that might take hundreds of words to explain otherwise. Maps reflect the great variety of knowledge covered by political science. To show such a variety of information maps are made in many different ways. Because of this variety, maps must be understood in order to make the best sense of them.

Skill 21.3   Locate places based on ordinal directions, latitude and longitude, the equator, prime meridian, the tropics, the hemispheres, time zones and the international dateline.

Physical **locations** of the earth's surface features include the four major hemispheres and the parts of the earth's continents in them. Political **locations** are the political divisions, if any, within each continent. Both physical and political locations are precisely determined in two ways: (1) Surveying is done to determine boundary lines and distance from other features. (2) Exact locations are precisely determined by imaginary lines of **latitude (parallels)** and **longitude** (meridians). The intersection of these lines at right angles forms a grid, making it impossible to pinpoint an exact location of any place using any two grip coordinates.   The earth is comprised of 24 wedge-shaped sections each 15° of longitude apart. Most adjacent **time zones** are one hour apart and compute their local time from Greenwich Mean Time (GMT).

The **Eastern Hemisphere**, located between the North and South Poles and between the **Prime Meridian** (0 degrees longitude) east to the **International Date Line** at 180 degrees longitude, consists of most of Europe, all of Australia, most of Africa, and all of Asia, except for a tiny piece of the easternmost part of Russia that extends east of 180 degrees longitude.

The Western Hemisphere, located between the North and South Poles and between the Prime Meridian (0 degrees longitude) west to the International Date Line at 180 degrees longitude, consists of all of North and South America, a tiny part of the easternmost part of Russia that extends east of 180 degrees longitude, and a part of Europe that extends west of the Prime Meridian (0 degrees longitude).

The **equator** is an imaginary circle drawn halfway between the poles around the earth and divides the earth into the Northern and Southern Hemispheres. Places near or along the equator experience a constant amount of day/night time of 12 hours of each every day and have quick sunrises and sunsets.   Many tropical regions are found at the equator and experience two seasons, wet and dry.

The **Northern Hemisphere**, located between the North Pole and the equator, contains all of the continents of Europe and North America and parts of South America, Africa, and most of Asia. The **Southern Hemisphere**, located between the South Pole and the equator, contains all of Australia, a small part of Asia, about one-third of Africa, most of South America, and all of Antarctica.

Of the seven continents, only one contains just one entire country and is the only island continent, Australia. Its political divisions consist of six states and one territory: Western Australia, South Australia, Tasmania, Victoria, New South Wales, Queensland, and Northern Territory.

Skill 21.4   Identify and interpret major geographical features of the earth's surface including continents and other large landmasses, mountain ranges, forested areas, grasslands, deserts and major bodies of water and rivers.

The earth's physical environment is divided into three major parts: the **atmosphere**, the **hydrosphere**, and the **lithosphere**: The atmosphere is the layer of air that surrounds the earth. The hydrosphere is the water portion of the planet (70% of the earth is covered by water) and the lithosphere is the solid portion of the earth.

World weather patterns are greatly influenced by ocean surface currents in the upper layer of the ocean. These current continuously move along the ocean surface in specific directions. Surface currents are caused by winds and classified by temperature. Cold currents originate in the Polar regions and flow through surrounding water that is measurably warmer. Those currents with a higher temperature than the surrounding water are called warm currents and can be found near the **equator**. These currents follow swirling routes around the ocean basins and the equator. The Gulf Stream and the California Current are the two main surface currents that flow along the coastlines of the United States. The California Current is a cold current that originates in the Artic regions and flows southward along the west coast of the United States.

Mountains are landforms with rather steep slopes at least 2,000 feet or more above sea level. Mountains are found in groups called mountain chains or mountain ranges. At least one range can be found on six of the earth's seven continents. North America has the Appalachian and Rocky Mountains; South America the Andes; Asia the Himalayas; Australia the Great Dividing Range; Europe the Alps; and Africa the Atlas, Ahaggar, and Drakensburg Mountains.

Hills are elevated landforms rising to an elevation of about 500 to 2000 feet. They are found everywhere on earth including Antarctica.

Plateaus are elevated landforms usually level on top. Depending on location, they range from being an area that is very cold to one that is cool and healthful. Some plateaus are dry because they are surrounded by mountains that keep out any moisture. Some examples include the Kenya Plateau in East Africa, which is very cool. The plateau extending north from the Himalayas is extremely dry while those in Antarctica and Greenland are covered with ice and snow.

Plains are described as areas of flat or slightly rolling land, usually lower than the landforms next to them. Sometimes called lowlands (and sometimes located along **seacoasts)** they support the majority of the world's people. Some are found inland and many have been formed by large rivers. This resulted in extremely fertile soil for successful cultivation of crops and numerous large settlements of people. In North America, the vast plains areas extend from the

Gulf of Mexico north to the Arctic Ocean and between the Appalachian and Rocky Mountains. In Europe, rich plains extend east from Great Britain into central Europe on into the Siberian region of Russia.

Valleys are land areas that are found between hills and mountains. Some have gentle slopes containing trees and plants; others have very steep walls and are referred to as canyons. One famous example is Arizona's Grand Canyon of the Colorado River.

Deserts are large dry areas of land receiving ten inches or less of rainfall each year. Among the better known deserts are Africa's large Sahara Desert, the Arabian Desert on the Arabian Peninsula, and the desert Outback covering roughly one third of Australia.

Deltas are areas of lowlands formed by soil and sediment deposited at the mouths of rivers. The soil is generally very fertile and most fertile river deltas are important crop-growing areas. One well-known example is the delta of Egypt's Nile River, known for its production of cotton.

Mesas are the flat tops of hills or mountains usually with steep sides. Sometimes plateaus are also called mesas. Basins are considered to be low areas drained by rivers or low spots in mountains. Foothills are generally considered a low series of hills found between a plain and a mountain range. Marshes and swamps are wet lowlands providing growth of such plants as rushes and reeds.

Oceans are the largest bodies of water on the planet. The four oceans of the earth are the **Atlantic Ocean**, the **Pacific Ocean**, the **Indian Ocean**, and the ice-filled **Arctic Ocean. Seas** are smaller than oceans and are surrounded by land. Some examples include the Mediterranean Sea found between Europe, Asia, and Africa; and the Caribbean Sea, touching the West Indies, South and Central America. A lake is a body of water surrounded by land. The Great Lakes in North America are a good example.

Rivers, considered a nation's lifeblood, usually begin as very small streams, formed by melting snow and rainfall, flowing from higher to lower land, emptying into a larger body of water, usually a sea or an ocean. Examples of important rivers for the people and countries affected by and/or dependent on them include the Nile River of Africa; the Thames River of Europe and the Orinoco in South America. River systems are made up of large rivers and numerous smaller rivers or tributaries flowing into them. Examples include the vast Amazon Rivers system in South America and the Mississippi River system in the United States.

Canals are man-made water passages constructed to connect two larger bodies of water. Famous examples include the **Panama Canal** across Panama's isthmus connecting the Atlantic and Pacific Oceans and the **Suez Canal** in the Middle East.

Skill 21.5   Describe the cultural, historical, economic and political characteristics of world regions, including human features of the regions such as population, land use patterns and settlement patterns.

A **population** is a group of people living within a certain geographic area. Populations are usually measured on a regular basis by census, which also measures age, economic, ethnic and other data. Populations change over time due to many factors, and these changes can have significant impact on cultures. When a population grows in size, it becomes necessary for it to either expand its geographic boundaries to make room for new people or to increase its density.

As a population grows, its economic needs change. More basic needs are required, and more workers are needed to produce them. If a population's production or purchasing power does not keep pace with its growth, its economy can be adversely affected. Growth in some areas may spur migration to other parts of a population's geographic region that are less densely populated. This redistribution of population also places demands on the economy, as infrastructure is needed to connect these new areas to older population centers, and land is put to new use.

Populations can grow naturally, when the rate of birth is higher than the rate of death, or by adding new people from other populations through **immigration**. Populations can also decline in number, when the death rate exceeds the birth rate or when people migrate to another area. War, famine, disease and natural disasters can also dramatically reduce a population.

Environmental and geographic factors have affected the pattern of **urban development** in the world. In turn, urban infrastructure and development patterns are interrelated factors, which affect one another.

The growth of urban areas is often linked to the advantages provided by its geographic location. Before the advent of efficient overland routes of commerce such as railroads and highways, water provided the primary means of transportation of commercial goods. Most large American cities are situated along bodies of water.

As **transportation** technology advanced, the supporting infrastructure was built to connect cities with one another and to connect remote areas to larger communities. The railroad, for example, allowed for the quick transport of agricultural products from rural areas to urban centers. For urban dwellers, improvements in building technology and advances in transportation allowed for larger cities. Growth brought with it a new set of problems unique to each location. The bodies of water that had made the development of cities possible in their early days also formed natural barriers to growth.

As cities grew in population, living conditions became more crowded. As roads and bridges became better, and transportation technology improved, many people began to look outside the city for living space. Along with the development of these new suburbs came the infrastructure to connect them to the city in the form of commuter railroads and highways. The growth of suburbs had the effect in many cities of creating a type of economic segregation. Working class people who could not afford new suburban homes and perhaps an automobile to carry them to and from work were relegated to closer, more densely populated areas. Frequently, these areas had to be passed through by those on their way to the suburbs, and rail lines and freeways sometimes bisected these urban communities.

In the modern age, advancements in **telecommunications** infrastructure may have an impact on urban growth patterns as information can pass instantly and freely between almost any two points on the globe, allowing access to some aspects of urban life to those in remote areas.

Land use is the function of the land – what use is made of it. Land use and development models are theories that attempt to explain the layout of urban areas, primarily in "more economically developed countries" or in "less economically developed countries".

Two primary land use models are generally applied to urban regions. These are: (1) The Burgess model (also called the concentric model), in which cities are seen to develop in a series of concentric circles with the central business district at the center, ringed by the factories and industrial usage area, ringed by the low class residential area, then the middle class residential area, and finally the high class residential area (often suburbs); and (2) The Hoyt model (also called the Sector Model), in which the central business district occupies a central area of a circle, with factories and industry occupying an elongated area that abuts the city center, and with the low class residential area surrounding the industrial area, and the middle class residential area forming a semi-circle toward the other side of the city center, and a small upper class residential sector extending from the city center out through the middle of the middle-class residential area.

In rural areas, land use will probably include agriculture, forestry, and possibly fishing. The Von Thunen Model observes a city as the center of a state or region, from which a series of concentric circles emanates, each devoted to particular rural land usage patterns: the first ring from the city would be devoted to dairy farming and intensive farming, which allows produce to reach the market quickly. The second zone would focus on timber and firewood for fuel and building materials, which, because of its weight, needs to be relatively close to the city. The third zone would be dedicated to extensive field crops such as grains. The fourth zone would be dedicated to ranching and/or animal husbandry. Beyond this unoccupied wilderness would remain.

Skill 21.6   Analyze, interpret and evaluate research evidence in history and the social sciences.

The world of social science research has never been so open to new possibilities. Where our predecessors were unable to tread for fear of exceeding the limits of the available data, data access and data transfer, analytic routines, or computing power, today's social scientists can advance with confidence. Where once social scientists of empirical bent struggled with punch cards, chattering computer terminals, and jobs disappearing into the black hole of remote mainframe processors, often never reappearing, we now enjoy massive arrays of data, powerful personal computers on our desks, online access to data, and suites of sophisticated analytic packages. Never before has the social scientist come so well armed. Advances in technology can free social scientists from the tyranny of simplification that has often hampered attempts to grasp the complexity of the world.

Refer to the content under **Competency 21.7** for a thorough discussion of primary and secondary sources. Primary sources for a study in social sciences may be obtained one-on-one: the children in the school where you are a teacher or via electronic means. For example, government sources contain much data for social sciences research such as census statistics, employment statistics, health statistics, etc., that can be readily accessed and manipulated.
Secondary sources may also be obtained in a hands-on fashion: interviews of people who had first-hand knowledge; books, journals, etc., that record primary statistics or analyses of primary statistics. However, the best source for obtaining that information is the Internet. An excellent resource for social science information is MOST (Management of Social Transformations) at http://portal. unesco.org/shs/en/ev.php-URL_ID=3511&URL_DO=DO_TOPIC&URL_ SECTION=201.html.

Skill 21.7   Interpret primary and secondary sources, including written documents, narratives, photographs, art and artifacts revealed through archeology.

The resources used in the study of history can be divided into two major groups: primary sources and secondary sources.

Primary sources are works, records, etc. that were created during the period being studied or immediately after it. Secondary sources are works written significantly after the period being studied and based upon primary sources. "Primary sources are the basic materials that provide the raw data and information for the historian. Secondary sources are the works that contain the explications of, and judgments on, this primary material." [Source: Norman F Cantor & Richard I. Schneider. HOW TO STUDY HISTORY, Harlan Davidson, Inc., 1967, pp. 23-24.]

Primary sources include the following kinds of materials:

- Documents that reflect the immediate, everyday concerns of people: memoranda, bills, deeds, charters, newspaper reports, pamphlets, graffiti, popular writings, journals or diaries, records of decision-making bodies, letters, receipts, snapshots, etc.
- Theoretical writings which reflect care and consideration in composition and an attempt to convince or persuade. The topic will generally be deeper and more pervasive values than is the case with "immediate" documents. These may include newspaper or magazine editorials, sermons, political speeches, philosophical writings, etc.
- Narrative accounts of events, ideas, trends, etc. written with intentionality by someone contemporary with the events described.
- Statistical data, although statistics may be misleading.
- Literature and nonverbal materials, novels, stories, poetry and essays from the period, as well as coins, archaeological artifacts, and art produced during the period.

Guidelines for the use of primary resources:

1. Be certain that you understand how language was used at the time of writing and that you understand the context in which it was produced.
2. Do not read history blindly; but be certain that you understand both explicit and implicit referenced in the material.
3. Read the entire text you are reviewing; do not simply extract a few sentences to read.
4. Although anthologies of materials may help you identify primary source materials, the full original text should be consulted.

Secondary sources include the following kinds of materials:

- Books written on the basis of primary materials about the period of time.
- Books written on the basis of primary materials about persons who played a major role in the events under consideration.
- Books and articles written on the basis of primary materials about the culture, the social norms, the language, and the values of the period.
- Quotations from primary sources.
- Statistical data on the period.
- The conclusions and inferences of other historians.
- Multiple interpretations of the ethos of the time.

Guidelines for the use of secondary sources:

1. Do not rely upon only a single secondary source.
2. Check facts and interpretations against primary sources whenever possible.
3. Do not accept the conclusions of other historians uncritically.
4. Place greatest reliance on secondary sources created by the best and most respected scholars.
5. Do not use the inferences of other scholars as if they were facts.
6. Ensure that you recognize any bias the writer brings to his/her interpretation of history.
7. Understand the primary point of the book as a basis for evaluating the value of the material presented in it to your questions.

Skill 21.8   Discuss confirmed research evidence and assess textbooks and contrast differing points of view on historic and current events.

The scientific method is the process by which researchers over time endeavor to construct an accurate (that is, reliable, consistent and non-arbitrary) representation of the world. Recognizing that personal and cultural beliefs influence both our perceptions and our interpretations of natural phenomena, standard procedures and criteria minimize those influences when developing a theory.

The scientific method has four steps:

1. Observation and description of a phenomenon or group of phenomena.
2. Formulation of a hypothesis to explain the phenomena.
3. Use of the hypothesis to predict the existence of other phenomena or to predict quantitatively the results of new observations.
4. Performance of experimental tests of the predictions by several independent experimenters and properly performed experiments.

While the researcher may bring certain biases to the study, it's important that bias not be permitted to enter into the interpretation. It's also important that data that doesn't fit the hypothesis not be ruled out. This is unlikely to happen if the researcher is open to the possibility that the hypothesis might turn out to be null.

Skill 21.9   Identify, explain and discuss multiple causes and effects.

Historic causation is the concept that events in history are linked to one another by an endless chain of cause and effect. The root causes of major historical events cannot always be seen immediately, and are only apparent when looking back from many years later.

When Columbus landed in the New World in 1492, the full effect of his discovery could not have been measured at that time. By opening the Western Hemisphere to economic and political development by Europeans, Columbus changed the face of the world. The native populations that had existed before Columbus arrived were quickly decimated by disease and warfare. Over the following century, the Spanish conquered most of South and Central America, and English and French settlers arrived in North America, eventually displacing the native people. This gradual displacement took place over many years and could not have been foreseen by those early explorers. Looking back it can be said that Columbus caused a series of events that greatly impacted world history.

In some cases, individual events can have an immediate, clear effect. In 1941, Europe was embroiled in war. On the Pacific Rim, Japan was engaged in military occupation of Korea and other Asian countries. The United States took a position of isolation, choosing not to become directly involved with the conflicts. This position changed rapidly, however, on the morning of December 7, 1941, when Japanese forces launched a surprise attack on the US naval base at Pearl Harbor in Hawaii. The United States immediately declared war on Japan and became involved in Europe shortly afterwards. The entry of the United States into the Second World War undoubtedly contributed to the eventual victory of the Allied forces in Europe, and the defeat of Japan after two atomic bombs were dropped there by the US. The surprise attack on Pearl Harbor affected the outcome of the war and the shape of the modern world.

Interaction between cultures, either by exploration and migration or war, often contribute directly to major historical events, but other forces can influence the course of history, as well. Religious movements such as the rise of Catholicism in the Middle Ages created social changes throughout Europe and culminated in the Crusades and the expulsion of Muslims from Spain. Technological developments can lead to major historical events, as in the case of the Industrial Revolution which was driven by the replacement of water power with steam power. Social movements can also cause major historical shifts. Between the Civil War and the early 1960s in the United States, racial segregation was practiced legally in many parts of the country through "Jim Crow" laws. Demonstrations and activism opposing segregation began to escalate during the late 1950s and early 1960s, eventually leading to the passage in the Congress of the Civil Rights Act of 1964, which ended legal segregation in the United States.

Skill 21.10   Recognize the differing ramifications of historical and current events for people of varying ethnic, racial, socio-economic, cultural and gender backgrounds.

Humans are social animals who naturally form groups based on familial, cultural, national and other lines. Conflicts and differences of opinion are just as natural between these groups.

One source of differing views among groups is ethnocentrism. **Ethnocentrism**, as the word suggests, is the belief that one's own culture is the central and usually superior culture. An ethnocentric view usually considers different practices in other cultures as inferior or even "savage."

Psychologists have suggested that ethnocentrism is a naturally occurring attitude. For the large part, people are most comfortable among other people who share their same upbringing, language and cultural background, and are likely to judge other cultural behaviors as alien or foreign.

Historical developments are likely to affect different groups in different ways, some positively and some negatively. These effects can strengthen the ties an individual feels to the group he belongs to, and solidify differences between groups.

Skill 21.11   Apply concepts from history and other social studies including political science and government, geography, economics, anthropology, and sociology.

The disciplines within the social sciences, sometimes referred to as social studies, include anthropology, geography, history, sociology, economics, and political science. Some programs include psychology, archaeology, philosophy, religion, law, and criminology. Also, the subjects of civics and government may be a part of an educational curriculum as separate from political science.

ANTHROPOLOGY is the scientific study of human culture and humanity, the relationship between man and his culture. Anthropologists study different groups and how they relate to other cultures, patterns of behavior, similarities and differences. Their research is two fold: cross-cultural and comparative. The major method of study is referred to as "participant observation." The anthropologist studies and learns about the people being studied by living among them and participating with them in their daily lives.

ARCHAEOLOGY is the scientific study of past human cultures by studying the remains they left behind--objects such as pottery, bones, buildings, tools, and artwork. Archaeologists locate and examine any evidence to help explain the way people lived in past times. They use special equipment and techniques to gather the evidence and make special effort to keep detailed records of their findings because a lot of their research results in destruction of the remains being studied.

CIVICS is the study of the responsibilities and rights of citizens with emphasis on such subjects as freedom, democracy, and individual rights. Students study local, state, national and international government structures, functions, and problems.

ECONOMICS generally is the study of the ways goods and services are produced and the ways they are distributed. It also includes the ways people and nations choose what they buy from what they want. Some of the methods of study include research, case studies, analysis, statistics, and mathematics.

GEOGRAPHY involves studying location and how living things and earth's features are distributed throughout the earth. It includes where animals, people, and plants live and the effects of their relationship with earth's physical features. Geographers also explore the locations of earth's features, how they got there, and why it is so important. Special research methods used by geographers include mapping, interviewing, field studies, mathematics, statistics, and scientific instruments.

HISTORY is the study of the past, especially the aspects of the human past, political and economic events as well as cultural and social conditions. Students study history through textbooks, research, field trips to museums and historical sights, and other methods. Most nations set the requirements in history to study the country's heritage, usually to develop an awareness and feeling of loyalty and patriotism. History is generally divided into the three main divisions: **(a) time periods, (b) nations, and (c) specialized topics.** Study is accomplished through research, reading, and writing.

POLITICAL SCIENCE is the study of political life, different forms of government including elections, political parties, and public administration. In addition, political science studies include values such as justice, freedom, power, and equality.

PSYCHOLOGY involves scientifically studying behavior and mental processes. The ways people and animals relate to each other are observed and recorded. Psychologists scrutinize specific patterns, which will enable them to discern and predict certain behaviors, using scientific methods to verify their ideas. In this way they have been able to learn how to help people fulfill their individual human potential and strengthen understanding between individuals as well as groups and in nations and cultures. The results of the research of psychologists have deepened our understanding of the reasons for people's behavior.

SOCIOLOGY is the study of human society: the individuals, groups, and institutions making up human society. It includes every feature of human social conditions. It deals with the predominant behaviors, attitudes, and types of relationships within a society, which is defined as a group of people with a similar cultural background living in a specific geographical area.

Skill 21.12   Explain concepts related to human, government and political institutions, including power and authority, monarchy, totalitarianism, republicanism, democracy, limited government and the roles and responsibilities of citizenship.

Government ultimately began as a form of protection. A strong person, usually one of the best warriors or someone who had the support of many strong men, assumed command of a people or a city or a land. The power to rule those people rested in his hands. **Laws** existed insofar as the pronouncements and decision of the ruler and were not, in practice, written down, leading to inconsistency Religious leaders had a strong hand in governing the lives of people. In many instances the political leader was also the primary religious figure.

First in Greece and then in Rome and then in other places throughout the world, the idea of government by more than one person or more than just a handful came to the fore. These governments still existed to keep the peace and protect their people from encroachments by both inside and outside forces.

Through the Middle Ages and on into even the twentieth century, many countries still had **monarchs** as their heads of state. These monarchs made laws (or, later, upheld laws), but the laws were still designed to protect the welfare of the people—and the state.

In the modern day, people are subject to **laws** made by many levels of government. Local governments such as city and county bodies are allowed to pass ordinances covering certain local matters, such as property taxation, school districting, civil infractions and business licensing.

State governments in the United States are mainly patterned after the federal government, with an elected legislative body, a judicial system, and a governor who oversees the executive branch. Like the federal government, state governments derive their authority from **constitutions**. State legislation applies to all residents of that state, and local laws must conform. State government funding is frequently from state income tax and sales taxes.

The national or federal government of the United States derives its power from the US Constitution and has three branches, the legislative, executive and judicial. The federal government exists to make national policy and to legislate matters that affect the residents of all states, and to settle matters between states. National income tax is the primary source for federal funding.

Anarchism - Political movement believing in the elimination of all government and its replacement by a cooperative community of individuals. Sometimes it has involved political violence such as assassinations of important political or governmental figures. The historical banner of the movement is a black flag.

Communism - A belief as well as a political system, characterized by the ideology of class conflict and revolution, one party state and dictatorship, repressive police apparatus, and government ownership of the means of production and distribution of goods and services. A revolutionary ideology that preaches the eventual overthrow of all other political orders and the establishment of a one world Communist government.

Dictatorship - The rule by an individual or small group of individuals (Oligarchy) that centralizes all political control in itself and enforces its will with a terrorist police force.

Fascism - A belief as well as a political system, opposed ideologically to Communism, though similar in basic structure, with a one party state, centralized political control and a repressive police system. It however tolerates private ownership of the means of production, though it maintains tight overall control. Central to its belief is the idolization of the Leader, a "Cult of the Personality," and most often an expansionist ideology. Examples have been German Nazism and Italian Fascism.

Monarchy - The rule of a nation by a Monarch, (a non-elected usually hereditary leader), most often a king or queen. It may or may not be accompanied by some measure of democratic open institutions and elections at various levels. A modern example is Great Britain, where it is called a Constitutional Monarchy.

Parliamentary System - A system of government with a legislature, usually involving a multiplicity of political parties and often coalition politics. There is division between the head of state and head of government. Head of government is usually known as a Prime Minister who is also usually the head of the largest party. The head of government and cabinet usually both sit and vote in the parliament. Head of state is most often an elected president, (though in the case of a constitutional monarchy, like Great Britain, the sovereign may take the place of a president as head of state).

Presidential System - A system of government with a legislature, can involve few or many political parties, no division between head of state and head of government. The President serves in both capacities. The President is elected either by direct or indirect election. A President and cabinet usually do not sit or vote in the legislature and the President may or may not be the head of the largest political party. A President can thus rule even without a majority in the legislature.

Socialism - Political belief and system in which the state takes a guiding role in the national economy and provides extensive social services to its population. It may or may not own outright means of production, but even where it does not, it exercises tight control.

A citizen in a democratic society is expected to do certain things in order to remain such a citizen. First a person is expected to follow the laws of that society. The vast majority of the laws of a democratic society have been enacted to facilitate the continuance of that society. Many of these laws also have the rights of the citizens in mind. Citizens have a responsibility to themselves as well and that if government is infringing on their basic rights, they have a natural right to speak up and do something about it. Related to this is the idea that the government of a democratic society exists in part to protect the rights of its citizens with civil and countrywide defense, and laws and the people who make them. Citizens of a democratic society are also expected to participate in the political process, either directly or indirectly. Other ways to participate in the political process include donating time and/or money to the political campaigns of others and speaking out on behalf of or against certain issues. The most basic level of participation in the political process is to **vote**. A democratic society is built on the theory of participatory government.

Skill 21.13   Define some basic economic concepts.

Economics is defined as a study of how scarce resources are allocated to satisfy unlimited wants. Resources refer to the four factors of production: **labor, capital, land and entrepreneurship**.

Scarcity means that choices have to be made. If society decides to produce more of one good, this means that there are fewer resources available for the production of other goods.

Opportunity cost is the value of the sacrificed alternative, the value of what had to be given up in order to have the output of good A. Opportunity cost does not just refer to production. Your opportunity cost of studying with this guide is the value of what you are not doing because you are studying, whether it is watching TV, spending time with family, working, or whatever. Every choice has an opportunity cost.

Marginal analysis is used greatly in the study of economics. The term marginal always means "the change in". There are benefits and costs associated with every decision. The benefits are the gains or the advantages of a decision or action.

The **production costs** involve the cost of the resources involved and the cost of their alternative uses.

Marginal cost is the increase in costs from producing one more unit of output, or the change in total cost divided by the change in quantity of output. Looking at costs and benefits in this way is referred to as making decisions at the margin and this is the methodology used in the study of economics.

A **market economy** functions on the basis of the financial incentive. Firms use society's scarce resources to produce the goods that consumers want.

In a **planned economy**, particularly one based on public ownership of the means of production, a planning entity substitutes for the market, to varying degrees from partial to total. Instead of consumers voting with their dollars, they have a bureaucratic entity trying to substitute for the functions of supply and demand in making production decisions.

Supply is defined as the quantity of a good or service that a producer is willing to make available at different prices during a specified period of time.

Demand is defined as the quantity of goods and services that a buyer is willing and able to buy at different prices during a specified period of time.

Market equilibrium occurs where the selling decisions of producers are equal to the buying decisions of consumers, or where the supply and demand curves intersect.

Incentives and **substitutes** affect the market situation. Incentives for consumers are things like sales, coupons, rebates, etc. The incentives results in increased sales for the firm, even though there is a cost to the incentives.

Skill 21.14 **Discuss basic concepts of sociology related to individuals, interpersonal relationships and institutions, including family and community; and concepts related to social structure, including occupation, socio-economic class, ethnicity and gender.**

Socialization also takes place among adults who change their environment and are expected to adopt new behaviors. Two primary ways that socialization takes place are through positive and negative sanctions. Positive sanctions are rewards for appropriate or desirable behavior, and negative sanctions are punishments for inappropriate behavior. Sanctions can be either formal or informal. Public awards and prizes are ways a society formally reinforces positive behaviors. Laws that punish specific infractions are formal negative sanctions.

Sociologists have identified five different types of institutions around which societies are structured: family, education, government, religion and economy. These institutions provide a framework for members of a society to learn about and participate in a society, and allow for a society to perpetuate its beliefs and values to succeeding generations.

The **family** is the primary social unit in most societies. It is through the family that children learn the most essential skills for functioning in their society such as language and appropriate forms of interaction. The family is connected to ethnicity, which is partly defined by a person's heritage.

Education is an important institution in a society, as it allows for the formal passing on of a culture's collected knowledge. The institution of education is connected to the family, as that is where a child's earliest education takes place. The United States has a public school system administered by the states that ensures a basic education and provides a common experience for most children.

A society's **governmental** institutions often embody its beliefs and values. Laws, for instance, reflect a society's values by enforcing its ideas of right and wrong. The structure of a society's government can reflect a society's ideals about the role of an individual in his society. The American form of democracy emphasizes the rights of the individual, but in return expects individuals to respect the rights of others, including those of ethnic or political minorities.

Religion is frequently the institution from which springs a society's primary beliefs and values, and can be closely related to other social institutions. Many religions have definite teachings on the structure and importance of the family, for instance. The U.S. Constitution guarantees the free practice of religion, which has led to a large number of denominations practicing in the U.S. today. Most Americans identify with Christian faiths.

A society's **economic** institutions define how an individual can contribute and receive economic reward from his society. The United States has a capitalist economy motivated by free enterprise. While this system allows for economic advancement for the individual, it can also produce areas of poverty and economic depression.

Skill 21.15 Discuss major concepts of philosophy and their impact on history and society.

Philosophy is a field of study where people question and theorize about the nature of reality, whether or not God exists, ethics, law, what is the nature of being and the universe, what is truth, consciousness and what makes actions right or wrong. The term philosophy comes from the Greek word, philosophia, which means "love of wisdom".

Belief systems, like other cultural elements or institutions, spread through human interaction. Religions and belief systems general originate in a particular region, with elements that are culturally or regionally defined or influenced. As belief systems are introduced to new groups or societies, some of those regional and cultural markers will also penetrate the new society. By the same token, as interaction between the originating society and the new society continues and the belief system finds new expression, some regional or cultural elements introduced by the new society will be carried back to the originating culture. One method is military and political conquest. As the originating society conquers a new territory and incorporates it into the political entity, belief systems are frequently either peaceably spread to the conquered people or forced upon them. The rise and spread of the Islamic Empire both converted and forced the conversion of conquered peoples to Islam. Another example may be seen in the conversion of the Emperor Constantine to Christianity and his imposition of Christianity upon Rome as the national religion.

Belief systems are also introduced through other types of human interaction. This occurs through commercial interaction, the identification of common or similar primitive mythologies (for example, similar creation and great flood myths). Educational interaction and cultural sharing between cultures also frequently carries religious belief systems, as well.

Judaism: the oldest of the eight and was the first to teach and practice the belief in one God, Yahweh.

Christianity: came from Judaism, grew and spread in the First Century throughout the Roman Empire, despite persecution. A later schism resulted in the Western (Roman Catholic) and Eastern (Orthodox) parts. Protestant sects developed as part of the Protestant Revolution. The name "Christian" means one who is a follower of Jesus Christ who started Christianity. Christians follow his teachings and examples, living by the laws and principles of the Bible.

Islam: founded in Arabia by Mohammed who preached about God, Allah. Islam spread through trade, travel, and conquest and followers of it fought in the Crusades. In addition, other wars against Christians and today against the Jewish nation of Israel. Followers of Islam, called Muslims, live by the teachings of the Koran, their holy book, and of their prophets.

Hinduism: begun by people called Aryans around 1500 BC and spread into India. The Aryans blended their culture with the culture of the Dravidians, natives they conquered. Today it has many sects, promotes worship of hundreds of gods and goddesses and belief in reincarnation. Though forbidden today by law, a prominent feature of Hinduism in the past was a rigid adherence to and practice of the infamous caste system.

Buddhism: developed in India from the teachings of Prince Gautama and spread to most of Asia. Its beliefs opposed the worship of numerous deities, the Hindu caste system and the supernatural. Worshippers must be free of attachment to all things worldly and devote themselves to finding release from life's suffering.

Confucianism: is a Chinese religion based on the teachings of the Chinese philosopher Confucius. There is no clergy, no organization, and no belief in a deity or in life after death. It emphasizes political and moral ideas with respect for authority and ancestors. Rulers were expected to govern according to high moral standards.

Taoism: a native Chinese religion with worship of more deities than almost any other religion. It teaches all followers to make the effort to achieve the two goals of happiness and immortality. Practices and ceremonies include meditation, prayer, magic, reciting scriptures, special diets, breath control, beliefs in witchcraft, fortune telling, astrology, and communicating with the spirits of the dead.

Shinto: the native religion of Japan developed from native folk beliefs worshipping spirits and demons in animals, trees, and mountains. According to its mythology, deities created Japan and its people, which resulted in worshipping the emperor as a god. Shinto was influenced by Buddhism and Confucianism but never had strong doctrines on salvation or life after death.

Skill 21.16 Explain basic concepts of demography including factors associated with human migration.

Demography is the branch of science of statistics most concerned with the social well being of people. **Demographic tables** may include: (1) Analysis of the population on the basis of age, parentage, physical condition, race, occupation and civil position, giving the actual size and the density of each separate area. (2) Changes in the population as a result of birth, marriage, and death. (3) Statistics on population movements and their effects and their relations to given economic, social and political conditions. (4) Statistics of crime, illegitimacy and suicide. (5) Levels of education and economic and social statistics.

Such information is also similar to that area of science known as **vital statistics** and as such is indispensable in studying social trends and making important legislative, economic, and social decisions. In collecting any such statistical information and data, care and adequate precautions must always be taken in order to assure that the knowledge obtained is complete and accurate. It is also important to be aware of just how much data is necessary to collect in order to establish the idea that is attempting to be formulated. One important idea to understand is that statistics usually deal with a specific **model**, **hypothesis**, or **theory** that is being attempted to be proven.

Though one should be aware that a theory can never actually be proved correct it can only really be corroborated. **Corroboration** meaning that the data presented is more consistent with this theory than with any other theory, so it makes sense to use this theory.) One should also be aware of what is known as **correlation** (the joint movement of various data points) does not infer **causation** (the change in one of those data points caused the other data points to change). It is important that one take these aspects into account so that one can be in a better position to appreciate what the collected data is really saying. **Tests of reliability** are used to explain real world events. Indeed the methods used and the inherent biases and reasons actually for doing the study by the individual(s) involved, must never be discounted.

Skill 21.17   Discuss basic concepts of anthropology.

ANTHROPOLOGY is the scientific study of human culture and humanity, the relationship between man and his culture. Anthropologists study different groups, how they relate to other cultures, and patterns of behavior, similarities and differences. Their research is two fold: cross-cultural and comparative. The major method of study is referred to as "participant observation." The anthropologist studies and learns about the people being studied by living among them and participating with them in their daily lives.

ARCHAEOLOGY is the scientific study of past human cultures by studying the remains they left behind--objects such as pottery, bones, buildings, tools, and artwork. Archaeologists locate and examine any evidence to help explain the way people lived in past times. They use special equipment and techniques to gather the evidence and make special effort to keep detailed records of their findings because a lot of their research results in destruction of the remains being studied. The first step is to locate an archaeological site using various methods. Next, surveying the site takes place starting with a detailed description of the site with notes, maps, photographs, and collecting artifacts from the surface. Excavating follows either by digging for buried objects or by diving and working in submersible decompression chambers, when underwater. They record and preserve the evidence for eventual classification, dating, and evaluating their find.

CONTENT AREA – MATHEMATICS

DOMAIN I – NUMBER SENSE

COMPETENCY 22.0 NUMBERS, RELATIONSHIPS AMONG NUMBERS AND NUMBER SYSTEMS

Skill 22.1 **Understand base ten place value, number theory concepts and the structure of the whole, integer, rational, and real number systems**

GCF is the abbreviation for the **greatest common factor**. The GCF is the largest number that is a factor of all the numbers given in a problem. The GCF can be no larger than the smallest number given in the problem. If no other number is a common factor, then the GCF will be the number 1. To find the GCF, list all possible factors of the smallest number given (include the number itself). Starting with the largest factor (which is the number itself), determine if it is also a factor of all the other given numbers. If so, that is the GCF. If that factor doesn't work, try the same method on the next smaller factor. Continue until a common factor is found. That is the GCF. Note: There can be other common factors besides the GCF.

Example: Find the GCF of 12, 20, and 36.

The smallest number in the problem is 12. The factors of 12 are 1,2,3,4,6 and 12. 12 is the largest factor, but it does not divide evenly into 20. Neither does 6, but 4 will divide into both 20 and 36 evenly.

Therefore, 4 is the GCF.

Example: Find the GCF of 14 and 15.

Factors of 14 are 1,2,7 and 14. 14 is the largest factor, but it does not divide evenly into 15. Neither does 7 or 2. Therefore, the only factor common to both 14 and 15 is the number 1, the GCF.

Skill 22.2   Order integers, mixed numbers, rational numbers and real numbers.

Rational numbers can be expressed as the ratio of two integers, $\frac{a}{b}$ where b ≠ 0, for example $\frac{2}{3}$, $-\frac{4}{5}$, 5 = $\frac{5}{1}$.

The rational numbers include integers, fractions and mixed numbers, terminating and repeating decimals. Every rational number can be expressed as a repeating or terminating decimal and can be shown on a number line.

Integers are positive and negative whole numbers and zero.
    ...-6, -5, -4, -3, -2, -1, 0, 1, 2, 3, 4, 5, 6, ...

Whole numbers are natural numbers and zero.
    0, 1, 2, 3, 4, 5, 6...

Natural numbers are the counting numbers.
    1, 2, 3, 4, 5, 6...

Irrational numbers are real numbers that cannot be written as the ratio of two integers. These are infinite non-repeating decimals.
    <u>Examples</u>: $\sqrt{5}$ = 2.2360..,   pi =$\prod$ = 3.1415927...

A **fraction** is an expression of numbers in the form of x/y, where **x** is the numerator and **y** is the denominator, which cannot be zero.

Example: $\dfrac{3}{7}$ 3 is the numerator; 7 is the denominator

If the fraction has common factors for the numerator and denominator, divide both by the common factor to reduce the fraction to its lowest form.

Example:

$$\frac{13}{39} = \frac{1 \times 13}{3 \times 13} = \frac{1}{3}$$ Divide by the common factor 13

A **mixed** number has an integer part and a fractional part.

Example: $2\dfrac{1}{4}$, $^-5\dfrac{1}{6}$, $7\dfrac{1}{3}$

Percent = per 100 (written with the symbol %). Thus 10% $= \dfrac{10}{100} = \dfrac{1}{10}$.

Decimals = deci = part of ten. To find the decimal equivalent of a fraction, use the denominator to divide the numerator as shown in the following example.

Example: Find the decimal equivalent of $\dfrac{7}{10}$.

Since 10 cannot divide into 7 evenly

Skill 22.3   Represent numbers in exponential and scientific notation.

The **exponent form** is a shortcut method to write repeated multiplication. Basic form: b^n, where b is called the base and n is the exponent. b and n are both real numbers. b^n implies that the base b is multiplied by itself n times.

Examples: $3^4 = 3 \times 3 \times 3 \times 3 = 81$

$2^3 = 2 \times 2 \times 2 = 8$

$(^-2)^4 = (^-2) \times (^-2) \times (^-2) \times (^-2) = 16$

$^-2^4 = ^-(2 \times 2 \times 2 \times 2) = ^-16$

Key exponent rules:
        For 'a' nonzero, and 'm' and 'n' real numbers:

  1) $a^m \cdot a^n = a^{(m+n)}$ Product rule

  2) $\dfrac{a^m}{a^n} = a^{(m-n)}$ Quotient rule

  3) $\dfrac{a^{-m}}{a^{-n}} = \dfrac{a^n}{a^m}$

When 10 is raised to any power, the exponent tells the numbers of zeroes in the product.

Example: $10^7 = 10{,}000{,}000$

Caution: Unless the negative sign is inside the parentheses and the exponent is outside the parentheses, the sign is not affected by the exponent.

  $(^-2)^4$ implies that -2 is multiplied by itself 4 times.

  $^-2^4$ implies that 2 is multiplied by itself 4 times, then the answer is negated.

Scientific notation is a more convenient method for writing very large and very small numbers. It employs two factors. The first factor is a number between 1 and 10. The second factor is a power of 10. This notation is "shorthand" for expressing large numbers (like the weight of 100 elephants) or small numbers (like the weight of an atom in pounds).

Recall that:

$10^n = (10)^n$ Ten multiplied by itself n times.

$10^0 = 1$ Any nonzero number raised to power of zero is 1.

$10^1 = 10$

$10^2 = 10 \times 10 = 100$

$10^3 = 10 \times 10 \times 10 = 1000$ (kilo)

$10^{-1} = 1/10$ (deci)

$10^{-2} = 1/100$ (centi)

$10^{-3} = 1/1000$ (milli)

$10^{-6} = 1/1,000,000$ (micro)

Example: Write 46,368,000 in scientific notation.

1)   Introduce a decimal point and decimal places.
46,368,000 = 46,368,000.0000

2)   Make a mark between the two digits that give a number between -9.9 and 9.9.
4 ∧ 6,368,000 .0000

3)   Count the number of digit places between the decimal point and the ∧ mark. This number is the 'n'-the power of ten.

So, $46,368,000 = 4.6368 \times 10^7$

Example: Write 0.00397 in scientific notation.

1)   Decimal place is already in place.

2)   Make a mark between 3 and 9 to get a one number between -9.9 and 9.9.

3)   Move decimal place to the mark (3 hops).

0.003 ∧ 97

Motion is to the right, so n of 10^n is negative.

Therefore, $0.00397 = 3.97 \times 10^{-3}$.

Skill 22.4   Describe the relationships between the algorithms for addition, subtraction, multiplication, and division.

Recognition and understanding of the relationships between concepts and topics is of great value in mathematical problem solving and the explanation of more complex processes.

For instance, multiplication is simply repeated addition. This relationship explains the concept of variable addition. We can show that the expression 4x + 3x = 7x is true by rewriting 4 times x and 3 times x as repeated addition, yielding the expression (x + x + x + x) + (x + x + x). Thus, because of the relationship between multiplication and addition, variable addition is accomplished by coefficient addition.

Skill 22.5   Understand properties of number systems and their relationship to the algorithms.

Properties are rules that apply for addition, subtraction, multiplication, or division of real numbers. These properties are:

Commutative: You can change the order of the terms or factors as follows.

For addition: $a + b = b + a$
For multiplication: $ab = ba$

Since addition is the inverse operation of subtraction and multiplication is the inverse operation of division, no separate laws are needed for subtraction and division.

Example: $5 + {}^-8 = {}^-8 + 5 = {}^-3$

Example: ${}^-2 \times 6 = 6 \times {}^-2 = {}^-12$

Associative: You can regroup the terms as you like.

For addition: $a + (b + c) = (a + b) + c$
For multiplication: $a(bc) = (ab)c$

This rule does not apply for division and subtraction.

Example: $({}^-2 + 7) + 5 = {}^-2 + (7 + 5)$
$5 + 5 = {}^-2 + 12 = 10$

Example: $(3 \times {}^-7) \times 5 = 3 \times ({}^-7 \times 5)$
${}^-21 \times 5 = 3 \times {}^-35 = {}^-105$

Identity: Finding a number so that when added to a term results in that number (additive identity); finding a number such that when multiplied by a term results in that number (multiplicative identity).

For addition: $a + 0 = a$ (zero is additive identity)
For multiplication: $a \cdot 1 = a$ (one is multiplicative)

Example: $17 + 0 = 17$

Example: ${}^-34 \times 1 = {}^-34$
The product of any number and one is that number.

Inverse: Finding a number such that when added to the number it results in zero; or when multiplied by the number results in 1.

For addition: $a + (-a) = 0$
For multiplication: $a \cdot (1/a) = 1$

$(-a)$ is the additive inverse of a; $(1/a)$, also called the reciprocal, is the multiplicative inverse of a.

Example: $25 + {}^-25 = 0$

Example: $5 \times \frac{1}{5} = 1$ The product of any number and its reciprocal is one.

Distributive: This technique allows us to operate on terms within parentheses without first performing operations within the parentheses. This is especially helpful when terms within the parentheses cannot be combined.

$$a\ (b + c) = ab + ac$$

Example: $6 \times (\ ^-4 + 9) = (6 \times\ ^-4) + (6 \times 9)$
$6 \times 5 =\ ^-24 + 54 = 30$

To multiply a sum by a number, multiply each addend by the number, then add the products.

Skill 22.6 **Perform operations with positive, negative, and fractional exponents, as they apply to whole numbers and fractions.**

Addition of whole numbers

Example: At the end of a day of shopping, a shopper had $24 remaining in his wallet. He spent $45 on various goods. How much money did the shopper have at the beginning of the day?

The total amount of money the shopper started with is the sum of the amount spent and the amount remaining at the end of the day.

$$\begin{array}{r} 24 \\ +\ 45 \\ \hline 69 \end{array}$$ → The original total was $69.

Example: A race took the winner 1 hr. 58 min. 12 sec. on the first half of the race and 2 hr. 9 min. 57 sec. on the second half of the race. How much time did the entire race take?

```
  1 hr. 58 min. 12 sec.
+ 2 hr.  9 min. 57 sec.    Add these numbers
  3 hr. 67 min. 69 sec.
+ 1 min -60 sec.           Change 60 seconds to 1
                              min.
  3 hr. 68 min.  9 sec.
+ 1 hr.-60 min.       .    Change 60 minutes to 1 hr.
  4 hr.  8 min.  9 sec.  ← final answer
```

Subtraction of Whole Numbers

Example: At the end of his shift, a cashier has $96 in the cash register. At the beginning of his shift, he had $15. How much money did the cashier collect during his shift?

The total collected is the difference of the ending amount and the starting amount.

$$
\begin{array}{r}
96 \\
-\ 15 \\
\hline
81
\end{array}
$$
→ The total collected was $81.

Multiplication of whole numbers

Multiplication is one of the four basic number operations. In simple terms, multiplication is the addition of a number to itself a certain number of times. For example, 4 multiplied by 3 is the equal to 4 + 4 + 4 or 3 + 3 + 3 +3. Another way of conceptualizing multiplication is to think in terms of groups. For example, if we have 4 groups of 3 students, the total number of students is 4 multiplied by 3. We call the solution to a multiplication problem the product.

The basic algorithm for whole number multiplication begins with aligning the numbers by place value with the number containing more places on top.

$$
\begin{array}{r}
172 \\
\times\ 43
\end{array}
$$
→ Note that we placed 122 on top because it has more places than 43 does.

Next, we multiply the ones' place of the second number by each place value of the top number sequentially.

$$
\begin{array}{r}
(2) \\
172 \\
\times\ 43 \\
\hline
516
\end{array}
$$
→ {3 x 2 = 6, 3 x 7 = 21, 3 x 1 = 3}
Note that we had to carry a 2 to the hundreds' column because 3 x 7 = 21. Note also that we add, not multiply, carried numbers to the product.

Next, we multiply the number in the tens' place of the second number by each place value of the top number sequentially. Because we are multiplying by a number in the tens' place, we place a zero at the end of this product.

$$
\begin{array}{r}
(2) \\
172 \\
\times\ 43 \\
\hline
516 \\
6880
\end{array}
$$
→ {4 x 2 = 8, 4 x 7 = 28, 4 x 1 = 4}

Finally, to determine the final product we add the two partial products.

$$
\begin{array}{r}
172 \\
\times\ \ 43 \\
\hline
516 \\
+\ 6880 \\
\hline
7396
\end{array}
$$
⟶ The product of 172 and 43 is 7396.

Example: A student buys 4 boxes of crayons. Each box contains 16 crayons. How many total crayons does the student have?

The total number of crayons is 16 x 4.

$$
\begin{array}{r}
16 \\
\times\ \ 4 \\
\hline
64
\end{array}
$$
⟶ Total number of crayons equals 64.

Division of whole numbers

Division, the inverse of multiplication, is another of the four basic number operations. When we divide one number by another, we determine how many times we can multiply the divisor (number divided by) before we exceed the number we are dividing (dividend). For example, 8 divided by 2 equals 4 because we can multiply 2 four times to reach 8 (2 x 4 = 8 or 2 + 2 + 2 + 2 = 8). Using the grouping conceptualization we used with multiplication, we can divide 8 into 4 groups of 2 or 2 groups of 4. We call the answer to a division problem the quotient.

If the divisor does not divide evenly into the dividend, we express the leftover amount either as a remainder or as a fraction with the divisor as the denominator. For example, 9 divided by 2 equals 4 with a remainder of 1 or 4 ½.

The basic algorithm for division is long division. We start by representing the quotient as follows.

$14\overline{)293}$ ⟶ 14 is the divisor and 293 is the dividend.
This represents 293 ÷ 14.

Next, we divide the divisor into the dividend starting from the left.

$14\overline{)293}^{\ 2}$ ⟶ 14 divides into 29 two times with a remainder.

Next, we multiply the partial quotient by the divisor, subtract this value from the first digits of the dividend, and bring down the remaining dividend digits to complete the number.

13.

$$
\begin{array}{r}
2 \\
14\overline{)293} \\
-28 \\
\hline
13
\end{array}
$$

$\longrightarrow$ 2 x 14 = 28, 29 – 28 = 1, and bringing down the 3 yields

Finally, we divide again (the divisor into the remaining value) and repeat the preceding process. The number left after the subtraction represents the remainder.

$$
\begin{array}{r}
20 \\
14\overline{)293} \\
-28 \\
\hline
13 \\
-0 \\
\hline
13
\end{array}
$$

$\longrightarrow$ The final quotient is 20 with a remainder of 13. We can also represent this quotient as 20 13/14.

Example: Each box of apples contains 24 apples. How many boxes must a grocer purchase to supply a group of 252 people with one apple each?

The grocer needs 252 apples. Because he must buy apples in groups of 24, we divide 252 by 24 to determine how many boxes he needs to buy.

12.

$$
\begin{array}{r}
10 \\
24\overline{)252} \\
-24 \\
\hline
12 \\
-0 \\
\hline
12
\end{array}
$$

$\longrightarrow$ The quotient is 10 with a remainder of

Thus, the grocer needs 10 boxes plus 12 more apples. Therefore, the minimum number of boxes the grocer can purchase is 11.

Example: At his job, John gets paid $20 for every hour he works. If John made $940 in a week, how many hours did he work?

This is a division problem. To determine the number of hours John worked, we divide the total amount made ($940) by the hourly rate of pay ($20). Thus, the number of hours worked equals 940 divided by 20.

$$
\begin{array}{r}
47 \\
20\overline{)940} \\
-80 \\
\hline
140 \\
-140 \\
\hline
0
\end{array}
$$

20 divides into 940, 47 times with no remainder.

John worked 47 hours.

Addition and Subtraction of Decimals

When adding and subtracting decimals, we align the numbers by place value as we do with whole numbers. After adding or subtracting each column, we bring the decimal down, placing it in the same location as in the numbers added or subtracted.

Example: Find the sum of 152.3 and 36.342.

$$
\begin{array}{r}
152.300 \\
+ 36.342 \\
\hline
188.642
\end{array}
$$

Note that we placed two zeroes after the final place value in 152.3 to clarify the column addition.

Example: Find the difference of 152.3 and 36.342.

$$
\begin{array}{cc}
\begin{array}{r}
2\ 9\ 10 \\
152.300 \\
- 36.342 \\
\hline
58
\end{array}
&
\begin{array}{r}
(4)11(12) \\
152.300 \\
- 36.342 \\
\hline
115.958
\end{array}
\end{array}
$$

Note how we borrowed to subtract from the zeroes in the hundredths' and thousandths' place of 152.300.

Multiplication of Decimals

When multiplying decimal numbers, we multiply exactly as with whole numbers and place the decimal moving in from the left the total number of decimal places contained in the two numbers multiplied. For example, when multiplying 1.5 and 2.35, we place the decimal in the product 3 places in from the left (3.525).

Example: Find the product of 3.52 and 4.1.

$$
\begin{array}{r}
3.52 \\
\times\ 4.1 \\
\hline
352 \\
+\ 14080 \\
\hline
14432
\end{array}
$$

Note that there are 3 total decimal places in the two numbers.

We place the decimal 3 places in from the left.

Thus, the final product is 14.432.

Example: A shopper has 5 one-dollar bills, 6 quarters, 3 nickels, and 4 pennies in his pocket. How much money does he have?

$$
5 \times \$1.00 = \$5.00
$$

$$
\begin{array}{r}
3 \\
\$0.25 \\
\times\ 6 \\
\hline
\$1.50
\end{array}
\qquad
\begin{array}{r}
\$0.05 \\
\times\ 3 \\
\hline
\$0.15
\end{array}
\qquad
\begin{array}{r}
\$0.01 \\
\times\ 4 \\
\hline
\$0.04
\end{array}
$$

Note the placement of the decimals in the multiplication products. Thus, the total amount of money in the shopper's pocket is:

$$
\begin{array}{r}
\$5.00 \\
1.50 \\
0.15 \\
+\ 0.04 \\
\hline
\$6.69
\end{array}
$$

Division of Decimals

When dividing decimal numbers, we first remove the decimal in the divisor by moving the decimal in the dividend the same number of spaces to the right. For example, when dividing 1.45 into 5.3 we convert the numbers to 145 and 530 and perform normal whole number division.

Example: Find the quotient of 5.3 divided by 1.45.
            Convert to 145 and 530.

            Divide.

$$
\begin{array}{r} 3 \\ 145\overline{)530} \\ -435 \\ \hline 95 \end{array}
\longrightarrow
\begin{array}{r} 3.65 \\ 145\overline{)530.00} \\ -435 \\ \hline 950 \\ -870 \\ \hline 800 \end{array}
\longrightarrow
$$

continue

Note that we insert the decimal to division.

Because one of the numbers divided contained one decimal place, we round the quotient to one decimal place. Thus, the final quotient is 3.7.

Operating with Percents

Example: 5 is what percent of 20?

            This is the same as converting $\dfrac{5}{20}$ to % form.

            $$\frac{5}{20} \times \frac{100}{1} = \frac{5}{1} \times \frac{5}{1} = 25\%$$

Example: There are 64 dogs in the kennel. 48 are collies. What percent are collies?

            Restate the problem.   48 is what percent of 64?
            Write an equation. $48 = n \times 64$
            Solve. $\frac{48}{64} = n$

            $n = \frac{3}{4} = 75\%$

            75% of the dogs are collies.

Example: The auditorium was filled to 90% capacity. There were 558 seats occupied. What is the capacity of the auditorium?

Restate the problem.   90% of what number is 558?
Write an equation. $0.9n = 558$
Solve. $n = \frac{558}{.9}$
                         $n = 620$

The capacity of the auditorium is 620 people.

Example: A pair of shoes costs $42.00. Sales tax is 6%. What is the total cost of the shoes?

Restate the problem.   What is 6% of 42?
Write an equation. $n = 0.06 \times 42$
Solve. $n = 2.52$

Add the sales tax to the cost. $42.00 + $2.52 = $44.52

The total cost of the shoes, including sales tax, is $44.52.

Addition and subtraction of fractions

<u>Key Points</u>

1. You need a common denominator in order to add and subtract reduced and improper fractions.

   Example: $\dfrac{1}{3} + \dfrac{7}{3} = \dfrac{1+7}{3} = \dfrac{8}{3} = 2\dfrac{2}{3}$

   Example: $\dfrac{4}{12} + \dfrac{6}{12} - \dfrac{3}{12} = \dfrac{4+6-3}{12} = \dfrac{7}{12}$

2. Adding an integer and a fraction of the <u>same</u> sign results directly in a mixed fraction.

   Example: $2 + \dfrac{2}{3} = 2\dfrac{2}{3}$

   Example: $^-2 - \dfrac{3}{4} = ^-2\dfrac{3}{4}$

3.   Adding an integer and a fraction with different signs involves the following steps.

-get a common denominator
-add or subtract as needed
-change to a mixed fraction if possible

Example: $2 - \dfrac{1}{3} = \dfrac{2 \times 3 - 1}{3} = \dfrac{6-1}{3} = \dfrac{5}{3} = 1\dfrac{2}{3}$

Example: Add $7\dfrac{3}{8} + 5\dfrac{2}{7}$

Add the whole numbers; add the fractions and combine the two results:

$$7\dfrac{3}{8} + 5\dfrac{2}{7} = (7+5) + (\dfrac{3}{8} + \dfrac{2}{7})$$

$$= 12 + \dfrac{(7 \times 3) + (8 \times 2)}{56} \quad \text{(LCM of 8 and 7)}$$

$$= 12 + \dfrac{21 + 16}{56} = 12 + \dfrac{37}{56} = 12\dfrac{37}{56}$$

Example: Perform the operation.

$$\dfrac{2}{3} - \dfrac{5}{6}$$

We first find the LCM of 3 and 6 which is 6.

$$\dfrac{2 \times 2}{3 \times 2} - \dfrac{5}{6} \rightarrow \dfrac{4-5}{6} = \dfrac{^{-}1}{6} \qquad \text{(Using method A)}$$

Example: $^-7\dfrac{1}{4}+2\dfrac{7}{8}$

$$^-7\dfrac{1}{4}+2\dfrac{7}{8}=(^-7+2)+(\dfrac{^-1}{4}+\dfrac{7}{8})$$

$$=(^-5)+\dfrac{(^-2+7)}{8}=(^-5)+(\dfrac{5}{8})$$

$$=(^-5)+\dfrac{5}{8}=\dfrac{^-5\times8}{1\times8}+\dfrac{5}{8}=\dfrac{^-40+5}{8}$$

$$=\dfrac{^-35}{8}=^-4\dfrac{3}{8}$$

Divide 35 by 8 to get 4, remainder 3.

Caution: Common error would be

$$^-7\dfrac{1}{4}+2\dfrac{7}{8}=^-7\dfrac{2}{8}+2\dfrac{7}{8}=^-5\dfrac{9}{8} \qquad \text{Wrong.}$$

It is correct to add -7 and 2 to get -5, but adding $\dfrac{2}{8}+\dfrac{7}{8}=\dfrac{9}{8}$

is wrong. It should have been $\dfrac{^-2}{8}+\dfrac{7}{8}=\dfrac{5}{8}$. Then,

$$^-5+\dfrac{5}{8}=^-4\dfrac{3}{8} \quad \text{as before.}$$

Multiplication of fractions

Using the following example: $3\dfrac{1}{4}\times\dfrac{5}{6}$

1. Convert each number to an improper fraction.

$$3\dfrac{1}{4}=\dfrac{(12+1)}{4}=\dfrac{13}{4} \qquad\qquad \dfrac{5}{6} \text{ is already in reduced form.}$$

2. Reduce (cancel) common factors of the numerator and denominator if they exist.

$$\dfrac{13}{4}\times\dfrac{5}{6} \qquad \text{No common factors exist.}$$

3. Multiply the numerators by each other and the denominators by each other.

$$\frac{13}{4} \times \frac{5}{6} = \frac{65}{24}$$

4. If possible, reduce the fraction back to its lowest term.

$$\frac{65}{24}$$ Cannot be reduced further.

5. Convert the improper fraction back to a mixed fraction by using long division.

$$\frac{65}{24} = 24\overline{)65} \qquad = 2\frac{17}{24}$$
$$\underline{48}$$
$$17$$

Summary of sign changes for multiplication:

a. $(+) \times (+) = (+)$

b. $(-) \times (+) = (-)$

c. $(+) \times (-) = (-)$

d. $(-) \times (-) = (+)$

Example: $\quad 7\frac{1}{3} \times \frac{5}{11} = \frac{22}{3} \times \frac{5}{11} \quad$ Reduce like terms (22 and 11)

$$= \frac{2}{3} \times \frac{5}{1} = \frac{10}{3} = 3\frac{1}{3}$$

Example: $\quad {}^{-}6\frac{1}{4} \times \frac{5}{9} = \frac{{}^{-}25}{4} \times \frac{5}{9}$

$$= \frac{{}^{-}125}{36} = {}^{-}3\frac{17}{36}$$

Example: $\quad \frac{{}^{-}1}{4} \times \frac{{}^{-}3}{7} \qquad$ Negative times a negative equals positive.

$$= \frac{1}{4} \times \frac{3}{7} = \frac{3}{28}$$

Division of fractions:

1. Change mixed fractions to improper fraction.

2. Change the division problem to a multiplication problem by using the reciprocal of the number after the division sign.
3. Find the sign of the final product.

4. Cancel if common factors exist between the numerator and the denominator.

5. Multiply the numerators together and the denominators together.

6. Change the improper fraction to a mixed number.

Example:
$$3\frac{1}{5} \div 2\frac{1}{4} = \frac{16}{5} \div \frac{9}{4}$$

$$= \frac{16}{5} \times \frac{4}{9} \qquad \text{Reciprocal of } \frac{9}{4} \text{ is } \frac{4}{9}.$$

$$= \frac{64}{45} = 1\frac{19}{45}$$

Example:
$$7\frac{3}{4} \div 11\frac{5}{8} = \frac{31}{4} \div \frac{93}{8}$$

$$= \frac{31}{4} \times \frac{8}{93} \qquad \text{Reduce like terms.}$$

$$= \frac{1}{1} \times \frac{2}{3} = \frac{2}{3}$$

Example:
$$\left(^-2\frac{1}{2}\right) \div 4\frac{1}{6} = \frac{^-5}{2} \div \frac{25}{6}$$

$$= \frac{^-5}{2} \times \frac{6}{25} \qquad \text{Reduce like terms.}$$

$$= \frac{^-1}{1} \times \frac{3}{5} = \frac{^-3}{5}$$

Example: $\left(-5\dfrac{3}{8}\right) \div \left(\dfrac{^-7}{16}\right) = \dfrac{^-43}{8} \div \dfrac{^-7}{16}$

$= \dfrac{^-43}{8} \times \dfrac{^-16}{7}$ Reduce like terms.

$= \dfrac{43}{1} \times \dfrac{2}{7}$ Negative times a negative equals a positive.

$= \dfrac{86}{7} = 12\dfrac{2}{7}$

Converting decimals, fractions and percents

A **decimal** can be converted to a **percent** by multiplying by 100, or merely moving the decimal point two places to the right. A **percent** can be converted to a **decimal** by dividing by 100, or moving the decimal point two places to the left.

Examples: 0.375 = 37.5%
0.7 = 70%
0.04 = 4 %
3.15 = 315 %
84% = 0.84
3 % = 0.03
60% = 0.6
110% = 1.1
$\frac{1}{2}$ % = 0.5% = 0.005

A **percent** can be converted to a **fraction** by placing it over 100 and reducing to simplest terms.

Example: Convert 0.056 to a fraction.

Multiplying 0.056 by $\dfrac{1000}{1000}$ to get rid of the decimal point:

$$0.056 \times \dfrac{1000}{1000} = \dfrac{56}{1000} = \dfrac{7}{125}$$

Example: Find 23% of 1000.

$$= \dfrac{23}{100} \times \dfrac{1000}{1} = 23 \times 10 = 230$$

Example: Convert 6.25% to a decimal and to a fraction.

$$6.25\% = 0.0625 = 0.0625 \times \frac{10000}{10000} = \frac{625}{10000} = \frac{1}{16}$$

An example of a type of problem involving fractions is the conversion of recipes. For example, if a recipe serves 8 people and we want to make enough to serve only 4, we must determine how much of each ingredient to use. The conversion factor, the number we multiply each ingredient by, is:

$$\text{Conversion Factor} = \frac{\text{Number of Servings Needed}}{\text{Number of Servings in Recipe}}$$

Example: Consider the following recipe.

3 cups flour
½ tsp. baking powder
2/3 cups butter
2 cups sugar
2 eggs

If the above recipe serves 8, how much of each ingredient do we need to serve only 4 people?

First, determine the conversion factor.

Conversion Factor = $\dfrac{4}{8} = \dfrac{1}{2}$

Next, multiply each ingredient by the conversion factor.

3 x ½ =	1 ½ cups flour
½ x ½ =	¼ tsp. baking powder
2/3 x ½ = 2/6 =	1/3 cups butter
2 x ½ =	1 cup sugar
2 x ½ =	1 egg

COMPETENCY 23.0 COMPUTATIONAL TOOLS, PROCEDURES AND STRATEGIES

Skill 23.1   Demonstrate fluency in standard algorithms for computation and evaluate the correctness of nonstandard algorithms.

1. Failing to distribute:
    ex. $4x - (2x - 3) = 4x - 2x + 3$ (**not** $4x - 2x - 3$)
    ex. $3(2x + 5) = 6x + 15$ (**not** $6x + 5$)
2. Distributing exponents:
    ex. $(x + y)^2 = x^2 + 2xy + y^2$ (**not** $x^2 + y^2$)
3. Canceling terms instead of factors:
    ex. $\dfrac{x^3 + 5}{x} \neq x^2 + 5 X^2 + 5$
4. Misunderstanding negative and fractional exponents:
    ex. $x^{\frac{1}{2}} = \sqrt{x}$ (**not** $\dfrac{1}{x^2}$)
    ex. $x^{-2} = \dfrac{1}{x^2}$ (**not** $\sqrt{x}$)

Skill 23.2   Demonstrate an understanding of the order of operations.

The Order of Operations are to be followed when evaluating algebraic expressions. Follow these steps in order:

1. Simplify inside grouping characters such as parentheses, brackets, square root, fraction bar, etc.

2. Multiply out expressions with exponents.

3. Do multiplication or division, from left to right.

4. Do addition or subtraction, from left to right.

Example: $2 - 4 \times 2^3 - 2(4 - 2 \times 3)$

$= 2 - 4 \times 2^3 - 2(4 - 6) = 2 - 4 \times 2^3 - 2(^-2)$

$= 2 - 4 \times 2^3 + 4 = 2 - 4 \times 8 + 4$

$= 2 - 32 + 4 = 6 - 32 = ^- 26$

Skill 23.3   Round numbers, estimate the results of calculations, and place numbers accurately on a number line.

Estimation and approximation may be used to check the reasonableness of answers.

<u>Example</u>:   Estimate the answer.

$$\frac{58 \times 810}{1989}$$

58 becomes 60, 810 becomes 800 and 1989 becomes 2000.

$$\frac{60 \times 800}{2000} = 24$$

Skill 23.4   Demonstrate the ability to use technology, such as calculators or software, for complex calculations.

Calculators are an important tool. They should be encouraged in the classroom and at home. They do not replace basic knowledge but they can relieve the tedium of mathematical computations, allowing students to explore more challenging mathematical directions. Students will be able to use calculators more intelligently if they are taught how. Students need to always check their work by estimating. The goal of mathematics is to prepare the child to survive in the real world. Technology is a reality in today's society

DOMAIN II – ALGEBRA AND FUNCTIONS

COMPETENCY 24.0 PATTERNS AND FUNCTIONAL RELATIONSHIPS

Skill 24.1 **Represent patterns, including relations and functions, through tables, graphs, verbal rules, or symbolic rules.**

Example:
Given two terms of an arithmetic sequence, find a_1 and d.

$a_4 = 21$	$a_6 = 32$
$a_n = a + (n-1)d$	$a_4 = 21, n = 4$
$21 = a_1 + (4-1)d$	$a_6 = 32, n = 6$
$32 = a_1 + (6-1)d$	

$21 = a_1 + 3d$ solve the system of equations
$32 = a_1 + 5d$

$21 = a_1 + 3d$
$\underline{-32 = -a_1 - 5d}$ multiply by -1
$-11 = -2d$ add the equations
$5.5 = d$

$21 = a_1 + 3(5.5)$ substitute $d = 5.5$, into one of the equations
$21 = a_1 + 16.5$
$a_1 = 4.5$

The sequence begins with 4.5 and has a common difference of 5.5 between numbers.

Geometric Sequences

When using geometric sequences, consecutive numbers are compared to find the common ratio.

$$r = \frac{a_{n+1}}{a_n}$$

where r = common ratio
a = the nth term

The ratio is then used in the geometric sequence formula:
$a_n = a_1 r^{n-1}$

Example:
Find the 8th term of the geometric sequence 2, 8, 32, 128 ...

$r = \dfrac{a_{n+1}}{a_n}$ use common ratio formula to find ratio

$r = \frac{8}{2}$ substitute $a_n = 2$ $a_{n+1} = 8$

$r = 4$

$a_n = a_1 \bullet r^{n-1}$ use $r = 4$ to solve for the 8th term

$a_n = 2 \bullet 4^{8-1}$

$a_n = 32{,}768$

Skill 24.2 **Use proportional reasoning such as ratios, equivalent fractions, and similar triangles, to solve numerical, algebraic, and geometric problems.**

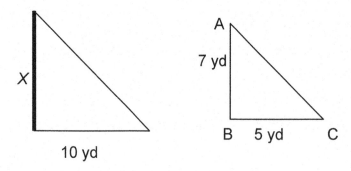

The problem can be determined by setting up the proportion below and solving for X.

$$\dfrac{X}{10 \text{ yd}} = \dfrac{7\text{yd}}{5\text{yd}}$$

After cross-multiplying, the equation can be written as $5X = 70$; X equals 14 yards. Without actually measuring the distance with a measuring tape or other tool, the distance between the points is determined.

COMPETENCY 25.0 LINEAR AND QUADRATIC EQUATIONS AND INEQUALITIES

Skill 25.1　　Able to find equivalent expressions for equalities and inequalities, explain the meaning of symbolic expressions, find the solutions, and represent them on graphs.

A first degree equation has an equation of the form $ax + by = c$. To graph this equation, find either one point and the slope of the line or find two points. To find a point and slope, solve the equation for y. This gets the equation in **slope intercept form**, $y = mx + b$. The point (0,b) is the y-intercept and m is the line's slope. To find any 2 points, substitute any 2 numbers for x and solve for y. To find the intercepts, substitute 0 for x and then 0 for y.

Remember that graphs will go up as they go to the right when the slope is positive. Negative slopes make the lines go down as they go to the right.

If the equation solves to $x =$ **any number**, then the graph is a **vertical line**. It only has an x intercept. Its slope is **undefined**.

If the equation solves to $y =$ **any number**, then the graph is a **horizontal line**. It only has a y intercept. Its slope is 0 (zero).

- When graphing a linear inequality, the line will be dotted if the inequality sign is $<$ or $>$. If the inequality signs are either $\geq$ or $\leq$, the line on the graph will be a solid line. Shade above the line when the inequality sign is $\geq$ or $>$. Shade below the line when the inequality sign is $<$ or $\leq$. Inequalities of the form $x >, x \leq, x <$, or $x \geq$ number, draw a vertical line (solid or dotted). Shade to the right for $>$ or $\geq$. Shade to the left for $<$ or $\leq$. Remember: **Dividing or multiplying by a negative number will reverse the direction of the inequality sign.**

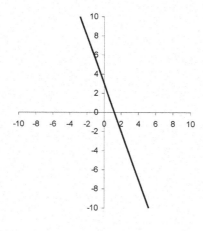

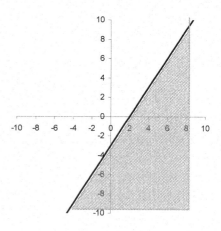

$$5x + 2y = 6$$

$$y = {}^-5/2\,x + 3$$

$$3x - 2y \geq 6$$

$$y \leq 3/2\,x - 3$$

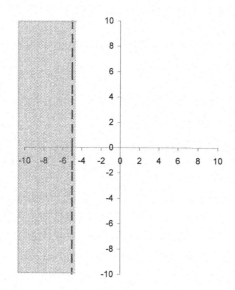

$$3x + 12 < -3$$

$$x < {}^-5$$

Skill 25.2 **Recognize and create equivalent algebraic expressions and represent geometric problems algebraically.**

Example:

A family wants to enclose 3 sides of a rectangular garden with 200 feet of fence. In order to have the maximum area possible, find the dimensions of the garden. Assume that the fourth side of the garden is already bordered by a wall or a fence.

Existing Wall

Solution:
Let x = distance
from the wall

x [rectangle diagram] x

Then $2x$ feet of fence is used for these 2 sides. The remaining side of the garden would use the rest of the 200 feet of fence, that is, $200-2x$ feet of fence. Therefore the width of the garden is x feet and the length is $200-2x$ ft. The area, called y, would equal length times width:

$$y = x(200 - 2x) = 200x - 2x^2$$

In this equation, a = $^-2$, b = 200, c = 0. The maximum area of this garden would occur at the vertex, where $x = {}^-b/2a$.
Substituting for a and b in this equation, this equation becomes $x = {}^-200/(2 \times {}^-2) = {}^-200/({}^-4) = 50$ feet. If x = 50 ft, then $200-2x$ equals the other 100 feet. The maximum area occurs when the length is 100 feet and each of the widths is 50 feet. The maximum area = $100 \times 50 = 5000$ square feet.

Example:

A family wants to enclose 3 sides of a rectangular garden with 200 feet of fence. In order to have a garden with an area of **at least 4800 square feet**, find the dimensions of the garden. Assume that the fourth side of the garden is already bordered by a wall or a fence.

Existing Wall

Solution:
Let $x =$ distance
from the wall

x ⬚ x

Then 2x feet of fence is used for these 2 sides. The remaining side of the garden would use the rest of the 200 feet of fence, that is, $200-2x$ feet of fence. Therefore the width of the garden is x feet and the length is $200-2x$ ft. The area, called y, would have to be greater than or equal to the length times the width:

$$y \geq x(200 - 2x) \text{ or } y \geq 200x - 2x^2$$

In this equation, a = $^-2$, b = 200, c = 0. The area, $200x - 2x^2$, needs to be greater than or equal to 4800 sq. ft. So, this problem uses the inequality $4800 \leq 200x - 2x^2$. This becomes $2x^2 - 200x + 4800 \leq 0$. Solving this, we get:

$$2(x^2 - 100x + 2400) \leq 0$$
$$2(x - 60)(x - 40) \leq 0$$

If x = 60 or x = 40, then the area is at least 4800 sq. ft. So the area will be at least 4800 square feet if the width of the garden is from 40 up to 60 feet. (The length of the rectangle would vary from 120 feet to 80 feet depending on the width of the garden.) **Graph relations involving quadratics and estimate zeros from the graphs.**

Quadratic equations can be used to model different real life situations. The graphs of these quadratics can be used to determine information about this real life situation.

Example:

The height of a projectile fired upward at a velocity of v meters per second from an original height of h meters is $y = h + vx - 4.9x^2$. If a rocket is fired from an original height of 250 meters with an original velocity of 4800 meters per second, find the approximate time the rocket would drop to sea level (a height of 0).

Solution:

The equation for this problem is: $y = 250 + 4800x - 4.9x^2$. If the height at sea level is zero, then $y = 0$ so $0 = 250 + 4800x - 4.9x^2$. Solving this for x could be done by using the quadratic formula. In addition, the approximate time in x seconds until the rocket would be at sea level could be estimated by looking at the graph. When the y value of the graph goes from positive to negative then there is a root (also called solution or x intercept) in that interval.

$$x = \frac{^-4800 \pm \sqrt{4800^2 - 4(^-4.9)(250)}}{2(^-4.9)} \approx 980 \text{ or } ^-0.05 \text{ seconds}$$

Since the time has to be positive, it will be about 980 seconds until the rocket is at sea level.

Skill 25.3 **Have a basic understanding of linear equations and their properties; the multiplication, division, and factoring of polynomials; and graphing and solving quadratic equations through factoring and completing the square.**

Exercise :

a)   One line passes through the points (-4, -6) and (4, 6); another line passes through the points (-5, -4) and (3, 8). Are these lines parallel, perpendicular or neither?

Find the slopes.

$$m = \frac{y_2 - y_1}{x_2 - x_1}$$

$$m_1 = \frac{6 - (-6)}{4 - (-4)} = \frac{6 + 6}{4 + 4} = \frac{12}{8} = \frac{3}{2}$$

$$m_2 = \frac{8 - (-4)}{3 - (-5)} = \frac{8 + 4}{3 + 5} = \frac{12}{8} = \frac{3}{2}$$

Since the slopes are the same, the lines are parallel.

b) One line passes through the points (1, -3) and (0, -6); another line passes through the points (4, 1) and (-2, 3). Are these lines parallel, perpendicular or neither?

Find the slopes.

$$m = \frac{y_2 - y_1}{x_2 - x_1}$$

$$m_1 = \frac{-6 - (-3)}{0 - 1} = \frac{-6 + 3}{-1} = \frac{-3}{-1} = 3$$

$$m_2 = \frac{3 - 1}{-2 - 4} = \frac{2}{-6} = -\frac{1}{3}$$

The slopes are negative reciprocals, so the lines are perpendicular.

c) One line passes through the points (-2, 4) and (2, 5); another line passes through the points (-1, 0) and (5, 4). Are these lines parallel, perpendicular or neither?

Find the slopes.

$$m = \frac{y_2 - y_1}{x_2 - x_1}$$

$$m_1 = \frac{5 - 4}{2 - (-2)} = \frac{1}{2 + 2} = \frac{1}{4}$$

$$m_2 = \frac{4 - 0}{5 - (-1)} = \frac{4}{5 + 1} = \frac{4}{6} = \frac{2}{3}$$

Since the slopes are not the same, the lines are not parallel. Since they are not negative reciprocals, they are not perpendicular, either. Therefore, the answer is "neither."

Slope – The slope of a line is the "slant" of a line. A downward left to right slant means a negative slope. An upward slant is a positive slope.
The formula for calculating the slope of a line with coordinates $(x_1, y_1) and (x_2, y_2)$ is:

$$\text{slope} = \frac{y_2 - y_1}{x_2 - x_1}$$

The top of the fraction represents the change in the y coordinates; it is called the **rise**. The bottom of the fraction represents the change in the x coordinates, it is called the **run.**

Example: Find the slope of a line with points at (2,2) and (7,8).

$$\frac{(8)-(2)}{(7)-(2)}$$ plug the values into the formula

$$\frac{6}{5}$$ solve the rise over run

$$= 1.2$$ solve for the slope

The y intercept is the y coordinate of the point where a line crosses the y axis. The equation can be written in slope-intercept form, which is $y = mx + b$, where m is the slope and b is the y intercept. To rewrite the equation into some other form, multiply each term by the common denominator of all the fractions. Then rearrange terms as necessary.

The equation of a line from its graph can be found by finding its slope (see Skill 3.2 for the slope formula) and its y intercept.

$$Y - y_a = m(X - x_a)$$

(x_a, y_a) can be (x_1, y_1) or (x_2, y_2) If **m**, the value of the slope, is distributed through the parentheses, the equation can be rewritten into other forms of the equation of a line.

Example: Find the equation of a line through $(9, {}^{-}6)$ and $({}^{-}1, 2)$.

$$\text{slope} = \frac{y_2 - y_1}{x_2 - x_1} = \frac{2 - {}^{-}6}{{}^{-}1 - 9} = \frac{8}{{}^{-}10} = \frac{{}^{-}4}{5}$$

$$Y - y_a = m(X - x_a) \rightarrow Y - 2 = {}^{-}4/5(X - {}^{-}1) \rightarrow$$
$$Y - 2 = {}^{-}4/5(X + 1) \rightarrow Y - 2 = {}^{-}4/5 X - 4/5 \rightarrow$$
$$Y = {}^{-}4/5 \, X + 6/5 \quad \text{This is the slope-intercept form.}$$

Multiplying by 5 to eliminate fractions, it is:

$$5Y = {}^{-}4X + 6 \rightarrow 4X + 5Y = 6 \quad \text{Standard form.}$$

Skill 25.4 **Interpret graphs of linear and quadratic equations and inequalities, including solutions to systems of equations.**

Word problems can sometimes be solved by using a system of two equations in 2 unknowns. This system can then be solved using **substitution**, or the **addition-subtraction method**.

Example: Farmer Greenjeans bought 4 cows and 6 sheep for $1700. Mr. Ziffel bought 3 cows and 12 sheep for $2400. If all the cows were the same price and all the sheep were another price, find the price charged for a cow or for a sheep.

Let x = price of a cow
Let y = price of a sheep

Then Farmer Greenjeans' equation would be: $4x + 6y = 1700$
Mr. Ziffel's equation would be: $\qquad\qquad 3x + 12y = 2400$

To solve by **addition-subtraction**:
Multiply the first equation by $^-2$: $\quad ^-2(4x + 6y = 1700)$
Keep the other equation the same : $\quad (3x + 12y = 2400)$
By doing this, the equations can be added to each other to eliminate one variable and solve for the other variable.

$$^-8x - 12y = {}^-3400$$
$$\underline{3x + 12y = 2400} \qquad \text{Add these equations.}$$
$$^-5x \qquad = {}^-1000$$

$x = 200 \leftarrow$ the price of a cow was $200.
Solving for y, $y = 150 \leftarrow$ the price of a sheep, $150.

To solve by **substitution**:

Solve one of the equations for a variable. (Try to make an equation without fractions if possible.) Substitute this expression into the equation that you have not yet used. Solve the resulting equation for the value of the remaining variable.

$$4x + 6y = 1700$$
$$3x + 12y = 2400 \leftarrow \text{Solve this equation for } x.$$

It becomes $x = 800 - 4y$. Now substitute $800 - 4y$ in place of x in the OTHER equation. $4x + 6y = 1700$ now becomes:

$$4(800 - 4y) + 6y = 1700$$
$$3200 - 16y + 6y = 1700$$
$$3200 - 10y = 1700$$
$$^-10y = \,^-1500$$
$$y = 150, \text{ or } \$150 \text{ for a sheep.}$$

Substituting 150 back into an equation for y, find x.

$$4x + 6(150) = 1700$$
$$4x + 900 = 1700$$
$$4x = 800 \text{ so } x = 200 \text{ for a cow.}$$

Word problems can sometimes be solved by using a system of three equations in 3 unknowns. This system can then be solved using **substitution** or the **addition-subtraction method**.

To solve by **substitution**:

Example: Mrs. Allison bought 1 pound of potato chips, a 2 pound beef roast, and 3 pounds of apples for a total of $ 8.19. Mr. Bromberg bought a 3 pound beef roast and 2 pounds of apples for $ 9.05. Kathleen Kaufman bought 2 pounds of potato chips, a 3 pound beef roast, and 5 pounds of apples for $ 13.25. Find the per pound price of each item.

Let x = price of a pound of potato chips
Let y = price of a pound of roast beef
Let z = price of a pound of apples

Mrs. Allison's equation would be: $1x + 2y + 3z = 8.19$
Mr. Bromberg's equation would be: $3y + 2z = 9.05$
K. Kaufman's equation would be: $2x + 3y + 5z = 13.25$

Take the first equation and solve it for x. (This was chosen because x is the easiest variable to get alone in this set of equations.) This equation would become:

$$x = 8.19 - 2y - 3z$$

Substitute this expression into the other equations in place of the letter x:

$$3y + 2z = 9.05 \leftarrow \text{equation 2}$$
$$2(8.19 - 2y - 3z) + 3y + 5z = 13.25 \leftarrow \text{equation 3}$$

Simplify the equation by combining like terms:

$$3y + 2z = 9.05 \leftarrow \text{equation 2}$$
$$* \ ^{-}1y - 1z = {}^{-}3.13 \leftarrow \text{equation 3}$$

Solve equation 3 for either y or z:

$$y = 3.13 - z \quad \text{Substitute this into equation 2 for } y:$$

$$3(3.13 - z) + 2z = 9.05 \leftarrow \text{equation 2}$$
$$^{-}1y - 1z = {}^{-}3.13 \leftarrow \text{equation 3}$$

Combine like terms in equation 2:

$$9.39 - 3z + 2z = 9.05$$
$$z = .34 \quad \text{per pound price of bananas}$$

Substitute .34 for z in the starred equation above to solve for y:

$$y = 3.13 - z \text{ becomes } y = 3.13 - .34, \text{ so}$$
$$y = 2.79 = \text{per pound price of roast beef}$$

Substituting .34 for z and 2.79 for y in one of the original equations, solve for x:

$$1x + 2y + 3z = 8.19$$
$$1x + 2(2.79) + 3(.34) = 8.19$$
$$x + 5.58 + 1.02 = 8.19$$
$$x + 6.60 = 8.19$$
$$x = 1.59 \quad \text{per pound of potato chips}$$

$$(x, y, z) = (\ 1.59, \ 2.79, \ .34)$$

To solve by **addition-subtraction**:

Choose a letter to eliminate. Since the second equation is already missing an x, let's eliminate x from equations 1 and 3.

1) $1x + 2y + 3x = 8.19 \leftarrow$ Multiply by $^-2$ below.
2) $3y + 2z = 9.05$
3) $2x + 3y + 5z = 13.25$

$^-2(1x + 2y + 3z = 8.19) \quad = \quad ^-2x - 4y - 6z = ^-16.38$
Keep equation 3 the same : $\quad 2x + 3y + 5z = 13.25$

By doing this, the equations $\qquad\qquad ^-y - z = ^-3.13 \leftarrow$ equation 4
can be added to each other to
eliminate one variable.

The equations left to solve are equations 2 and 4:

$\quad ^-y - z = ^-3.13 \leftarrow$ equation 4

$\quad 3y + 2z = 9.05 \leftarrow$ equation 2

Multiply equation 4 by 3: $\quad 3(^-y - z = ^-3.13)$
Keep equation 2 the same: $\quad 3y + 2z = 9.05$

$\quad ^-3y - 3z = ^-9.39$

$\quad 3y + 2z = 9.05 \qquad$ Add these equations.

$\qquad ^-1z = ^-.34$

$\qquad z = .34 \leftarrow$ the per pound price of bananas

solving for y, $y = 2.79 \leftarrow$ the per pound roast beef price

solving for x, $x = 1.59 \leftarrow$ potato chips, per pound price

To solve by **substitution**:

Solve one of the 3 equations for a variable. (Try to make an equation without fractions if possible.) Substitute this expression into the other 2 equations that you have not yet used.

1) $1x + 2y + 3z = 8.19 \leftarrow$ Solve for x.
2) $3y + 2z = 9.05$
3) $2x + 3y + 5z = 13.25$
  Equation 1 becomes $x = 8.19 - 2y - 3z$.

Substituting this into equations 2 and 3, they become:

2) $3y + 2z = 9.05$
3) $2(8.19 - 2y - 3z) + 3y + 5z = 13.25$

$$16. \ 38 - 4y - 6z + 3y + 5z = 13.25$$

$$^-y - z = \ ^-3.13$$

The equations left to solve are :

$$3y + 2z = 9.05$$

$$^-y - z = \ ^-3.13 \leftarrow \text{Solve for either } y \text{ or } z.$$

It becomes $y = 3.13 - z$. Now substitute $3.13 - z$ in place of y in the OTHER equation. $3y + 2z = 9.05$ now becomes:

$$3(3.13 - z) + 2z = 9.05$$

$$9.39 - 3z + 2z = 9.05$$

$$9.39 - z = 9.05$$

$$^-z = \ ^-.34$$

$$z = .34, \text{ or } \$.34/\text{lb of bananas}$$

Substituting .34 back into an equation for z, find y.

$$3y + 2z = 9.05$$

$$3y + 2(.34) = 9.05$$

$$3y + .68 = 9.05 \text{ so } y = 2.79/\text{lb of roast beef}$$

Substituting .34 for z and 2.79 for y into one of the original equations, it becomes:

$$2x + 3y + 5z = 13.25$$

$$2x + 3(2.79) + 5(.34) = 13.25$$

$$2x + 8.37 + 1.70 = 13.25$$

$$2x + 10.07 = 13.25, \text{ so } x = 1.59/\text{lb of potato chips}$$

DOMAIN III: MEASUREMENT AND GEOMETRY

COMPETENCY 26.0 Two- and Three-dimensional Geometric Objects.

Skill 26.1 **Understand characteristics of common two- and three-dimensional figures, such as triangles, quadrilaterals, and spheres.**

A **triangle** is a polygon with three sides.

Triangles can be classified by the types of angles or the lengths of their sides.

Classifying by angles:

An **acute** triangle has exactly three *acute* angles.
A **right** triangle has one *right* angle.
An **obtuse** triangle has one *obtuse* angle.

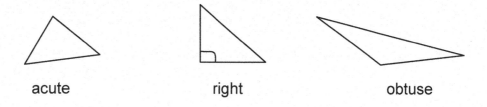

acute   right   obtuse

Classifying by sides:

All *three* sides of an **equilateral** triangle are the same length.
Two sides of an **isosceles** triangle are the same length.
None of the sides of a **scalene** triangle are the same length.

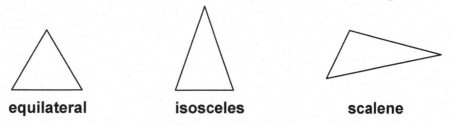

equilateral   **isosceles**   **scalene**

A **polygon** is a simple closed figure composed of line segments. In a **regular polygon** all sides are the same length and all angles are the same measure.

The sum of the measures of the **interior angles** of a polygon can be determined using the following formula, where n represents the number of angles in the polygon.

$$\text{Sum of } \angle s = 180(n - 2)$$

The measure of each angle of a regular polygon can be found by dividing the sum of the measures by the number of angles.

$$\text{Measure of } \angle = \frac{180(n - 2)}{n}$$

Example: Find the measure of each angle of a regular octagon. Since an octagon has eight sides, each angle equals:

$$\frac{180(8 - 2)}{8} = \frac{180(6)}{8} = 135°$$

The sum of the measures of the **exterior angles** of a polygon, taken one angle at each vertex, equals 360°.

The measure of each exterior angle of a regular polygon can be determined using the following formula, where n represents the number of angles in the polygon.

$$\text{Measure of exterior } \angle \text{ of regular polygon} = 180 - \frac{180(n - 2)}{n}$$

$$\text{or, more simply} = \frac{360}{n}$$

Example: Find the measure of the interior and exterior angles of a regular pentagon.

Since a pentagon has five sides, each exterior angle measures:

$$\frac{360}{5} = 72°$$

Since each exterior angle is supplementary to its interior angle, the interior angle measures 180 - 72 or 108°.

Skill 26.2   Able to draw conclusions based on the congruence, similarity, or lack thereof, of two figures.

Example:

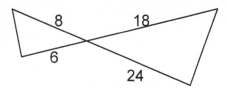

The two triangles are similar since the sides are proportional and vertical angles are congruent.

Example: Given two similar quadrilaterals. Find the lengths of sides x, y, and z.

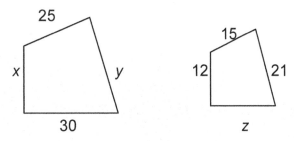

Since corresponding sides are proportional:

$$\frac{15}{25} = \frac{3}{5} \text{ so the scale is } \frac{3}{5}$$

$$\frac{12}{x} = \frac{3}{5} \qquad\qquad \frac{21}{y} = \frac{3}{5} \qquad\qquad \frac{z}{30} = \frac{3}{5}$$

$$3x = 60 \qquad\qquad 3y = 105 \qquad\qquad 5z = 90$$
$$x = 20 \qquad\qquad y = 35 \qquad\qquad z = 18$$

*   *   *

Polygons are similar if and only if there is a one-to-one correspondence between their vertices such that the corresponding angles are congruent and the lengths of corresponding sides are proportional.

Given the rectangles below, compare the area and perimeter.

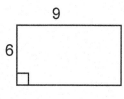

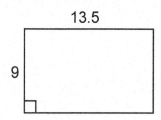

$A = LW$	$A = LW$	1. write formula
$A = (6)(9)$	$A = (9)(13.5)$	2. substitute known
values		
$A = 54$ sq. units	$A = 121.5$ sq. units	3. compute
$P = 2(L + W)$	$P = 2(L + W)$	1. write formula
$P = 2(6 + 9)$	$P = 2(9 + 13.5)$	2. substitute known
values		
$P = 30$ units	$P = 45$ units	3. compute

Notice that the areas relate to each other in the following manner:

Ratio of sides $9/13.5 = 2/3$

Multiply the first area by the square of the reciprocal $(3/2)^2$ to get the second area.

$$54 \times (3/2)^2 = 121.5$$

The perimeters relate to each other in the following manner:

Ratio of sides $9/13.5 = 2/3$

Multiply the perimeter of the first by the reciprocal of the ratio to get the perimeter of the second.

$$30 \times 3/2 = 45$$

Skill 26.3 **Identify different forms of symmetry, translations, rotations, and reflections.**

A **transformation** is a change in the position, shape, or size of a geometric figure. **Transformational geometry** is the study of manipulating objects by flipping, twisting, turning and scaling. **Symmetry** is exact similarity between two parts or halves, as if one were a mirror image of the other.

A **translation** is a transformation that "slides" an object a fixed distance in a given direction. The original object and its translation have the same shape and size, and they face in the same direction.

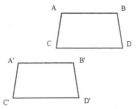

An example of a translation in architecture would be stadium seating. The seats are the same size and the same shape and face in the same direction.

A **rotation** is a transformation that turns a figure about a fixed point called the center of rotation. An object and its rotation are the same shape and size, but the figures may be turned in different directions. Rotations can occur in either a clockwise or a counterclockwise direction.

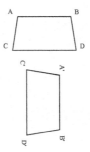

Rotations can be seen in wallpaper and art, and a Ferris wheel is an example of rotation.

An object and its **reflection** have the same shape and size, but the figures face in opposite directions.

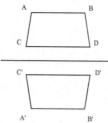

The line (where a mirror may be placed) is called the **line of reflection**. The distance from a point to the line of reflection is the same as the distance from the point's image to the line of reflection.

A **glide reflection** is a combination of a reflection and a translation.

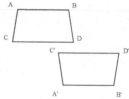

Another type of transformation is **dilation**. Dilation is a transformation that "shrinks" or "makes it bigger."

Example:
Using dilation to transform a diagram.

Starting with a triangle whose center of dilation is point P,

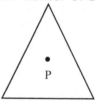

we dilate the lengths of the sides by the same factor to create a n

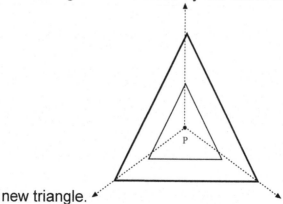

new triangle.

Skill 26.4   Understand the Pythagorean theorem and its converse.

Pythagorean theorem states that the square of the length of the hypotenuse is equal to the sum of the squares of the lengths of the legs. Symbolically, this is stated as:

$$c^2 = a^2 + b^2$$

Given the right triangle below, find the missing side.

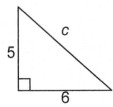

$c^2 = a^2 + b^2$	1. write formula
$c^2 = 5^2 + 6^2$	2. substitute known values
$c^2 = 61$	3. take square root
$c = \sqrt{61}$ or 7.81	4. solve

*   *   *

The Converse of the Pythagorean Theorem states that if the square of one side of a triangle is equal to the sum of the squares of the other two sides, then the triangle is a right triangle.

Example:
Given △XYZ, with sides measuring 12, 16 and 20 cm. Is this a right triangle?

$$c^2 = a^2 + b^2$$
$$20^2 \ \underline{?} \ 12^2 + 16^2$$
$$400 \ \underline{?} \ 144 + 256$$
$$400 \ = 400$$

Yes, the triangle is a right triangle.

This theorem can be expanded to determine if triangles are obtuse or acute.

If the square of the longest side of a triangle is greater than the sum of the squares of the other two sides, then the triangle is an obtuse triangle.

and

If the square of the longest side of a triangle is less than the sum of the squares of the other two sides, then the triangle is an acute triangle.

<u>Example</u>:
Given △LMN with sides measuring 7, 12, and 14 inches. Is the triangle right, acute, or obtuse?

$$14^2 \; \underline{\; ? \;} \; 7^2 + 12^2$$
$$196 \; \underline{\; ? \;} \; 49 + 144$$
$$196 > 193$$

Therefore, the triangle is obtuse.

<u>Real-World Example:</u> Find the area and perimeter of a rectangle if its length is 12 inches and its diagonal is 15 inches.

1. Draw and label sketch.

2. Since the height is still needed use Pythagorean formula to find missing leg of the triangle.

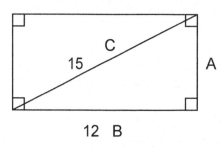

$$A^2 + B^2 = C^2$$
$$A^2 + 12^2 = 15^2$$
$$A^2 = 15^2 - 12^2$$
$$A^2 = 81$$
$$A = 9$$

Now use this information to find the area and perimeter.

$A = LW$	$P = 2(L + W)$	1. write formula
$A = (12)(9)$	$P = 2(12 + 9)$	2. substitute
$A = 108 \text{ in}^2$	$P = 42 \text{ inches}$	3. solve

<u>Real-World Example:</u> Given the figure below, find the area by dividing the polygon into smaller shapes.

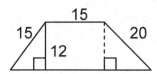

1. divide the figure into two triangles and a rectangle.

2. find the missing lengths.

3. find the area of each part.

4. find the sum of all areas.

Find base of both right triangles using Pythagorean Formula:

$$a^2 + b^2 = c^2$$
$$a^2 + 12^2 = 15^2$$
$$a^2 = 225 - 144$$
$$a^2 = 81$$
$$a = 9$$

$$a^2 + b^2 = c^2$$
$$a^2 + 12^2 = 20^2$$
$$a^2 = 400 - 144$$
$$a^2 = 256$$
$$a = 16$$

Area of triangle 1   Area of triangle 2   Area of rectangle

$$A = \frac{1}{2}bh$$
$$A = \frac{1}{2}(9)(12)$$
$$A = 54 \text{ sq. units}$$

$$A = \frac{1}{2}bh$$
$$A = \frac{1}{2}(16)(12)$$
$$A = 96 \text{ sq. units}$$

$$A = LW$$
$$A = (15)(12)$$
$$A = 180 \text{ sq. units}$$

Find the sum of all three figures.

$$54 + 96 + 180 = 330 \text{ square units}$$

Skill 26.5   Able to work with properties of parallel lines.

Corresponding angles are in the same corresponding position on two parallel lines cut by a transversal.

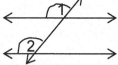

Alternate interior angles are diagonal angles on the inside of two parallel lines cut by a transversal.

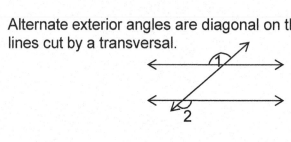

Alternate exterior angles are diagonal on the outside of two parallel lines cut by a transversal.

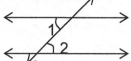

COMPETENCY 27.0   Representational Systems, Including Concrete Models, Drawings, and Coordinate Geometry.

Skill 27.1   Use concrete representations, such as manipulatives, drawings, and coordinate geometry to represent geometric objects.

We can represent any two-dimensional geometric figure in the **Cartesian** or **rectangular coordinate system**. The Cartesian or rectangular coordinate system is formed by two perpendicular axes (coordinate axes): the X-axis and the Y-axis. If we know the dimensions of a two-dimensional, or planar, figure, we can use this coordinate system to visualize the shape of the figure.

Example: Represent an isosceles triangle with two sides of length 4.

Draw the two sides along the x- and y- axes and connect the points (vertices).

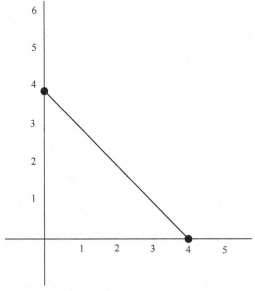

Skill 27.2   **Construct basic geometric figures using a compass and straightedge, and represent three-dimensional objects through two-dimensional drawings.**

In order to represent three-dimensional figures, we need three coordinate axes (X, Y, and Z) which are all mutually perpendicular to each other. Since we cannot draw three mutually perpendicular axes on a two-dimensional surface, we use oblique representations.

Example: Represent a cube with sides of 2.

Once again, we draw three sides along the three axes to make things easier.

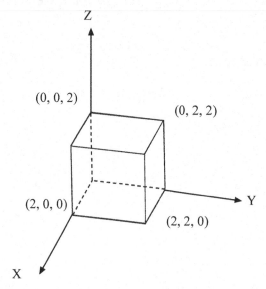

Each point has three coordinates (x, y, z).

Skill 27.3   **Combine and dissect two- and three-dimensional figures into familiar shapes, such as dissecting a parallelogram and rearranging the pieces to form a rectangle of equal area.**

The union of all points on a simple closed surface and all points in its interior form a space figure called a **solid**. The five regular solids, or **polyhedra**, are the cube, tetrahedron, octahedron, icosahedron, and dodecahedron. A **net** is a two-dimensional figure that can be cut out and folded up to make a three-dimensional solid. Below are models of the five regular solids with their corresponding face polygons and nets.

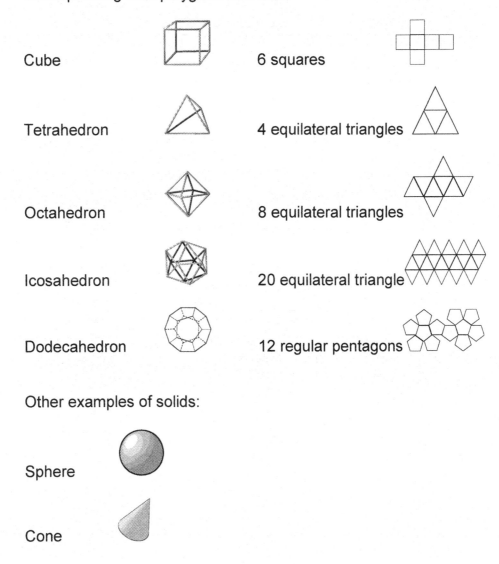

Cube   6 squares

Tetrahedron   4 equilateral triangles

Octahedron   8 equilateral triangles

Icosahedron   20 equilateral triangle

Dodecahedron   12 regular pentagons

Other examples of solids:

Sphere

Cone

COMPETENCY 28.0   TECHNIQUES, TOOLS AND FORUMULAS FOR DETERMINING MEASUREMENTS.

Skill 28.1   Estimate and measure time, length, angles, perimeter, area, surface area, volume, weight/mass, and temperature through appropriate units and scales.

It is necessary to be familiar with the metric and customary system in order to estimate measurements.

Some common equivalents include:

ITEM	APPROXIMATELY EQUAL TO	
	METRIC	IMPERIAL
large paper clip	1 gram	1 ounce
1 quart	1 liter	
average sized man	75 kilograms	170 pounds
1 yard	1 meter	
math textbook	1 kilogram	2 pounds
1 mile	1 kilometer	
1 foot	30 centimeters	
thickness of a dime	1 millimeter	0.1 inches

Estimate the measurement of the following items:

The length of an adult cow = _____ meters
The thickness of a compact disc = _____ millimeters
Your height = _____ meters
length of your nose = _____ centimeters
weight of your math textbook = _____ kilograms
weight of an automobile = _____ kilograms
weight of an aspirin = _____ grams

Skill 28.2   Identify relationships between different measures within the metric or customary systems of measurements and estimate an equivalent measurement across the two systems.

The units of **length** in the customary system are inches, feet, yards and miles.

> 12 inches (in.) = 1 foot (ft.)
> 36 in. = 1 yard (yd.)
> 3 ft. = 1 yd.
> 5280 ft. = 1 mile (mi.)
> 760 yd. = 1 mi.

To change from a **larger unit to a smaller unit, multiply**.
To change from a **smaller unit to a larger unit, divide**.

Example:
    4 mi. = _____ yd.
    Since 1760 yd. = 1 mile, multiply $4 \times 1760 = 7040$ yd.

Example:
    21 in. = _____ ft.
    $21 \div 12 = 1\frac{3}{4}$ ft.

The units of **weight** are ounces, pounds and tons.

> 16 ounces (oz.) = 1 pound (lb.)
> 2,000 lb. = 1 ton (T.)

Example: $2\frac{3}{4}$ T. = _____ lb.
    $2\frac{3}{4} \times 2,000 = 5,500$ lb.

The units of **capacity** are fluid ounces, cups, pints, quarts, and gallons.

8 fluid ounces (fl. oz.) = 1 cup (c.)
2 c. = 1 pint (pt.)
4 c. = 1 quart (qt.)
2 pt. = 1 qt.
4 qt. = 1 gallon (gal.)

Example1: 3 gal. = _____ qt.
       $3 \times 4 = 12$ qt.

Example: $1\frac{1}{4}$ cups = _____ oz.
       $1\frac{1}{4} \times 8 = 10$ oz.

Example: 7 c. = _____ pt.
       $7 \div 2 = 3\frac{1}{2}$ pt.

Square units can be derived with knowledge of basic units of length by squaring the equivalent measurements.

1 square foot (sq. ft.) = 144 sq. in.
1 sq. yd. = 9 sq. ft.
1 sq. yd. = 1296 sq. in.

Example: 14 sq. yd. = _____ sq. ft.
       $14 \times 9 = 126$ sq. ft.

METRIC UNITS

The metric system is based on multiples of <u>ten</u>. Conversions are made by simply moving the decimal point to the left or right.

kilo-   1000 thousands
hecto-   100 hundreds
deca-   10 tens
nit
deci-   .1 tenths
centi-   .01 hundredths
milli-   .001 thousandths

The basic unit for **length** is the meter. One meter is approximately one yard.

The basic unit for **weight** or mass is the gram.   A paper clip weighs about one gram.

The basic unit for **volume** is the liter. One liter is approximately a quart.

These are the most commonly used units.

1 m = 100 cm	1000 mL= 1 L	1000
mg = 1 g		
1 m = 1000 mm	1 kL = 1000 L	1 kg = 1000 g
1 cm = 10 mm		
1000 m = 1 km		

The prefixes are commonly listed from left to right for ease in conversion.

K H D U D C M

Example: 63 km = _____ m
Since there are 3 steps from Kilo to Unit, move the decimal point 3 places to the right.
        63 km = 63,000 m

Example: 14 mL = _____ L
Since there are 3 steps from Milli to Unit, move the decimal point 3 places to the left.
        14 mL = 0.014 L

Example: 56.4 cm = _____ mm
        56.4 cm = 564 mm

Example: 9.1 m = _____ km
        9.1 m = 0.0091 km

Example 5:   75 kg = _____ m
        75 kg = 75,000,000 m

Skill 28.3 **Calculate perimeters and areas of two-dimensional objects and surface areas and volumes of three-dimensional objects.**

The **perimeter** of any polygon is the sum of the lengths of the sides.

P = sum of sides

Since the opposite sides of a rectangle are congruent, the perimeter of a rectangle equals twice the sum of the length and width or

$P_{rect} = 2l + 2w$ or $2(l + w)$

Similarly, since all the sides of a square have the same measure, the perimeter of a square equals four times the length of one side or

$P_{square} = 4s$

The **area** of a polygon is the number of square units covered by the figure.

$A_{rect} = l \times w$
$A_{square} = s^2$

Example: Find the perimeter and the area of this rectangle.

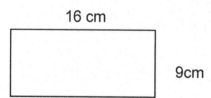

16 cm

9cm

$P_{rect} = 2l + 2w$
$\quad = 2(16) + 2(9)$
$\quad = 32 + 18 = 50$ cm

$A_{rect} = l \times w$
$\quad = 16(9)$
$\quad = 144$ cm^2

Example: Find the perimeter and area of this square.

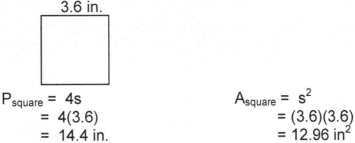

3.6 in.

$P_{square} = 4s$
$= 4(3.6)$
$= 14.4$ in.

$A_{square} = s^2$
$= (3.6)(3.6)$
$= 12.96$ in^2

In the following formulas, b = the base and h = the height of an altitude drawn to the base.

$A_{parallelogram} = bh$
$A_{triangle} = \frac{1}{2}bh$
$A_{trapezoid} = \frac{1}{2}h(b_1 + b_2)$

Example: Find the area of a parallelogram whose base is 6.5 cm and the height of the altitude to that base is 3.7 cm.

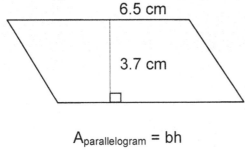

6.5 cm

3.7 cm

$A_{parallelogram} = bh$

$= (3.7)(6.5)$
$= 24.05$ cm^2

Example: Find the area of this triangle.

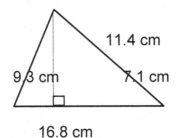

11.4 cm

9.3 cm   7.1 cm

16.8 cm

$A_{triangle} = \frac{1}{2}bh$
$= 0.5\,(16.8)\,(7.1)$
$= 59.64$ cm^2

Note that the altitude is drawn to the base measuring 16.8 cm. The lengths of the other two sides are unnecessary information.

Example: Find the area of a right triangle whose sides measure 10 inches, 24 inches and 26 inches.

Since the hypotenuse of a right triangle must be the longest side, then the two perpendicular sides must measure 10 and 24 inches.

$$A_{triangle} = \tfrac{1}{2}bh$$
$$= \tfrac{1}{2}(10)(24)$$
$$= 120 \text{ sq. in.}$$

Example: Find the area of this trapezoid.

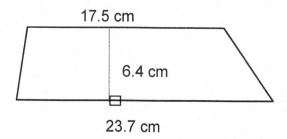

17.5 cm

6.4 cm

23.7 cm

The area of a trapezoid equals one-half the sum of the bases times the altitude.

$$A_{trapezoid} = \tfrac{1}{2}h(b_1 + b_2)$$
$$= 0.5(6.4)(17.5 + 23.7)$$
$$= 131.84 \text{ cm}^2$$

Compute the area remaining when sections are cut out of a given figure composed of triangles, squares, rectangles, parallelograms, trapezoids, or circles.

Example: You have decided to fertilize your lawn. The shapes and dimensions of your lot, house, pool and garden are given in the diagram below. The shaded area will not be fertilized. If each bag of fertilizer costs $7.95 and covers 4,500 square feet, find the total number of bags needed and the total cost of the fertilizer.

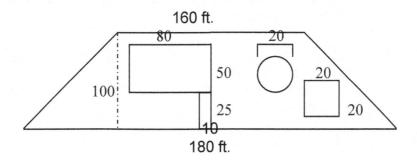

Area of Lot
$A = \frac{1}{2} h(b_1 + b_2)$
$A = \frac{1}{2}(100)(180 + 160)$
$A = 17,000$ sq ft

Area of House
$A = LW$
$A = (80)(50)$
$A = 4,000$ sq ft

Area of Driveway
$A = LW$
$A = (10)(25)$
$A = 250$ sq ft

Area of Pool
$A = \pi r^2$
$A = \pi(10)^2$
$A = 314.159$ sq. ft.

Area of Garden
$A = s^2$
$A = (20)^2$
$A = 400$ sq. ft.

Total area to fertilize = Lot area - (House + Driveway + Pool + Garden)
  = 17,000 - (4,000 + 250 + 314.159 + 400)
      = 12,035.841 sq ft

Number of bags needed = Total area to fertilize$/$4,500 sq.ft. bag

$= 12,035.841/$4,500

= 2.67 bags

Since we cannot purchase 2.67 bags we must purchase 3 full bags.

Total cost = Number of bags * $7.95
      = 3 * $7.95
      = $23.85

The **lateral** area is the area of the faces excluding the bases.

The **surface area** is the total area of all the faces, including the bases.

The **volume** is the number of cubic units in a solid. This is the amount of space a figure holds.

Right prism

V = Bh   (where B = area of the base of the prism and h = the height of the prism)

Rectangular right prism

S = 2(lw + hw + lh) (where l = length, w = width and h = height)
V = lwh

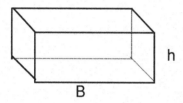

B

Example: Find the height of a box whose volume is 120 cubic meters and the area of the base is 30 square meters.

V = Bh
120 = 30h
h = 4 meters

Regular pyramid

V = 1/3Bh

h

B

Right circular cylinder

$S = 2\Pi r(r + h)$ (where r is the radius of the base)
$V = \Pi r^2 h$

Right circular cone

$V = \frac{1}{3} Bh$

Skill 28.4   Relate proportional reasoning to the construction of scale drawings or models.

Example: The scale on a map is $\frac{3}{4}$ inch = 6 miles. What is the actual distance between two cities if they are $1\frac{1}{2}$ inches apart on the map?

Write a proportion comparing the scale to the actual distance.

$$\begin{array}{cc} \text{scale} & \text{actual} \end{array}$$

$$\frac{\frac{3}{4}}{1\frac{1}{2}} = \frac{6}{x}$$

$$\frac{3}{4}x = 1\frac{1}{2} \times 6$$

$$\frac{3}{4}x = 9$$

$$x = 12$$

Thus, the actual distance between the cities is 12 miles.

*   *   *

When graphing a first degree equation, solve for the variable. The graph of this solution will be a single point on the number line. There will be no arrows.

When graphing a linear inequality, the dot will be hollow if the inequality sign is < or >. If the inequality signs is either $\geq$ or $\leq$, the dot on the graph will be solid. The arrow goes to the right for $\geq$ or >. The arrow goes to the left for < or $\leq$.

Example:
$$5(x + 2) + 2x = 3(x - 2)$$
$$5x + 10 + 2x = 3x - 6$$
$$7x + 10 = 3x - 6$$
$$4x = -16$$
$$x = -4$$

$$-10\ ^-8\ ^-6\ ^-4\ ^-2\ \mathbf{0}\ 2\ 4\ 6\ 8\ 10$$

Example:
$$2(3x - 7) > 10x - 2$$
$$6x - 14 > 10x - 2$$
$$-4x > 12$$
$$x < -3$$

$$^-10\ ^-8\ ^-6\ ^-4\ ^-2\ \mathbf{0}\ 2\ 4\ 6\ 8\ 10$$

Skill 28.5   Use measures such as miles per hour to analyze and solve problems.

Some problems can be solved using equations with rational expressions. First write the equation. To solve it, multiply each term by the LCD of all fractions. This will cancel out all of the denominators and give an equivalent algebraic equation that can be solved.

1. The denominator of a fraction is two less than three times the numerator. If 3 is added to both the numerator and denominator, the new fraction equals 1/2 .

original fraction: $\dfrac{x}{3x-2}$ revised fraction: $\dfrac{x+3}{3x+1}$

$$\dfrac{x+3}{3x+1} = \dfrac{1}{2}$$ $$2x+6 = 3x+1$$

$$x = 5$$

original fraction: $\dfrac{5}{13}$

2. Elly Mae can feed the animals in 15 minutes. Jethro can feed them in 10 minutes. How long will it take them if they work together?

Solution: If Elly Mae can feed the animals in 15 minutes, then she could feed 1/15 of them in 1 minute, 2/15 of them in 2 minutes, $x/15$ of them in x minutes. In the same fashion Jethro could feed $x/10$ of them in x minutes. Together they complete 1 job. The equation is:

$$\frac{x}{15} + \frac{x}{10} = 1$$

Multiply each term by the LCD of 30:

$$2x + 3x = 30$$
$$x = 6 \text{ minutes}$$

3. A salesman drove 480 miles from Pittsburgh to Hartford. The next day he returned the same distance to Pittsburgh in half an hour less time than his original trip took, because he increased his average speed by 4 mph. Find his original speed.

Since distance = rate x time then time = $\dfrac{\text{distance}}{\text{rate}}$

original time $- 1/2$ hour = shorter return time

$$\frac{480}{x} - \frac{1}{2} = \frac{480}{x+4}$$

Multiplying by the LCD of $2x(x+4)$, the equation becomes:

$$480\big[2(x+4)\big] - 1\big[x(x+4)\big] = 480(2x)$$
$$960x + 3840 - x^2 - 4x = 960x$$
$$x^2 + 4x - 3840 = 0$$
$$(x+64)(x-60) = 0$$
$$x = 60 \qquad \text{60 mph is the original speed}$$
$$\qquad\qquad\qquad\text{64 mph is the faster return speed}$$

Try these:

1. Working together, Larry, Moe, and Curly can paint an elephant in 3 minutes. Working alone, it would take Larry 10 minutes or Moe 6 minutes to paint the elephant. How long would it take Curly to paint the elephant if he worked alone?

2. The denominator of a fraction is 5 more than twice the numerator. If the numerator is doubled, and the denominator is increased by 5, the new fraction is equal to 1/2. Find the original number.

3. A trip from Augusta, Maine to Galveston, Texas is 2108 miles. If one car drove 6 mph faster than a truck and got to Galveston 3 hours before the truck, find the speeds of the car and truck.

DOMAIN IV: STATISTICS, DATA ANALYSIS AND PROBABILITY

COMPETENCY 29.0   Collection, Organization, and Representation of Data.

Skill 29.1   **Represent a collection of data through graphs, tables, or charts.**

BAR, LINE, PICTO-, AND CIRCLE GRAPHS

	Test 1	Test 2	Test 3	Test 4	Test 5
Evans, Tim	75	66	80	85	97
Miller, Julie	94	93	88	97	98
Thomas, Randy	81	86	88	87	90

Bar graphs are used to compare various quantities.

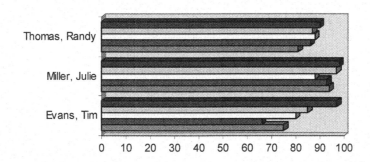

Line graphs are used to show trends, often over a period of time.

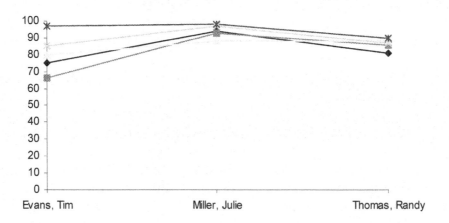

A **pictograph** shows comparison of quantities using symbols. Each symbol represents a number of items.

Circle graphs show the relationship of various parts to each other and the whole. Percents are used to create circle graphs.

Julie spends 8 hours each day in school, 2 hours doing homework, 1 hour eating dinner, 2 hours watching television, 10 hours sleeping and the rest of the time doing other things.

Skill 29.2   Understand the mean, median, mode, and range of a collection of data.

Mean, median and mode are three measures of central tendency. The **mean** is the average of the data items. The **median** is found by putting the data items in order from smallest to largest and selecting the item in the middle (or the average of the two items in the middle). The **mode** is the most frequently occurring item.

Range is a measure of variability. It is found by subtracting the smallest value from the largest value.

Sample problem:

Find the mean, median, mode and range of the test score listed below:

85	77	65
92	90	54
88	85	70
75	80	69
85	88	60
72	74	95

Mean (X) = sum of all scores ÷ number of scores
      = 78

Median = put numbers in order from smallest to largest. Pick middle number.
54, 60, 65, 69, 70, 72, 74, 75, 77, 80, 85, 85, 85, 88, 88, 90, 92, 95
                    --   --
                 both in middle
Therefore, median is average of two numbers in the middle or 78.5

Mode = most frequent number
      = 85

Range = largest number minus the smallest number
      = 95 − 54 = 41

Skill 29.3   Have a basic understanding of the design of surveys, such as the role of a random sample.

In cases where the number of events or individuals is too large to collect data on each one, scientists collect information from only a small percentage. This is known as sampling or surveying. If sampling is done correctly, it should give the investigator nearly the same information he would've obtained by testing the entire population. The survey must be carefully designed, considering both the sampling technique and the size of the sample.

There are a variety of sampling techniques: random, systematic, stratified, cluster, and quota are just a few. A truly random sample must chose events or individuals without regard to time, place, or result. Stratified, quota, and cluster sampling all involve the definition of sub-populations; those subpopulations are then samples randomly, in an attempt to represent many segments of a data population evenly. Systemic sampling involves the collection of a sample at defined intervals (for instance, every 10th part to come off a manufacturing line). While random sampling is typically viewed as the "gold standard", sometimes compromises must be made to save time, money, or effort. For instance, when conducting a phone survey, calls are typically only made in a certain geographical area and at a certain time of day. This is an example of cluster sampling.

Another important consideration in sampling is sample size. Again, a large sample will yield the most accurate information, but other factors often limit sample size. Statistical methods may be used to determine how large a sample is necessary to give an investigator a specified level of certainty (95% is a typical confidence interval). Conversely, if a scientist has a sample of certain size, those same statistical methods can be used to determine how confident the scientist can be that the sample accurately reflects the whole population.

COMPETENCY 30.0   Inferences, Predictions, and Arguments Based on
                   Data.

Skill 30.1   Interpret a graph, table, or chart representing a data set.

Correlation is a measure of association between two variables. It
varies from -1 to 1, with 0 being a random relationship, 1 being a
perfect positive linear relationship, and -1 being a perfect negative
linear relationship.

The **correlation coefficient** (r) is used to describe the strength of
the association between the variables and the direction of the
association.
Example:

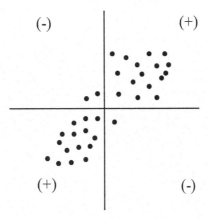

Horizontal and vertical lines are drawn through the point of
averages which is the point on the averages of the x and y values.
This divides the scatter plot into four quadrants. If a point is in the
lower left quadrant, the product of two negatives is positive; in the
upper right, the product of two positives is positive. The positive
quadrants are depicted with the positive sign (+). In the two
remaining quadrants (upper left and lower right), the product of a
negative and a positive is negative. The negative quadrants are
depicted with the negative sign (-). If r is positive, then there are
more points in the positive quadrants and if r is negative, then there
are more points in the two negative quadrants.

Regression is a form of statistical analysis used to predict a
dependent variable (y) from values of an independent variable (x).
A regression equation is derived from a known set of data.

The simplest regression analysis models the relationship between two variables using the following equation: $y = a + bx$, where y is the dependent variable and x is the independent variable. This simple equation denotes a linear relationship between x and y. This form would be appropriate if, when you plotted a graph of x and y, you tended to see the points roughly form along a straight line.

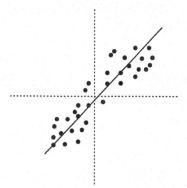

The line can then be used to make predictions.

If all of the data points fell on the line, there would be a perfect correlation ($r = 1.0$) between the x and y data points. These cases represent the best scenarios for prediction. A positive or negative r value represents how y varies with x. When r is positive, y increases as x increases. When r is negative y decreases as x increases.

Skill 30.2   **Draw conclusions about a population from a random sample, and identify potential sources and effects of bias.**

Different situations require different information. If we examine the circumstances under which an ice cream store owner may use statistics collected in the store, we find different uses for different information.

Over a 7-day period, the store owner collected data on the ice cream flavors sold. He found the mean number of scoops sold was 174 per day. The most frequently sold flavor was vanilla. This information was useful in determining how much ice cream to order in all and in what amounts for each flavor.

In the case of the ice cream store, the median and range had little business value for the owner.

Consider the set of test scores from a math class: 0, 16, 19, 65, 65, 65, 68, 69, 70, 72, 73, 73, 75, 78, 80, 85, 88, and 92. The mean is 64.06 and the median is 71. Since there are only three scores less than the mean out of the eighteen score, the median (71) would be a more descriptive score.

Retail store owners may be most concerned with the most common dress size so they may order more of that size than any other.

COMPETENCY 31.0 BASIC NOTIONS OF CHANCE AND PROBABILITY.

Skill 31.1 Define the concept of probability in terms of a sample space of equally likely outcomes.

In probability, the **sample space** is a list of all possible outcomes of an experiment. For example, the sample space of tossing two coins is the set {HH, HT, TT, TH}, the sample space of rolling a six-sided die is the set {1, 2, 3, 4, 5, 6}, and the sample space of measuring the height of students in a class is the set of all real numbers {R}.

The **fundamental counting principle** states that if there are m possible outcomes for one task and n possible outcomes of another, there are (m x n) possible outcomes of the two tasks together.

Skill 31.2 Use their understanding of complementary, mutually exclusive, dependent, and independent events to calculate probabilities of simple events.

Example:

1. Find the size of the sample space of rolling two six-sided die and flipping two coins.

> Solution:
> List the possible outcomes of each event:
> > each dice: {1, 2, 3, 4, 5, 6}
> > each coin: {Heads, Tails}
>
> Apply the fundamental counting principle:
> > size of sample space = 6 x 6 x 2 x 2 = 144

Skill 31.3 **Express probabilities in a variety of ways, including ratios, proportions, decimals, and percents.**

Odds are defined as the ratio of the number of favorable outcomes to the number of unfavorable outcomes. The sum of the favorable outcomes and the unfavorable outcomes should always equal the total possible outcomes.

For example, given a bag of 12 red and 7 green marbles compute the odds of randomly selecting a red marble.

$$\text{Odds of red} = \frac{12}{19} : \frac{7}{19} \text{ or } 12:7.$$

$$\text{Odds of not getting red} = \frac{7}{19} : \frac{12}{19} \text{ or } 7:12.$$

In the case of flipping a coin, it is equally likely that a head or a tail will be tossed. The odds of tossing a head are 1:1. This is called even odds.

COMPETENCY 32.0 SUBJECT MATTER SKILLS AND ABILITIES APPLICABLE TO THE CONTENT DOMAINS IN MATHEMATICS.

Skill 32.1 Identify and prioritize relevant and missing information in mathematical problems.

The unit rate for purchasing an item is its price divided by the number of pounds/ ounces, etc. in the item. The item with the lower unit rate is the lower price.

Example: Find the item with the best unit price:

$1.79 for 10 ounces
$1.89 for 12 ounces
$5.49 for 32 ounces

$$\frac{1.79}{10} = .179 \text{ per ounce} \qquad \frac{1.89}{12} = .1575 \text{ per ounce} \qquad \frac{5.49}{32} = .172 \text{ per ounce}$$

$1.89 for 12 ounces is the best price.

A second way to find the better buy is to make a proportion with the price over the number of ounces, etc. Cross multiply the proportion, writing the products above the numerator that is used. The better price will have the smaller product.

Example: Find the better buy:

$8.19 for 40 pounds or $4.89 for 22 pounds

Find the unit price.

$$\frac{40}{8.19} = \frac{1}{x} \qquad\qquad\qquad \frac{22}{4.89} = \frac{1}{x}$$
$$40x = 8.19 \qquad\qquad\qquad 22x = 4.89$$
$$x = .20475 \qquad\qquad\qquad x = .22\overline{227}$$

Since $.20475 < .22\overline{227}$, $8.19 is less and is a better buy.

To find the amount of sales tax on an item, change the percent of sales tax into an equivalent decimal number. Then multiply the decimal number times the price of the object to find the sales tax. The total cost of an item will be the price of the item plus the sales tax.

Example: A guitar costs $120 plus 7% sales tax. How much are the sales tax and the total bill?

7% = .07 as a decimal   (.07)(120) = $8.40 sales tax
$120 + $8.40 = $128.40 ← total price

Example: A suit costs $450 plus 6½% sales tax. How much are the sales tax and the total bill?

6½% = .065 as a decimal
(.065)(450) = $29.25 sales tax
$450 + $29.25 = $479.25 ← total price

Skill 32.2   **Analyze complex problems to identify similar simple problems that might suggest solution strategies.**

Examining the change in area or volume of a given figure requires first to find the existing area given the original dimensions and then finding the new area given the increased dimensions.

Sample problem:

Given the rectangle below determine the change in area if the length is increase by 5 and the width is increased by 7.

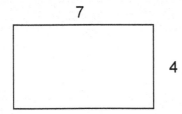

Draw and label a sketch of the new rectangle.

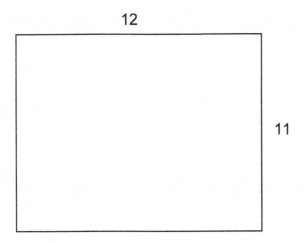

Find the areas.

Area of original = LW   Area of enlarged shape = LW
          = (7)(4)   = (12)(11)
          = 28 units^2 = 132 units^2

The change in area is 132 – 28 = 104 units^2.

Skill 32.3 **Represent a problem in alternate ways, such as words, symbols, concrete models, and diagrams, to gain greater insight.**

MANIPULATIVES

<u>Example</u>:
Using tiles to demonstrate both geometric ideas and number theory.

Give each group of students 12 tiles and instruct them to build rectangles. Students draw their rectangles on paper.

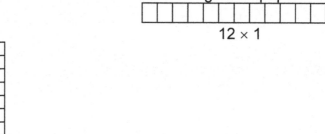
12 × 1

1 × 12

3 × 4

4 × 3

6 × 2

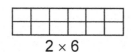
2 × 6

Skill 32.4   Consider examples and patterns as means to formulating a conjecture.

What conclusion, if any, can be reached? Assume each statement is true, regardless of any personal beliefs.

1. If the Red Sox win the World Series, I will die.
   I died.

2. If an angle's measure is between 0° and 90°, then the angle is acute. Angle B is not acute.

3. Students who do well in geometry will succeed in college.
   Annie is doing extremely well in geometry.

4. Left-handed people are witty and charming.
   You are left-handed.

Skill 32.5   Apply logical reasoning and techniques from arithmetic, algebra, geometry, and probability/statistics to solve mathematical problems.

Suppose that these statements were given to you, and you are asked to try to reach a conclusion. The statements are:

All rectangles are parallelograms.
Quadrilateral ABCD is not a parallelogram.

In "if-then" form, the first statement would be:
    If a figure is a rectangle, then it is also a parallelogram.

Note that the second statement is the negation of the conclusion of statement one. Remember also that the contrapositive is logically equivalent to a given conditional. That is, **"If ~ q, then ~ p"**. Since" ABCD is NOT a parallelogram " is like saying **"If ~ q,"** then you can come to the conclusion **"then ~ p"**. Therefore, the conclusion is ABCD is not a rectangle. Looking at the Venn diagram below, if all rectangles are parallelograms, then rectangles are included as part of the parallelograms. Since quadrilateral ABCD is not a parallelogram, that it is excluded from anywhere inside the parallelogram box. This allows you to conclude that ABCD can not be a rectangle either.

PARALLELOGRAMS	quadrilateral
	ABCD rectangles

Skill 32.6   **Analyze problems to identify alternative solution strategies.**

Elapsed time problems are usually one of two types. One type of problem is the elapsed time between 2 times given in hours, minutes, and seconds. The other common type of problem is between 2 times given in months and years.

For any time of day past noon, change it into military time by adding 12 hours. For instance, 1:15 p.m. would be 13:15. Remember when you borrow a minute or an hour in a subtraction problem that you have borrowed 60 more seconds or minutes.

<u>Example:</u> Find the time from 11:34:22 a.m. until 3:28:40 p.m.

> First change 3:28:40 p.m. to   15:28:40 p.m.
> Now subtract   - <u>11:34:22</u> a.m.
>   :18

Borrow an hour and add 60 more minutes. Subtract
> 14:88:40 p.m.
> - <u>11:34:22</u> a.m.
>   3:54:18   ↔ 3 hours, 54 minutes, 18 seconds

<u>Example:</u> John lived in Arizona from September 91 until March 95. How long is that?

>   year month
> March 95   =   95   03
> September 91   = - <u>91   09</u>

Borrow a year, change it into 12 more months, and subtract.

>   year month
> March 95   =   94   15
> September 91   = - <u>91   09</u>
>   3 yr 6 months

<u>Example:</u> A race took the winner 1 hr. 58 min. 12 sec. on the first half of the race and 2 hr. 9 min. 57 sec. on the second half of the race. How much time did the entire race take?

>   1 hr. 58 min. 12 sec.
> + <u>2 hr. 9 min. 57 sec.</u>   Add these numbers
>   3 hr. 67 min. 69 sec.
> + <u>1 min -60 sec.</u>   Change 60 seconds to 1 min.
>   3 hr. 68 min. 9 sec.
> + <u>1 hr.-60 min.   .</u>   Change 60 minutes to 1 hr.
>   4 hr. 8 min. 9 sec. ←final answer

Skill 32.7   Evaluate the truth of mathematical statements.

Conditional statements are frequently written in "**if-then**" form. The "if" clause of the conditional is known as the **hypothesis**, and the "then" clause is called the **conclusion**. In a proof, the hypothesis is the information that is assumed to be true, while the conclusion is what is to be proven true. A conditional is considered to be of the form:

If p, then q

p is the hypothesis. q is the conclusion.

Conditional statements can be diagrammed using a **Venn diagram**. A diagram can be drawn with one circle inside another circle. The inner circle represents the hypothesis. The outer circle represents the conclusion. If the hypothesis is taken to be true, then you are located inside the inner circle. If you are located in the inner circle then you are also inside the outer circle, so that proves the conclusion is true.

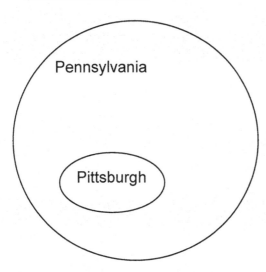

Example:
If an angle has a measure of 90 degrees, then it is a right angle.

> In this statement "an angle has a measure of 90 degrees" is the hypothesis.
> In this statement "it is a right angle" is the conclusion.

Example:
If you are in Pittsburgh, then you are in Pennsylvania.
> In this statement "you are in Pittsburgh" is the hypothesis.
> In this statement "you are in Pennsylvania" is the conclusion.

Skill 32.8 **Apply different solution strategies to check the reasonableness of a solution.**

Estimation and approximation may be used to check the reasonableness of answers.

Example: Estimate the answer.

$$\frac{58 \times 810}{1989}$$

58 becomes 60, 810 becomes 800 and 1989 becomes 2000.

$$\frac{60 \times 800}{2000} = 24$$

Word problems: An estimate may sometimes be all that is needed to solve a problem.

Example: Janet goes into a store to purchase a CD on sale for $13.95. While shopping, she sees two pairs of shoes, prices $19.95 and $14.50. She only has $50. Can she purchase everything?

Solve by rounding:

$19.95 \rightarrow $20.00
$14.50 \rightarrow $15.00
$13.95 \rightarrow \underline{$14.00}
$49.00   Yes, she can purchase the CD and the shoes.

Skill 32.9   **Demonstrate that a solution is correct.**

ERROR ANALYSIS

A simple method for analyzing student errors is to ask how the answer was obtained. The teacher can then determine if a common error pattern has resulted in the wrong answer. There is a value to having the students explain how the arrived at the correct as well as the incorrect answers.

Many errors are due to simple **carelessness**. Students need to be encouraged to work slowly and carefully. They should check their calculations by redoing the problem on another paper, not merely looking at the work. Addition and subtraction problems need to be written neatly so the numbers line up. Students need to be careful regrouping in subtraction. Students must write clearly and legibly, including erasing fully. Use estimation to ensure that answers make sense.

Many students' computational skills exceed their **reading** level. Although they can understand basic operations, they fail to grasp the concept or completely understand the question. Students must read directions slowly.

Fractions are often a source of many errors. Students need to be reminded to use common denominators when adding and subtracting and to always express answers in simplest terms. Again, it is helpful to check by estimating.

The most common error that is made when working with **decimals** is failure to line up the decimal points when adding or subtracting or not moving the decimal point when multiplying or dividing. Students also need to be reminded to add zeroes when necessary. Reading aloud may also be beneficial. Estimation, as always, is especially important.

Students need to know that it is okay to make mistakes. The teacher must keep a positive attitude, so they do not feel defeated or frustrated.

Skill 32.10 **Explain their mathematical reasoning through a variety of methods, such as words, numbers, symbols, charts, graphs, tables, diagrams, and concrete models.**

A valid argument is a statement made about a pattern or relationship between elements, thought to be true, which is subsequently justified through repeated examples and logical reasoning. Another term for a valid argument is a proof.

For example, the statement that the sum of two odd numbers is always even could be tested through actual examples.

Two Odd Numbers	Sum	Validity of Statement
1+1	2 (even)	Valid
1+3	4 (even)	Valid
61+29	90 (even)	Valid
135+47	182 (even)	Valid
253+17	270 (even)	Valid
1,945+2,007	3,952 (even)	Valid
6,321+7,851	14,172 (even)	Valid

Adding two odd numbers always results in a sum that is even. It is a valid argument based on the justifications in the table above.

Here is another example. The statement that a fraction of a fraction can be determined by multiplying the numerator by the numerator and the denominator by the denominator can be proven through logical reasoning. For example, one-half of one-quarter of a candy bar can be found by multiplying ½ * ¼. The answer would be one-eighth. The validity of this argument can be demonstrated as valid with a model.

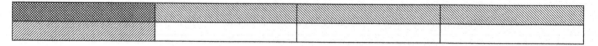

The entire rectangle represents one whole candy bar. The top half section of the model is shaded in one direction to demonstrate how much of the candy bar remains from the whole candy bar. The left quarter, shaded in a different direction, demonstrates that one-quarter of the candy bar has been given to a friend. Since the whole candy bar is not available to give out, the area that is double-shaded is the fractional part of the ½ candy bar that has been actually given away. That fractional part is one-eighth of the whole candy bar as shown in both the sketch and the algorithm.

Skill 32.11   Use appropriate mathematical notation with clear and accurate language.

Mathematical operations include addition, subtraction, multiplication and division.

Addition can be indicated by the expressions: sum, greater than, and, more than, increased by, added to.

Subtraction can be expressed by: difference, fewer than, minus, less than, decreased by.

Multiplication is shown by: product, times, multiplied by, twice.

Division is used for: quotient, divided by, ratio.

Examples: 7 added to a number $\qquad n + 7$
a number decreased by 8 $\qquad n - 8$
12 times a number divided by 7 $\qquad 12n \div 7$
28 less than a number $\qquad n - 28$
the ratio of a number to 55 $\qquad \dfrac{n}{55}$
4 times the sum of a number and 21 $4(n + 21)$

Mathematical operations can be shown using manipulatives or drawings.
Multiplication can be shown using arrays.

3×4 □□□□□□ □ □ □
□ □ □ □
□ □ □ □

Addition and subtractions can be demonstrated with symbols.

ψ ψ ψ ξ ξ ξ
$3 + 4 = 7$
$7 - 3 = 4$

Fractions can be clarified using pattern blocks, fraction bars, or paper folding.

Skill 32.12   **Explain how to derive a result based on previously developed ideas, and explain how a result is related to other ideas.**

Recognition and understanding of the relationships between concepts and topics is of great value in mathematical problem solving and the explanation of more complex processes.

For instance, multiplication is simply repeated addition. This relationship explains the concept of variable addition. We can show that the expression $4x + 3x = 7x$ is true by rewriting 4 times x and 3 times x as repeated addition, yielding the expression $(x + x + x + x) + (x + x + x)$. Thus, because of the relationship between multiplication and addition, variable addition is accomplished by coefficient addition.

CONTENT AREA – SCIENCE

DOMAIN I – PHYSICAL SCIENCE

COMPETENCY 33.0 STRUCTURE AND PROPERTIES OF MATTER

Skill 33.1   **Understand the physical properties of solids, liquids, and gases, such as color, mass, density, hardness, and electrical and thermal conductivity.**

Everything in our world is made up of **matter**, whether it is a rock, a building, an animal, or a person. Matter is defined by its characteristics: It takes up space and it has mass.

Mass is a measure of the amount of matter in an object. Two objects of equal mass will balance each other on a simple balance scale no matter where the scale is located. For instance, two rocks with the same amount of mass that are in balance on earth will also be in balance on the moon. They will feel heavier on earth than on the moon because of the gravitational pull of the earth. So, although the two rocks have the same mass, they will have different **weight.**

Weight is the measure of the earth's pull of gravity on an object. It can also be defined as the pull of gravity between other bodies. The units of weight measurement commonly used are the pound (English measure) and the kilogram (metric measure).

In addition to mass, matter also has the property of volume. **Volume** is the amount of cubic space that an object occupies. Volume and mass together give a more exact description of the object. Two objects may have the same volume, but different mass, or the same mass but different volumes, etc. For instance, consider two cubes that are each one cubic centimeter, one made from plastic, one from lead. They have the same volume, but the lead cube has more mass. The measure that we use to describe the cubes takes into consideration both the mass and the volume. **Density** is the mass of a substance contained per unit of volume. If the density of an object is less than the density of a liquid, the object will float in the liquid. If the object is denser than the liquid, then the object will sink.

Density is stated in grams per cubic centimeter (g/cm^3) where the gram is the standard unit of mass. To find an object's density, you must measure its mass and its volume. Then divide the mass by the volume ($D = m/V$).
To discover an object's density, first use a balance to find its mass. Then calculate its volume. If the object is a regular shape, you can find the volume by multiplying the length, width, and height together. However, if it is an irregular shape, you can find the volume by seeing how much water it displaces. Measure the water in the container before and after the object is submerged. The difference will be the volume of the object.

Specific gravity is the ratio of the density of a substance to the density of water. For instance, the specific density of one liter of turpentine is calculated by comparing its mass (0.81 kg) to the mass of one liter of water (1 kg):

$$\frac{\text{mass of 1 L alcohol}}{\text{mass of 1 L water}} = \frac{0.81 \text{ kg}}{1.00 \text{ kg}} = 0.81$$

Physical properties and chemical properties of matter describe the appearance or behavior of a substance. A **physical property** can be observed without changing the identity of a substance. For instance, you can describe the color, mass, shape, and volume of a book. **Chemical properties** describe the ability of a substance to be changed into new substances. Baking powder goes through a chemical change as it changes into carbon dioxide gas during the baking process.

Matter constantly changes. A **physical change** is a change that does not produce a new substance. The freezing and melting of water is an example of physical change. A **chemical change** (or chemical reaction) is any change of a substance into one or more other substances. Burning materials turn into smoke; a seltzer tablet fizzes into gas bubbles.

Skill 33.2   Know that matter can undergo physical changes and chemical changes.

The **phase of matter** (solid, liquid, or gas) is identified by its shape and volume.

A **solid** has a definite shape and volume. A **liquid** has a definite volume, but no shape. A **gas** has no shape or volume because it will spread out to occupy the entire space of whatever container it is in.

While plasma is really a type of gas, its properties are so unique that it is considered a unique phase of matter. **Plasma is a gas that has been ionized**, meaning that at least on electron has been removed from some of its atoms. Plasma shares some characteristics with gas, specifically, the **high kinetic energy** of its molecules. Thus, plasma exists as a diffuse "cloud," though it sometimes includes tiny grains (this is termed dusty plasma). What most distinguishes plasma from gas is that it is **electrically conductive** and exhibits a strong response to electromagnetic fields. This property is a consequence of the **charged particles that result from the removal of electrons** from the molecules in the plasma.

Energy is the ability to cause change in matter. Applying heat to a frozen liquid changes it from solid back to liquid. Continue heating it and it will boil and give off steam, a gas.

Evaporation is the change in phase from liquid to gas. **Condensation** is the change in phase from gas to liquid.

Skill 33.3   Know that matter consists of atoms and molecules in various arrangements, and can give the location and motions of the parts of an atom.

An **atom** is a nucleus surrounded by a cloud with moving electrons.

The **nucleus** is the center of the atom. The positive particles inside the nucleus are called **protons.** The mass of a proton is about 2,000 times that of the mass of an electron. The number of protons in the nucleus of an atom is called the **atomic number**. All atoms of the same element have the same atomic number.

Neutrons are another type of particle in the nucleus. Neutrons and protons have about the same mass, but neutrons have no charge. Neutrons were discovered because scientists observed that not all atoms in neon gas have the same mass. They had identified isotopes. **Isotopes** of an element have the same number of protons in the nucleus, but have different masses. Neutrons explain the difference in mass. They have mass but no charge.

The mass of matter is measured against a standard mass such as the gram. Scientists measure the mass of an atom by comparing it to that of a standard atom. The result is relative mass. The **relative mass** of an atom is its mass expressed in terms of the mass of the standard atom. The isotope of the element carbon is the standard atom. It has six (6) neutrons and is called carbon-12. It is assigned a mass of 12 atomic mass units (amu). Therefore, the **atomic mass unit (amu)** is the standard unit for measuring the mass of an atom. It is equal to the mass of a carbon atom.

The **mass number** of an atom is the sum of its protons and neutrons. In any element, there is a mixture of isotopes, some having slightly more or slightly fewer protons and neutrons. The **atomic mass** of an element is an average of the mass numbers of its atoms.

The following table summarizes the terms used to describe atomic nuclei:

Term	Example	Meaning	Characteristic
Atomic Number	# protons (p)	same for all atoms of a given element	Carbon (C) atomic number = 6 (6p)
Mass number	# protons + # neutrons (p + n)	changes for different isotopes of an element	C-12 (6p + 6n) C-13 (6p + 7n)
Atomic mass carbon	average mass of the atoms of the element	usually not a whole number	atomic mass of equals 12.011

Each atom has an equal number of electrons (negative) and protons (positive). Therefore, atoms are neutral. Electrons orbiting the nucleus occupy energy levels that are arranged in order and the electrons tend to occupy the lowest energy level available. A **stable electron arrangement** is an atom that has all of its electrons in the lowest possible energy levels.

Each energy level holds a maximum number of electrons. However, an atom with more than one level does not hold more than 8 electrons in its outermost shell.

Level	Name	Max. # of Electrons
First	K shell	2
Second	L shell	8
Third	M shell	18
Fourth	N shell	32

This can help explain why chemical reactions occur. Atoms react with each other when their outer levels are unfilled. When atoms either exchange or share electrons with each other, these energy levels become filled and the atom becomes more stable.

As an electron gains energy, it moves from one energy level to a higher energy level. The electron can not leave one level until it has enough energy to reach the next level. **Excited electrons** are electrons that have absorbed energy and have moved farther from the nucleus.

Electrons can also lose energy. When they do, they fall to a lower level. However, they can only fall to the lowest level that has room for them. This explains why atoms do not collapse.

Skill 33.4 **Describe the constituents of molecules and compounds, naming common elements, and explain how elements are organized on the Periodic Table on the basis of their atomic and chemical properties.**

The **periodic table of elements** is an arrangement of the elements in rows and columns so that it is easy to locate elements with similar properties. The elements of the modern periodic table are arranged in numerical order by atomic number.

The **periods** are the rows down the left side of the table. They are called first period, second period, etc. The columns of the periodic table are called **groups**, or **families.** Elements in a family have similar properties.

There are three types of elements that are grouped by color: metals, nonmetals, and metalloids.

Element Key

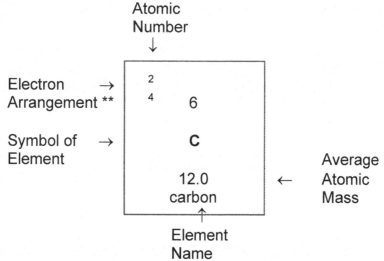

** Number of electrons on each level. Top number represents the innermost level.

The periodic table arranges metals into families with similar properties. The periodic table has its columns marked IA - VIIIA. These are the traditional group numbers. Arabic numbers 1 - 18 are also used, as suggested by the Union of Physicists and Chemists. The Arabic numerals will be used in this text.

Metals:
With the exception of hydrogen, all elements in Group 1 are **alkali metals**. These metals are shiny, softer and less dense than other metals, and are the most chemically active.

Group 2 metals are the **alkaline earth metals.** They are harder, denser, have higher melting points, and are chemically active.

The **transition elements** can be found by finding the periods (rows) from 4 to 7 under the groups (columns) 3 - 12. They are metals that do not show a range of properties as you move across the chart. They are hard and have high melting points. Compounds of these elements are colorful, such as silver, gold, and mercury.

Elements can be combined to make metallic objects. An **alloy** is a mixture of two or more elements having properties of metals. The elements do not have to be all metals. For instance, steel is made up of the metal iron and the non-metal carbon.

Nonmetals:
Nonmetals are not as easy to recognize as metals because they do not always share physical properties. However, in general the properties of nonmetals are the opposite of metals. They are dull, brittle, and are not good conductors of heat and electricity.

Nonmetals include solids, gases, and one liquid (bromine).

Nonmetals have four to eight electrons in their outermost energy levels and tend to attract electrons. As a result, the outer levels are usually filled with eight electrons. This difference in the number of electrons is what caused the differences between metals and nonmetals. The outstanding chemical property of nonmetals is that they react with metals.

The **halogens** can be found in Group 17. Halogens combine readily with metals to form salts. Table salt, fluoride toothpaste, and bleach all have an element from the halogen family.

The **Noble Gases** got their name from the fact that they did not react chemically with other elements, much like the nobility did not mix with the masses. These gases (found in Group 18) will only combine with other elements under very specific conditions. They are **inert** (inactive).

In recent years, scientists have found this to be only generally true, since chemists have been able to prepare compounds of krypton and xenon.
Metalloids:
Metalloids have properties in between metals and nonmetals. They can be found in Groups 13 - 16, but do not occupy the entire group. They are arranged in stair steps across the groups.

Physical Properties:
1. All are solids having the appearance of metals.
2. All are white or gray, but not shiny.
3. They will conduct electricity, but not as well as a metal.

Chemical Properties:
1. Have some characteristics of metals and nonmetals.
2. Properties do not follow patterns like metals and nonmetals. Each must be studied individually.

Boron is the first element in Group 13. It is a poor conductor of electricity at low temperatures. However, increase its temperature and it becomes a good conductor. By comparison, metals, which are good conductors, lose their ability as they are heated. It is because of this property that boron is so useful. Boron is a semiconductor. **Semiconductors** are used in electrical devices that have to function at temperatures too high for metals.

Silicon is the second element in Group 14. It is also a semiconductor and is found in great abundance in the earth's crust. Sand is made of a silicon compound, silicon dioxide. Silicon is also used in the manufacture of glass and cement.

Skill 33.5   Describe characteristics of solutions and they know examples with different pH levels such as soft drinks, liquid detergents, and water.

An **element** is a substance that can not be broken down into other substances. To date, scientists have identified 109 elements: 89 are found in nature and 20 are synthetic.

An **atom** is the smallest particle of the element that retains the properties of that element. All of the atoms of a particular element are the same. The atoms of each element are different from the atoms of other elements.
Elements are assigned an identifying symbol of one or two letters. The symbol for oxygen is O and stands for one atom of oxygen. However, because oxygen atoms in nature are joined together is pairs, the symbol O_2 represents oxygen. This pair of oxygen atoms is a molecule. A **molecule** is the smallest particle of substance that can exist independently and has all of the properties of that substance. A molecule of most elements is made up of one atom. However, oxygen, hydrogen, nitrogen, and chlorine molecules are made of two atoms each.

A **compound** is made of two or more elements that have been chemically combined. Atoms join together when elements are chemically combined. The result is that the elements lose their individual identities when they are joined. The compound that they become has different properties.

We use a formula to show the elements of a chemical compound. A **chemical formula** is a shorthand way of showing what is in a compound by using symbols and subscripts. The letter symbols let us know what elements are involved and the number subscript tells how many atoms of each element are involved. No subscript is used if there is only one atom involved. For example, carbon dioxide is made up of one atom of carbon (C) and two atoms of oxygen (O_2), so the formula would be represented as CO_2.

Substances can combine without a chemical change. A **mixture** is any combination of two or more substances in which the substances keep their own properties. A fruit salad is a mixture. So is an ice cream sundae, although you might not recognize each part if it is stirred together. Colognes and perfumes are the other examples. You may not readily recognize the individual elements. However, they can be separated.

Compounds and **mixtures** are similar in that they are made up of two or more substances. However, they have the following opposite characteristics:

Compounds:
1. Made up of one kind of particle
2. Formed during a chemical change
3. Broken down only by chemical changes
4. Properties are different from its parts
5. Has a specific amount of each ingredient.

Mixtures:
1. Made up of two or more particles
2. Not formed by a chemical change
3. Can be separated by physical changes
4. Properties are the same as its parts.
5. Does not have a definite amount of each ingredient.

Common compounds are **acids, bases, salts**, and **oxides** and are classified according to their characteristics.

An **acid** contains one element of hydrogen (H). Although it is never wise to taste a substance to identify it, acids have a sour taste. Vinegar and lemon juice are both acids, and acids occur in many foods in a weak state. Strong acids can burn skin and destroy materials. Common acids include:

Sulfuric acid (H_2SO_4)	-	Used in medicines, alcohol, dyes, and car batteries.
Nitric acid (HNO_3)	-	Used in fertilizers, explosives, cleaning materials.
Carbonic acid (H_2CO_3)	-	Used in soft drinks.
Acetic acid ($HC_2H_3O_2$)	-	Used in making plastics, rubber, photographic film, and as a solvent.

Bases have a bitter taste and the stronger ones feel slippery. Like acids, strong bases can be dangerous and should be handled carefully. All bases contain the elements oxygen and hydrogen (OH). Many household cleaning products contain bases. Common bases include:

Sodium hydroxide	NaOH	-	Used in making soap, paper, vegetable oils, and refining petroleum.
Ammonium hydroxide	NH_4OH	-	Making deodorants, bleaching compounds, cleaning compounds.
Potassium hydroxide	KOH	-	Making soaps, drugs, dyes, alkaline batteries, and purifying industrial gases.
Calcium hydroxide	$Ca(OH)_2$	-	Making cement and plaster

An **indicator** is a substance that changes color when it comes in contact with an acid or a base. Litmus paper is an indicator. Blue litmus paper turns red in an acid. Red litmus paper turns blue in a base.

A substance that is neither acid nor base is **neutral**. Neutral substances do not change the color of litmus paper.

Salt is formed when an acid and a base combine chemically. Water is also formed. The process is called **neutralization**. Table salt (NaCl) is an example of this process. Salts are also used in toothpaste, epsom salts, and cream of tartar. Calcium chloride ($CaCl_2$) is used on frozen streets and walkways to melt the ice. **Oxides** are compounds that are formed when oxygen combines with another element. Rust is an oxide formed when oxygen combines with iron.

Skill 33.6   Know that mixtures may often be separated based on physical or chemical properties.

A mixture is the combination of pure substances (elements or compounds). It is the result of mechanical mixing, not chemical bonding. Therefore, each element or compound retains its own unique properties. This means that the components of the mixture can often be separated back out. Both mechanical and chemical techniques exist to accomplish this and these are termed separation processes. Separation processes may utilize differences in size, charge, chemical affinity or physical properties of the components. A few of the more common techniques are listed below:

Distillation involves heating the mixture slowly such that those compounds with the lowest boiling point become gas first. The gas can then be collected and condensed.

Fractional freezing utilizes differences in freezing point by lowering the temperature of a liquid mixture until one substance becomes a solid.

Extraction involves introducing another solvent to the mixture (typically an aqueous solvent to an organic mixture). The compounds will then separate between the two phases, depending on their relative solubilities.

Centrifugation relies on differences in density. When the mixture is rapidly spun, centrifugal forces draw the more dense components to the bottom.

Gel electrophoresis uses as electrical gradient to separate compounds by size or charge; this is a very gentle separation techniques that is typically used for proteins and other biomolecules.

Precipitation and filtration involves introducing another substance that will bind with one or more of the compounds in the mixture and form a solid. These solids can then be filtered out of the solution.

Chromatography techniques include many specific technologies, but all involve passing the mixture through a stationary phase. The various components in the mixture will have different degrees of affinity for this stationary phase and will thus be separated. This affinity may be based upon charge, relative solubility or adsorption. The major types of chromatography are capillary-action (paper and thin layer), column, gas-liquid, and counter-current.

COMPETENCY 34.0 PRINCIPLES OF MOTION AND ENERGY

Skill 34.1 Describe an object's motion based on position, displacement, speed, velocity, and acceleration.

Dynamics is the study of the relationship between motion and the forces affecting motion. **Force** causes motion.

Mass and weight are not the same quantities. An object's **mass** gives it a reluctance to change its current state of motion. It is also the measure of an object's resistance to acceleration. The force that the earth's gravity exerts on an object with a specific mass is called the object's weight on earth. Weight is a force that is measured in Newtons. Weight (W) = mass times acceleration due to gravity (**W = mg**). To illustrate the difference between mass and weight, picture two rocks of equal mass on a balance scale. If the scale is balanced in one place, it will be balanced everywhere, regardless of the gravitational field.

However, the weight of the stones would vary on a spring scale, depending upon the gravitational field. In other words, the stones would be balanced both on earth and on the moon. However, the weight of the stones would be greater on earth than on the moon.

Inertia is the continuation of an object at rest to remain at rest. Conversely, **momentum** is the likelihood that an object in motion will remain in motion.

Speed is a scalar quantity that refers to how fast an object is moving (ex. the car was traveling 60 mi/hr). **Velocity** is a vector quantity that refers to the rate at which an object changes its position. In other words, velocity is speed with direction (ex. the car was traveling 60 mi./hr east).

$$\text{Average speed} = \frac{\text{Distance traveled}}{\text{Time of travel}}$$

$$v = \frac{d}{t}$$

$$\text{Average velocity} = \frac{\Delta \text{position}}{\text{time}} = \frac{\text{displacement}}{\text{time}}$$

Instantaneous Speed - speed at any given instant in time.

Average Speed - average of all instantaneous speeds, found simply by a distance/time ratio.

Acceleration is a vector quantity defined as the rate at which an object changes its velocity.

$$a = \frac{\Delta velocity}{time} = \frac{v_f - v_i}{t}$$ where f represents the final velocity and i

represents the initial velocity

Since acceleration is a vector quantity, it always has a direction associated with it. The direction of the acceleration vector depends on

- whether the object is speeding up or slowing down
- whether the object is moving in the positive or negative direction.

Skill 34.2   Know that forces such as gravity, magnetism, and friction act on objects and may change their motion if these forces are not in balance.

Push and pull –Pushing a volleyball or pulling a bowstring applies muscular force when the muscles expand and contract. Elastic force is when any object returns to its original shape (for example, when a bow is released).

Rubbing – Friction opposes the motion of one surface past another. Friction is common when slowing down a car or sledding down a hill.

Pull of gravity – is a force of attraction between two objects. Gravity questions can be raised not only on earth but also between planets and even black hole discussions.

Forces on objects at rest – The formula **F= m/a** is shorthand for force equals mass over acceleration. An object will not move unless the force is strong enough to move the mass. Also, there can be opposing forces holding the object in place. For instance, a boat may want to be forced by the currents to drift away but an equal and opposite force is a rope holding it to a dock.

Forces on a moving object - Overcoming inertia is the tendency of any object to oppose a change in motion. An object at rest tends to stay at rest. An object that is moving tends to keep moving.

Inertia and circular motion – The centripetal force is provided by the high banking of the curved road and by friction between the wheels and the road. This inward force that keeps an object moving in a circle is called centripetal force.

Skill 34.3   Know that "like" electrical charges or magnetic poles produce repulsive forces and "unlike" charges or poles produce attractive forces.

Electrostatics is the study of stationary electric charges. A plastic rod that is rubbed with fur or a glass rod that is rubbed with silk will become electrically charged and will attract small pieces of paper. The charge on the plastic rod rubbed with fur is negative and the charge on glass rod rubbed with silk is positive.

Electrically charged objects share these characteristics:

1. Like charges repel one another.
2. Opposite charges attract each other.
3. Charge is conserved. A neutral object has no net change. If the plastic rod and fur are initially neutral, when the rod becomes charged by the fur a negative charge is transferred from the fur to the rod. The net negative charge on the rod is equal to the net positive charge on the fur.

Materials through which electric charges can easily flow are called conductors. On the other hand, an **insulator** is a material through which electric charges do not move easily, if at all. A simple device used to indicate the existence of a positive or negative charge is called an **electroscope**. An electroscope is made up of a conducting knob and attached to it are very lightweight conducting leaves usually made of foil (gold or aluminum). When a charged object touches the knob, the leaves push away from each other because like charges repel. It is not possible to tell whether if the charge is positive or negative.

Charging by induction:
Touch the knob with a finger while a charged rod is nearby. The electrons will be repulsed and flow out of the electroscope through the hand. If the hand is removed while the charged rod remains close, the electroscope will retain the charge.

When an object is rubbed with a charged rod, the object will take on the same charge as the rod. However, charging by induction gives the object the opposite charge as that of the charged rod.

Grounding charge:
Charge can be removed from an object by connecting it to the earth through a conductor. The removal of static electricity by conduction is called **grounding**.

An **electric circuit** is a path along which electrons flow. A simple circuit can be created with a dry cell, wire, a bell, or a light bulb. When all are connected, the electrons flow from the negative terminal, through the wire to the device and back to the positive terminal of the dry cell. If there are no breaks in the circuit, the device will work. The circuit is closed. Any break in the flow will create an open circuit and cause the device to shut off.

The device (bell, bulb) is an example of a **load**. A load is a device that uses energy. Suppose that you also add a buzzer so that the bell rings when you press the buzzer button. The buzzer is acting as a **switch**. A switch is a device that opens or closes a circuit. Pressing the buzzer makes the connection complete and the bell rings. When the buzzer is not engaged, the circuit is open and the bell is silent.

A **series circuit** is one where the electrons have only one path along which they can move. When one load in a series circuit goes out, the circuit is open. An example of this is a set of Christmas tree lights that is missing a bulb. None of the bulbs will work.

A **parallel circuit** is one where the electrons have more than one path to move along. If a load goes out in a parallel circuit, the other load will still work because the electrons can still find a way to continue moving along the path.

When an electron goes through a load, it does work and therefore loses some of its energy. The measure of how much energy is lost is called the **potential difference**. The potential difference between two points is the work needed to move a charge from one point to another.

Potential difference is measured in a unit called the volt. **Voltage** is potential difference. The higher the voltage, the more energy the electrons have. This energy is measured by a device called a voltmeter. To use a voltmeter, place it in a circuit parallel with the load you are measuring.
Current is the number of electrons per second that flow past a point in a circuit. Current is measured with a device called an ammeter. To use an ammeter, put it in series with the load you are measuring.

As electrons flow through a wire, they lose potential energy. Some is changed into heat energy because of resistance. **Resistance** is the ability of the material to oppose the flow of electrons through it. All substances have some resistance, even if they are a good conductor such as copper. This resistance is measured in units called **ohms**. A thin wire will have more resistance than a thick one because it will have less room for electrons to travel. In a thicker wire, there will be more possible paths for the electrons to flow. Resistance also depends upon the length of the wire. The longer the wire, the more resistance it will have.

Potential difference, resistance, and current form a relationship know as **Ohm's Law**. Current **(I)** is measured in amperes and is equal to potential difference **(V)** divided by resistance **(R)**.

$$I = V / R$$

If you have a wire with resistance of 5 ohms and a potential difference of 75 volts, you can calculate the current by

I = 75 volts / 5 ohms
I = 15 amperes

A current of 10 or more amperes will cause a wire to get hot. 22 amperes is about the maximum for a house circuit. Anything above 25 amperes can start a fire.

Skill 34.4 **Describe simple machines in which small forces are exerted over long distances to accomplish difficult tasks.**

Forces on objects at rest – The formula F= m/a is shorthand for force equals mass over acceleration. An object will not move unless the force is strong enough to move the mass. Also, there can be opposing forces holding the object in place. For instance, a boat may want to be forced by the currents to drift away but an equal and opposite force is a rope holding it to a dock.

Forces on a moving object - Overcoming inertia is the tendency of any object to oppose a change in motion. An object at rest tends to stay at rest. An object that is moving tends to keep moving.

Inertia and circular motion – The centripetal force is provided by the high banking of the curved road and by friction between the wheels and the road. This inward force that keeps an object moving in a circle is called centripetal force.

Work is done on an object when an applied force moves through a distance.

Power is the work done divided by the amount of time that it took to do it. (Power = Work / time)

Simple machines include the following:

1.   Inclined plane
2.   Lever
3.   Wheel and axle
4.   Pulley

Compound machines are two or more simple machines working together. A wheelbarrow is an example of a complex machine. It uses a lever and a wheel and axle. Machines of all types ease workload by changing the size or direction of an applied force. The amount of effort saved when using simple or complex machines is called mechanical advantage or MA.

Skill 34.5   Identify forms of energy including solar, chemical, electrical, magnetic, nuclear, sound, light, and electromagnetic.

Dynamics is the study of the relationship between motion and the forces affecting motion. **Force** causes motion.

Mass and weight are not the same quantities. An object's **mass** gives it a reluctance to change its current state of motion. It is also the measure of an object's resistance to acceleration. The force that the earth's gravity exerts on an object with a specific mass is called the object's weight on earth. Weight is a force that is measured in Newtons. Weight (W) = mass times acceleration due to gravity (**W = mg**). To illustrate the difference between mass and weight, picture two rocks of equal mass on a balance scale. If the scale is balanced in one place, it will be balanced everywhere, regardless of the gravitational field. However, the weight of the stones would vary on a spring scale, depending upon the gravitational field. In other words, the stones would be balanced both on earth and on the moon. However, the weight of the stones would be greater on earth than on the moon.

Surfaces that touch each other have a certain resistance to motion. This resistance is **friction.**

1. The materials that make up the surfaces will determine the magnitude of the frictional force.
2. The frictional force is independent of the area of contact between the two surfaces.
3. The direction of the frictional force is opposite to the direction of motion.
4. The frictional force is proportional to the normal force between the two surfaces in contact.

Static friction describes the force of friction of two surfaces that are in contact but do not have any motion relative to each other, such as a block sitting on an inclined plane. **Kinetic friction** describes the force of friction of two surfaces in contact with each other when there is relative motion between the surfaces. When an object moves in a circular path, a force must be directed toward the center of the circle in order to keep the motion going. This constraining force is called **centripetal force**. Gravity is the centripetal force that keeps a satellite circling the earth.

Electrical force is the influential power resulting from electricity as an attractive or repulsive interaction between two charged objects. The electric force is determined using Coulomb's law. As shown below, the appropriate unit on charge is the Coulomb (C) and the appropriate unit on distance is meters (m). Use of these units will result in a force expressed in units of Newtons. The demand for these units emerges from the units on Coulomb's constant.

$$F_{elect} = k \cdot Q_1 \cdot Q_2 / d^2$$

There is something of a mystery as to how objects affect each other when they are not in mechanical contact. Newton wrestled with the concept of "action-at-a-distance" (as Electrical Force is now classified) and eventually concluded that it was necessary for there to be some form of ether, or intermediate medium, which made it possible for one object to transfer force to another. We now know that no ether exists. It is possible for objects to exert forces on one another without any medium to transfer the force. From our fluid notion of electrical forces, however, we still associate forces as being due to the exchange of something between the two objects. The electrical field force acts between two charges, in the same way that the gravitational field force acts between two masses.

Magnetic Force- Magnetized items interact with other items in very specific ways. If a magnet is brought close enough to a ferromagnetic material (that is not magnetized itself) the magnet will strongly attract the ferromagnetic material regardless of orientation. Both the north and south pole of the magnet will attract the other item with equal strength. IN opposition, diamagnetic materials weakly repel a magnetic field. This occurs regardless of the north/south orientation of the field. Paramagnetic materials are weakly attracted to a magnetic field. This occurs regardless of the north/south orientation of the field. **Calculating** the attractive or repulsive magnetic force between two magnets is, in the general case, an extremely complex operation, as it depends on the shape, magnetization, orientation and separation of the magnets

In the **Nuclear Force** the protons in the nucleus of an atom are positively charged. If protons interact, they are usually pushed apart by the electromagnetic force. However, when two or more nuclei come VERY close together, the nuclear force comes into play. The nuclear force is a hundred times stronger than the electromagnetic force so the nuclear force may be able to "glue" the nuclei together so fusion can happen. The nuclear force is also known as the strong force. The nuclear force keeps together the most basic of elementary particles, the quarks. Quarks combine together to form the protons and neutrons in the atomic nucleus.

The **force of gravity** is the force at which the earth, moon, or other massively large object attracts another object towards itself. By definition, this is the weight of the object. All objects upon earth experience a force of gravity that is directed "downward" towards the center of the earth. The force of gravity on earth is always equal to the weight of the object as found by the equation:

Fgrav = m * g

where g = 9.8 m/s^2 (on Earth)

and m = mass (in kg)

Skill 34.6 Know that total energy in a system is conserved but may be changed from one form to another, as in an electrical motor or generator.

Electricity can be used to change the chemical composition of a material. For instance, when electricity is passed through water, it breaks the water down into hydrogen gas and oxygen gas.

Circuit breakers in a home monitor the electric current. If there is an overload, the circuit breaker will create an open circuit, stopping the flow of electricity. Computers can be made small enough to fit inside a plastic credit card by creating what is known as a solid state device. In this device, electrons flow through solid material such as silicon.

Resistors are used to regulate volume on a television or radio or through a dimmer switch for lights.

A bird can sit on an electrical wire without being electrocuted because the bird and the wire have about the same potential. However, if that same bird would touch two wires at the same time he would not have to worry about flying south next year.

When caught in an electrical storm, a car is a relatively safe place from lightening because of the resistance of the rubber tires. A metal building would not be safe unless there was a lightening rod that would attract the lightening and conduct it into the ground.

Skill 34.7   Understand the difference between heat and temperature, and understand temperature measurement systems.

Heat and temperature are different physical quantities. **Heat** is a measure of energy. **Temperature** is the measure of how hot (or cold) a body is with respect to a standard object.

Two concepts are important in the discussion of temperature changes. Objects are in thermal contact if they can affect each other's temperatures. Set a hot cup of coffee on a desk top. The two objects are in thermal contact with each other and will begin affecting each other's temperatures. The coffee will become cooler and the desktop warmer. Eventually, they will have the same temperature. When this happens, they are in **thermal equilibrium.**

We can not rely on our sense of touch to determine temperature because the heat from a hand may be conducted more efficiently by certain objects, making them feel colder. **Thermometers** are used to measure temperature. A small amount of mercury in a capillary tube will expand when heated. The thermometer and the object whose temperature it is measuring are put in contact long enough for them to reach thermal equilibrium. Then the temperature can be read from the thermometer scale.
Three temperature scales are used:

Celsius: The freezing point of water is set at 0 and the steam (boiling) point is 100. The interval between the two is divided into 100 equal parts called degrees Celsius.

Fahrenheit: The freezing point of water is 32 degrees and the boiling point is 212. The interval between is divided into 180 equal parts called degrees Fahrenheit.

Temperature readings can be converted from one to the other as follows.

Fahrenheit to Celsius	**Celsius to Fahrenheit**
$C = 5/9 (F - 32)$	$F = (9/5) C + 32$

Kelvin Scale has degrees the same size as the Celsius scale, but the zero point is moved to the triple point of water. Water inside a closed vessel is in thermal equilibrium in all three states (ice, water, and vapor) at 273.15 degrees Kelvin. This temperature is equivalent to .01 degrees Celsius. Because the degrees are the same in the two scales, temperature changes are the same in Celsius and Kelvin.

Temperature readings can be converted from Celsius to Kelvin:

Celsius to Kelvin	**Kelvin to Celsius**
K = C + 273.15	C = K - 273.15

Heat is a measure of energy. If two objects that have different temperatures come into contact with each other, heat flows from the hotter object to the cooler.

Heat Capacity of an object is the amount of heat energy that it takes to raise the temperature of the object by one degree.

Heat capacity (C) per unit mass (m) is called **specific heat** (c):

$$c = \frac{C}{m} = \frac{Q / \Delta}{m}$$

Specific heats for many materials have been calculated and can be found in tables.

There are a number of ways that heat is measured. In each case, the measurement is dependent upon raising the temperature of a specific amount of water by a specific amount. These conversions of heat energy and work are called the **mechanical equivalent of heat**.

The **calorie** is the amount of energy that it takes to raise one gram of water one degree Celsius.

The **kilocalorie** is the amount of energy that it takes to raise one kilogram of water by one degree Celsius. Food calories are kilocalories.

In the International System of Units **(SI),** the calorie is equal to 4.184 **joules**.

A **British thermal unit (BTU)** = 252 calories = 1.054 kJ

Skill 34.8   Know how heat may be transferred by conduction, convection, and radiation.

Electrostatics is the study of stationary electric charges. A plastic rod that is rubbed with fur or a glass rod that is rubbed with silk will become electrically charged and will attract small pieces of paper. The charge on the plastic rod rubbed with fur is negative and the charge on glass rod rubbed with silk is positive.

Electrically charged objects share these characteristics:

1. Like charges repel one another.
2. Opposite charges attract each other.
3. Charge is conserved. A neutral object has no net change. If the plastic rod and fur are initially neutral, when the rod becomes charged by the fur a negative charge is transferred from the fur to the rod. The net negative charge on the rod is equal to the net positive charge on the fur.

Materials through which electric charges can easily flow are called conductors. On the other hand, an **insulator** is a material through which electric charges do not move easily, if at all. A simple device used to indicate the existence of a positive or negative charge is called an **electroscope**. An electroscope is made up of a conducting knob and attached to it are very lightweight conducting leaves usually made of foil (gold or aluminum). When a charged object touches the knob, the leaves push away from each other because like charges repel. It is not possible to tell whether if the charge is positive or negative.

Charging by induction:
Touch the knob with a finger while a charged rod is nearby. The electrons will be repulsed and flow out of the electroscope through the hand. If the hand is removed while the charged rod remains close, the electroscope will retain the charge.

When an object is rubbed with a charged rod, the object will take on the same charge as the rod. However, charging by induction gives the object the opposite charge as that of the charged rod.

Grounding charge:
Charge can be removed from an object by connecting it to the earth through a conductor. The removal of static electricity by conduction is called **grounding**.

An **electric circuit** is a path along which electrons flow. A simple circuit can be created with a dry cell, wire, a bell, or a light bulb. When all are connected, the electrons flow from the negative terminal, through the wire to the device and back to the positive terminal of the dry cell. If there are no breaks in the circuit, the device will work. The circuit is closed. Any break in the flow will create an open circuit and cause the device to shut off.

The device (bell, bulb) is an example of a **load**. A load is a device that uses energy. Suppose that you also add a buzzer so that the bell rings when you press the buzzer button. The buzzer is acting as a **switch**. A switch is a device that opens or closes a circuit. Pressing the buzzer makes the connection complete and the bell rings. When the buzzer is not engaged, the circuit is open and the bell is silent.

A **series circuit** is one where the electrons have only one path along which they can move. When one load in a series circuit goes out, the circuit is open. An example of this is a set of Christmas tree lights that is missing a bulb. None of the bulbs will work.

A **parallel circuit** is one where the electrons have more than one path to move along. If a load goes out in a parallel circuit, the other load will still work because the electrons can still find a way to continue moving along the path.

When an electron goes through a load, it does work and therefore loses some of its energy. The measure of how much energy is lost is called the **potential difference**. The potential difference between two points is the work needed to move a charge from one point to another.

Potential difference is measured in a unit called the volt. **Voltage** is potential difference. The higher the voltage, the more energy the electrons have. This energy is measured by a device called a voltmeter. To use a voltmeter, place it in a circuit parallel with the load you are measuring.

Current is the number of electrons per second that flow past a point in a circuit. Current is measured with a device called an ammeter. To use an ammeter, put it in series with the load you are measuring.

As electrons flow through a wire, they lose potential energy. Some is changed into heat energy because of resistance. **Resistance** is the ability of the material to oppose the flow of electrons through it. All substances have some resistance, even if they are a good conductor such as copper. This resistance is measured in units called **ohms**. A thin wire will have more resistance than a thick one because it will have less room for electrons to travel. In a thicker wire, there will be more possible paths for the electrons to flow. Resistance also depends upon the length of the wire. The longer the wire, the more resistance it will have.

Potential difference, resistance, and current form a relationship know as **Ohm's Law**. Current **(I)** is measured in amperes and is equal to potential difference **(V)** divided by resistance **(R)**.

$$I = V / R$$

If you have a wire with resistance of 5 ohms and a potential difference of 75 volts, you can calculate the current by

I = 75 volts / 5 ohms
I = 15 amperes

A current of 10 or more amperes will cause a wire to get hot. 22 amperes is about the maximum for a house circuit. Anything above 25 amperes can start a fire.

Skill 34.9   Describe sources of light including the sun, light bulbs, or excited atoms and interactions of light with matter.

There are several types of light and they derive from many sources. A few of the more common ones are listed below:

Thermal emissions- Thermal light is emitted from a body at a characteristic temperature. This phenomenon is known as black body radiation. For example, the Sun is a star at 6000 K that emits visible light, sunlight. Similarly, incandescent light bulbs reach a certain temperature and emit visible light. The same phenomenon can be observed in coals glowing in an open fire. The color of visible light emitted depends upon the temperature of the body; as temperature increases, the wavelengths become shorter and so the color of the lights changes from red to white to blue.

Atomic emissions- Atoms can both emit and absorb light. Atoms of each element emit unique energies. The emissions can be spontaneous, as in neon lamps and signs or stimulated, as in lasers and masers.

Chemo-luminescence- Particular chemicals produce visible light and this phenomenon is known as chemo-luminescence. This is also sometimes seen in living things, where it is known as bioluminescence (fireflies, certain species of plankton).
Fluorescence- Some substances produce light when they are exposed to more energetic radiation. This phenomenon is seen in fluorescent light bulbs.

An entire field of science, optics, is devoted to the study of interaction of light and matter. There are applications for optics in eyeglasses, cameras, and microscopes. In all these technologies, light interacts with lenses and other optical equipment to magnify and/or clarify images. There are also natural examples of light-matter interaction such as rainbows (sunlight shining on droplets of water in the atmosphere) and photosynthesis (interaction of sunlight with chlorophyll to fix carbon and harness energy). Vision itself is caused by the interaction of light and photoreceptor cells in the retina.

Skill 34.10 Know and can apply the optical properties of waves, especially light and sound, including reflection or refraction.

Shadows illustrate one of the basic properties of light. Light travels in a straight line. If you put your hand between a light source and a wall, you will interrupt the light and produce a shadow.

When light hits a surface, it is **reflected.** The angle of the incoming light (angle of incidence) is the same as the angle of the reflected light (angle of reflection). It is this reflected light that allows you to see objects. You see the objects when the reflected light reaches your eyes.

Different surfaces reflect light differently. Rough surfaces scatter light in many different directions. A smooth surface reflects the light in one direction. If it is smooth and shiny (like a mirror) you see your image in the surface.
When light enters a different medium, it bends. This bending, or change of speed, is called **refraction**.

Light can be **diffracted**, or bent around the edges of an object. Diffraction occurs when light goes through a narrow slit. As light passes through it, the light bends slightly around the edges of the slit. You can demonstrate this by pressing your thumb and forefinger together, making a very thin slit between them. Hold them about 8 cm from your eye and look at a distant source of light. The pattern you observe is caused by the diffraction of light.

Wave **interference** occurs when two waves meet while traveling along the same medium. The medium takes on a shape resulting from the net effect of the individual waves upon the particles of the medium. There are two types of interference: constructive and destructive.

Constructive interference occurs when two crests or two troughs of the same shape meet. The medium will take on the shape of a crest or a trough with twice the amplitude of the two interfering crests or troughs. If a trough and a crest of the same shape meet, the two pulses will cancel each other out, and the medium will assume the equilibrium position. This is called **destructive** interference.

Destructive interference in sound waves will reduce the loudness of the sound. This is a disadvantage in rooms, such as auditoriums, where sound needs to be at its optimum. However, it can be used as an advantage in noise reduction systems. When two sound waves differing slightly in frequency are superimposed, beats are created by the alternation of constructive and destructive interference. The frequency of the beats is equal to the difference between the frequencies of the interfering sound waves.

Wave interference occurs with light waves in much the same manner that it does with sound waves. If two light waves of the same color, frequency, and amplitude are combined, the interference shows up as fringes of alternating light and dark bands. In order for this to happen, the light waves must come from the same source.

Wave-particle duality is the exhibition of both wavelike and particle-like properties by a single entity. Wave-particle duality is usually a quantum phenomenon relating to photons, electrons, and protons. Quantum mechanics shows that such objects sometimes behave like particles, sometimes like waves, and sometimes both. All objects exhibit wave-particle duality to some extent, but the larger the object the harder it is to observe. Individual molecules are often too large to show their quantum mechanical behavior.

An everyday example of wave-particle duality is sunlight. When standing in the sun, the shadow your body makes suggests that the light travels straight from the sun and is blocked by your body. Here the light is behaving like a collection of particles sent from the sun. However, if you take two pieces of glass with a little water between them and hold them in the sun, you will see fringes; these are formed by the interference of waves.

When a piano tuner tunes a piano, he only uses one tuning fork, even though there are many strings on the piano. He adjusts to first string to be the same as that of the tuning fork. Then he listens to the beats that occur when both the tuned and un-tuned strings are struck. He adjusts the un-tuned string until he can hear the correct number of beats per second. This process of striking the un-tuned and tuned strings together and timing the beats is repeated until all the piano strings are tuned.

Pleasant sounds have a regular wave pattern that is repeated over and over. Sounds that do not happen with regularity are unpleasant and are called **noise**. Change in experienced frequency due to relative motion of the source of the sound is called the **Doppler Effect.** When a siren approaches, the pitch is high. When it passes, the pitch drops. As a moving sound source approaches a listener, the sound waves are closer together, causing an increase in frequency in the sound that is heard. As the source passes the listener, the waves spread out and the sound experienced by the listener is lower.

Skill 34.11   Explain conservation of energy resources in terms of renewable and non-renewable natural resources and their use in society.

Humans have a tremendous impact on the world's natural resources. The world's natural water supplies are affected by human use. Waterways are major sources for recreation and freight transportation. Oil and wastes from boats and cargo ships pollute the aquatic environment. The aquatic plant and animal life is affected by this contamination. To obtain drinking water, contaminants such as parasites, pollutants and bacteria are removed from raw water through a purification process involving various screening, conditioning and chlorination steps. Most uses of water resources, such as drinking and crop irrigation, require fresh water. Only 2.5% of water on Earth is fresh water, and more than two thirds of this fresh water is frozen in glaciers and polar ice caps. Consequently, in many parts of the world, water use greatly exceeds supply. This problem is expected to increase in the future.

Plant resources also make up a large part of the world's natural resources. Plant resources are renewable and can be re-grown and restocked. Plant resources can be used by humans to make clothing, buildings and medicines, and can also be directly consumed. Forestry is the study and management of growing forests. This industry provides the wood that is essential for use as construction timber or paper. Cotton is a common plant found on farms of the Southern United States. Cotton is used to produce fabric for clothing, sheets, furniture, etc. Another example of a plant resource that is not directly consumed is straw, which is harvested for use in plant growth and farm animal care. The list of plants grown to provide food for the people of the world is extensive. Major crops include corn, potatoes, wheat, sugar, barley, peas, beans, beets, flax, lentils, sunflowers, soybeans, canola, and rice. These crops may have alternate uses as well. For example, corn is used to manufacture cornstarch, ethanol fuel, high fructose corn syrup, ink, biodegradable plastics, chemicals used in cosmetics and pharmaceuticals, adhesives, and paper products.

Other resources used by humans are known as "non-renewable" resources. Such resources, including fossil fuels, cannot be re-made and do not naturally reform at a rate that could sustain human use. Non-renewable resources are therefore depleted and not restored. Presently, non-renewable resources provide the main source of energy for humans. Common fossil fuels used by humans are coal, petroleum and natural gas, which all form from the remains of dead plants and animals through natural processes after millions of years. Because of their high carbon content, when burnt these substances generate high amounts of energy as well as carbon dioxide, which is released back into the atmosphere increasing global warming. To create electricity, energy from the burning of fossil fuels is harnessed to power a rotary engine called a turbine. Implementation of the use of fossil fuels as an energy source provided for large-scale industrial development.

Mineral resources are concentrations of naturally occurring inorganic elements and compounds located in the Earth's crust that are extracted through mining for human use. Minerals have a definite chemical composition and are stable over a range of temperatures and pressures. Construction and manufacturing rely heavily on metals and industrial mineral resources. These metals may include iron, bronze, lead, zinc, nickel, copper, tin, etc. Other industrial minerals are divided into two categories: bulk rocks and ore minerals. Bulk rocks, including limestone, clay, shale and sandstone, are used as aggregate in construction, in ceramics or in concrete. Common ore minerals include calcite, barite and gypsum. Energy from some minerals can be utilized to produce electricity fuel and industrial materials. Mineral resources are also used as fertilizers and pesticides in the industrial context.

Deforestation for urban development has resulted in the extinction or relocation of several species of plants and animals. Animals are forced to leave their forest homes or perish amongst the destruction. The number of plant and animal species that have become extinct due to deforestation is unknown. Scientists have only identified a fraction of the species on Earth. It is known that if the destruction of natural resources continues, there may be no plants or animals successfully reproducing in the wild.

The current energy crisis is largely centered on the uncertain future of fossil fuels. The supplies of fossil fuels are limited and fast declining. Additionally, most oil is now derived from a highly politically volatile area of the world. Finally, continuing to produce energy from fossils fuels is unwise given the damage done by both the disruption to the environment necessary to harvest them and the byproducts of their combustion cause pollution. The various detrimental effects of fossil fuels are listed later in this section.

It is important to recognize that a real energy crisis has vast economic implications. Oil, currently the most important fossil fuel, is needed for heating, electricity, and as a raw material for the manufacture of many items, particularly plastics. Additionally, the gasoline made from oil is important in transporting people and goods, including food and other items necessary for life. A disruption in the oil supply often causes rising prices in all sectors and may eventually trigger recession.

Alternative, sustainable energy sources must be found for both economic and ecological reasons.

DOMAIN II – LIFE SCIENCE

COMPETENCY 35.0 STRUCTURE OF LIVING ORGANISMS AND THEIR FUNCTION

Skill 35.1 **Describe levels of organization and related functions in plants and animals, including, organ systems, organs, tissues, cells, and sub-cellular organelles.**

The structure of the cell is often related to the cell's function. Root hair cells differ from flower stamens or leaf epidermal cells. They all have different functions.

Animal cells – begin a discussion of the nucleus as a round body inside the cell. It controls the cell's activities. The nuclear membrane contains threadlike structures called chromosomes. The genes are units that control cell activities found in the nucleus. The cytoplasm has many structures in it. Vacuoles contain the food for the cell. Other vacuoles contain waste materials. Animal cells differ from plant cells because they have cell membranes.

Plant cells – have cell walls. A cell wall differs from cell membranes. The cell membrane is very thin and is a part of the cell. The cell wall is thick and is a nonliving part of the cell. Chloroplasts are bundles of chlorophyll.

Skill 35.2 **Know structures and related functions of systems in plants and animals, such as reproductive, respiratory, circulatory, and digestive.**

Plant Tissues - specialization of tissues enabled plants to grow larger. Be familiar with the following tissues and their functions.

Xylem - transports water.

Phloem - transports food (glucose).

Cortex - storage of food and water.

Epidermis – protective covering.

Endodermis - controls movement between the cortex and the cell interior.

Pericycle - meristematic tissue which can divide when necessary.

Pith - storage in stems.

Sclerenchyma and collenchyma - support in stems.

Stomata - openings on the underside of leaves. They let carbon dioxide in and water out (transpiration).

Guard cells - control the size of the stomata. If the plant has to conserve water, the stomata will close.

Palisade mesophyll - contain chloroplasts in leaves. Site of photosynthesis.

Spongy mesophyll - open spaces in the leaf that allows for gas circulation.

Seed coat - protective covering on a seed.

Cotyledon - small seed leaf that emerges when the seed germinates.

Endosperm - food supply in the seed.

Apical meristem - this is an area of cell division allowing for growth.
Flowers are the reproductive organs of the plant. Know the following functions and locations:

Pedicel - supports the weight of the flower.

Receptacle - holds the floral organs at the base of the flower.

Sepals - green leaf like parts that cover the flower prior to blooming.

Petals - contain coloration by pigments, whose purpose is to attract insects to assist in pollination.

Anther - male part that produces pollen.

Filament - supports the anther; the filament and anther make up the **stamen**.

Stigma - female part that holds pollen grains that came from the male part.

Style - tube that leads to the ovary (female).

Ovary - contains the ovules; the stigma, style and ovary make up the **carpel**.

Skill 35.3   **Understand principles of chemistry underlying the functioning of biological systems.**

DNA and DNA REPLICATION

The modern definition of a gene is a unit of genetic information. DNA makes up genes which in turn make up the chromosomes. DNA is wound tightly around proteins in order to conserve space. The DNA/protein combination makes up the chromosome. DNA controls the synthesis of proteins, thereby controlling the total cell activity. DNA is capable of making copies of itself.

Review of DNA structure:

1. Made of nucleotides; a five carbon sugar, phosphate group and nitrogen base (either adenine, guanine, cytosine or thymine).
2. Consists of a sugar/phosphate backbone which is covalently bonded. The bases are joined down the center of the molecule and are attached by hydrogen bonds which are easily broken during replication.
3. The amount of adenine equals the amount of thymine and the amount of cytosine equals the amount of guanine.
4. The shape is that of a twisted ladder called a double helix. The sugar/phosphates make up the sides of the ladder and the base pairs make up the rungs of the ladder.

DNA Replication

Enzymes control each step of the replication of DNA. The molecule untwists. The hydrogen bonds between the bases break and serve as a pattern for replication. Free nucleotides found inside the nucleus join on to form a new strand. Two new pieces of DNA are formed which are identical. This is a very accurate process. There is only one mistake for every billion nucleotides added. This is because there are enzymes (polymerases) present that proofread the molecule. In eukaryotes, replication occurs in many places along the DNA at once. The molecule may open up at many places like a broken zipper. In prokaryotic circular plasmids, replication begins at a point on the plasmid and goes in both directions until it meets itself.

Base pairing rules are important in determining a new strand of DNA sequence. For example say our original strand of DNA had the sequence as follows:

1. A T C G G C A A T A G C   This may be called our sense strand as it contains a sequence that makes sense or codes for something. The complementary strand (or other side of the ladder) would follow base pairing rules (A bonds with T and C bonds with G) and would read:

2. T A G C C G T T A T C G   When the molecule opens up and nucleotides join on, the base pairing rules create two new identical strands of DNA

A T C G G C A A T A G C   and   A T C G G C A A T A G C
T A G C C G T T A T C G   T A G C C G T T A T C G

Protein Synthesis

It is necessary for cells to manufacture new proteins for growth and repair of the organism. Protein Synthesis is the process that allows the DNA code to be read and carried out of the nucleus into the cytoplasm in the form of RNA. This is where the ribosomes are found, which are the sites of protein synthesis. The protein is then assembled according to the instructions on the DNA. There are several types of RNA. Familiarize yourself with where they are found and their function.

Messenger RNA - (mRNA) copies the code from DNA in the nucleus and takes it to the ribosomes in the cytoplasm.

Transfer RNA - (tRNA) free floating in the cytoplasm. Its job is to carry and position amino acids for assembly on the ribosome.

Ribosomal RNA - (rRNA) found in the ribosomes. They make a place for the proteins to be made. rRNA is believed to have many important functions, so much research is currently being done currently in this area.

Along with enzymes and amino acids, the RNA's function is to assist in the building of proteins. There are two stages of protein synthesis:

Transcription - this phase allows for the assembly of mRNA and occurs in the nucleus where the DNA is found. The DNA splits open and the mRNA reads the code and "transcribes" the sequence onto a single strand of mRNA. For example, if the code on the DNA is T A C C T C G T A C G A , the mRNA will make a complementary strand reading: A U G G A G C A U G C U (Remember that uracil replaces thymine in RNA.) Each group of three bases is called a **codon**. The codon will eventually code for a specific amino acid to be carried to the ribosome. "Start" codons begin the building of the protein and "stop" codons end transcription. When the stop codon is reached, the mRNA separates from the DNA and leaves the nucleus for the cytoplasm.

Translation - this is the assembly of the amino acids to build the protein and occurs in the cytoplasm. The nucleotide sequence is translated to choose the correct amino acid sequence. As the rRNA translates the code at the ribosome, tRNA's that contain an **anticodon** seek out the correct amino acid and bring it back to the ribosome. For example, using the codon sequence from the example above:

the mRNA reads A U G / G A G / C A U / G C U
the anticodons are U A C / C U C / G U A / C G A
the amino acid sequence would be: Methionine (start) - Glu - His - Ala.

*Be sure to note if the table you are given is written according to the codon sequence or the anticodon sequence. It will be specified.

This whole process is accomplished through the assistance of **activating enzymes**. Each of the twenty amino acids has their own enzyme. The enzyme binds the amino acid to the tRNA. When the amino acids get close to each other on the ribosome, they bond together using peptide bonds. The start and stop codons are called nonsense codons. There is one start codon (AUG) and three stop codons. (UAA, UGA and UAG). Addition mutations will cause the whole code to shift, thereby producing the wrong protein or, at times, no protein at all.

COMPETENCY 36.0 LIVING AND NON-LIVING COMPONENTS IN ENVIRONMENTS

Skill 36.1 Know the characteristics of many living organisms.

Members of the five different kingdoms of the classification system of living organisms often differ in their basic life functions. Here we compare and analyze how members of the five kingdoms obtain nutrients, excrete waste, and reproduce.

Bacteria are prokaryotic, single-celled organisms that lack cell nuclei. The different types of bacteria obtain nutrients in a variety of ways. Most bacteria absorb nutrients from the environment through small channels in their cell walls and membranes (chemotrophs) while some perform photosynthesis (phototrophs). Chemo-organotrophs use organic compounds as energy sources while chemo-lithotrophs can use inorganic chemicals as energy sources. Depending on the type of metabolism and energy source, bacteria release a variety of waste products (e.g. alcohols, acids, carbon dioxide) to the environment through diffusion.

All bacteria reproduce through binary fission (asexual reproduction) producing two identical cells. Bacteria reproduce very rapidly, dividing or doubling every twenty minutes in optimal conditions. Asexual reproduction does not allow for genetic variation, but bacteria achieve genetic variety by absorbing DNA from ruptured cells and conjugating or swapping chromosomal or plasmid DNA with other cells.

Animals are multi-cellular, eukaryotic organisms. All animals obtain nutrients by eating food (ingestion). Different types of animals derive nutrients from eating plants, other animals, or both. Animal cells perform respiration that converts food molecules, mainly carbohydrates and fats, into energy. The excretory systems of animals, like animals themselves, vary in complexity. Simple invertebrates eliminate waste through a single tube, while complex vertebrates have a specialized system of organs that process and excrete waste.

Most animals, unlike bacteria, exist in two distinct sexes. Members of the female sex give birth or lay eggs. Some less developed animals can reproduce asexually. For example, flatworms can divide in two and some unfertilized insect eggs can develop into viable organisms. Most animals reproduce sexually through various mechanisms. For example, aquatic animals reproduce by external fertilization of eggs, while mammals reproduce by internal fertilization. More developed animals possess specialized reproductive systems and cycles that facilitate reproduction and promote genetic variation.

Plants, like animals, are multi-cellular, eukaryotic organisms. Plants obtain nutrients from the soil through their root systems and convert sunlight into energy through photosynthesis. Many plants store waste products in vacuoles or organs (e.g. leaves, bark) that are discarded. Some plants also excrete waste through their roots.

More than half of the plant species reproduce by producing seeds from which new plants grow. Depending on the type of plant, flowers or cones produce seeds. Other plants reproduce by spores, tubers, bulbs, buds, and grafts. The flowers of flowering plants contain the reproductive organs. Pollination is the joining of male and female gametes that is often facilitated by movement by wind or animals.

Fungi are eukaryotic, mostly multi-cellular organisms. All fungi are heterotrophs, obtaining nutrients from other organisms. More specifically, most fungi obtain nutrients by digesting and absorbing nutrients from dead organisms. Fungi secrete enzymes outside of their body to digest organic material and then absorb the nutrients through their cell walls.

Most fungi can reproduce asexually and sexually. Different types of fungi reproduce asexually by mitosis, budding, sporification, or fragmentation. Sexual reproduction of fungi is different from sexual reproduction of animals. The two mating types of fungi are plus and minus, not male and female. The fusion of hyphae, the specialized reproductive structure in fungi, between plus and minus types produces and scatters diverse spores.

Protists are eukaryotic, single-celled organisms. Most protists are heterotrophic, obtaining nutrients by ingesting small molecules and cells and digesting them in vacuoles. All protists reproduce asexually by either binary or multiple fission. Like bacteria, protists achieve genetic variation by exchange of DNA through conjugation.

Behavioral responses to external and internal stimuli in a variety of organisms

Response to stimuli is one of the key characteristics of any living thing. Any detectable change in the internal or external environment (the stimulus) may trigger a response in an organism. Just like physical characteristics, organisms" responses to stimuli are adaptations that allow them to better survive. While these responses may be more noticeable in animals that can move quickly, all organisms are actually capable of responding to changes.

Single celled organisms

These organisms are able to respond to basic stimuli such as the presence of light, heat, or food. Changes in the environment are typically sensed via cell surface receptors. These organisms may respond to such stimuli by making changes in internal biochemical pathways or initiating reproduction or phagocytosis. Those capable of simple motility, using flagella for instance, may respond by moving toward food or away from heat.

Plants

Plants typically do not possess sensory organs and so individual cells recognize stimuli through a variety of pathways. When many cells respond to stimuli together, a response becomes apparent. Logically then, the responses of plants occur on a rather longer timescale that those of animals. Plants are capable of responding to a few basic stimuli including light, water and gravity. Some common examples include the way plants turn and grow toward the sun, the sprouting of seeds when exposed to warmth and moisture, and the growth of roots in the direction of gravity.

Animals

Lower members of the animal kingdom have responses similar to those seen in single celled organisms. However, higher animals have developed complex systems to detect and respond to stimuli. The nervous system, sensory organs (eyes, ears, skin, etc), and muscle tissue all allow animals to sense and quickly respond to changes in their environment. As in other organisms, many responses to stimuli in animals are involuntary. For example, pupils dilate in response to the reduction of light. Such reactions are typically called reflexes. However, many animals are also capable of voluntary response. In many animal species, voluntary reactions are instinctual. For instance, a zebra's response to a lion is a voluntary one, but, instinctually, it will flee quickly as soon as the lion's presence is sensed. Complex responses, which may or may not be instinctual, are typically termed behavior. An example is the annual migration of birds when seasons change. Even more complex social behavior is seen in animals that live in large groups.

Skill 36.2   Understand the basic needs of all living organisms and can distinguish between environmental adaptations and accommodations.

See Skill 36.1

Skill 36.3   Describe the relationship between the number and types of organisms an ecosystem can support and relationships among members of a species and across species.

There are many interactions that may occur between different species living together. Predation, parasitism, competition, commensalisms, and mutualism are the different types of relationships populations have amongst each other.

Predation and **parasitism** result in a benefit for one species and a detriment for the other. Predation is when a predator eats its prey. The common conception of predation is of a carnivore consuming other animals. This is one form of predation. Although not always resulting in the death of the plant, herbivory is a form of predation. Some animals eat enough of a plant to cause death. Parasitism involves a predator that lives on or in their hosts, causing detrimental effects to the host. Insects and viruses living off and reproducing in their hosts is an example of parasitism. Many plants and animals have defenses against predators. Some plants have poisonous chemicals that will harm the predator if ingested and some animals are camouflaged so they are harder to detect.

Competition is when two or more species in a community use the same resources. Competition is usually detrimental to both populations. Competition is often difficult to find in nature because competition between two populations is not continuous. Either the weaker population will no longer exist, or one population will evolve to utilize other available resources.

Symbiosis is when two species live close together. Parasitism is one example of symbiosis described above. Another example of symbiosis is commensalisms. **Commensalism** occurs when one species benefits from the other without harmful effects. **Mutualism** is when both species benefit from the other. Species involved in mutualistic relationships must co-evolve to survive. As one species evolves, the other must as well if it is to be successful in life. The grouper and a species of shrimp live in a mutualistic relationship. The shrimp feed off parasites living on the grouper; thus the shrimp are fed and the grouper stays healthy. Many microorganisms are in mutualistic relationships.

The concepts of niche and carrying capacity
The term 'Niche' describes the relational position of a species or population in an ecosystem. Niche includes how a population responds to the abundance of its resources and enemies (e.g., by growing when resources are abundant and predators, parasites and pathogens are scarce).

Niche also indicates the life history of an organism, habitat and place in the food chain. According to the competitive exclusion principle, no two species can occupy the same niche in the same environment for a long time.

The full range of environmental conditions (biological and physical) under which an organism can exist describes its fundamental niche. Because of the pressure from superior competitors, superior are driven to occupy a niche much narrower than their previous niche. This is known as the 'realized niche'

Examples of niche:

1. Oak trees:
* live in forests
* absorb sunlight by photosynthesis
* provide shelter for many animals
* act as support for creeping plants
* serve as a source of food for animals
* cover their ground with dead leaves in the autumn
If the oak trees were cut down or destroyed by fire or storms they would no longer be doing their job and this would have a disastrous effect on all the other organisms living in the same habitat.

2. Hedgehogs:
* eat a variety of insects and other invertebrates which live underneath the dead leaves and twigs in the garden
* the spines are a superb environment for fleas and ticks
* put the nitrogen back into the soil when they urinate
* eat slugs and protect plants from them
If there were no hedgehogs around, the population of slugs would explode and the nutrients in the dead leaves and twigs will not recycled.

A **population** is a group of individuals of one species that live in the same general area. Many factors can affect the population size and its growth rate. Population size can depend on the total amount of life a habitat can support. This is the carrying capacity of the environment. Once the habitat runs out of food, water, shelter, or space, the carrying capacity decreases, and then stabilizes.

Limiting factors can affect population growth. As a population increases, the competition for resources is more intense, and the growth rate declines. This is a **density-dependent** growth factor. The carrying capacity can be determined by the density-dependent factor. **Density-independent factors** affect the individuals regardless of population size. The weather and climate are good examples. Too hot or too cold temperatures may kill many individuals from a population that has not reached its carrying capacity.

Human population increased slowly until 1650. Since 1650, the human population has grown almost exponentially, reaching its current population of over 6 billion. Factors that have led to this increased growth rate include improved nutrition, sanitation, and health care. In addition, advances in technology, agriculture, and scientific knowledge have made the use of resources more efficient and increased their availability.

While the Earth's ultimate carrying capacity for humans is uncertain, some factors that may limit growth are the availability of food, water, space, and fossil fuels. There is a finite amount of land on Earth available for food production. In addition, providing clean, potable water for a growing human population is a real concern. Finally, fossil fuels, important energy sources for human technology, are scarce. The inevitable shortage of energy in the Earth's future will require the development of alternative energy sources to maintain or increase human population growth.

Skill 36.4   Illustrate the flow of energy and matter through an ecosystem from sunlight to food chains and food webs.

Trophic levels are based on the feeding relationships that determine energy flow and chemical cycling.

Autotrophs are the primary produc[ ]   **Producers** mainly consist of plant[Decomposers]ers are [Tertiary Consumers] The primary consumers are the h[ ]ants or a[ ]sumers are the carnivores that eat the primary consumers. Tertiary consumers eat the secondary consumer. These trophic levels may go higher depending on the ecosystem. **Decomposers** are consumers that feed off animal waste and dead organisms. This pathway of food transfer is known as the food chain.

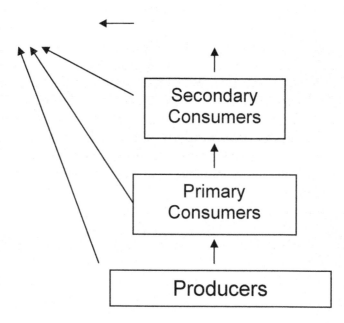

Most food chains are more elaborate, becoming food webs.

Energy is lost as the trophic levels progress from producer to tertiary consumer. The amount of energy that is transferred between trophic levels is called the ecological efficiency. The visual of this energy flow is represented in a **pyramid of productivity**.

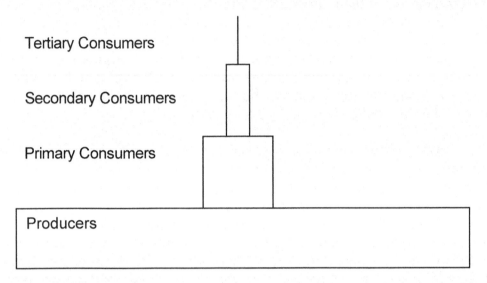

The **biomass pyramid** represents the total dry weight of organisms in each trophic level. A **pyramid of numbers** is a representation of the population size of each trophic level. The producers, being the most populous, are on the bottom of this pyramid with the tertiary consumers on the top with the fewest numbers.

Skill 36.5   Identify the resources available in an ecosystem, and describe the environmental factors that support the ecosystem, such as temperature, water, and soil composition.

Humans have a tremendous impact on the world's natural resources. The world's natural water supplies are affected by human use. Waterways are major sources for recreation and freight transportation. Oil and wastes from boats and cargo ships pollute the aquatic environment. The aquatic plant and animal life is affected by this contamination. To obtain drinking water, contaminants such as parasites, pollutants and bacteria are removed from raw water through a purification process involving various screening, conditioning and chlorination steps. Most uses of water resources, such as drinking and crop irrigation, require fresh water. Only 2.5% of water on Earth is fresh water, and more than two thirds of this fresh water is frozen in glaciers and polar ice caps. Consequently, in many parts of the world, water use greatly exceeds supply. This problem is expected to increase in the future.

Plant resources also make up a large part of the world's natural resources. Plant resources are renewable and can be re-grown and restocked. Plant resources can be used by humans to make clothing, buildings and medicines, and can also be directly consumed. Forestry is the study and management of growing forests. This industry provides the wood that is essential for use as construction timber or paper. Cotton is a common plant found on farms of the Southern United States. Cotton is used to produce fabric for clothing, sheets, furniture, etc. Another example of a plant resource that is not directly consumed is straw, which is harvested for use in plant growth and farm animal care. The list of plants grown to provide food for the people of the world is extensive. Major crops include corn, potatoes, wheat, sugar, barley, peas, beans, beets, flax, lentils, sunflowers, soybeans, canola, and rice. These crops may have alternate uses as well. For example, corn is used to manufacture cornstarch, ethanol fuel, high fructose corn syrup, ink, biodegradable plastics, chemicals used in cosmetics and pharmaceuticals, adhesives, and paper products.

Other resources used by humans are known as "non-renewable" resources. Such resources, including fossil fuels, cannot be re-made and do not naturally reform at a rate that could sustain human use. Non-renewable resources are therefore depleted and not restored. Presently, non-renewable resources provide the main source of energy for humans. Common fossil fuels used by humans are coal, petroleum and natural gas, which all form from the remains of dead plants and animals through natural processes after millions of years. Because of their high carbon content, when burnt these substances generate high amounts of energy as well as carbon dioxide, which is released back into the atmosphere increasing global warming. To create electricity, energy from the burning of fossil fuels is harnessed to power a rotary engine called a turbine. Implementation of the use of fossil fuels as an energy source provided for large-scale industrial development.

Mineral resources are concentrations of naturally occurring inorganic elements and compounds located in the Earth's crust that are extracted through mining for human use. Minerals have a definite chemical composition and are stable over a range of temperatures and pressures. Construction and manufacturing rely heavily on metals and industrial mineral resources. These metals may include iron, bronze, lead, zinc, nickel, copper, tin, etc. Other industrial minerals are divided into two categories: bulk rocks and ore minerals. Bulk rocks, including limestone, clay, shale and sandstone, are used as aggregate in construction, in ceramics or in concrete. Common ore minerals include calcite, barite and gypsum. Energy from some minerals can be utilized to produce electricity fuel and industrial materials. Mineral resources are also used as fertilizers and pesticides in the industrial context.

Deforestation for urban development has resulted in the extinction or relocation of several species of plants and animals. Animals are forced to leave their forest homes or perish amongst the destruction. The number of plant and animal species that have become extinct due to deforestation is unknown. Scientists have only identified a fraction of the species on Earth. It is known that if the destruction of natural resources continues, there may be no plants or animals successfully reproducing in the wild.

The current energy crisis is largely centered on the uncertain future of fossil fuels. The supplies of fossil fuels are limited and fast declining. Additionally, most oil is now derived from a highly politically volatile area of the world. Finally, continuing to produce energy from fossils fuels is unwise given the damage done by both the disruption to the environment necessary to harvest them and the byproducts of their combustion cause pollution. The various detrimental effects of fossil fuels are listed later in this section.

It is important to recognize that a real energy crisis has vast economic implications. Oil, currently the most important fossil fuel, is needed for heating, electricity, and as a raw material for the manufacture of many items, particularly plastics. Additionally, the gasoline made from oil is important in transporting people and goods, including food and other items necessary for life. A disruption in the oil supply often causes rising prices in all sectors and may eventually trigger recession.

Alternative, sustainable energy sources must be found for both economic and ecological reasons.

COMPETENCY 37.0 LIFE CYCLE, REPRODUCTION AND EVOLUTION

Skill 37.1   Diagram life cycles of familiar organisms.

A diagram of an organism's life cycle simply reveal the various stages through which it progresses from the time it is conceived until it reaches sexual maturity and reproduces, starting the cycle over again.   However, the various types of animals pass through very different phases of life.   The different species may either lay eggs or give life birth, pass through metamorphosis or be born in a form similar to that of an adult, and have aquatic and terrestrial phases or spend their entire lives on land. The diagrams of the sample animals listed above will give us a feel for the life cycles of insects, amphibians, and mammals. These diagrams also include the features of each life stage that make it unique.

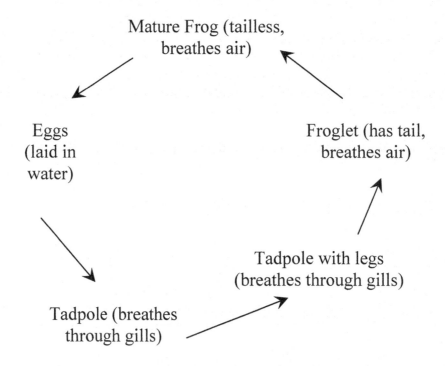

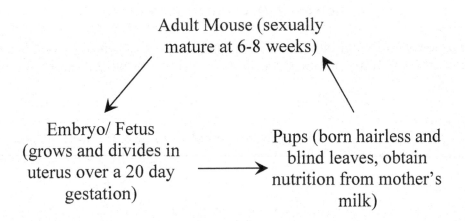

Adult Mouse (sexually mature at 6-8 weeks)

Embryo/ Fetus (grows and divides in uterus over a 20 day gestation)

Pups (born hairless and blind leaves, obtain nutrition from mother's milk)

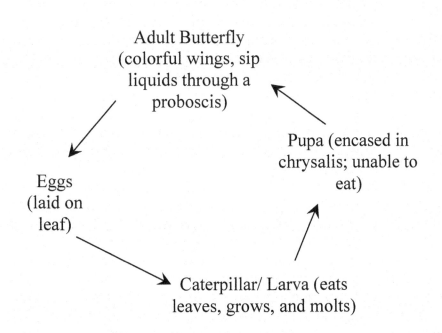

Adult Butterfly (colorful wings, sip liquids through a proboscis)

Pupa (encased in chrysalis; unable to eat)

Eggs (laid on leaf)

Caterpillar/ Larva (eats leaves, grows, and molts)

Skill 37.2   Explain the factors that affect the growth and development of plants, such as light, gravity, and stress.

While responses to stimuli may appear less dramatic in plants than in animals, they do occur at many points in the growth and development of plants.

A growth in response to stimuli is known as tropism. The actual growth associated with tropism is typically signaled by auxin, a plant hormone that stimulates cell elongation. Movements toward stimulus are termed positive tropisms and those away from a stimulus are negative tropisms. Below are a few examples:

Phototropism: This term refers the growth of plants in response to light. Phototropism is a positive tropism because a plant will bend and grow toward light. In this case, auxin moves to the side of plant away from the light, causing it to grown and bend the entire plant in the direction of the light.

Gravitropism: Gravity can act as either a positive or negative tropism: plant shoots grow away from gravity but plant roots grow toward it. Auxin is also involved in this tropism, though its role is less clearly understood.

Thigmotropism: This is the movement of plants in response to touch or contact with a surface. Thigmotropism occurs when plants grow on a surface, such as ivy or climb up a structure, such as sweet peas

Thigmorphogenesis: This term indicates a more significant change in the plant's growth that ultimately causes a change in its entire morphology. Thigmorphogensis is also a result pressure/touch. It occurs, for instance, in plants growing in windy areas and makes them short and fat and therefore, less susceptible to being blown down.

Similar stimuli trigger the development of a plant from a seed. That is, a seed may lie dormant for months or years, until the right combination of light, moisture, and temperature cause it to sprout and begin the growth of a new plant.

Finally, there are various natural and man-made stressors that can trigger changes in plants. These include: drought, low or high temperature, pH imbalance in the soil, too much or too little light, and phytotoxic compounds. How plants respond to these stimuli is largely dependant on the species of plant in question and may include mechanism to avoid, tolerate, or acclimate to the stress. Some examples include:

- Osmotic adjustments in response to drought; the vacuoles in the plants cells lose water and the plant wilts, freeing water for other purposes
- Production of antioxidants to repair damage done by oxidizing compounds such as ozone
- Production of heat shock proteins in response to excessively high temperatures

Skill 37.3 **Distinguish between sexual and asexual reproduction, and understand the process of cell division (mitosis), the types of cells and their functions, and the replication of plants and animals.**

The purpose of cell division is to provide growth and repair in body (somatic) cells and to replenish or create sex cells for reproduction. There are two forms of cell division. Mitosis is the division of somatic cells and **meiosis** is the division of sex cells (eggs and sperm).

Mitosis is divided into two parts: the **mitotic (M) phase** and **interphase**. In the mitotic phase, mitosis and cytokinesis divide the nucleus and cytoplasm, respectively. This phase is the shortest phase of the cell cycle. Interphase is the stage where the cell grows and copies the chromosomes in preparation for the mitotic phase. Interphase occurs in three stages of growth: **G1** (growth) period is when the cell is growing and metabolizing, the **S** period (synthesis) is where new DNA is being made and the **G2** phase (growth) is where new proteins and organelles are being made to prepare for cell division.

The mitotic phase is a continuum of change, although it is described as occurring in five stages: prophase, prometaphase, metaphase, anaphase, and telophase. During **prophase**, the cell proceeds through the following steps continuously, with no stopping. The chromatin condenses to become visible chromosomes. The nucleolus disappears and the nuclear membrane breaks apart. Mitotic spindles are formed which will eventually pull the chromosomes apart. They are composed of microtubules. The cytoskeleton breaks down and the spindles are pushed to the poles or opposite ends of the cell by the action of centrioles. During **prometaphase**, the nuclear membrane fragments and allows the spindle microtubules to interact with the chromosomes. Kinetochore fibers attach to the chromosomes at the centromere region. (Sometimes prometaphase is grouped with metaphase). When the centrosomes are at opposite ends of the cell, the division is in **metaphase**. The centromeres of all the chromosomes are aligned with one another. During **anaphase**, the centromeres split in half and homologous chromosomes separate. The chromosomes are pulled to the poles of the cell, with identical sets at either end. The last stage of mitosis is **telophase**. Here, two nuclei form with a full set of DNA that is identical to the parent cell. The nucleoli become visible and the nuclear membrane reassembles. A cell plate is seen in plant cells, whereas a cleavage furrow is formed in animal cells. The cell is pinched into two cells. Cytokinesis, or division of the cytoplasm and organelles, occurs.

Below is a diagram of mitosis.

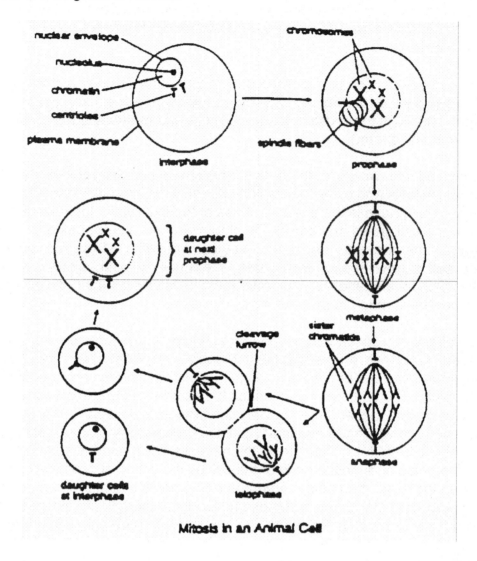

Mitosis in an Animal Cell

Meiosis is similar to mitosis, but there are two consecutive cell divisions, meiosis I and meiosis II in order to reduce the chromosome number by one half. This way, when the sperm and egg join during fertilization, the haploid number is reached.

Similar to mitosis, meiosis is preceded by an interphase during which the chromosome replicates. The steps of meiosis are as follows:

Prophase I – the replicated chromosomes condense and pair with homologues in a process called synapsis. This forms a tetrad. Crossing over, the exchange of genetic material between homologues to further increase diversity, occurs during prophase I.

Metaphase I – the homologous pairs attach to spindle fibers after lining up in the middle of the cell.

Anaphase I – the sister chromatids remain joined and move to the poles of the cell.

Telophase I – the homologous chromosome pairs continue to separate. Each pole now has a haploid chromosome set. Telophase I occurs simultaneously with cytokinesis. In animal cells, cleavage furrows form and cell plate appear in plant cells.

Prophase II – a spindle apparatus forms and the chromosomes condense.

Metaphase II – sister chromatids line up in center of cell. The centromeres divide and the sister chromatids begin to separate.

Anaphase II – the separated chromosomes move to opposite ends of the cell.

Telophase II – cytokinesis occurs, resulting in four haploid daughter cells.

Next you will find a diagram of meiosis.

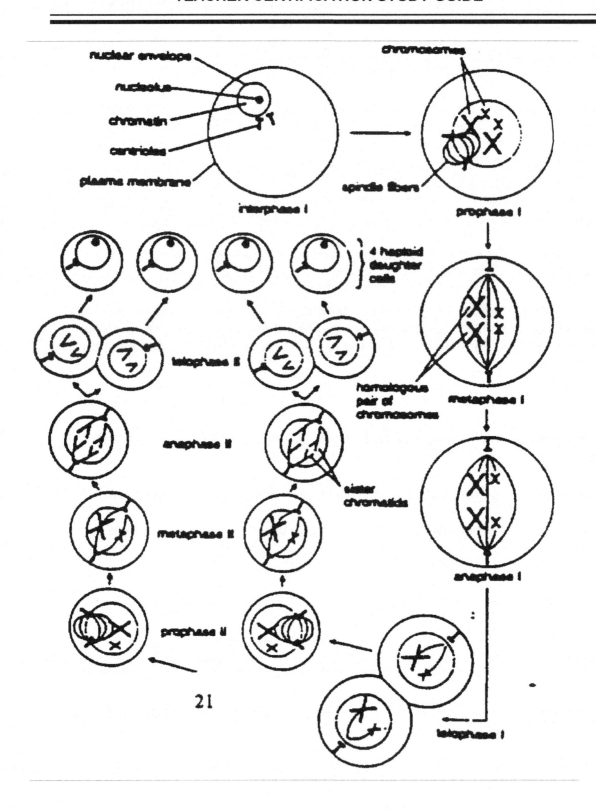

21

Skill 37.4   Distinguish between environmental and genetic sources of variation and understand the principles of natural and artificial selection.

Charles Darwin proposed a mechanism for his theory of evolution, which he termed natural selection. Natural selection describes the process by which favorable traits accumulate in a population, changing the population's genetic make-up over time. Darwin theorized that all individual organisms, even those of the same species, are different and those individuals that happen to possess traits favorable for survival would produce more offspring. Thus, in the next generation, the number of individuals with the favorable trait increases and the process continues. Darwin, in contrast to other evolutionary scientists, did not believe that traits acquired during an organism's lifetime (e.g. increased musculature) or the desires and needs of the organism affected evolution of populations. For example, Darwin argued that the evolution of long trunks in elephants resulted from environmental conditions that favored those elephants that possessed longer trunks. The individual elephants did not stretch their trunks to reach food or water and pass on the new, longer trunks to their offspring.

Jean Baptiste Lamarck proposed an alternative mechanism of evolution. Lamarck believed individual organisms developed traits in response to changing environmental conditions and passed on these new, favorable traits to their offspring. For example, Lamarck argued that the trunks of individual elephants lengthen as a result of stretching for scarce food and water, and elephants pass on the longer trunks to their offspring. Thus, in contrast to Darwin's relatively random natural selection, Lamarck believed the mechanism of evolution followed a predetermined plan and depended on the desires and needs of individual organisms.

Different molecular and environmental processes and conditions drive the evolution of populations. The various mechanisms of evolution either introduce new genetic variation or alter the frequency of existing variation.

Mutations, random changes in nucleotide sequence, are a basic mechanism of evolution. Mutations in DNA result from copying errors during cell division, exposure to radiation and chemicals, and interaction with viruses. Simple point mutations, deletions, or insertions can alter the function or expression of existing genes but do not contribute greatly to evolution. On the other hand, gene duplication, the duplication of an entire gene, often leads to the creation of new genes that may contribute to the evolution of a species. Because gene duplication results in two copies of the same gene, the extra copy is free to mutate and develop without the selective pressure experienced by mutated single-copy genes. Gene duplication and subsequent mutation often leads to the creation of new genes. When new genes resulting from mutations lend the mutated organism a reproductive advantage relative to environmental conditions, natural selection and evolution can occur.

Recombination is the exchange of DNA between a pair of chromosomes during meiosis. Recombination does not introduce new genes into a population, but does affect the expression of genes and the combination of traits expressed by individuals. Thus, recombination increases the genetic diversity of populations and contributes to evolution by creating new combinations of genes that nature selects for or against.

Isolation is the separation of members of a species by environmental barriers that the organisms cannot cross. Environmental change, either gradual or sudden, often results in isolation. An example of gradual isolation is the formation of a mountain range or dessert between members of a species. An example of sudden isolation is the separation of species members by a flood or earthquake. Isolation leads to evolution because the separated groups cannot reproduce together and differences arise. In addition, because the environment of each group is different, the groups adapt and evolve differently. Extended isolation can lead to speciation, the development of new species.

Sexual reproduction and selection contributes to evolution by consolidating genetic mutations and creating new combinations of genes. Genetic recombination during sexual reproduction, as previously discussed, introduces new combinations of traits and patterns of gene expression. Consolidation of favorable mutations through sexual reproduction speeds the processes of evolution and natural selection. On the other hand, consolidation of deleterious mutations creates completely unfit individuals that are readily eliminated from the population.

Genetic drift is, along with natural selection, one of the two main mechanisms of evolution. Genetic drift refers to the chance deviation in the frequency of alleles (traits) resulting from the randomness of zygote formation and selection. Because only a small percentage of all possible zygotes become mature adults, parents do not necessarily pass all of their alleles on to their offspring. Genetic drift is particularly important in small populations because chance deviations in allelic frequency can quickly alter the genotypic make-up of the population. In extreme cases, certain alleles may completely disappear from the gene pool. Genetic drift is particularly influential when environmental events and conditions produce small, isolated populations.

Plate tectonics is the theory that the Earth's surface consists of large plates. Movement and shifting of the plates dictate the location of continents, formation of mountains and seas, and volcanic and earthquake activity. Such contributions to environmental conditions influence the evolution of species. For example, tectonic activity resulting in mountain formation or continent separation can cause genetic isolation. In addition, the geographic distribution of species is indicative of evolutionary history and related tectonic activity.

Skill 37.5   Know how evidence from the fossil record, comparative anatomy, and DNA sequences can be used to support the theory that life gradually evolved on earth over billions of years.

The wide range of evidence of evolution provides information on the natural processes by which the variety of life on earth developed.

1. Paleontology: Paleontology is the study of past life based on fossil records and their relation to different geologic time periods. When organisms die, they often decompose quickly or are consumed by scavengers, leaving no evidence of their existence. However, occasionally some organisms are preserved. The remains or traces of the organisms from a past geological age embedded in rocks by natural processes are called fossils. They are very important for the understanding the evolutionary history of life on earth as they provide evidence of evolution and detailed information on the ancestry of organisms.

Petrification is the process by which a dead animal gets fossilized. For this to happen, a dead organism must be buried quickly to avoid weathering and decomposition. When the organism is buried, the organic matter decays. The mineral salts from the mud (in which the organism is buried) will infiltrate into the bones and gradually fill up the pores. The bones will harden and be preserved as fossils. If dead organisms are covered by wind- blown sand and if the and is subsequently turned into mud by heavy rain or floods, the same process of mineral infiltration may occur. Besides petrification, the organisms may be well preserved in ice, in hardened resin of coniferous trees (amber), in tar, in anaerobic acidic peat. Fossilization can sometimes be a trace, an impression of a form – e.g., leaves and footprints.

From the horizontal layers of sedimentary rocks (these are formed by silt or mud on top of each other) called strata and each layer consists of fossils. The oldest layer is the one at the bottom of the pile and the fossils found in this layer are the oldest and this is how the paleontologists determine the relative ages of these fossils.

Some organisms appear in some layers only indicating that thy lived only during that period and became extinct. A succession of animals and plants can also be seen in fossil records, which supports the theory that organisms tend to progressively increase in complexity.

According to fossil records, some modern species of plants and animals are found to be almost identical to the species that lived in ancient geological ages. They are existing species of ancient lineage that have remained unchanged morphologically and may be physiologically as well. Hence they're called "living fossils". Some examples of living fossils are tuatara, nautilus, horseshoe crab, gingko and metasequoia.

2. Anatomy: Comparative anatomical studies reveal that some structural features are basically similar – e.g., flowers generally have sepals, petals, stigma, style and ovary but the size, color, number of petals, sepals etc., may differ from species to species.

The degree of resemblance between two organisms indicates how closely they are related in evolution. Groups with little in common are supposed to have diverged from a common ancestor much earlier in geological history than groups which have more in common. To decide how closely two organisms are related, anatomists look for the structures which may serve different purpose in the adult, but are basically similar (homologous). In cases where similar structures serve different functions in adults, it is important to trace their origin and embryonic development

When a group of organisms share a homologous structure, which is specialized, to perform a variety of functions in order to adapt to different environmental conditions are called adaptive radiation. The gradual spreading of organisms with adaptive radiation is known as divergent evolution. Examples of divergent evolution are – pentadactyl limb and insect mouthparts.

Under similar environmental conditions, fundamentally different structures in different groups of organisms may undergo modifications to serve similar functions. This is called convergent evolution. The structures, which have no close phylogenetic links but showing adaptation to perform the same functions, are called analogous. Examples are – wings of bats, bird and insects, jointed legs of insects and vertebrates, eyes of vertebrates and cephalopods.

Vestigial organs: Organs that are smaller and simpler in structure than corresponding parts in the ancestral species are called vestigial organs. They are usually degenerated or underdeveloped. These were functional in ancestral species but no have become non functional, e.g., vestigial hind limbs of whales, vestigial leaves of some xerophytes, vestigial wings of flightless birds like ostriches, etc.

3. Geographical distribution:

Continental distribution: All organisms are adapted to their environment to a greater or lesser extent. It is generally assumed that the same type of species would be found in a similar habitat in a similar geographic area.

Examples: Africa has short tailed (old world) monkeys, elephants, lions and giraffes. South America has long-tailed monkeys, pumas, jaguars and llamas

Evidence for migration and isolation: The fossil record shows that evolution of camels started in North America, from which they migrated across the Bering strait into Asia and Africa and through the Isthmus o Panama into south America.

Continental drift: Fossils of the ancient amphibians, arthropods and ferns are found in South America, Africa, India, Australia and Antarctica which can be dated to the Paleozoic Era, at which time they were all in a single landmass called Gondwana.

Oceanic Island distribution: Most small isolated islands only have native species. Plant life in Hawaii could have arrived as airborne spores or as seeds in the droppings of birds. A few large mammals present in remote islands were brought by human settlers.

4. Evidence from comparative embryology: Comparative embryology shows how embryos start off looking the same. As they develop their similarities slowly decrease until they take the form of their particular class.
Example: Adult vertebrates are diverse, yet their embryos are quite similar at very early stages. Fishlike structures still form in early embryos of reptiles, birds and mammals. In fish embryos, a two-chambered heart, some veins, and parts of arteries develop and persist in adult fishes. The same structures form early in human embryos but do not persist as in adults.

5. Physiology and Biochemistry:
Evolution of widely distributed proteins and molecules: All organisms make use of DNA and/or RNA. ATP is the metabolic currency. Genetic code is same for almost every organism. A piece of RNA in a bacterium cell codes for the same protein as in a human cell.

Comparison of the DNA sequence allows organisms to be grouped by sequence similarity, and the resulting phylogenetic trees are typically consistent with traditional taxonomy, and are often used to strengthen or correct taxonomic classifications. DNA sequence comparison is considered strong enough to b used to correct erroneous assumptions in the phylogenetic tree in cases where other evidence is missing. The sequence of the 168rRNA gene, a vital gene encoding a part of the ribosome was used to find the broad phylogenetic relationships between all life.

The proteomic evidence also supports the universal ancestry of life. Vital proteins such as ribosome, DNA polymerase, and RNA polymerase are found in the most primitive bacteria to the most complex mammals. Since metabolic processes do not leave fossils, research into the evolution of the basic cellular processes is done largely by comparison of existing organisms.

Skill 37.6   Understand the basis of Darwin's theory, that species evolved by a process of natural selection.

See Skill 36.4.

DOMAIN III – EARTH AND SPACE SCIENCE

COMPETENCY 38.0 THE SOLAR SYSTEM AND THE UNIVERSE

Skill 38.1   **Identify and describe the planets, their motion, and that of other planetary bodies around the sun.**

There are eight established planets in our solar system; Mercury, Venus, Earth, Mars, Jupiter, Saturn, Uranus, and Neptune. Pluto was an established planet in our solar system, but as of Summer 2006, it's status is being reconsidered. The planets are divided into two groups based on distance from the sun. The inner planets include: Mercury, Venus, Earth, and Mars. The outer planets include: Jupiter, Saturn, Uranus, and Neptune.

Mercury -- the closest planet to the sun. Its surface has craters and rocks. The atmosphere is composed of hydrogen, helium and sodium. Mercury was named after the Roman messenger god.

Venus -- has a slow rotation when compared to Earth. Venus and Uranus rotate in opposite directions from the other planets. This opposite rotation is called retrograde rotation. The surface of Venus is not visible due to the extensive cloud cover. The atmosphere is composed mostly of carbon dioxide. Sulfuric acid droplets in the dense cloud cover give Venus a yellow appearance. Venus has a greater greenhouse effect than observed on Earth. The dense clouds combined with carbon dioxide trap heat. Venus was named after the Roman goddess of love.

Earth -- considered a water planet with 70% of its surface covered by water. Gravity holds the masses of water in place. The different temperatures observed on earth allow for the different states (solid. Liquid, gas) of water to exist. The atmosphere is composed mainly of oxygen and nitrogen. Earth is the only planet that is known to support life.

Mars -- the surface of Mars contains numerous craters, active and extinct volcanoes, ridges, and valleys with extremely deep fractures. Iron oxide found in the dusty soil makes the surface seem rust colored and the skies seem pink in color. The atmosphere is composed of carbon dioxide, nitrogen, argon, oxygen and water vapor. Mars has polar regions with ice caps composed of water. Mars has two satellites. Mars was named after the Roman war god.

Jupiter -- largest planet in the solar system. Jupiter has 16 moons. The atmosphere is composed of hydrogen, helium, methane and ammonia. There are white colored bands of clouds indicating rising gas and dark colored bands of clouds indicating descending gases. The gas movement is caused by heat resulting from the energy of Jupiter's core. Jupiter has a Great Red Spot that is thought to be a hurricane type cloud. Jupiter has a strong magnetic field.

Saturn -- the second largest planet in the solar system. Saturn has rings of ice, rock, and dust particles circling it. Saturn's atmosphere is composed of hydrogen, helium, methane, and ammonia. Saturn has 20 plus satellites. Saturn was named after the Roman god of agriculture.

Uranus -- the second largest planet in the solar system with retrograde revolution. Uranus is a gaseous planet. It has 10 dark rings and 15 satellites. Its atmosphere is composed of hydrogen, helium, and methane. Uranus was named after the Greek god of the heavens.

Neptune -- another gaseous planet with an atmosphere consisting of hydrogen, helium, and methane. Neptune has 3 rings and 2 satellites. Neptune was named after the Roman sea god because its atmosphere is the same color as the seas.

Pluto – once considered the smallest planet in the solar system; its status as a planet is being reconsidered . Pluto's atmosphere probably contains methane, ammonia, and frozen water. Pluto has 1 satellite. Pluto revolves around the sun every 250 years. Pluto was named after the Roman god of the underworld.

Comets, asteroids, and meteors

Astronomers believe that rocky fragments may have been the remains of the birth of the solar system that never formed into a planet. **Asteroids** are found in the region between Mars and Jupiter.

Comets are masses of frozen gases, cosmic dust, and small rocky particles. Astronomers think that most comets originate in a dense comet cloud beyond Pluto. Comet consists of a nucleus, a coma, and a tail. A comet's tail always points away from the sun. The most famous comet, **Halley's Comet,** is named after the person whom first discovered it in 240 B.C. It returns to the skies near earth every 75 to 76 years.

Meteoroids are composed of particles of rock and metal of various sizes. When a meteoroid travels through the earth's atmosphere, friction causes its surface to heat up and it begins to burn. The burning meteoroid falling through the earth's atmosphere is called a **meteor** (also known as a "shooting star").

Meteorites are meteors that strike the earth's surface. A physical example of a meteorite's impact on the earth's surface can be seen in Arizona. The Barringer Crater is a huge meteor crater. There are many other meteor craters throughout the world.

Oort Cloud and Kuiper Belt

The **Oort Cloud** is a hypothetical spherical cloud surrounding our solar system. It extends approximately 3 light years or 30 trillion kilometers from the Sun. The cloud is believed to be made up of materials ejected out of the inner solar system because of interaction with Uranus and Neptune, but is gravitationally bound to the Sun. It is named the Oort Cloud after Jan Oort who suggested its existence in 1950. Comets from the Oort Cloud exhibit a wide range of sizes, inclinations and eccentricities and are often referred to as Long-Period Comets because they have a period of greater than 200 years.

It seems that the Oort Cloud objects were formed closer to the Sun than the Kuiper Belt objects. Small objects formed near the giant planets would have been ejected from the solar system by gravitational encounters. Those that didn't escape entirely formed the distant Oort Cloud. Small objects formed farther out had no such interactions and remained as the Kuiper Belt objects.

The **Kuiper Belt** is the name given to a vast population of small bodies orbiting the sun beyond Neptune. There are more than 70,000 of these small bodies with diameters larger than 100 km extending outwards from the orbit of Neptune to 50AU. They exist mostly within a ring or belt surrounding the sun. It is believed that the objects in the Kuiper Belt are primitive remnants of the earliest phases of the solar system. It is also believed that the Kuiper Belt is the source of many Short-Period Comets (periods of less then 200 years). It is a reservoir for the comets in the same way that the Oort Cloud is a reservoir for Long-Period Comets.

Occasionally the orbit of a Kuiper Belt object will be disturbed by the interactions of the giant planets in such a way as to cause the object to cross the orbit of Neptune. It will then very likely have a close encounter with Neptune sending it out of the solar system or into an orbit crossing those of the other giant planets or even into the inner solar system. Prevailing theory states that scattered disk objects began as Kuiper belt objects, which were scattered through gravitational interactions with the giant planets.

Skill 38.2   Explain time zones in terms of longitude and the rotation of the earth, and understand the reasons for changes in the observed position of the sun and moon in the sky during the course of the day and from season to season.

Earth is the third planet away from the sun in our solar system. Earth's numerous types of motion and states of orientation greatly effect global conditions, such as seasons, tides and lunar phases. The Earth orbits the Sun with a period of 365 days. During this orbit, the average distance between the Earth and Sun is 93 million miles. The shape of the Earth's orbit around the Sun deviates from the shape of a circle only slightly. This deviation, known as the Earth's eccentricity, has a very small affect on the Earth's climate. The Earth is closest to the Sun at perihelion, occurring around January 2nd of each year, and farthest from the Sun at aphelion, occurring around July 2nd. Because the Earth is closest to the sun in January, the northern winter is slightly warmer than the southern winter.

Seasons
The rotation axis of the Earth is not perpendicular to the orbital (ecliptic) plane. The axis of the Earth is tilted 23.45° from the perpendicular. The tilt of the Earth's axis is known as the obliquity of the ecliptic, and is mainly responsible for the four seasons of the year by influencing the intensity of solar rays received by the Northern and Southern Hemispheres. The four seasons, spring, summer, fall and winter, are extended periods of characteristic average temperature, rainfall, storm frequency and vegetation growth or dormancy. The effect of the Earth's tilt on climate is best demonstrated at the solstices, the two days of the year when the Sun is farthest from the Earth's equatorial plane. At the Summer Solstice (June Solstice), the Earth's tilt on its axis causes the Northern Hemisphere to the lean toward the Sun, while the southern hemisphere leans away. Consequently, the Northern Hemisphere receives more intense rays from the Sun and experiences summer during this time, while the Southern Hemisphere experiences winter. At the Winter Solstice (December Solstice), it is the Southern Hemisphere that leans toward the sun and thus experiences summer. Spring and fall are produced by varying degrees of the same leaning toward or away from the Sun.

Tides
The orientation of and gravitational interaction between the Earth and the Moon are responsible for the ocean tides that occur on Earth. The term "tide" refers to the cyclic rise and fall of large bodies of water. Gravitational attraction is defined as the force of attraction between all bodies in the universe. At the location on Earth closest to the Moon, the gravitational attraction of the Moon draws seawater toward the Moon in the form of a tidal bulge. On the opposite side of the Earth, another tidal bulge forms in the direction away from the Moon because at this point, the Moon's gravitational pull is the weakest.

"Spring tides" are especially strong tides that occur when the Earth, Sun and Moon are in line, allowing both the Sun and the Moon to exert gravitational force on the Earth and increase tidal bulge height. These tides occur during the full moon and the new moon. "Neap tides" are especially weak tides occurring when the gravitational forces of the Moon and the Sun are perpendicular to one another. These tides occur during quarter moons.

Lunar Phases

The Earth's orientation in respect to the solar system is also responsible for our perception of the phases of the moon. As the Earth orbits the Sun with a period of 365 days, the Moon orbits the Earth every 27 days. As the moon circles the Earth, its shape in the night sky appears to change. The changes in the appearance of the moon from Earth are known as "lunar phases." These phases vary cyclically according to the relative positions of the Moon, the Earth and the Sun. At all times, half of the Moon is facing the Sun and is thus illuminated by reflecting the Sun's light. As the Moon orbits the Earth and the Earth orbits the Sun, the half of the moon that faces the Sun changes. However, the Moon is in synchronous rotation around the Earth, meaning that nearly the same side of the moon faces the Earth at all times. This side is referred to as the near side of the moon. Lunar phases occur as the Earth and Moon orbit the Sun and the fractional illumination of the Moon's near side changes.

When the Sun and Moon are on opposite sides of the Earth, observers on Earth perceive a "full moon," meaning the moon appears circular because the entire illuminated half of the moon is visible. As the Moon orbits the Earth, the Moon "wanes" as the amount of the illuminated half of the Moon that is visible from Earth decreases. A gibbous moon is between a full moon and a half moon, or between a half moon and a full moon. When the Sun and the Moon are on the same side of Earth, the illuminated half of the moon is facing away from Earth, and the moon appears invisible. This lunar phase is known as the "new moon." The time between each full moon is approximately 29.53 days.

A list of all lunar phases includes:
- New Moon: the moon is invisible or the first signs of a crescent appear
- Waxing Crescent: the right crescent of the moon is visible
- First Quarter: the right quarter of the moon is visible
- Waxing Gibbous: only the left crescent is not illuminated
- Full Moon: the entire illuminated half of the moon is visible
- Waning Gibbous: only the right crescent of the moon is not illuminated
- Last Quarter: the left quarter of the moon is illuminated
- Waning Crescent: only the left crescent of the moon is illuminated

Viewing the moon from the Southern Hemisphere would cause these phases to occur in the opposite order.

Skill 38.3   **Name and describe bodies in the universe including the sun, stars, and galaxies.**

Astronomers use groups or patterns of stars called **constellations** as reference points to locate other stars in the sky. Familiar constellations include: Ursa Major (also known as the big bear) and Ursa Minor (known as the little bear). Within the Ursa Major, the smaller constellation, The Big Dipper is found. Within the Ursa Minor, the smaller constellation, The Little Dipper is found.

Different constellations appear as the earth continues its revolution around the sun with the seasonal changes.

Magnitude stars are 21 of the brightest stars that can be seen from earth. These are the first stars noticed at night. In the Northern Hemisphere there are 15 commonly observed first magnitude stars.

A vast collection of stars are defined as **galaxies**. Galaxies are classified as irregular, elliptical, and spiral. An irregular galaxy has no real structured appearance; most are in their early stages of life. An elliptical galaxy consists of smooth ellipses, containing little dust and gas, but composed of millions or trillion stars. Spiral galaxies are disk-shaped and have extending arms that rotate around its dense center. Earth's galaxy is found in the Milky Way and it is a spiral galaxy.

A **pulsar** is defined as a variable radio source that emits signals in very short, regular bursts; believed to be a rotating neutron star.

A **quasar** is defined as an object that photographs like a star but has an extremely large redshift and a variable energy output; believed to be the active core of a very distant galaxy.

Black holes are defined as an object that has collapsed to such a degree that light can not escape from its surface; light is trapped by the intense gravitational field.

Origin of the Solar System
Two main hypotheses of the origin of the solar system are: (1) the tidal hypothesis and (2) the condensation hypothesis.

The tidal hypothesis proposes that the solar system began with a near collision of the sun and a large star. Some astronomers believe that as these two stars passed each other, the great gravitational pull of the large star extracted hot gases out of the sun. The mass from the hot gases started to orbit the sun, which began to cool then condensing into the nine planets. (Few astronomers support this example).

The condensation hypothesis proposes that the solar system began with rotating clouds of dust and gas. Condensation occurred in the center forming the sun and the smaller parts of the cloud formed the nine planets. (This example is widely accepted by many astronomers).

Two main theories to explain the origins of the universe include: (1) **The Big Bang Theory** and (2) **The Steady-State Theory.**

The Big Bang Theory has been widely accepted by many astronomers. It states that the universe originated from a magnificent explosion spreading mass, matter and energy into space. The galaxies formed from this material as it cooled during the next half-billion years.

The Steady-State Theory is the least accepted theory. It states that the universe is a continuously being renewed. Galaxies move outward and new galaxies replace the older galaxies. Astronomers have not found any evidence to prove this theory.

The future of the universe is hypothesized with the Oscillating Universe Hypothesis. It states that the universe will oscillate or expand and contract. Galaxies will move away from one another and will in time slow down and stop. Then a gradual moving toward each other will again activate the explosion or The Big Bang theory.

The stages of life for a star starts with a mass of gas and dust that becomes a nebula, then a main sequence star. Next it becomes a red giant, then a nova and then in its final stages, a white dwarf (the dying core of a giant star), a neutron star or a black hole.

The forces of gravity acting on particles of gas and dust in a cloud in an area of space produce stars. This cloud is called a nebula. Particles in this cloud attract each other and as it grows its temperature increases. With the increased temperature the star begins to glow. Fusion occurs in the core of the star releasing radiant energy at the star's surface.

When hydrogen becomes exhausted in a small, or even an average star, its core will collapse and cause its temperature to rise. This released heat causes nearby gases to heat, contract, carry out fusion, and produce helium. Stars at this stage are nearing the end of their life. These stars are called red giants; also called supergiants. A white dwarf is the dying core of a giant star. A nova is an ordinary star that experiences a sudden increase in brightness and then fades back to its original brightness. A supernova radiates even greater light energy. A neutron star is the result of mass left behind after a supernova. A black hole is a star with condensed matter and gravity so intense that light can not escape.

COMPETENCY 39.0 THE STRUCTURE AND COMPOSITION OF THE EARTH

Skill 39.1 Describe the formation and observable physical characteristics of minerals and different types of rocks.

A fossil is the remains or trace of an ancient organism that has been preserved naturally in the Earth's crust. Sedimentary rocks usually are rich sources of fossil remains. Those fossils found in layers of sediment were embedded in the slowly forming sedimentary rock strata. The oldest fossils known are the traces of 3.5 billion year old bacteria found in sedimentary rocks. Few fossils are found in metamorphic rock and virtually none found in igneous rocks. The magma is so hot that any organism trapped in the magma is destroyed.

The fossil remains of a woolly mammoth embedded in ice were found by a group of Russian explorers. However, the best-preserved animal remains have been discovered in natural tar pits. When an animal accidentally fell into the tar, it became trapped sinking to the bottom. Preserved bones of the saber-toothed cat have been found in tar pits.

Prehistoric insects have been found trapped in ancient amber or fossil resin that was excreted by some extinct species of pine trees.
Fossil molds are the hollow spaces in a rock previously occupied by bones or shells. A fossil cast is a fossil mold that fills with sediments or minerals that later hardens forming a cast.

Fossil tracks are the imprints in hardened mud left behind by birds or animals.

The three major subdivisions of rocks are sedimentary, metamorphic and igneous.

Lithification of sedimentary rocks
When fluid sediments are transformed into solid sedimentary rocks, the process is known as **lithification**. One very common process affecting sediments is compaction where the weights of overlying materials compress and compact the deeper sediments. The compaction process leads to cementation. **Cementation** is when sediments are converted to sedimentary rock.
Factors in crystallization of igneous rocks

Igneous rocks can be classified according to their texture, their composition, and the way they formed.

Molten rock is called magma. When molten rock pours out onto the surface of Earth, it is called lava.

As magma cools, the elements and compounds begin to form crystals. The slower the magma cools, the larger the crystals grow. Rocks with large crystals are said to have a coarse-grained texture. Granite is an example of a coarse grained rock. Rocks that cool rapidly before any crystals can form have a glassy texture such as obsidian, also commonly known as volcanic glass.

Metamorphic rocks are formed by high temperatures and great pressures. The process by which the rocks undergo these changes is called metamorphism. The outcome of metamorphic changes include deformation by extreme heat and pressure, compaction, destruction of the original characteristics of the parent rock, bending and folding while in a plastic stage, and the emergence of completely new and different minerals due to chemical reactions with heated water and dissolved minerals.

Metamorphic rocks are classified into two groups, foliated (leaf-like) rocks and unfoliated rocks. Foliated rocks consist of compressed, parallel bands of minerals, which give the rocks a striped appearance. Examples of such rocks include slate, schist, and gneiss. Unfoliated rocks are not banded and examples of such include quartzite, marble, and anthracite rocks.

Minerals are natural, non-living solids with a definite chemical composition and a crystalline structure. **Ores** are minerals or rock deposits that can be mined for a profit. **Rocks** are earth materials made of one or more minerals. A **Rock Facies** is a rock group that differs from comparable rocks (as in composition, age or fossil content).

Characteristics by which minerals are classified.

Minerals must adhere to five criteria. They must be (1) non-living, (2) formed in nature, (3) solid in form, (4) their atoms form a crystalline pattern, (5) its chemical composition is fixed within narrow limits.
There are over 3000 minerals in Earth's crust. Minerals are classified by composition. The major groups of minerals are silicates, carbonates, oxides, sulfides, sulfates, and halides. The largest group of minerals is the silicates. Silicates are made of silicon, oxygen, and one or more other elements.

Soil
Soils are composed of particles of sand, clay, various minerals, tiny living organisms, and humus, plus the decayed remains of plants and animals. Soils are divided into three classes according to their texture. These classes are sandy soils, clay soils, and loamy soils.

Sandy soils are gritty, and their particles do not bind together firmly. Sandy soils are porous- water passes through them rapidly. Sandy soils do not hold much water.

Clay soils are smooth and greasy, their particles bind together firmly. Clay soils are moist and usually do not allow water to pass through easily.
Loamy soils feel somewhat like velvet and their particles clump together. Loamy soils are made up of sand, clay, and silt. Loamy soils holds water but some water can pass through.

In addition to three main classes, soils are further grouped into three major types based upon their composition. These groups are pedalfers, pedocals, and laterites.

Pedalfers form in the humid, temperate climate of the eastern United States. Pedalfer soils contain large amounts of iron oxide and aluminum-rich clays, making the soil a brown to reddish brown color. This soil supports forest type vegetation.

Pedocals are found in the western United States where the climate is dry and temperate. These soils are rich in calcium carbonate. This type of soil supports grasslands and brush vegetation.

Laterites are found where the climate is wet and tropical. Large amounts of water flows through this soil. Laterites are red-orange soils rich in iron and aluminum oxides. There is little humus and this soil is not very fertile.

Minerals

Minerals are natural inorganic compounds. They are solid with homogenous crystal structures. Crystal structures are the 3-D geometric arrangements of atoms within minerals. Though these mineral grains are often too small to see, they can be visualized by X-ray diffraction. Both chemical composition and crystal structure determine mineral type. The chemical composition of minerals can vary from purely elemental to simple salts to complex compounds. However, it is possible for two or more minerals to have identical chemical composition, but varied crystal structure. Such minerals are known as polymorphs. One example of polymorphs demonstrates how crystal structures influence the physical properties of minerals with the same chemical composition: diamonds and graphite. Both are made from carbon, but diamonds are extremely hard because the carbon atoms are arranged in a strong 3-D network while graphite is soft because the carbon atoms are present in sheets that slide past one another. There are over 4,400 minerals on Earth, which are organized into the following classes:

Silicate minerals are composed mostly of silicon and oxygen. This is the most abundant class of minerals on Earth and includes quartz, garnets, micas, and feldspars.

Carbonate class are formed from compounds including carbonate ions (including calcium carbonate, magnesium carbonate, and iron carbonate). They are common in marine environments, in caves (stalactite and stalagmites), and anywhere minerals can form via dissolution and precipitation. Nitrate and borate minerals are also in this class.

Sulfate minerals contain sulfate ions and are formed near bodies of water where slow evaporation allows precipitation of sulfates and halides. Sulfates include celestite, barite, and gypsum.

Halide minerals include all minerals formed from natural salts including calcium fluoride, sodium chloride, and ammonium chloride. Like the sulfides, these minerals are typically formed in evaporative settings. Minerals in this class include fluorite, halite, and sylvite.

Oxide class minerals contain oxide compounds including iron oxide, magnetite oxide, and chromium oxide. They are formed by various processes including precipitation and oxidation of other minerals. These minerals form many ores and are important in mining. Hematite, chromite, rutile, and magnetite are all examples of oxide minerals.

Sulfide minerals are formed from sulfide compounds such as iron sulfide, nickel iron sulfide and lead sulfide. Several important metal ores are members of this class. Minerals in this class include pyrite (fool's gold) and galena. Phosphate class includes not only those containing phosphate ions, but any mineral with a tetrahedral molecular geometry in which an element is surrounded by four oxygen atoms. This can include elements such as phosphorous, arsenic, and antimony. Minerals in this class are important biologically, as they are common in teeth and bones. Phosphate, arsenate, vanadate, and antimonite minerals are all in this class.

Element class minerals are formed from pure elements, whether they are metallic, semi-metallic or non-metallic. Accordingly, minerals in this class include gold, silver, copper, bismuth, and graphite as well as natural alloys such as electrum and carbides.

Rocks
Rocks are simply aggregates of minerals. Rocks are classified by their differences in chemical composition and mode of formation. Generally, three classes are recognized: igneous, sedimentary, and metamorphic. However, it is common that one type of rock is transformed into another and this is known as the rock cycle.

Igneous rocks are formed from molten magma. There are two types of igneous rock: volcanic and plutonic. As the name suggest, volcanic rock is formed when magma reaches the Earth's surface as lava. Plutonic rock is also derived from magma, but it is formed when magma cools and crystallizes beneath surface of the Earth. Thus, both types of igneous rock are magma that has cooled either above (volcanic) or below (plutonic) the Earth's crust. Examples of this type of rock include granite and obsidian glass.

Sedimentary rocks are formed by the layered deposition of inorganic and/or organic matter. Layers, or strata, of rock are laid down horizontally to form sedimentary rocks. Sedimentary rocks that form as mineral solutions (i.e., sea water) evaporate are called precipitate. Those that contain the remains of living organisms are termed biogenic. Finally, those that form from the freed fragments of other rocks are called clastic. Because the layers of sedimentary rocks reveal chronology and often contain fossils, these types of rock have been key in helping scientists understand the history of the earth. Chalk, limestone, sandstone, and shale are all examples of sedimentary rock.

Metamorphic rocks are created when rocks are subjected to high temperatures and pressures. The original rock, or protolith, may have been igneous, sedimentary or even an older metamorphic rock. The temperatures and pressures necessary to achieve transformation are higher than those observed on the Earth's surface and are high enough to alter the minerals in the protolith. Because these rocks are formed within the Earth's crust, studying metamorphic rocks gives us clues to conditions in the Earth's mantle. In some metamorphic rocks, different colored bands are apparent. These result from strong pressures being applied from specific directions and is termed foliation. Examples of metamorphic rock include slate and marble.

Skill 39.2   Identify characteristics of landforms, such as mountains, rivers, deserts, and oceans.

See Skill 39.5

Skill 39.3   Explain chemical and physical weathering, erosion, deposition, and other rock forming and soil changing processes and the formation and properties of different types of soils and rocks.

Erosion is the inclusion and transportation of surface materials by another moveable material, usually water, wind, or ice. The most important cause of erosion is running water. Streams, rivers, and tides are constantly at work removing weathered fragments of bedrock and carrying them away from their original location.

A stream erodes bedrock by the grinding action of the sand, pebbles and other rock fragments. This grinding against each other is called abrasion.

Streams also erode rocks by dissolving or absorbing their minerals. Limestone and marble are readily dissolved by streams.

The breaking down of rocks at or near to the earth's surface is known as **weathering**. Weathering breaks down these rocks into smaller and smaller pieces. There are two types of weathering: physical weathering and chemical weathering.

Physical weathering is the process by which rocks are broken down into smaller fragments without undergoing any change in chemical composition. Physical weathering is mainly caused by the freezing of water, the expansion of rock, and the activities of plants and animals.

Frost wedging is the cycle of daytime thawing and refreezing at night. This cycle causes large rock masses, especially the rocks exposed on mountain tops, to be broken into smaller pieces.

The peeling away of the outer layers from a rock is called exfoliation. Rounded mountain tops are called exfoliation domes and have been formed in this way. Chemical weathering is the breaking down of rocks through changes in their chemical composition. An example would be the change of feldspar in granite to clay. Water, oxygen, and carbon dioxide are the main agents of chemical weathering. When water and carbon dioxide combine chemically, they produce a weak acid that breaks down rocks.

Deposition, also known as sedimentation, is the term for the process by which material from one area is slowly deposited into another area. This is usually due to the movement of wind, water, or ice containing particles of matter. When the rate of movement slows down, particles filter out and remain behind, causing a build up of matter. Note that this is a result of matter being eroded and removed from another site.

Skill 39.4 Describe layers of the earth and plate tectonics, including its convective source.

Data obtained from many sources led scientists to develop the theory of plate tectonics. This theory is the most current model that explains not only the movement of the continents, but also the changes in the earth's crust caused by internal forces.

Plates are rigid blocks of earth's crust and upper mantle. These rigid solid blocks make up the lithosphere. The earth's lithosphere is broken into nine large sections and several small ones. These moving slabs are called plates. The major plates are named after the continents they are "transporting."

The plates float on and move with a layer of hot, plastic-like rock in the upper mantle. Geologists believe that the heat currents circulating within the mantle cause this plastic zone of rock to slowly flow, carrying along the overlying crustal plates.

Movement of these crustal plates creates areas where the plates diverge as well as areas where the plates converge. A major area of divergence is located in the Mid-Atlantic. Currents of hot mantle rock rise and separate at this point of divergence creating new oceanic crust at the rate of 2 to 10 centimeters per year. Convergence is when the oceanic crust collides with either another oceanic plate or a continental plate. The oceanic crust sinks forming an enormous trench and generating volcanic activity. Convergence also includes continent to continent plate collisions. When two plates slide past one another a transform fault is created.

These movements produce many major features of the earth's surface, such as mountain ranges, volcanoes, and earthquake zones. Most of these features are located at plate boundaries, where the plates interact by spreading apart, pressing together, or sliding past each other. These movements are very slow, averaging only a few centimeters a year.

Boundaries form between spreading plates where the crust is forced apart in a process called rifting. Rifting generally occurs at mid-ocean ridges. Rifting can also take place within a continent, splitting the continent into smaller landmasses that drift away from each other, thereby forming an ocean basin between them. The Red Sea is a product of rifting. As the seafloor spreading takes place, new material is added to the inner edges of the separating plates. In this way the plates grow larger, and the ocean basin widens. This is the process that broke up the super continent Pangaea and created the Atlantic Ocean.
Boundaries between plates that are colliding are zones of intense crustal activity. When a plate of ocean crust collides with a plate of continental crust, the more dense oceanic plate slides under the lighter continental plate and plunges into the mantle. This process is called **subduction**, and the site where it takes place is called a subduction zone. A subduction zone is usually seen on the sea-floor as a deep depression called a trench.

The crustal movement which is identified by plates sliding sideways past each other produces a plate boundary characterized by major faults that are capable of unleashing powerful earth-quakes. The San Andreas Fault forms such a boundary between the Pacific Plate and the North American Plate.

Skill 39.5   **Explain how mountains are created and why volcanoes and earthquakes occur, and describe their mechanisms and effects.**

Orogeny is the term given to natural mountain building.

A mountain is terrain that has been raised high above the surrounding landscape by volcanic action, or some form of tectonic plate collisions. The plate collisions could be intercontinental or ocean floor collisions with a continental crust (subduction). The physical composition of mountains would include igneous, metamorphic, or sedimentary rocks; some may have rock layers that are tilted or distorted by plate collision forces.

There are many different types of mountains. The physical attributes of a mountain range depends upon the angle at which plate movement thrust layers of rock to the surface. Many mountains (Adirondacks, Southern Rockies) were formed along high angle faults.
Folded mountains (Alps, Himalayas) are produced by the folding of rock layers during their formation. The Himalayas are the highest mountains in the world and contain Mount Everest which rises almost 9 km above sea level. The Himalayas were formed when India collided with Asia. The movement which created this collision is still in process at the rate of a few centimeters per year.

Fault-block mountains (Utah, Arizona, and New Mexico) are created when plate movement produces tension forces instead of compression forces. The area under tension produces normal faults and rock along these faults is displaced upward.

Dome mountains are formed as magma tries to push up through the crust but fails to break the surface. Dome mountains resemble a huge blister on the earth's surface.

Upwarped mountains (Black Hills of S.D.) are created in association with a broad arching of the crust. They can also be formed by rock thrust upward along high angle faults.

Volcanism is the term given to the movement of magma through the crust and its emergence as lava onto the earth's surface. Volcanic mountains are built up by successive deposits of volcanic materials.

An active volcano is one that is presently erupting or building to an eruption. A dormant volcano is one that is between eruptions but still shows signs of internal activity that might lead to an eruption in the future. An extinct volcano is said to be no longer capable of erupting. Most of the world's active volcanoes are found along the rim of the Pacific Ocean, which is also a major earthquake zone. This curving belt of active faults and volcanoes is often called the Ring of Fire.

The world's best known volcanic mountains include: Mount Etna in Italy and Mount Kilimanjaro in Africa. The Hawaiian Islands are actually the tops of a chain of volcanic mountains that rise from the ocean floor.

There are three types of volcanic mountains: shield volcanoes, cinder cones and composite volcanoes.

Shield Volcanoes are associated with quiet eruptions. Lava emerges from the vent or opening in the crater and flows freely out over the earth's surface until it cools and hardens into a layer of igneous rock. A repeated lava flow builds this type of volcano into the largest volcanic mountain. Mauna Loa found in Hawaii, is the largest volcano on earth.

Cinder Cone Volcanoes are associated with explosive eruptions as lava is hurled high into the air in a spray of droplets of various sizes. These droplets cool and harden into cinders and particles of ash before falling to the ground. The ash and cinder pile up around the vent to form a steep, cone-shaped hill called the cinder cone. Cinder cone volcanoes are relatively small but may form quite rapidly.

Composite Volcanoes are described as being built by both lava flows and layers of ash and cinders. Mount Fuji in Japan, Mount St. Helens in Washington, USA and Mount Vesuvius in Italy are all famous composite volcanoes.

Mechanisms of producing mountains

Mountains are produced by different types of mountain-building processes. Most major mountain ranges are formed by the processes of folding and faulting.

Folded Mountains are produced by the folding of rock layers. Crustal movements may press horizontal layers of sedimentary rock together from the sides, squeezing them into wavelike folds. Up-folded sections of rock are called anticlines; down-folded sections of rock are called synclines. The Appalachian Mountains are an example of folded mountains with long ridges and valleys in a series of anticlines and synclines formed by folded rock layers.

Faults are fractures in the earth's crust which have been created by either tension or compression forces transmitted through the crust. These forces are produced by the movement of separate blocks of crust.

Faultings are categorized on the basis of the relative movement between the blocks on both sides of the fault plane. The movement can be horizontal, vertical or oblique.

A dip-slip fault occurs when the movement of the plates is vertical and opposite. The displacement is in the direction of the inclination, or dip, of the fault. Dip-slip faults are classified as normal faults when the rock above the fault plane moves down relative to the rock below.

Reverse faults are created when the rock above the fault plane moves up relative to the rock below. Reverse faults having a very low angle to the horizontal are also referred to as thrust faults.

Faults in which the dominant displacement is horizontal movement along the trend or strike (length) of the fault are called **strike-slip faults**. When a large strike-slip fault is associated with plate boundaries it is called a **transform fault**. The San Andreas Fault in California is a well-known transform fault.

Faults that have both vertical and horizontal movement are called **oblique-slip faults**.

When lava cools, igneous rock is formed. This formation can occur either above ground or below ground.

Intrusive rock includes any igneous rock that was formed below the earth's surface. Batholiths are the largest structures of intrusive type rock and are composed of near granite materials; they are the core of the Sierra Nevada Mountains.

Extrusive rock includes any igneous rock that was formed at the earth's surface.

Dikes are old lava tubes formed when magma entered a vertical fracture and hardened. Sometimes magma squeezes between two rock layers and hardens into a thin horizontal sheet called a **sill**. A **laccolith** is formed in much the same way as a sill, but the magma that creates a laccolith is very thick and does not flow easily. It pools and forces the overlying strata creating an obvious surface dome.

A **caldera** is normally formed by the collapse of the top of a volcano. This collapse can be caused by a massive explosion that destroys the cone and empties most if not all of the magma chamber below the volcano. The cone collapses into the empty magma chamber forming a caldera.

An inactive volcano may have magma solidified in its pipe. This structure, called a volcanic neck, is resistant to erosion and today may be the only visible evidence of the past presence of an active volcano.

When lava cools, igneous rock is formed. This formation can occur either above ground or below ground.

Glaciation

A continental glacier covered a large part of North America during the most recent ice age. Evidence of this glacial coverage remains as abrasive grooves, large boulders from northern environments dropped in southerly locations, glacial troughs created by the rounding out of steep valleys by glacial scouring, and the remains of glacial sources called **cirques** that were created by frost wedging the rock at the bottom of the glacier. Remains of plants and animals found in warm climate have been discovered in the moraines and out wash plains help to support the theory of periods of warmth during the past ice ages.

The Ice Age began about 2 -3 million years ago. This age saw the advancement and retreat of glacial ice over millions of years. Theories relating to the origin of glacial activity include Plate Tectonics, where it can be demonstrated that some continental masses, now in temperate climates, were at one time blanketed by ice and snow. Another theory involves changes in the earth's orbit around the sun, changes in the angle of the earth's axis, and the wobbling of the earth's axis. Support for the validity of this theory has come from deep ocean research that indicates a correlation between climatic sensitive micro-organisms and the changes in the earth's orbital status.

About 12,000 years ago, a vast sheet of ice covered a large part of the northern United States. This huge, frozen mass had moved southward from the northern regions of Canada as several large bodies of slow-moving ice, or glaciers. A time period in which glaciers advance over a large portion of a continent is called an ice age. A glacier is a large mass of ice that moves or flows over the land in response to gravity. Glaciers form among high mountains and in other cold regions.

There are two main types of glaciers: valley glaciers and continental glaciers. Erosion by valley glaciers is characteristic of U-shaped erosion. They produce sharp peaked mountains such as the Matterhorn in Switzerland. Erosion by continental glaciers often rides over mountains in their paths leaving smoothed, rounded mountains and ridges.

Skill 39.6 Know the commonly cited evidence supporting the theory of plate tectonics.

See Skill 39.4

Skill 39.7 **Identify factors influencing the location and intensity of earthquakes, and describe the effects of plate tectonic motion over time on climate, geography, and distribution of organisms, as well as more general changes on the earth over geologic time as evidenced in landforms and the rock and fossil records, including plant and animal extinction.**

What is an earthquake?
An earthquake is a destructive force, brought about by the interactions and movements between the earth's tectonic plates. Often occurring among the plate edges, earthquakes range from being destructive to barely noticeable. If the intensity is high, there could be loss of life and damage to properties.

Factors influencing the location of earthquakes:
1. Plate convergence, divergence or sliding past one another: These are the most important reasons for earthquakes to occur.
2. Volcanic activity: Areas with earthquakes coincide with areas with volcanic activity.
3. Percent Distribution of earthquakes: 70% of the earthquakes occur in the Circum - Pacific region and 20% in the belt stretching from the Himalayan mountains to the Mediterranean Sea. The remaining 10% occur in divergent plate boundaries such as the Mid - Atlantic Ridge.

Factors influencing the intensity of the earthquakes:
1. Magnitude of earthquake: Of the estimated 6000earthquakes a year, only 50 cause huge damage to people and properties and these are above 6.0 on the Richter scale.
2. Depth of focus: Earthquakes which have a focus around 70 Km deep are the most devastating and destructive.
3. Proximity to the epicenter: Areas closer to the epicenter suffer huge damages than the areas farther away.
4. Geology of epicenter: An epicenter made of soft rocks will suffer more damage than epicenter made of hard rocks.
5. Types of buildings: Weaker and older buildings are a threat many lives as opposed to buildings reinforced to withstand earthquakes.

Before we discuss Plate tectonics and their effect on climate etc. it is important for us to understand the meaning for Plate tectonics.

Plate tectonics is a theory of geology which was developed to explain the observed evidence for large scale motion within the earth's crust. This theory superseded the older theory of Continental Drift by Alfred Wagener of Germany. The outermost part of the earth's crust is made up of two layers: above is the lithosphere, comprising the rigid uppermost part of the mantle. Below the lithosphere lies the athenosphere, which is a more viscous zone of the mantle.

The influence of plate tectonics on climate, geography and distribution of organisms:

Plate boundaries are commonly associated with geological events such as earthquakes, mountains, volcanoes, and oceanic trenches.

The left or right lateral motion of one plate against another along transform faults can cause highly visible surface effects such as earthquakes along transform boundaries. A good example of this is the San Andreas Fault in North America.

The evidence for the movement of plates is found in the observations of the distribution of same species of plants in areas like western Africa and the eastern part of South America. The same type of fossils and fauna were also found in areas, which were supposed to be one piece before the continents drifted away. Similar observations were recorded regarding the climate.

Basing on all these, we can conclude that the earth is made up of several plates and the plates got separated and are in the present form as continents and we have evidences in the distribution of flora and fauna.

COMPETENCY 40.0 THE EARTH'S ATMOSPHERE

Skill 40.1   **Explain the influence and role of the sun and oceans in weather and climate and the role of the water cycle and describe the causes and effects of air movements and ocean currents on daily and seasonal weather.**

El Niño refers to a sequence of changes in the ocean and atmospheric circulation across the Pacific Ocean. The water around the equator is unusually hot every two to seven years. Trade winds normally blow east to west across the equatorial latitudes, piling warm water into the western Pacific. A huge mass of heavy thunderstorms usually forms in the area and produces vast currents of rising air that displace heat poleward. This helps create the strong mid-latitude jet streams. The world's climate patterns are disrupted by this change in location of thunderstorm activity.

Air masses moving toward or away from the Earth's surface are called air currents. Air moving parallel to Earth's surface is called **wind**. Weather conditions are generated by winds and air currents carrying large amounts of heat and moisture from one part of the atmosphere to another. Wind speeds are measured by instruments called anemometers.

The wind belts in each hemisphere consist of convection cells that encircle Earth like belts. There are three major wind belts on Earth: (1) trade winds (2) prevailing westerlies, and (3) polar easterlies. Wind belt formation depends on the differences in air pressures that develop in the doldrums, the horse latitudes, and the polar regions. The Doldrums surround the equator. Within this belt heated air usually rises straight up into Earth's atmosphere. The Horse latitudes are regions of high barometric pressure with calm and light winds and the polar regions contain cold dense air that sinks to the Earth's surface.

Winds caused by local temperature changes include sea breezes, and land breezes.

Sea breezes are caused by the unequal heating of the land and an adjacent, large body of water. Land heats up faster than water. The movement of cool ocean air toward the land is called a sea breeze. Sea breezes usually begin blowing about mid-morning; ending about sunset.
A breeze that blows from the land to the ocean or a large lake is called a **land breeze.**

Monsoons are huge wind systems that cover large geographic areas and that reverse direction seasonally. The monsoons of India and Asia are examples of these seasonal winds. They alternate wet and dry seasons. As denser cooler air over the ocean moves inland, a steady seasonal wind called a summer or wet monsoon is produced.

The air temperature at which water vapor begins to condense is called the **dew point.**

Relative humidity is the actual amount of water vapor in a certain volume of air compared to the maximum amount of water vapor this air could hold at a given temperature.

Knowledge of types of storms

A **thunderstorm** is a brief, local storm produced by the rapid upward movement of warm, moist air within a cumulonimbus cloud. Thunderstorms always produce lightning and thunder, and are accompanied by strong wind gusts and heavy rain or hail.

A severe storm with swirling winds that may reach speeds of hundreds of km per hour is called a **tornado**. Such a storm is also referred to as a "twister". The sky is covered by large cumulonimbus clouds and violent thunderstorms; a funnel-shaped swirling cloud may extend downward from a cumulonimbus cloud and reach the ground. Tornadoes are storms that leave a narrow path of destruction on the ground.

A swirling, funnel-shaped cloud that **extends** downward and touches a body of water is called a **waterspout.**

Hurricanes are storms that develop when warm, moist air carried by trade winds rotates around a low-pressure "eye". A large, rotating, low-pressure system accompanied by heavy precipitation and strong winds is called a tropical cyclone (better known as a hurricane). In the Pacific region, a hurricane is called a typhoon.

Storms that occur only in the winter are known as blizzards or ice storms. A **blizzard** is a storm with strong winds, blowing snow and frigid temperatures. An **ice storm** consists of falling rain that freezes when it strikes the ground, covering everything with a layer of ice.

COMPETENCY 41.0 THE EARTH'S WATER

Skill 41.1   **Compare the characteristics of bodies of water, such as rivers, lakes, oceans, and estuaries, describe and explain the tides mechanisms causing and modifying them, such as the gravitational attraction of the moon, sun, and coastal topography.**

Seventy percent of the earth's surface is covered with saltwater which is termed the hydrosphere. The mass of this saltwater is about 1.4×10^{24} grams. The ocean waters continuously circulate among different parts of the hydrosphere. There are seven major oceans: the North Atlantic Ocean, South Atlantic Ocean, North Pacific Ocean, South Pacific Ocean, Indian Ocean, Arctic Ocean, and the Antarctic Ocean.

Pure water is a combination of the elements hydrogen and oxygen. These two elements make up about 96.5% of ocean water. The remaining portion is made up of dissolved solids. The concentration of these dissolved solids determines the water's salinity.

Salinity is the number of grams of these dissolved salts in 1,000 grams of sea water. The average salinity of ocean water is about 3.5%. In other words, one kilogram of sea water contains about 35 grams of salt. Sodium Chloride or salt (NaCl) is the most abundant of the dissolved salts. The dissolved salts also include smaller quantities of magnesium chloride, magnesium and calcium sulfates, and traces of several other salt elements. Salinity varies throughout the world oceans; the total salinity of the oceans varies from place to place and also varies with depth. Salinity is low near river mouths where the ocean mixes with fresh water, and salinity is high in areas of high evaporation rates.

The temperature of the ocean water varies with different latitudes and with ocean depths. Ocean water temperature is about constant to depths of 90 meters (m). The temperature of surface water will drop rapidly from 28° C at the equator to -2° C at the Poles. The freezing point of sea water is lower than the freezing point of pure water. Pure water freezes at 0° C. The dissolved salts in the sea water keep sea water at a freezing point of -2° C. The freezing point of sea water may vary depending on its salinity in a particular location.

The ocean can be divided into three temperature zones. The surface layer consists of relatively warm water and exhibits most of the wave action present. The area where the wind and waves churn and mix the water is called the mixed layer. This is the layer where most living creatures are found due to abundant sunlight and warmth. The second layer is called the thermocline and it becomes increasingly cold as its depth increases. This change is due to the lack of energy from sunlight. The layer below the thermocline continues to the deep dark, very cold, and semi-barren ocean floor.

Oozes - the name given to the sediment that contains at least 30% plant or animal shell fragments. Ooze contains calcium carbonate. Deposits that form directly from sea water in the place where they are found are called authigenic deposits. Manganese nodules are authigenic deposits found over large areas of the ocean floor.

Causes for the formation of ocean floor features

The surface of the earth is in constant motion. This motion is the subject of Plate Tectonics studies. Major plate separation lines lie along the ocean floors. As these plates separate, molten rock rises, continuously forming new ocean crust and creating new and taller mountain ridges under the ocean. The Mid-Atlantic Range, which divides the Atlantic Ocean basin into two nearly equal parts, shows evidence of these deep-ocean floor changes using mapping.

Seamounts are formed by underwater volcanoes. Seamounts and volcanic islands are found in long chains on the ocean floor. They are formed when the movement of an oceanic plate positions a plate section over a stationary hot spot located deep in the mantle. Magma rising from the hot spot punches through the plate and forms a volcano. The Hawaiian Islands are examples of volcanic island chains.

Magma that rises to produce a curving chain of volcanic islands is called an island arc. An example of an island arc is the Lesser Antilles chain in the Caribbean Sea.

COMPETENCY 42.0 SKILLS AND ABILITIES

Skill 42.1   Know how to plan and conduct a scientific investigation to test a hypothesis.

Science may be defined as a body of knowledge that is systematically derived from study, observations and experimentation. Its goal is to identify and establish principles and theories that may be applied to solve problems. Pseudoscience, on the other hand, is a belief that is not warranted. There is no scientific methodology or application. Some of the more classic examples of pseudoscience include witchcraft, alien encounters, or any topics that are explained by hearsay.

Scientific inquiry starts with observation. Observation is a very important skill by itself, since it leads to experimentation and finally communicating the experimental findings to the society / public. After observing, a question is formed, which starts with "why" or "how." To answer these questions, experimentation is necessary. Between observation and experimentation, there are three more important steps. These are: gathering information (or researching about the problem), hypothesis, and designing the experiment.

Designing an experiment is very important since it involves identifying control, constants, independent variables and dependent variables. A control / standard is something we compare our results with at the end of the experiment. It is like a reference. Constants are the factors we have to keep constant in an experiment to get reliable results. Independent variables are factors we change in an experiment. It is very important to bear in mind that there should be more constants than variables to obtain reproducible results in an experiment.

Classifying is grouping items according to their similarities. It is important for students to realize relationships and similarity as well as differences to reach a reasonable conclusion in a lab experience. After the experiment is done, it is repeated and results are graphically presented. The results are then analyzed and conclusions drawn. It is the responsibility of the scientists to share the knowledge they obtain through their research.

After the conclusion is drawn, the final step is communication. In this age, lot of emphasis is put on the way and the method of communication. The conclusions must be communicated by clearly describing the information using accurate data, visual presentation like graphs (bar/line/pie), tables/charts, diagrams, artwork, and other appropriate media like power point presentation. Modern technology must be used whenever it is necessary. The method of communication must be suitable to the audience.

Written communication is as important as oral communication. This is essential for submitting research papers to scientific journals, newspapers, and magazines.

Skill 42.2   Apply principles of experimental design, including formulation of testable questions and hypotheses, and evaluation of the accuracy and reproducibility of data.

The scientific method is the basic process behind science. It involves several steps beginning with hypothesis formulation and working through to the conclusion.

Posing a question Although many discoveries happen by chance, the standard thought process of a scientist begins with forming a question to research. The more limited the question, the easier it is to set up an experiment to answer it.

Form a hypothesis
Once the question is formulated take an educated guess about the answer to the problem or question. This 'best guess' is your hypothesis.

Doing the test
To make a test fair, data from an experiment must have a **variable** or any condition that can be changed such as temperature or mass. A good test will try to manipulate as few variables as possible so as to see which variable is responsible for the result. This requires a second example of a **control**. A control is an extra setup in which all the conditions are the same except for the variable being tested.

Observe and record the data
Reporting of the data should state specifics of how the measurements were calculated. A graduated cylinder needs to be read with proper procedures. As beginning students, technique must be part of the instructional process so as to give validity to the data.

Drawing a conclusion
After recording data, you compare your data with that of other groups. A conclusion is the judgment derived from the data results.

Graphing data
Graphing utilizes numbers to demonstrate patterns. The patterns offer a visual representation, making it easier to draw conclusions.

Apply knowledge of designing and performing investigations.
Normally, knowledge is integrated in the form of a lab report. A report has many sections. It should include a specific **title** and tell exactly what is being studied. The **abstract** is a summary of the report written at the beginning of the paper. The **purpose** should always be defined and will state the problem. The purpose should include the **hypothesis** (educated guess) of what is expected from the outcome of the experiment. The entire experiment should relate to this problem. It is important to describe exactly what was done to prove or disprove a hypothesis. A **control** is necessary to prove that the results occurred from the

changed conditions and would not have happened normally. Only one variable should be manipulated at a time. **Observations** and **results** of the experiment should be recorded including all results from data. Drawings, graphs and illustrations should be included to support information. Observations are objective, whereas analysis and interpretation is subjective. A **conclusion** should explain why the results of the experiment either proved or disproved the hypothesis.

A scientific theory is an explanation of a set of related observations based on a proven hypothesis. A scientific law usually lasts longer than a scientific theory and has more experimental data to support it.

Skill 42.3   **Distinguish between dependent and independent variables and controlled parameters, and between linear and nonlinear relationships on a graph of data.**

Science uses the metric system as it is accepted worldwide and allows easier comparison among experiments done by scientists around the world. Learn the following basic units and prefixes:

> **meter** - measure of length
> **liter** - measure of volume
> **gram** - measure of mass

deca-(meter, liter, gram)= 10X the base unit   **deci** = 1/10 the base unit
hecto-(meter, liter, gram)= 100X the base unit   **centi** = 1/100 the base unit
kilo-(meter, liter, gram) = 1000X the base unit   **milli** = 1/1000 the base unit

Graphing is an important skill to visually display collected data for analysis. The two types of graphs most commonly used are the **line graph** and the **bar graph** (histogram). Line graphs are set up to show two variables represented by one point on the graph. The X axis is the horizontal axis and represents the dependent variable. Dependent variables are those that would be present independently of the experiment. A common example of a dependent variable is time. Time proceeds regardless of anything. The Y axis is the vertical axis and represents the independent variable. Independent variables are manipulated by the experiment, such as the amount of light, or the height of a plant. Graphs should be calibrated at equal intervals. If one space represents one day, the next space may not represent ten days. A "best fit" line is drawn to join the points and may not include all the points in the data. Axes must always be labeled, for the graph to be meaningful. A good title will describe both the dependent and the independent variable.

Bar graphs are set up similarly in regards to axes, but points are not plotted. Instead, the dependent variable is set up as a bar where the X axis intersects with the Y axis. Each bar is a separate item of data and is not joined by a continuous line.

Skill 42.4   Use scientific vocabulary appropriately.

Science may be defined as a body of knowledge that is systematically derived from study, observations, and experimentation. Its goal is to identify and establish principles and theories that may be applied to solve problems. Pseudoscience, on the other hand, is a belief that is not warranted. There is no scientific methodology or application. Some of the more classic examples of pseudoscience include witchcraft, alien encounters or any topic that is explained by hearsay.

Scientific theory and experimentation must be repeatable. It is also possible to be disproved and is capable of change. Science depends on communication, agreement, and disagreement among scientists. It is composed of theories, laws, and hypotheses.

theory - the formation of principles or relationships which have been verified and accepted.

law - an explanation of events that occur with uniformity under the same conditions (laws of nature, law of gravitation).

hypothesis - an unproved theory or educated guess followed by research to best explain a phenomena. A theory is a proven hypothesis.

Science is limited by the available technology. An example of this would be the relationship of the discovery of the cell and the invention of the microscope. As our technology improves, more hypotheses will become theories and possibly laws. Science is also limited by the data that is able to be collected. Data may be interpreted differently on different occasions. Science limitations cause explanations to be changeable as new technologies emerge.

An **independent variable** is one that is changed or manipulated by the researcher. This could be the amount of light given to a plant or the temperature at which bacteria is grown. The dependent variable is that which is influenced by the independent variable.

Science investigation is a very important part of science. Science investigation consists of a number of steps designed to solve a problem. This is important because it helps in solving scientific problems and to gather new information. Scientists start with a problem and solve it in an orderly fashion called the scientific method. This is made up of a series of steps, which, when applied properly, solve scientific problems. The key to the success of this method lies in minimizing human prejudice. As human beings, we tend to have bias. The steps consist of identifying the problem, gathering information, formulating a hypothesis, experimental design, interpreting data, and drawing conclusions.

The first step in a science investigation is identifying the problem. As we observe, we notice interesting things that arouse our curiosity. We ask ourselves the basic questions of enquiry – how, why, what, when, which and where. The two most important questions are how and why. We can classify observations into two types. The first is qualitative, which we describe in words. No mention of numbers or quantities is made – the water is very hot, the solution is sour, etc. The second type is quantitative, where numbers and quantities are used. This more precise –mass: format is 125 kg., distance: 500 km, etc.

The second step is gathering information. As information as possible is collected from various sources like internet, books, journals, knowledgeable people, newspapers etc. This lays a solid foundation for formulating a hypothesis. The third step is hypothesizing. This is making statement about the problem with the knowledge acquired and using the two important words, 'if' and 'when'. The next step is designing an experiment. Before this is done, we need to identify the control, the constants, the independent variables and the dependent variable.

For beginners, the simplest investigation would be to manipulate only one variable at a time. In this way, the experiment doesn't get too complicated and is easier to handle. The control has to be identified and then the variable which can effect the outcome of the results. For an experiment to be authentic and reliable, constants have to be identified and kept constant throughout the experiment. Finally, the dependent variable, which is dependent on the independent variable, has to be identified. The dependent variable is the factor that is being measured in an experiment – e.g. height of plant, number of leaves, etc. For an experiment to be successful, it should be completed in 10-12 days. The results are noted carefully. At the end of the experiment, the data have to be analyzed and searched for patterns. Any science investigation has to be repeated at least twice to get reproducible results. After the analysis, conclusions must be drawn based on the data.

In order to draw conclusions, we need to study the data on hand. The data tell us whether or not the hypothesis is correct. If the hypothesis is not correct, another hypothesis has to be formulated and an experiment has to be done.

If the hypothesis is tested and the results are repeated in further experimentation, a theory could be formulated. A theory is a hypothesis that is tested repeatedly by different scientists and has yielded the same results. A theory has more validity because it could be used to predict future events.

Scientific inquiries should end in formulating an explanation or model. Models should be physical, conceptual, and mathematical. While drawing conclusions, a lot of discussion and arguments are generated. There may be several possible explanations for any given sets of results: not all of them are reasonable. Carefully evaluating and analyzing the data creates a reasonable conclusion. The conclusion needs to be backed up by scientific criteria.

Skill 42.5   Select and use a variety of scientific tools.

Bunsen burners - Hot plates should be used whenever possible to avoid the risk of burns or fire. If Bunsen burners are used, the following precautions should be followed:
1. Know the location of fire extinguishers and safety blankets and train students in their use. Long hair and long sleeves should be secured and out of the way.
2. Turn the gas all the way on and make a spark with the striker. The preferred method to light burners is to use strikers rather than matches.
3. Adjust the air valve at the bottom of the Bunsen burner until the flame shows an inner cone.
4. Adjust the flow of gas to the desired flame height by using the adjustment valve.
5. Do not touch the barrel of the burner (it is hot).

Graduated Cylinder - These are used for precise measurements. They should always be placed on a flat surface. The surface of the liquid will form a meniscus (lens-shaped curve). The measurement is read at the <u>bottom</u> of this curve.

Balance - Electronic balances are easier to use, but more expensive. An electronic balance should always be tarred (returned to zero) before measuring and used on a flat surface. Substances should always be placed on a piece of paper to avoid spills and/or damage to the instrument. Triple beam balances must be used on a level surface. There are screws located at the bottom of the balance to make any adjustments. Start with the largest counterweight first and proceed toward the last notch that does not tip the balance. Do the same with the next largest, etc until the pointer remains at zero. The total mass is the total of all the readings on the beams. Again, use paper under the substance to protect the equipment.

Buret – A buret is used to dispense precisely measured volumes of liquid. A stopcock is used to control the volume of liquid being dispensed at a time.

Light microscopes are commonly used in laboratory experiments. Several procedures should be followed to properly care for this equipment:

- Clean all lenses with lens paper only.
- Carry microscopes with two hands; one on the arm and one on the base.
- Always begin focusing on low power, then switch to high power.
- Store microscopes with the low power objective down.
- Always use a coverslip when viewing wet mount slides.
- Bring the objective down to its lowest position then focus by moving up to avoid breaking the slide or scratching the lens.

Wet mount slides should be made by placing a drop of water on the specimen and then putting a glass coverslip on top of the drop of water. Dropping the coverslip at a forty-five degree angle will help in avoiding air bubbles. Total magnification is determined by multiplying the ocular (usually 10X) and the objective (usually 10X on low, 40X on high).

Skill 42.6   Know how to record length, mass, and volume measurements using the metric system.

See Skill 42.3.

Let's examine some examples of length measurement to show how this system makes the expression of values simple:

The height of a person: 1.82 meters
   We can easily record this in the basic unit for length, the meter.

Diameter of a cell: 0.00003 meters= 30 micrometers
   Expressing this value in meters means using an extremely small number and so it is more logical to express the quantity in micrometers (1 micrometer=0.000001 meters)

Distance from earth to the moon: 360,000,000 meters = 360,000 kilometers
   Similarly, expressing this quantity as in meters is unwieldy, so kilometers is a better choice.

Skill 42.7   Interpret results of experiments and interpret events by sequence and time from evidence of natural phenomena.

Some things happen at too fast or too slow a rate, or are too small or too large for use to see. In these cases, we have to rely on indirect evidence to develop models of what is intangible. Once data has been collected and analyzed, it is useful to generalize the information by creating a model. A model is a conceptual representation of a phenomenon. Models are useful in that they clarify relationships, helping us to understand the phenomenon and make predictions about future outcomes. The natural sciences and social sciences employ modeling for this purpose.

Many scientific models are mathematical in nature and contain a set of variables linked by logical and quantitative relationships. These mathematical models may include functions, tables, formulas, graphs, and etc. Typically, such mathematical models include assumptions that restrict them to very specific situations. Often this means they can only provide an approximate description of what occurs in the natural world. These assumptions, however, prevent the model from become overly complicated. For a mathematical model to fully explain a natural or social phenomenon, it would have to contain many variables and could become too cumbersome to use. Accordingly, it is critical that assumptions be carefully chosen and thoroughly defined.

Certain models are abstract and simply contain sets of logical principles rather than relying on mathematics. These types of models are generally vague and are more useful for discovering and understanding new ideas. Abstract models can also include actual physical models built to make concepts more tangible. Abstract models, to an even greater extent than mathematical models, make assumptions and simplify actual phenomena.

Proper scientific models must be able to be tested and verified using experimental data. Often these experimental results are necessary to demonstrate the superiority of a model when two or more conflicting models seek to explain the same phenomenon. Computer simulations are increasingly used in both testing and developing mathematical and even abstract models. These types of simulations are especially useful in situations, such as ecology or manufacturing, where experiments are not feasible or variables are not fully under control.

Skill 42.8   Communicate the steps in an investigation, record data, and interpret and analyze numerical and non-numerical results using charts, maps, tables, models, graphs, and labeled diagrams.

Some things happen at too fast or too slow a rate, or are too small or too large for use to see. In these cases, we have to rely on indirect evidence to develop models of what is intangible. Once data has been collected and analyzed, it is useful to generalize the information by creating a model. A model is a conceptual representation of a phenomenon. Models are useful in that they clarify relationships, helping us to understand the phenomenon and make predictions about future outcomes. The natural sciences and social sciences employ modeling for this purpose.

Many scientific models are mathematical in nature and contain a set of variables linked by logical and quantitative relationships. These mathematical models may include functions, tables, formulas, graphs, and etc. Typically, such mathematical models include assumptions that restrict them to very specific situations. Often this means they can only provide an approximate description of what occurs in the natural world. These assumptions, however, prevent the model from become overly complicated. For a mathematical model to fully explain a natural or social phenomenon, it would have to contain many variables and could become too cumbersome to use. Accordingly, it is critical that assumptions be carefully chosen and thoroughly defined.

Certain models are abstract and simply contain sets of logical principles rather than relying on mathematics. These types of models are generally more vague and are more useful for discovering and understanding new ideas. Abstract models can also include actual physical models built to make concepts more tangible. Abstract models, to an even greater extent than mathematical models, make assumptions and simplify actual phenomena.

Proper scientific models must be able to be tested and verified using experimental data. Often these experimental results are necessary to demonstrate the superiority of a model when two or more conflicting models seek to explain the same phenomenon. Computer simulations are increasingly used in both testing and developing mathematical and even abstract models. These types of simulations are especially useful in situations, such as ecology or manufacturing, where experiments are not feasible or variables are not fully under control.

Skill 42.9 Make appropriate use of print and electronic resources, including the World Wide Web, in preparing for an investigative activity.

Knowledge of appropriate use of laboratory materials
Light microscopes are commonly used in high school laboratory experiments. Total magnification is determined by multiplying the ocular (usually 10X) and the objective (usually 10X on low, 40X on high) lenses. Several procedures should be followed to properly care for this equipment.

-Clean all lenses with lens paper only.
-Carry microscopes with two hands; one on the arm and one on the base.
-Always begin focusing on low power, then switch to high power.
-Store microscopes with the low power objective down.
-Always use a coverslip when viewing wet mount slides.
-Bring the objective down to its lowest position then focus moving up to avoid
-breaking the slide or scratching the lens.

Wet mount slides should be made by placing a drop of water on the specimen and then putting a glass coverslip on top of the drop of water. Dropping the coverslip at a forty-five degree angle will help in avoiding air bubbles.

Chromatography uses the principles of capillarity to separate substances such as plant pigments. Molecules of a larger size will move slower up the paper, whereas smaller molecules will move more quickly producing lines of pigment.

An **indicator** is any substance used to assist in the classification of another substance. An example of an indicator is litmus paper. Litmus paper is a way to measure whether a substance is acidic or basic. Blue litmus turns pink when an acid is placed on it and pink litmus turns blue when a base is placed on it. pH paper is a more accurate measure of pH, with the paper turning different colors depending on the pH value.

Spectrophotometry measures percent of light at different wavelengths absorbed and transmitted by a pigment solution.

Centrifugation involves spinning substances at a high speed. The more dense part of a solution will settle to the bottom of the test tube, where the lighter material will stay on top. Centrifugation is used to separate blood into blood cells and plasma, with the heavier blood cells settling to the bottom.

Electrophoresis uses electrical charges of molecules to separate them according to their size. The molecules, such as DNA or proteins are pulled through a gel towards either the positive end of the gel box (if the material has a negative charge) or the negative end of the gel box (if the material has a positive charge). DNA is negatively charged and moves towards the positive charge.

Storing, identifying, and disposing of chemicals and biological materials
All laboratory solutions should be prepared as directed in the lab manual. Care should be taken to avoid contamination. All glassware should be rinsed thoroughly with distilled water before using and cleaned well after use. All solutions should be made with distilled water as tap water contains dissolved particles that may affect the results of an experiment. Unused solutions should be disposed of according to local disposal procedures.

The "Right to Know Law" covers science teachers who work with potentially hazardous chemicals. Briefly, the law states that employees must be informed of potentially toxic chemicals. An inventory must be made available if requested. The inventory must contain information about the hazards and properties of the chemicals. This inventory is to be checked against the "Substance List". Training must be provided on the safe handling and interpretation of the Material Safety Data Sheet.

The following chemicals are potential carcinogens and not allowed in school facilities: Acrylonitriel, Arsenic compounds, Asbestos, Bensidine, Benzene, Cadmium compounds, Chloroform, Chromium compounds, Ethylene oxide, Ortho-toluidine, Nickle powder, and Mercury.

Chemicals should not be stored on bench tops or heat sources. They should be stored in groups based on their reactivity with one another and in protective storage cabinets. All containers within the lab must be labeled. Suspect and known carcinogens must be labeled as such and segregated within trays to contain leaks and spills.

Chemical waste should be disposed of in properly labeled containers. Waste should be separated based on their reactivity with other chemicals.

Biological material should never be stored near food or water used for human consumption. All biological material should be appropriately labeled. All blood and body fluids should be put in a well-contained container with a secure lid to prevent leaking. All biological waste should be disposed of in biological hazardous waste bags.

Material safety data sheets are available for every chemical and biological substance. These are available directly from the company of acquisition or the internet. The manuals for equipment used in the lab should be read and understood before using them.

Use of live specimens

No dissections may be performed on living mammalian vertebrates or birds. Lower order life and invertebrates may be used. Biological experiments may be done with all animals except mammalian vertebrates or birds. No physiological harm may result to the animal. All animals housed and cared for in the school must be handled in a safe and humane manner. Animals are not to remain on school premises during extended vacations unless adequate care is provided. Any instructor who intentionally refuses to comply with the laws may be suspended or dismissed.

Pathogenic organisms must never be used for experimentation. Students should adhere to the following rules at all times when working with microorganisms to avoid accidental contamination:

1.   Treat all microorganisms as if they were pathogenic.
2.   Maintain sterile conditions at all times

Dissection and alternatives to dissection

Animals which are not obtained from recognized sources should not be used. Decaying animals or those of unknown origin may harbor pathogens and/or parasites. Specimens should be rinsed before handling. Latex gloves are desirable. If not available, students with sores or scratches should be excused from the activity. Formaldehyde is likely carcinogenic and should be avoided or disposed of according to district regulations. Students objecting to dissections for moral reasons should be given an alternative assignment. Interactive dissections are available online or from software companies for those students who object to performing dissections. There should be no penalty for those students who refuse to physically perform a dissection.

Laboratory safety procedures

All science labs should contain the following items of **safety equipment**. Those marked with an asterisk are requirements by state laws.

* fire blanket which is visible and accessible
*Ground Fault Circuit Interrupters (GCFI) within two feet of water supplies
*signs designating room exits
*emergency shower providing a continuous flow of water
*emergency eye wash station which can be activated by the foot or forearm
*eye protection for every student and a means of sanitizing equipment
*emergency exhaust fans providing ventilation to the outside of the building
*master cut-off switches for gas, electric and compressed air. Switches must have permanently attached handles. Cut-off switches must be clearly labeled.
*an ABC fire extinguisher
*storage cabinets for flammable materials
*chemical spill control kit
*fume hood with a motor which is spark proof
*protective laboratory aprons made of flame retardant material
*signs which will alert potential hazardous conditions
*containers for broken glassware, flammables, corrosives, and waste. Containers should be labeled.

Students should wear safety goggles when performing dissections, heating, or while using acids and bases. Hair should always be tied back and objects should never be placed in the mouth. Food should not be consumed while in the laboratory. Hands should always be washed before and after laboratory experiments. In case of an accident, eye washes and showers should be used for eye contamination or a chemical spill that covers the student's body. Small chemical spills should only be contained and cleaned by the teacher. Kitty litter or a chemical spill kit should be used to clean spill. For large spills, the school administration and the local fire department should be notified. Biological spills should also be handled only by the teacher. Contamination with biological waste can be cleaned by using bleach when appropriate.

Accidents and injuries should always be reported to the school administration and local health facilities. The severity of the accident or injury will determine the course of action to pursue.

It is the responsibility of the teacher to provide a safe environment for their students. Proper supervision greatly reduces the risk of injury and a teacher should never leave a class for any reason without providing alternate supervision. After an accident, two factors are considered; **foreseeability** and **negligence**. Foreseeability is the anticipation that an event may occur under certain circumstances. Negligence is the failure to exercise ordinary or reasonable care. Safety procedures should be a part of the science curriculum and a well managed classroom is important to avoid potential lawsuits.

Skill 42.10 Communicate the steps and results of a scientific investigation in both verbal and written formats.

After the conclusion is drawn, the final step is communication. In this age, much emphasis is put on the method of communication. The conclusions must be communicated by clearly describing the information using accurate data, visual presentation like graphs (bar/line/pie), tables/charts, diagrams, artwork, and other appropriate media like power point presentation. Modern technology must be used whenever it is necessary. The method of communication must be suitable to the audience.

Written communication is as important as oral communication. This is essential for submitting research papers to scientific journals, newspapers, other magazines etc.

Knowledge of appropriate and effective graphic representation of data

The type of graphic representation used to display observations depends on the data that is collected. **Line graphs** are used to compare different sets of related data or to predict data that has not yet be measured. An example of a line graph would be comparing the rate of activity of different enzymes at varying temperatures. A **bar graph** or **histogram** is used to compare different items and make comparisons based on this data. An example of a bar graph would be comparing the ages of children in a classroom. A **pie chart** is useful when organizing data as part of a whole. A good use for a pie chart would be displaying the percent of time students spend on various after school activities.

Knowledge of labeling graphs with independent and dependent variables

As noted before, the independent variable is controlled by the experimenter. This variable is placed on the x-axis (horizontal axis). The dependent variable is influenced by the independent variable and is placed on the y-axis (vertical axis). It is important to choose the appropriate units for labeling the axes. It is best to take the largest value to be plotted and divide it by the number of block, and rounding to the nearest whole number.

Appropriate measuring devices

The common instrument used for measuring volume is the graduated cylinder. The unit of measurement is usually in milliliters (mL). It is important for accurate measure to read the liquid in the cylinder at the bottom of the meniscus, the curved surface of the liquid.

The common instrument used is measuring mass is the triple beam balance. The triple beam balance is measured in as low as tenths of a gram and can be estimated to the hundredths of a gram.

The ruler or meter sticks are the most commonly used instruments for measuring length. Measurements in science should always be measured in metric units. Be sure when measuring length that the metric units are used.

CONTENT AREA – VISUAL AND PERFORMING ARTS

DOMAIN I – DANCE

COMPETENCY 43.0 DANCE

Skill 43.1   Identify the components and strands of dance education found in the Visual and Performing Arts Framework and Student Academic Content Standards.

Students are expected to be able to meet a variety of standards set forth for performing arts and dance. It is necessary for young students to master skills such as walking, running, galloping, jumping, hopping, and balance. Students must also learn to discriminate between opposites used to describe performance activities such a high/low, forward/backward, and move/freeze. Creative movements and expressions are necessary tools for dance as well. Students must be able to recall a feeling or personal experience they have had and perform accordingly. Students must learn to discern between different types of dance and dance experiences as well as learn what to expect from performances regarding staging, costume, setting and music.

Skill 43.2   Demonstrate a basic fluency with the elements of dance such as space, time, levels, and force/energy.

Dance is an artistic form of self expression that uses the various elements of dance such as use of space, time, levels, and force which form a composition.

The primary grades have a gross understanding of their motor movements whereas the older children are more apt to have a more refined concept of their bodies. Individual movements are developed by the instructor when attention to various aspects such as:

1. the range of movement or gestures through space,
2. or direction of the action or imaginary lines the body flows through space.
3. The timing of when movements form the dramatic effects.
4. Students are made aware of the planes formed by any two areas such as height and width or width and depth.
5. levels are introduced so that the composition incorporates sit, stand, and kneeling, etc.
6. elevation is the degree of lift as in leaping and the movements that are done under that allusion of suspension gives character to the dance.
7. the force and energy of dance can be a reflection of the music such as adagio (slow music) or allegro (quickening steps).

Skill 43.3 Use basic techniques to create dance/movement with children.

The primary grades have a gross understanding of their motor movements whereas the older children are more apt to have a more refined concept of their bodies. Begin with primitive patterns of **rhythm**. Rhythm is the basis of dance. A child can sit in a chair and clap or tap their hands on their legs to express thoughts of rhythm. With older children imagery enables a dancer to visualize and internalize the particular qualities of a specific movement.

Because the younger child is more unsteady the initial level emphasis is not on gracefulness but rather to develop **body awareness**. The uniqueness of dance is that it is self –expression that can be guided through instruction. The student is taught the elements that are available such as **time and space.** Therefore, the student is incorporating **listening skills** to develop a sense of tempo.

Practice, dedication and focus are essential in training for serious participation in dance. Each practice should begin with a warm-up consisting of stretches and movements to prevent muscular injury and to prepare the muscles for strenuous activity. The rehearsal period of individual movements, gestures and phrases of dance would comprise the major portion of the practice period ending with relaxation exercises enabling the individual to return gradually to normal metabolic levels. The rehearsal period stresses the individual characteristics of the steps and dances being performed. Each genre of dance has its own unique techniques. Fitness is important in developing a body that is flexible , strong, and fluid in movement. Dedication and commitment to dance as a profession is paramount where long hours on a daily basis develop expertise.

Skill 43.4 Identify and explain styles of dance from a variety of times, places, and cultures.

The various styles of dance can be explained as follows:
- Creative dance
- Modern dance
- Social dance
- Dance of other cultures
- Structured dance
- Ritual Dance
- Ballet

Creative dance is the one that is most natural to a young child. Creative dance depicts feelings through movement. It is the initial reaction to sound and movement. The older elementary student will incorporate mood and expressiveness. Stories can be told to release the dancer into imagination.

Isadora Duncan is credited with being the mother of modern dance. **Modern dance** today refers to a concept of dance where the expressions of opposites are developed such as fast-slow, contract- release, vary height and level to fall and recover. Modern dance is based on four principles which are substance, dynamism, metakinesis, and form.

Social dance requires a steadier capability that the previous levels. The social aspect of dance rather than romantic aspect representing customs and pastimes. Adults laugh when they hear little ones go "eweeee". Changing partners frequently within the dance is something that is subtly important to maintain. Social dances refer to a cooperative form of dance with respect to one sharing the dance floor with others and to have respect for ones partner. Social dance may be in the form of marches, waltz, and the two-step.

The upper level elementary student can learn dance in connection with historical **cultures** such as the minuet. The minuet was introduced to the court in Paris in 1650, and it dominated the ballroom until the end of the eighteenth century. The waltz was introduced around 1775 and was an occasion of fashion and courtship. The pomp and ceremony of it all makes for fun classroom experiences. Dance traditionally is central to many cultures and the interrelatedness of teaching history such as the Native American Indians dance, or the Mexican hat dance, or Japanese theater that incorporates both theater of masks and dance are all important exposures to dance and culture.

Structured dances are recognized by particular patterns such as the Tango, or waltz and were made popular in dance studios and gym classes alike. Arthur Murray promoted dance lessons for adults.

Ritual dance are often of a religious nature that celebrate a significant life event such as a harvest season, the rain season, glorifying the gods, asking for favors in hunting, birth and death dances. Many of these themes are carried out in movies and theaters today but they have their roots in Africa where circle dances and chants summoned the gods and sometimes produced trance like states where periods of divine contact convey the spiritual cleansing of the experience.

Dancing at weddings today is a prime example of ritual dance. The father dances with the bride. Then the husband dances with the bride. The two families dance with each other.

Ballet uses a barre to hold onto to practice the five basic positions used in ballet. Alignment is the way in which various parts of the dancer's body are in line with one another while the dancer is moving. It is very precise and executed with grace and form. The mood and expressions of the music are very important to ballet and form the canvas upon which the dance is performed.

Skill 43.5 **Able to make judgments about dance works based on the elements of dance.**

Students should be able to judge the effectiveness of a dance composition based on the intent, structure, meaning and purpose. Dance is a way of expressing everything from feelings of mood to appreciation of cultures and historical time periods. Students express empathy for others as they take on various roles within the dance. The application and participation in dances helps students develop self confidence, body awareness, and communication skills and provide experiences in areas otherwise left undiscovered. School settings for dance have a feel of community. Therefore, a good way to evaluate dance in a school setting is as a group experience rather than a technical skill level of individuals which is best left to dance schools. Dance is a way of expressing the connections and relationships between the dancers and appreciation of dance as creative expression.

DOMAIN II – MUSIC

COMPETENCY 44.0 MUSIC

Skill 44.1 **Understand the components and strands of music education found in the Visual and Performing Arts Framework and Student Academic Content Standards.**

The Visual and Performing Arts Framework and Student Academic Content Standards in music education consists of a multi-faceted approach assisting the learning of the methods, concepts and understanding making up the total content of musical instruction. Aiming to achieve the awareness of music through fostering personal aptitudes and talent as well as knowing what roles may be possibly accomplished or fulfilled throughout culture and society are main ideas addressed throughout the different grade levels and their changing standards.

The Visual and Performing Arts Framework and Student Academic Content Standards are denoted as consisting of Artistic Perception; Creative Expression; Historical and Cultural Context; Aesthetic Valuing; Connections, Relationships, and Applications. The maturation of these different topics, taken by the teacher and manifested by his or her instruction, composes the accomplishments by which guidance should be founded.

Core skills such as reading and writing music notation; composing, arranging and improvising music are continuously improved and complimented by other musical activities and information. Students become part of the musical process by ascertaining the natural evolution of their capabilities by the experience the teacher provides.

The increase of substance in the students' performance, both instrumental and vocal, is connected to the context provided by the teacher. Relating the students' musical inclinations to a working context of existing and current musical production creates a viable pathway for motivation and progress.

Amplifying the context in which music is performed through exercises and analysis that is grounded through knowledge of the historical and cultural context; aesthetic value; connections, relationships and applications of music lends the broad appreciation that is intrinsic in successfully interpreting the performer's role. Success in the music industry is appreciated according to the knowledge absorbed about the function of music in the social and cultural environment.

For more information on **The Visual Performing Arts Framework and Student Academic Content Standards**: http://www.cde.ca.gov/be/st/ss/

Skill 44.2 Demonstrate a basic fluency with the elements of music such as pitch, rhythm, and timbre and music concepts, including music notation.

The resources available to man to make music has varied throughout different ages and eras and has given the chance for a musical style or type to be created or invented due to diverse factors. Social changes, cultural features and historical purpose have all shared a part in giving birth to a multitude of different musical forms in every part of the earth.

Music can be traced to the people who created it by the instruments, melodies, rhythms and records of performance (songs) that are composed in human communities. Starting from early musical developments, as far back as nomadic cave dwellers playing the flute and beating on hand drums, to the different electric instruments and recording technology of the modern music industry, the style and type music produced has been closely related to the human beings who choose it for their particular lifestyle and way of existence.

Western music, rising chiefly from the fusion of classical and folkloric forms, has always been the pocket of a large variety of instruments and music generating new techniques to fit the change in expression provided by the expansion of its possibilities. Instruments such as the piano and the organ; stringed instruments like the violin, viola, cello, guitar and bass; wind instruments like the flute, saxophone, trumpet, trombone, tuba and saxophone; electronic instruments like the synthesizer and electric guitar have all provided for the invention of new styles and types of music created and used by different people in different times and places.

The rites of Christianity during the early middle ages were the focus of social and cultural aspiration and became a natural meeting place for communities to come together consistently for the purpose of experiencing God, through preaching and music. Composers and performers fulfilled their roles with sacred music with Gregorian chants and Oratorios. The art patron's court in the 15th and 14th centuries; the opera house of the 19th century satisfied the need of nascent, progressive society looking to experience grander and more satisfying music. New forms were generated such as the concerto, symphony, sonata and string quartet that employed a zeal and zest for creation typical of the burgeoning intellect at the end of the middle ages and the beginning of modern society.

Traditional types and styles of music in America, India, China, throughout the Middle East and Africa, using a contrasting variety of stringed instruments and percussion to typical Western instruments, began a long and exciting merging to the Western musical world with the beginning of widespread colonialism and the eventual integration it would achieve between disparate cultures. Western musical instruments were adopted to play the traditional musical styles of different cultures.

Blues music, arising from the southern black community in the United States would morph into Rock n' Roll and Hip Hop, alongside the progression of the traditional folk music of European settlers. Hispanic music would come about by Western musical instruments being imbued with African rhythms throughout the Caribbean in different forms like Salsa, Merengue, Cumbia and Son Cubano.

Skill 44.3 Use basic techniques to create vocal and instrumental music with children.

Music education is important throughout a child's elementary education. A comprehensive music curriculum not only teaches elements and appreciation of music, but also skills such as concentration, counting, listening, and cooperation. In addition, music has been connected with creating an effective educational environment that is more conducive to learning in other academic areas.

Basic Music Techniques

Some of the most basic music techniques include learning about rhythm, tempo, melody, and harmony. **Rhythm** refers to the pattern of regular or irregular pulses in music that result from the melodic beats of the music. When rhythm is measured and divided into parts of equal time value, it is called **meter**. Simple techniques to teach and practice rhythm include clapping hands and tapping feet to the beat of the music. Teachers can also incorporate the use of percussion instruments to examine rhythmic patters which also increases students' awareness of rhythm. As a result of exercises such as these, students learn the basics of conducting music, and through conducting, students learn to appreciate and develop musical awareness. Understanding rhythm also introduces students to the concept of **tempo**, or the speed of a given musical piece. Practicing with well-known songs with a strong musical beat such as "Happy Birthday" helps students become aware of patterns and speed.

The **melody** of a musical piece refers to the pattern of single tones in a composition that is distinguished from rhythm and harmony. The melody of a musical piece is often considered the "horizontal" aspect of the piece that flows from start to finish. **Harmony** refers to the combination of single tones at one time in a musical piece, or the full sound of different notes at the same time. To practice these concepts, students can compose their own ascending and descending melodies on staff paper. Students should be able to sing the melodies by reading the notation.

Other Musical Components and Terms

mood, expression, dynamics, nocturne, orchestra, tenor, clef, baritone, sonata, soprano, measure, cantata, march, alto, concerto, octave, staccato and legato

Skill 44.4   Able to identify and explain styles and types of music and instruments from a variety of times, places and cultures.

When we listen to certain music styles, they often connect us to a memory, a time in the past, or even an entire historical period. Very often, classical pieces, such as Bach or Beethoven, create a picture in our minds of the Baroque Period. The historical perspective of music can deepen one's musical understanding.

Throughout history, different cultures have developed different styles of music. Most of the written records of music developed from Western civilization.

Music styles varied across cultures as periods in history. As in the opening discussion, classical music, although still popular and being created today, is often associated with traditional classical periods in history such as the Renaissance.

As world contact merged more and more as civilizations developed and prospered, more and more influence from various cultural styles emerged across music styles. For example, African drums emerged in some Contemporary and Hip Hop music. Also, the Bluegrass music in the United States developed from the "melting pot" contributions from Irish, Scottish, German and African-American instrumental and vocal traditions.

In addition, the purposes for music changed throughout cultures and times. Music has been used for entertainment, but also for propaganda, worship, ceremonies, and communication.

Below is a list of some of the most common categories of musical styles.

Common Musical Styles
Medieval
Classical Music (loosely encompassing Renaissance and Baroque)
Gospel Music
Jazz
Latin Music
Rhythm and Blues
Funk
Rock
Country
Folk
Bluegrass
Electronic (Techno)
Melodic
Island (Ska, Reggae and other)
Hip Hop
Pop

African
Contemporary

Types of Musical Instruments
Instruments are categorized by the mechanism that creates its sound. Musical instruments can be divided into four basic categories.

1. String
2. Percussion
3. Brass
4. Wind

String Instruments
String instruments all make their sounds through strings. The sound of the instrument depends on the thickness and length of the strings. The slower a string vibrates, the lower the resulting pitch. Also, the way the strings are manipulated varies among string instruments. Some strings are plucked (e.g., guitar) while others use a bow to cause the strings to vibrate (e.g., violin). Some are even connected to keys (e.g., piano). Other common string instruments include the viola, double bass, cello and piano.

Wind Instruments
The sound of wind instruments is caused by wind vibrating in a pipe or tube. Air blows into one end of the instrument, and in many wind instruments, air passes over a reed which causes the air to vibrate. The pitch depends on the air's frequency as it passes through the tube, and the frequency depends on the tube's length or size. Larger tubes create deeper sounds in a wind instrument. The pitch is also controlled by holes or values. As fingers cover the holes or press the valve, the pitch changes for the notes the musician intends. Other common wind instruments include pipe organ, oboe, clarinet and saxophone.

Brass Instruments
Brass instruments are similar to wind instruments since music from brass instruments also results from air passing through an air chamber. They are called brass instruments, however, because they are made from metal or brass. Pitch on a brass instrument is controlled by the size or length of the air chamber. Many brass instruments are twisted or coiled which lengthens the air chamber without making the instrument unmanageably long. Like wind instruments, larger air chambers create deeper sounds, and the pitch can be controlled by valves on the instrument. In addition, some brass instruments also control the pitch by the musician's mouth position on the mouthpiece. Common brass instruments include the French horn, trumpet, trombone and tuba.

Percussion Instruments

To play a percussion instrument, the musician hits or shakes the instrument. The sound is created from sound vibrations as a result of shaking or striking the instrument. Many materials, such as metal or wood, are used to create percussion instruments, and different thicknesses or sizes of the material help control the sound. Thicker or heavier materials like drum membranes make deeper sounds, while thinner, metal materials (e.g., triangle) make higher-pitched sounds. Other common percussion instruments include the cymbals, tambourine, bells, xylophone and wood block.

Skill 44.5   Able to make judgments about musical works based on the elements and concepts of music.

Music education is a tremendous asset to all students. The study of music not only enhances students' well-rounded education, but also increases their evaluative, concentration, and recall skills. At the elementary level, students are taught the basics of music education and are given opportunities to explore music. For example, many students take music class, learn to play instruments and perform in concerts. At the secondary level, classes, choirs, bands and concerts and orchestras become even more involved, providing students with a deeper exposure to music.

Learning to judge, evaluate and appreciate music is a skill students develop throughout their educational careers. Through gaining basic and extended musical knowledge, students equip themselves with the knowledge base necessary to evaluate quality artistic performances.

In some schools, computer-assisted programs provide students with opportunities to evaluate music. Programs are designed to present two performances of one or more musical pieces so they can work with the teacher to compare and contrast the pieces. The Internet allows students to collect musical information for evaluation and provide information about studied or performed compositions. Knowledge of these resources and tools enable teachers to provide the richest education in music.

DOMAIN III – THEATRE

COMPETENCY 45.0 THEATRE

Skill 45.1 Identify the components and strands of theatre education found in the Visual and Performing Arts Framework and Student Academic Content Standards.

The framework and academic content in the area of theatre requires that teachers are able to express the various venues of the arts. In theatre students should learn to use all of their five senses to observe their environment and recreate experiences through drama and other theatre skills. Using role play and prior knowledge of experiences students should develop the ability to react to a feeling or a situation to expand their ability to develop character. Using sight, smell, taste, touch, hearing and memory recall students should become proficient with these skills so that they are able to retell stories, myths, and fables. Some experiences that the teacher should provide are costuming and props for performances. Many students can relate to familiar jobs that are relevant to their everyday experiences. Some experiences that should be offered but not limited to the following: firefighters, police officers, teachers, doctors, nurses, postal employees, clerks, and other service related professions that students may have witnessed.

Skill 45.2 Demonstrate a basic fluency in acting, directing, design, and scriptwriting and applying these elements and principles in order to create dramatic activities with children including improvisation and character development.

It is vital that teachers be trained in critical areas that focus on important principles of theatre education. The basic course of study should include state mandated topics in arts education, instructional materials, products in arts, both affective and cognitive processes of art, world and traditional cultures, and the most recent teaching tools, media and technology.

Areas that should in included but not limited to are as follows:

acting- Acting requires the student to demonstrate the ability to effectively communicate using skillful speaking, movement, rhythm, and sensory awareness.

directing- Direction requires the management skills to produce and perform an onstage activity. This requires guiding and inspiring students as well as script and stage supervision.

designing- Designing involves creating and initiating the onsite management of the art of acting.

scriptwriting- Scriptwriting demands that a leader be able to produce original material and staging an entire production through the writing and designing a story that has performance value.

Each of the above mentioned skills should be incorporated in daily activities with young children. It is important that children are exposed to character development through stories, role-play, and modeling through various teacher guided experiences. Some of these experiences that are age appropriate for early childhood level include puppet theatre, paper dolls, character sketches, storytelling, and re-telling of stories in a student's own words.

Skill 45.3   Able to identify and explain styles of theatre from a variety of times, places and cultures.

Greek History

The history of theatre can be dated back to early sixth century B.C. in Greece. The Greek theatre was the earliest known theater experience. Drama was expressed in many Greek spiritual ceremonies. There are two main forms of dramatic forms that have both evolved in their own time.

Tragedy- typically conflict between characters

Comedy- typically paradoxical relationships between humans and the unknown gods such as Sophocles and Euripides

Comedies and Tragedies were seldom mixed playwrights. Plays such as these were designed to entertain and contained little violence and were based on knowledge and the teachings of Aristotle.

Roman History

The history of theatre in Roman times was discovered in the third century. These theatre shows were too based on religious aspects of the lives of Roman gods and goddesses. Drama wasn't able to withstand the fall of the Roman Empire in 476 A.D. By the end of the sixth century drama was nearly dead in Rome.

Medieval Drama

Medieval theatre was a new revelation of drama that appeared in around the tenth century. New phases of religion were introduced in many holiday services such as Christmas and Easter. In the church itself drama was noticed in many troupes that toured churches presenting religious narratives and life stories of moral deeds. Over time the once small traveling groups grew into full sized plays, presentations, and elaborate passions. Performances became spectacles at outdoor theaters, marketplaces, and any place large audiences could gather. The main focus of these presentations of drama was to glorify God and humanity and to celebrate local artisan trades.

Puritan Commonwealth

The Puritan Commonwealth was ruled by Oliver Cromwell outlawed dramatic performances and that ban lasted for nearly twenty years. Following the Puritan era was the restoration of the English monarchy and new more well rounded plays became the focus of art. For the first time in history women were allowed to participate.

Melodrama

Melodrama eventually took over the stage of acting, in which the good always triumphed over the evil. This form of acting was usually pleasing to the audience yet sometimes unrealistic.

Serious Drama

Serious Drama emerged late in the nineteenth and twentieth centuries it came following the movement of realism. Realism attempted to combine the dealings of nature with realistic and ordinary situations on stage.

Realism

Today realism is the most common form of stage presence. The techniques used today to stage drama combine many of the past histories and cultures of drama.

Skill 45.4   Able to make judgments about dramatic works based on the elements of theatre.

Students would be exposed to a wide variety of dramatic works to enhance the theatre experience and provide endless opportunities for growth in the area of art and drama. Producers of plays need critics to enable them to better reach their audiences. Students need to judge the effectiveness of the plot, characters, and overall mood of the drama. Students have the opportunity to relate to the characters in the play and can express feelings such as empathy, and compassion. Drama is an expression that can be portrayed by the actors but can affect the audience in many aspects. To determine the level of performance by actors it is important to use technology to video the stage performance so that students can self-assess and also it is important to use a tool such as a rubric to make sure characters are meeting objectives during their performances, practices, and during peer assessments.

DOMAIN IV – VISUAL ART

COMPETENCY 46.0 VISUAL ART

Skill 46.1 **Identify the components and strands of visual arts education found in the Visual and Performing Arts Framework and Student Academic Content Standards.**

The components and strands of visual art encompass many areas. Students are expected to fine tune observation skills and be able to identify and recreate the experiences that teachers provide for them as learning tools. For example, students may walk as a group on a nature hike taking in the surrounding elements and then begin to discuss the repetition found in the leaves of trees, or the bricks of the sidewalk, or the size and shapes of the buildings and how they may relate. The may also use such an experience to describe lines, colors, shapes, forms and textures. Beginning elements of perspective are noticed at an early age. The questions of why buildings look smaller when they are at a far distance and bigger when they are closer are sure to spark the imagination of early childhood students. Students can then take their inquiry to higher level of learning with some hands-on activities such as building three dimensional buildings and construction using paper and geometric shapes. Eventually students should acquire higher level thinking skills such as analysis in which they will begin to questions artists, art work, and analyze many different aspects of visual art.

Skill 46.2 **Demonstrate a basic fluency with the principles of art such as balance, repetition, contrast, emphasis, and unity and are able to explain how works of art are organized in terms of line, color, value, space, texture, shape, and form.**

Students should have en early introduction to the principles of visual art and should become familiar with the basic level of the following terms:

abstract
> An image that reduces a subject to its essential visual elements, such as lines, shapes, and colors.

background
> Those portions or areas of composition that are back of the primary or dominant subject matter or design areas.

balance
> A principle of art and design concerned with the arrangement of one or more elements in a work of art so that they appear symmetrical or asymmetrical in design and proportion.

contrast
> A principle of art and design concerned with juxtaposing one or more elements in opposition, so as to show their differences.

emphasis
> A principle of art and design concerned with making one or more elements in a work of art stand out in such a way as to appear more important or significant.

sketch
> An image-development strategy; a preliminary drawing.

texture
> An element of art and design that pertains to the way something feels by representation of the tactile character of surfaces.

unity
> A principle of art and design concerned with the arrangement of one or more of the elements used to create a coherence of parts and a feeling of completeness or wholeness.

Following the learning the generic ideas for the above terms and how they relate to the use of line, color, value, space, texture and shape. An excellent opportunity is to create with the students an "art sample book."
Such books could include the different variety of material that would serve as examples for students to make connections to such as sandpaper to and cotton balls to represent texture elements. Samples of square pieces of construction paper designed into various shapes to represent shape. String samples to represent the element of lines, and other examples to cover all areas. The sampling of art should also focus clearly on colors necessary for the early childhood student. Color can be introduced more in-depth when discussing intensity or the strength of the color and value which relates to the lightness or darkness of the colors. Another valuable tool regarding color is the use of a color wheel and allowing students to experiment with the mixing of colors to create their own art experience.

Skill 46.3   Able to identify and explain styles of visual arts from a variety of times, places, and cultures.

The greatest works in art, literature, music, theater, and dance, all mirror universal themes. Universal themes are themes which reflect the human experience, regardless of time period, location, or socio-economic standing. Universal themes tend to fall into broad categories, such as Man vs. Society, Man vs. Himself, Man vs. God, Man vs. Nature, and Good vs. Evil, to name the most obvious. The general themes listed below all fall into one of these broad categories.

Prehistoric Arts, (circa 1,000,000-circa 8,000 B.C)

Major themes of this vast period appear to center around religious fertility rites and sympathetic magic, consisting of imagery of pregnant animals and faceless, pregnant women.

Mesopotamian Arts, (circa 8,000-400 B.C.)

The prayer statues and cult deities of the period point to the theme of polytheism in religious worship.

Egyptian Arts, (circa 3,000-100 B.C.)

The predominance of funerary art from ancient Egypt illustrates the theme of preparation for the afterlife and polytheistic worship. Another dominant theme, reflected by artistic convention, is the divinity of the pharaohs. In architecture, the themes were monumentality and adherence to ritual.

Greek Arts, (800-100 B.C.)

The sculpture of ancient Greece is replete with human figures, most nude and some draped. Most of these sculptures represent athletes and various gods and goddesses. The predominant theme is that of the ideal human, in both mind and body. In architecture, the theme was scale based on the ideal human proportions.

Roman Arts, (circa 480 B.C.- 476 A.D.)

Judging from Roman arts, the predominant themes of the period deal with the realistic depiction of human beings, and how they relate to Greek classical ideals. The emphasis is on practical realism. Another major theme is the glory in serving the Roman state. In architecture, the theme was rugged practicality mixed with Greek proportions and elements.

Middle Ages Arts, (300-1400 A.D.)

Although the time span is expansive, the major themes remain relatively constant. Since the Roman Catholic Church was the primary patron of the arts, most work was religious in nature. The purpose of much of the art was to educate. Specific themes varied from the illustration of Bible stories to interpretations of theological allegory, to lives of the saints, to consequences of good and evil. Depictions of the Holy Family were popular. Themes found in secular art and literature centered around chivalric love and warfare. In architecture, the theme was glorification of God, and education of congregation to religious principles.

Renaissance Arts, (circa 1400-1630 A.D.)

Renaissance themes include Christian religious depiction (see Middle Ages), but tend to reflect a renewed interest in all things classical. Specific themes include Greek and Roman mythological and philosophic figures, ancient battles and legends. Dominant themes mirror the philosophic beliefs of Humanism, emphasizing individuality and human reason, such as those of the High Renaissance which center around the psychological attributes of individuals. In architecture, the theme was scale based on human proportions.

Baroque Arts, (1630-1700 A.D.)

The predominant themes found in the arts of the Baroque period include the dramatic climaxes of well-known stories, legends and battles, and the grand spectacle of mythology. Religious themes are found frequently, but it is drama and insight that are emphasized and not the medieval "salvation factor". Baroque artists and authors incorporated various types of characters into their works, careful to include minute details. Portraiture focused on the psychology of the sitters. In architecture, the theme was large scale grandeur and splendor.

Eighteenth Century Arts, (1700-1800 A.D.)

Rococo themes of this century focused on religion, light mythology, portraiture of aristocrats, pleasure and escapism, and occasionally, satire. In architecture, the theme was artifice and gaiety, combined with an organic quality of form. Neo-classical themes centered on examples of virtue and heroism, usually in classical settings and historical stories. In architecture, classical simplicity and utility of design was regained.

Nineteenth Century Arts, (1800-1900 A.D.)

Romantic themes include human freedom, equality, and civil rights, a love for nature, and a tendency toward the melancholic and mystic. The underlying theme is that the most important discoveries are made within the self, and not in the exterior world. In architecture, the theme was fantasy and whimsy, known as "picturesque". Realistic themes included social awareness, and a focus on society victimizing individuals. The themes behind Impressionism were the constant flux of the universe and the immediacy of the moment. In architecture, the themes were strength, simplicity, and upward thrust as skyscrapers entered the scene.

Twentieth Century Arts, (1900-2000 A.D.)
> Diverse artistic themes of the century reflect a parting with traditional religious values, and a painful awareness of man's inhumanity to man. Themes also illustrate a growing reliance on science, while simultaneously expressing disillusionment with man's failure to adequately control science. A constant theme is the quest for originality and self-expression, while seeking to express the universal in human experience. In architecture, "form follows function".

Genres By Historical Periods

Ancient Greek Art, (circa 800-323 B.C.)
> Dominant genres from this period were vase paintings, both black-figure and red-figure, and classical sculpture.

Roman Art, (circa 480 B.C.- 476 A.D.)
> Major genres from the Romans include frescoes (murals done in fresh plaster to affix the paint), classical sculpture, funerary art, state propaganda art, and relief work on cameos.

Middle Ages Art, (circa 300-1400 A.D.)
> Significant genres during the Middle Ages include Byzantine mosaics, illuminated manuscripts, ivory relief, altarpieces, cathedral sculpture, and fresco paintings in various styles.

Renaissance Art, (1400-1630 A.D.)
> Important genres from the Renaissance included Florentine fresco painting (mostly religious), High Renaissance painting and sculpture, Northern oil painting, Flemish miniature painting, and Northern printmaking.

Baroque Art, (1630-1700 A.D.)
> Pivotal genres during the Baroque era include Mannerism, Italian Baroque painting and sculpture, Spanish Baroque, Flemish Baroque, and Dutch portraiture. Genre paintings in still-life and landscape appear prominently in this period.

Eighteenth Century Art, (1700-1800 A.D.)
> Predominant genres of the century include Rococo painting, portraiture, social satire, Romantic painting, and Neoclassic painting and sculpture.

Nineteenth Century Art, (1800-1900 A.D.)
> Important genres include Romantic painting, academic painting and sculpture, landscape painting of many varieties, realistic painting of many varieties, impressionism, and many varieties of post-impressionism.

Twentieth Century Art, (1900-2000 A.D.)

Major genres of the twentieth century include symbolism, art nouveau, fauvism, expressionism, cubism (both analytical and synthetic), futurism, non-objective art, abstract art, surrealism, social realism, constructivism in sculpture, Pop and Op art, and conceptual art.

Skill 46.4   Interpret works of art to derive meaning and are able to make judgments based on the principles of art as they are used to organize line, color, value, space, texture, shape, and form in works of art.

Works of art should most often be interpreted through a wide variety of rich art and literature experience. Students will be able to react to art experiences by understanding the definitions of the basic principles such as line, color, value, space, texture, and shape and form in art. Early Childhood students are most greatly affected by these experiences resource is the author Eric Carle. His books are age appropriate for young children and include a wide variety of shape, color, line, and media for young students to explore. Once students have been introduced to a wide range of materials they are able to better relate and explain the elements they have observed through art work and generously illustrated literature. Literature is the most common form of exposure for young students but video and other types of media also provided rich art experiences as well.

COMPETENCY 47.0 SKILLS AND ABILITIES

Skill 47.1   Able to make informed judgments about the quality of works in the arts based on the elements, principles, and/or concepts of the art form.

Teachers must be able to make judgments regarding the quality of arts using their prior knowledge of the concepts and principles that are standards for effective art. Each teacher must develop a system that can be used for judging art and that will provide a framework for students to follow. Clearly explained expectations help guide students in their art lessons. Early Childhood students often need very clear standards to follow. Not only is it important for young students to make connections between the vocabulary of art but the pictures or examples are always helpful too. For example when instructing a young pupil to used their scissors and glue in a project, the words "glue" and "scissors" should be clearly defined with a picture of each object next to the instructions. Once the tasks are clearly explained and labeled it important to develop a testing system to evaluate how accurately each student meets the standards. The most appropriate evaluation tool for young students in typically a rubric designed by the teacher. Evaluations using rubrics make is very simple for the teacher to check off each standard met by the students with little or no effort. By monitoring each student while working, teachers are able to identify the skills mastered with ease.

Skill 47 .2   Develop criteria for their judgments and justify their interpretations with plausible reasoning.

See Skill 47.1

Skill 47.3   Analyze the components and strands of the Visual and Performing Arts Framework and Student Academic Content Standards, and examine the connections among them.

The standards set forth by the Visual and Performing Arts Framework and Standards fully integrate the necessary competencies for teaching and evaluating all areas of art.

Component Strand 1.0 involves artistic perception which relates directly to processing, analyzing, and responding to sensory in the arts. This strand also involves expression of art through vocabulary and dialogue by direct observation. Students are also expected to become familiar with art media.

Component Strand 2.0 requires students to apply artistic skills and processes using a variety of means of communication. Skills that should be mastered involve drawing or painting human like subjects, mixing colors, early sculpting such as clay and paper Mache'. Students should be able to respond to observations of every day experiences and environment and scenes. Component Strand 3.0 includes the historical and cultural context of art. Students should be exposed to the early history or art and how art came to be. World art culture and a vast variety of visual arts and artists should be presented to early childhood students. The diversity of art should be portrayed by including various art pieces and artists works. A few examples are Japanese screen art, Mexican tin art, and African masks.

Component Strand 4.0 incorporates the aesthetic valuing of art. Students should be able to analyze, assess and conclude meaning from many different areas of art including their own and the art of their peers. The assessments should include the principles of art as well as how pleasing the design is to look at. Classroom discussions should focus on the media and technique of artists and should include the strengths and weaknesses of the artist's work.

Component Strand 5.0 connects and applies the visual art form to all other art forms. Students should be able to apply what they have learned and developed through all the competences, through problem solving, communication, and artistic experiences. Students should also be introduced to careers in the visual arts.

Skill 47.4   Consider the origins, meaning, and significance of works in the visual and performing arts; raise questions that have been asked by people, past and present; and determine how their responses have varied in significant ways over the years.

It is important for teachers to understand and relate to students the significance of early art forms and how the have developed over time. Many early folk art tales were scarce in their art and media. However now media and illustration is a tremendous part of any literature experience for young children. Another useful example is to have students describe the early days such as cave man art and compare it to art today. Examples such as early car designs compared to today's designs. There are many types of visual art that have gown in all areas. Teachers should incorporate themed units that are easily related cross-curriculum studies. Using themed units such as a theme on vehicles can show students early models of cars, trucks, motorcycles, air planes and how they have developed over time in to the models we use today.

Performing art has too developed over time. A great experience for young students is to have a Tribal performer demonstrate for students the dance, and rituals performed by Native American dancers. These dances and ceremonies have evolved over hundreds of years. Students could then compare that performance to a ballet performance and discuss the similarities and differences and how each art has evolved over time.

Skill 47.5   **Able to consider, weigh, and express ideas about aesthetic issues in the visual and performing arts.**

Although the elements of design have remained consistent throughout history, the emphasis on specific aesthetic principles has periodically shifted. Aesthetic standards or principles vary from time period to time period and from society to society.

An obvious difference in aesthetic principles occurs between works created by eastern and western cultures. Eastern works of art are more often based on spiritual considerations, while much western art is secular in nature. In attempting to convey reality, eastern artists generally prefer to use line, local color, and a simplistic view. Western artists tend toward a literal use of line, shape, color, and texture to convey a concise, detailed, complicated view. Eastern artists portray the human figure with symbolic meanings and little regard for muscle structure, resulting in a mystical view of the human experience. Western artists use the "principle of ponderation", which requires the knowledge of both human anatomy and an expression of the human spirit.

In attempts to convey the illusion of depth or visual space in a work of art, eastern and western artists use different techniques. Eastern artists prefer a diagonal projection of eye movement into the picture plane, and often leave large areas of the surface untouched by detail. The result is the illusion of vast space, an infinite view that coincides with the spiritual philosophies of the Orient. Western artists rely on several techniques, such as overlapping planes, variation of object size, object position on the picture plane, linear and aerial perspective, color change, and various points of perspective to convey the illusion of depth. The result is space that is limited and closed.

In the application of color, eastern artists use arbitrary choices of color. Western artists generally rely on literal color usage or emotional choices of color. The end result is that eastern art tends to be more universal in nature, while western art is more individualized.

An interesting change in aesthetic principles occurred between the Renaissance period (1400-1630 A.D.) and the Baroque period (1630-1700 A.D.) in Europe. The shift is easy to understand when viewed in the light of Wolfflin's categories of stylistic development (see 5.3).

The Renaissance period was concerned with the rediscovery of the works of classical Greece and Rome. The art, literature, and architecture were inspired by classical orders, which tended to be formal, simple, and concerned with the ideal human proportions. This means that the painting, sculpture, and architecture was of a teutonic, or closed nature, composed of forms that were restrained and compact. For example, consider the visual masterpieces of the period: Raphael's painting The School of Athens, with its highly precisioned use of space, Michelangelo's sculpture David, with its compact mass, and the facade of the Palazzo Strozzi, with its defined use of the rectangle, arches, and rustication of the masonry.

Compare the Renaissance characteristics to those of the Baroque period. The word "baroque" means "grotesque", which was the contemporary criticism of the new style. In comparison to the styles of the Renaissance, the Baroque was concerned with the imaginative flights of human fancy. The painting, sculpture and architecture were of a teutonic, or open nature, composed of forms that were whimsical and free-flowing. Consider again the masterpieces of the period: Ruben's painting The Elevation of the Cross, with its turbulent forms of light and dark tumbling diagonally through space, Puget's sculpture Milo of Crotona, with its use of open space and twisted forms, and Borromini's Chapel of St. Ivo, with a facade that plays convex forms against concave ones.

Although artists throughout time have used the same elements of design to compose their various artistic works, the emphasis on specific aesthetic principles has periodically shifted. Aesthetic principles vary from time period to time period, and from society to society.

In the 1920s and 30s, the German art historian, Professor Wolfflin outlined these shifts in aesthetic principles in his influential book <u>Principles of Art History</u>. He arranged these changes into five categories of "visual analysis", sometimes referred to as the "categories of stylistic development". Wolfflin was careful to point out that no style is inherently superior to any other. They are simply indicators of the phase of development of that particular time or society. However, Wolfflin goes on to state, correctly or not, that once the evolution occurs, it is impossible to regress. These modes of perception apply to drawing, painting, sculpture and architecture. They are as follows:

1. From a linear mode to a painterly mode.
This shift refers to stylistic changes that occur when perception or expression evolves from a linear form that is concerned with the contours and boundaries of objects, to perception or expression that stresses the masses and volumes of objects. From viewing objects in isolation, to seeing the relationships between objects are an important change in perception. Linear mode implies that objects are stationary and unchanging, while the painterly mode implies that objects and their relationships to other objects is always in a state of flux.

2. From plane to recession.

This shift refers to perception or expression that evolves from a planar style, when the artist views movement in the work in an "up and down" and "side to side" manner, to a recessional style, when the artist views the balance of a work in an "in and out" manner. The illusion of depth may be achieved through either style, but only the recessional style uses an angular movement forward and backward through the visual plane.

3. From closed to open form.

This shift refers to perception or expression that evolves from a sense of enclosure, or limited space, in "closed form", to a sense of freedom in "open form". The concept is obvious in architecture, as in buildings which clearly differentiate between "outside" and "inside" space, and buildings which open up the space to allow the outside to interact with the inside.

4. From multiplicity to unity.

This shift refers to an evolution from expressing unity through the use of balancing many individual parts, to expressing unity by subordinating some individual parts to others. Multiplicity stresses the balance between existing elements, whereas unity stresses emphasis, domination, and accent of some elements over other elements.

5. From absolute to relative clarity.

This shift refers to an evolution from works which clearly and thoroughly express everything there is to know about the object, to works that express only part of what there is to know, and leave the viewer to fill in the rest from his own experiences. Relative clarity, then, is a sophisticated mode, because it requires the viewer to actively participate in the "artistic dialogue". Each of the previous four categories is reflected in this, as linearity is considered to be concise while painterliness is more subject to interpretation. Planarity is more factual, while recessional movement is an illusion, and so on.

CONTENT AREA – PHYSICAL EDUCATION

DOMAIN I – MOVEMENT SKILLS AND MOVEMENT KNOWLEDGE

COMPETENCY 48.0 BASIC MOVEMENT SKILLS

Skill 48.1 **Identify movement concepts including body awareness, space awareness, and movement exploration.**

Body Awareness
Body awareness is a person's understanding of his or her own body parts and their capability of movement.

Instructors can assess body awareness by playing and watching a game of "Simon Says" and asking the students to touch different body parts. You can also instruct students to make their bodies into various shapes, from straight to round to twisted, and varying sizes, to fit into different sized spaces.

In addition, you can instruct children to touch one part of their body to another and to use various body parts to stamp their feet, twist their neck, clap their hands, nod their heads, wiggle their noses, snap their fingers, open their mouths, shrug their shoulders, bend their knees, close their eyes, bend their elbows, or wiggle their toes.

Spatial Awareness
Spatial awareness is the ability to make decisions about an object's positional changes in space (i.e. awareness of three-dimensional space position changes). Developing spatial awareness requires two sequential phases: 1) identifying the location of objects in relation to one's own body in space, and 2) locating more than one object in relation to each object and independent of one's own body.

Plan activities using different size balls, boxes, or hoops and have children move towards and away; under and over; in front of and behind; and inside, outside, and beside the objects.

Effort Qualities
Effort qualities are the qualities of movement that apply the mechanical principles of balance, time, and force).

Balance - activities for balance include having children move on their hands and feet, lean, move on lines, and balance and hold shapes while moving.
Time - activities using the concept of time can include having children move as fast as they can and as slow as they can in specified, timed movement patterns.

Force - activities using the concept of force can include having students use their bodies to produce enough force to move them through space. They can also paddle balls against walls and jump over objects of various heights.

Skill 48.2   List locomotor skills such as skipping, nonlocomotor skills such as static balancing, and object manipulation such as catching.

Locomotor Skills

Locomotor skills move an individual from one point to another.

1. **Crawling** - A form of locomotion where the person moves in a prone position with the body resting on or close to the ground or on the hands and knees.
2. **Creeping** - A slightly more advanced form of locomotion in which the person moves on the hands and knees.
3. **Walking** - with one foot contacting the surface at all times, walking shifts one's weight from one foot to the other while legs swing alternately in front of the body.
4. **Running** - an extension of walking that has a phase where the body is propelled with no base of support (speed is faster, stride is longer, and arms add power).
5. **Jumping** - projectile movements that momentarily suspend the body in midair.
6. **Vaulting** - coordinated movements that allow one to spring over an obstacle.
7. **Leaping** - similar to running, but leaping has greater height, flight, and distance.
8. **Hopping** - using the same foot to take off from a surface and land.
9. **Galloping** - forward or backward advanced elongation of walking combined and coordinated with a leap.
10. **Sliding** - sideward stepping pattern that is uneven, long, or short.
11. **Body Rolling** - moving across a surface by rocking back and forth, by turning over and over, or by shaping the body into a revolving mass.

12. **Climbing** - ascending or descending using the hands and feet with the upper body exerting the most control.

Nonlocomotor Skills

Nonlocomotor skills are stability skills where the movement requires little or no movement of one's base of support and does not result in change of position.

1. **Bending** - movement around a joint where two body parts meet.
2. **Dodging** - sharp change of direction from original line of movement such as away from a person or object.
3. **Stretching** - extending/hyper-extending joints to make body parts as straight or as long as possible.
4. **Twisting** - rotating body/body parts around an axis with a stationary base.
5. **Turning** - circular moving the body through space releasing the base of support.
6. **Swinging** - circular/pendular movements of the body/body parts below an axis.
7. **Swaying** - same as swinging but movement is above an axis.
8. **Pushing** - applying force against an object or person to move it away from one's body or to move one's body away from the object or person.
9. **Pulling** - executing force to cause objects/people to move toward one's body.

Manipulative Skills

Manipulative skills use body parts to propel or receive an object, controlling objects primarily with the hands and feet. Two types of manipulative skills are receptive (catch + trap) and propulsive (throw, strike, kick).

1. **Bouncing/Dribbling** - projecting a ball downwards.
2. **Catching** - stopping momentum of an object (for control) using the hands.
3. **Kicking** - striking an object with the foot.
4. **Rolling** - initiating force to an object to instill contact with a surface.
5. **Striking** - giving impetus to an object with the use of the hands or an object.
6. **Throwing** - using one or both arms to project an object into midair away from the body.
7. **Trapping** - without the use of the hands, receiving and controlling a ball.

Skill 48.3 Recognize basic concepts of biomechanics that affect movement, such as how the body moves and how such movement is influenced by gravity, friction, and the laws of motion.

When body segments move independently, body mass redistributes, changing the location of the body's center of gravity. Segments also move to change the body's base of support from one moment to the next to cope with imminent loss of balance.

The entire center of gravity of the body shifts in the same direction of movement of the body's segments. As long as the center of gravity remains over the base of support, the body will remain in a state of equilibrium. The more the center of gravity is situated over the base, the greater the stability. A wider base of support and/or a lower center of gravity enhances stability. To be effective, the base of support must widen in the direction of the force produced or opposed by the body. Shifting weight in the direction of the force in conjunction with widening the base of support further enhances stability.

Constant interaction of forces that move the body in the elected direction results in dynamic balance. The smooth transition of the center of gravity changing from one base of support to the next produces speed.

Concept of Force

Force is any influence that can change the state of motion of an object; we must consider the objective of movement.

Magnitude of Force – force must overcome the inertia of the object and any other resisting forces for movement to occur.

For linear movement, force applied close to the center of gravity requires a smaller magnitude of force to move the object than does force applied farther from the center of gravity.

For rotational movement, force applied farther from the center of gravity requires a smaller magnitude of force to rotate the object than does force applied closer to the center of gravity.

For objects with a fixed point, force applied anywhere other than through the point of fixation results in object rotation.

Energy – the capacity to do work. (The more energy a body has the greater the force with which it can move something [or change its shape] and/or the farther it can move it).

Movement (mechanical energy) has two types:

1. Potential energy (energy possessed by virtue of position, absolute location in space or change in shape).
   A. Gravitational potential energy - potential energy of an object that is in a position where gravity can act on it.
   B. Elastic (strain) potential energy - energy potential of an object to do work while recoiling (or reforming) after stretching, compressing, or twisting.
2. Kinetic energy (energy possessed by virtue of motion that increases with speed).

Force Absorption - maintaining equilibrium while receiving a moving object's kinetic energy without sustaining injury or without losing balance while rebounding. The force of impact is dependent on an object's weight and speed. The more abruptly kinetic energy is lost, the more likely injury or rebound occurs. Thus, **absorbing force requires gradually decelerating a moving mass by utilization of smaller forces over a longer period of time**. Stability is greater when the force is received closer to the center of gravity.

Striking resistive surfaces - the force of impact per unit area decreases when the moving object's area of surface making contact increases and the surface area that the object strikes increases.

Striking non-resistive surfaces - the force of impact decreases if the moving object's area of surface making contact decreases because it is more likely to penetrate.

The more time and distance that motion stops for a moving object to strike any surface, the more gradually the surface absorbs the force of impact, and the reaction forces acting upon the moving object decrease.

Equilibrium returns easily when the moving body (striking a resistive surface) aligns the center of gravity more vertically over the base of support.

Angular force against a body decreases when the distance between a contacting object and the body decreases and the contact occurs closer to the center of gravity. Also, widening the base of support in the direction of the moving object increases stability.

Force and Physical Education

1. **Inertia** - tendency of a body or object to remain in its present state of motion; an object will stay in a prescribed straight path and will move at its given speed unless some force acts to change it.

2. **Projecting objects for vertical distance** - the forces of gravity and air resistance prevent vertically projected objects from continuing at their initial velocities. The downward, resistive force of gravity slows a projectile directed upward until it halts (at the peak of vertical path). At this point, the downward force of gravity becomes an incentive force that increases the speed of the object until it confronts another force (the earth or other external object) that slows the object until it stops. When the object stops ascending and begins to descend, gravity alters the object's direction of motion. Air resistance (of still air) always opposes the object's motion. Therefore, an ascending object's air resistance is downward and a descending object's air resistance is upward. An increase in velocity increases air-drag force that decreases the magnitude of the drag as the object moves upward, slowing in velocity. The magnitude of the drag increases as the object moves faster and faster downward. Moreover, the direction and magnitude of the object's acceleration, due to the force of gravity, are constant while direction and magnitude of changes, due to air resistance, are dependent on the object's speed and direction.

An object travels the highest when projected with the greatest velocity, and the object's weight affects neither gravity's upward deceleration nor its downward acceleration. The object's weight, however, is a factor in calculating the net force acting on the object's vertical movement through the air.

If an object's acceleration is proportional to the applied force, greater force produces greater acceleration. An object's acceleration is inversely proportional to its mass (the greater the mass, the less the acceleration).

- **Angular acceleration** (rate that an object's angular speed or direction changes) - angular acceleration is great when there is a large change in angular velocity in a short amount of time. A rigid body (or segment) encounters angular acceleration or deceleration only when a net external torque is applied. When torque stops, the body reaches and maintains a new velocity until another torque occurs. Acceleration is always in the direction of the acting torque, and the greater the torque, the greater the angular acceleration.

- **Linear acceleration** (time rate of change in velocity) - an object's magnitude of acceleration is significant if there is a large change of velocity in a small amount of time. When the same velocity changes over a longer period of time, acceleration is small. Acceleration occurs only when force is applied. When the force stops, the object/body reaches a new and the object/body continues at the new speed until that a force changes that speed or direction. In addition, the direction of acceleration is the same direction as the applied net force. A large force produces a large acceleration. A small force produces a modest acceleration.
- **Zero/Constant Acceleration** (constant velocity) - there is no change in a system's velocity when the object/body moves at a given velocity and encounters equal, opposing forces. Hence, velocity is constant since no force causes acceleration or deceleration.
- **Acceleration caused by gravity** - a falling object/body continues to accelerate at the rate of 9.8 m/sec. (32 ft/sec.) throughout its fall.
- **Radial acceleration (direction change caused by centripetal force)** - centripetal force is aimed along an illusory line (the circular path) at any instant. Therefore, it is the force responsible for change of direction. The bigger the mass, the greater the centripetal force required. A tighter turn magnifies direction change (radial acceleration), so friction must increase to offset the increased acceleration. Maximum friction (centrifugal force) reduces speed. A combination of the variables mass, radius of curvature, speed of travel, and centripetal force cause radial acceleration.

Action/Reaction - every action has an equal and opposite reaction.

- **Linear motion** - the larger the mass, the more it resists motion change initiated by an outside force.

Body segments exert forces against surfaces they contact. These forces and the reaction of the surfaces result in body movement. For example, a runner propels himself forward by exerting a force on the ground (as long as the surface has sufficient friction and resistance to slipping). The force of the contact of the runner's foot with the ground and the equal and opposite reaction of the ground produces movement. A canoe paddler or swimmer exerts a backward force by pushing the water backwards, causing a specific velocity that is dependent on the stroke's force - as well as the equal and opposite force made by the water pushing forward against the canoe paddle or arm moving the canoe or swimmer forward.

Every torque (angular motion) exerted by one body/object on another has another torque equal in magnitude and opposite direction exerted by the second body/object on the first. Changing angular momentum requires a force that is equal and opposite to the change in momentum.

Performing actions in a standing position requires the counter pressure of the ground against the feet for accurate movement of one or more parts of the body.

Newton's Laws of Motion

Sir Isaac Newton developed three laws of motion that describe the movement of objects. Newton's three laws are as follows:

1. Concept of Inertia – an object in motion maintains its motion until an external force acts on it

2. $F = ma$ – The force applied to an object is equal to the mass of the object multiplied by the acceleration of the object.

3. For every action there is an equal and opposite reaction.

Newton's laws of motion are important to movement activities. The concept of inertia comes into play in any activity that involves a moving ball or other object. For example, when playing tennis, it is more difficult to hit a shot that changes the direction of the ball because you must overcome the ball's inertia. In other words, it is difficult to take a ball hit crosscourt and return it down the line, because you must factor in the ball's tendency to continue on its present path. Force and acceleration are important concepts in many sports, including striking sports, contact sports, and net/wall sports. Finally, action/reaction is an important concept in basic movement activities such as running and walking. The reactive force that occurs when a runner's foot strikes the ground helps propel the runner forward.

Skill 48.4 Describe critical elements of basic movement skills, such as stepping in opposition when throwing and/or following through when kicking a ball.

Research shows that the concepts of space, direction, and speed are interrelated with movement concepts. Such concepts are extremely important for students to understand, as they need to know movement skills with regard to direction in order to move with confidence and avoid collisions.

Space, direction, speed, and vision all relate to movement, as a student or player must take all of these elements into consideration in order to perform and understand a sport. A player must decide how to handle their space as well as numerous other factors that arise on the field.

For a player, the concepts are all interconnected. She has to understand how to maintain or change pathways with speed. This refers to the ability to change motion and perform well in space (or the area that the players occupy on the field).

Evaluating Fundamental Movement Skills

In all physical activity or training, there are certain fundamental movement skills that involve patterns necessary for the development of the body. We define them as the foundation movements or precursor patterns to the more specialized complex skills that are useful in all types of sports, dance, and play.

Fundamental movement skills form an indispensable part of all physical activity and physical education. Such basic movement skills are extremely important for children in their early years. These particular skills include running, stopping, changing direction, starting, hopping, skipping, and rolling.

These fundamental movement skills play an important role in the physical well-being of all growing children and are important for adults as well. These skills create the framework of every physical activity and sport.

Physical education instructors should be able to identify mature and immature motor patterns. For example, when observing an overhand throw, there are certain universal characteristics of immature throwing patterns. These include stepping with the foot on the same side of the body as the throwing arm, using only the elbow to propel the object, and facing the target throughout the throwing process. Conversely, characteristics of a mature overhand throwing pattern include leading with the foot opposite the throwing hand, using the entire body and arm to propel the ball, and starting the throwing motion facing perpendicular to the target.

Basic Movement Patterns

Overhand Throw
The overhand throw consists of a sequence of four movements: a stride, hip rotation, trunk rotation, and forward arm movement. The thrower should align his body sideways to the target (with opposite shoulder pointing towards the target). The overhand throw begins with a step or stride with the opposite foot (i.e. left foot for a right-handed thrower). As the stride foot contacts the ground, the pivot foot braces against the ground and provides stability for the subsequent movements. Hip rotation is the natural turning of the hips toward the target. Trunk rotation follows hip rotation. The hips should rotate before the trunk because the stretching of the torso muscles allows for stronger muscle contraction during trunk rotation. Following trunk rotation, the arm moves forward in two phases. In the first phase the elbow is bent. In the second phase, the elbow joint straightens and the thrower releases the ball.

Development of the overhand throwing motion in children occurs in three stages: elementary, mature, and advanced. In the elementary stage, the child throws mainly with the arm and does not incorporate the other body movements. The signature characteristic of this stage is striding with the foot on the same side of the body as the throwing arm (i.e. placing the right foot in front when throwing with the right hand). In the mature stage, the thrower brings the arm backward in preparation for the throw. Use of body rotation is still limited. Children in the advanced stage incorporate all the elements of the overhand throw. The thrower displays an obvious stride and body rotation.

Underhand Throw
The thrower places the object in the dominant hand. When drawing the arm back the triceps straighten the elbow and, depending on the amount of power behind the throw, the shoulder extends or hyperextends using the posterior deltoid, latissimus dorsi, and the teres major. At the time of drawback, the thrower takes a step forward with the leg opposite of the throwing arm. When coming back down, the thrower moves the shoulder muscles (primarily the anterior deltoid) into flexion. When the object in hand moves in front of the body, the thrower releases the ball. The wrist may be firm or slightly flexed. The thrower releases the object shortly after the planting the foot and the biceps muscle contracts, moving the elbow into flexion during follow through.

Kick
In executing a kick, the object needs to be in front of the body and in front of the dominant leg. The kicker steps and plants with the opposite leg while drawing the kicking leg back. During draw back, the hamstring muscle group flexes the knee. When the kicker plants the opposite foot, the hips swing forward for power and the knee moves into extension using the quadriceps muscle group. The contact point is approximately even with the plant foot and a comfortable follow through completes the action.

COMPETENCY 49.0 EXERCISE PHYSIOLOGY: HEALTH AND PHYSICAL FITNESS

Skill 49.1   Identify health and fitness benefits and associated risks, supporting a physically active lifestyle, related to safety and medical factors.

Dangers of Inactivity

Hypertension, atherosclerosis, arteriosclerosis, heart attack, stroke, congestive heart failure, angina, osteoporosis, osteoarthritis, adult on-set diabetes, gout, gall bladder disorders, ulcers, osteoporosis, cancer, lordosis, poor posture, neck, leg, knee, and foot problems are all diseases and conditions caused in part by a lack of physical activity.

Physiological benefits of physical activity include:
- improved cardio-respiratory fitness
- improved muscle strength
- improved muscle endurance
- improved flexibility
- more lean muscle mass and less body fat
- quicker rate of recovery
- improved ability of the body to utilize oxygen
- lower resting heart rate
- increased cardiac output
- improved venous return and peripheral circulation
- reduced risk of musculoskeletal injuries
- lower cholesterol levels
- increased bone mass
- cardiac hypertrophy and size and strength of blood vessels
- increased number of red cells
- improved blood-sugar regulation
- improved efficiency of thyroid gland
- improved energy regulation
- increased life expectancy

Considerations for Dealing with Specific Illnesses
Diabetes

Most children with diabetes suffer from Type 1 (insulin-dependent or juvenile) diabetes. Type 1 diabetes limits the pancreas' ability to produce insulin, a hormone vital to life. Without insulin, the body cannot use the sugar found in blood. In order to stay alive, an individual suffering from Type 1 diabetes must take one or more injections of insulin daily.

Diabetics control their disease by keeping the level of sugar (glucose) in the blood as close to normal as possible. The means to achieve diabetes control include proper nutrition, exercise, and insulin. Most children with diabetes self-monitor blood glucose levels to track their condition and respond to changes.

Some rules of thumb to keep in mind when dealing with a diabetic child are:

- Food makes the glucose level rise
- Exercise and insulin make the glucose level fall
- Hypoglycemia occurs when the blood sugar level is low
- Hyperglycemia occurs when the blood sugar level is high

Low Blood Sugar (Hypoglycemia)
This is the diabetic emergency most likely to occur. Low blood sugar may result from eating too little, engaging in too much physical activity without eating, or by injecting too much insulin.

Symptoms:
- Headache
- Sweating
- Shakiness
- Pale, moist skin
- Fatigue/Weakness
- Loss of coordination

Treatment:
Provide sugar immediately. You may give the student ½ cup of fruit juice, non-diet soda, or two to four glucose tablets. The child should feel better within the next 10 minutes. If so, the child should eat some additional food (e.g. half a peanut butter, meat, or cheese sandwich). If the child's status does not improve, treat the reaction again.

High Blood Sugar (Hyperglycemia)
Hyperglycemia can result from eating too much, engaging in too little physical activity, not injecting enough insulin, or illness. You can confirm high blood sugar levels by testing with a glucose meter.

Symptoms:
- Increased thirst
- Weakness/Fatigue
- Blurred vision
- Frequent urination
- Loss of appetite

Treatment:
If hyperglycemia occurs, the instructor should contact the student's parent or guardian immediately.

Dehydration
Dehydration occurs when a person loses more fluids than he/she takes in. The amount of water present in the body subsequently drops below the level needed for normal body functions. The two main causes of dehydration are gastrointestinal illness (vomiting, diarrhea) and sports. It is essential to replace fluids lost by sweating to prevent dehydration, especially on a hot day.

Symptoms:
- Thirst
- Dizziness
- Dry mouth
- Producing less/darker urine

Prevention/Treatment:
- Drink lots of fluids. Water is usually the best choice.
- Dress appropriately (i.e., loose-fitting clothes and a hat).
- If you begin to feel thirsty/dizzy, take a break and sit in the shade.
- Drink fluids prior to physical activity and then in 20-minute intervals after activity commences.
- Play sports or train in the early morning or late afternoon. You will avoid the hottest part of the day.

Skill 49.2   Recognize exercise principles such as frequency, intensity, and time to select activities that promote physical fitness.

Basic Training Principles
The **Overload Principle** is exercising at an above normal level to improve physical or physiological capacity (a higher than normal workload).

The **Specificity Principle** is overloading a particular fitness component. In order to improve a component of fitness, you must isolate and specifically work on a single component. Metabolic and physiological adaptations depend on the type of overload; hence, specific exercise produces specific adaptations, creating specific training effects.

The **Progression Principle** states that once the body adapts to the original load/stress, no further improvement of a component of fitness will occur without the addition of an additional load.

There is also a **Reversibility-of-Training Principle** in which all gains in fitness are lost with the discontinuance of a training program.

Modifications of Overload

We can modify overload by varying **frequency, intensity, and time**. Frequency is the number of times we implement a training program in a given period (e.g. three days per week). Intensity is the amount of effort put forth or the amount of stress placed on the body. Time is the duration of each training session.

Principles of Overload, Progressions, Specificity, and FIT Applied to Improvement of Health-Related Components of Fitness

1. Cardio-respiratory Fitness:

Overloading for cardio-respiratory fitness:
- **Frequency** = minimum of 3 days/week
- **Intensity** = exercising in target heart-rate zone
- **Time** = minimum of 15 minutes rate

Progression for cardiovascular fitness:
- begin at a frequency of 3 days/week and work up to no more than 6 days/week
- begin at an intensity near THR threshold and work up to 80% of THR
- begin at 15 minutes and work up to 60 minutes

Specificity for cardiovascular fitness:
- To develop cardiovascular fitness, you must perform aerobic (with oxygen) activities for at least fifteen minutes without developing an oxygen debt. Aerobic activities include, but are not limited to brisk walking, jogging, bicycling, and swimming.

2. Muscle Strength:

Overloading for muscle strength:
- **Frequency** = every other day
- **Intensity** = 60% to 90% of assessed muscle strength
- **Time** = 3 sets of 3 - 8 reps (high resistance with a low number of repetitions)

Progression for muscle strength:
- begin 3 days/week and work up to every other day
- begin near 60% of determined muscle strength and work up to no more than 90% of muscle strength
- begin with 1 set with 3 reps and work up to 3 sets with 8 reps

Specificity for muscle strength:
- to increase muscle strength for a specific part(s) of the body, you must target that/those part(s) of the body

3. Muscle endurance:

Overloading for muscle endurance:
- **Frequency** = every other day
- **Intensity** = 30% to 60% of assessed muscle strength
- **Time** = 3 sets of 12 - 20 reps (low resistance with a high number of repetitions)
-

Progression for muscle endurance:

- begin 3 days/week and work up to every other day
- begin at 20% to 30% of muscle strength and work up to no more than 60% of muscle strength
- begin with 1 set with 12 reps and work up to 3 sets with 20 reps

Specificity for muscle endurance:

- same as muscle strength

Skill 49.3   **Describe physical fitness components, such as flexibility, muscular strength and endurance, cardio-respiratory endurance, and body composition, which are included in comprehensive personal fitness development programs.**

Health-related Components of Physical Fitness
There are five health related components of physical fitness: **cardio-respiratory or cardiovascular endurance, muscle strength, muscle endurance, flexibility, and body composition.**

Cardiovascular endurance – the ability of the body to sustain aerobic activities (activities requiring oxygen utilization) for extended periods.

Muscle strength – the ability of muscle groups to contract and support a given amount of weight.

Muscle endurance – the ability of muscle groups to contract continually over a period of time and support a given amount of weight.

Flexibility – the ability of muscle groups to stretch and bend.

Body composition – an essential measure of health and fitness. The most important aspects of body composition are body fat percentage and ratio of body fat to muscle.

COMPETENCY 50.0 MOVEMENT FORMS: CONTENT AREAS

Skill 50.1   Know a variety of traditional and nontraditional games, sports, dance, and other physical activities.

Overview of Net/Wall Sports

Badminton – Students in a badminton class will have to master the strokes as basic skills and should learn at least some of them by name (e.g. types of serves, net shot, net kills, drive, push, lift). Students should also know which strokes are appropriate from which areas of the court.

Tennis – Skills that students will learn when studying tennis include the proper grips of the racket and stroke techniques, which they should know by name (e.g. flat serve, topspin serve, twist serve, forehand, backhand, volley, overhead).

Volleyball – Students studying volleyball should master six basic skills: the serve, pass, set, attack, block, and dig. Each of these skills comprises a number of specific techniques that are standard volleyball practice.

Overview of Striking/Fielding Sports

Softball – Skills students in softball classes will acquire include accurate throwing and catching, and the correct way to swing and hit with a softball bat.

Softball is similar in strategy to baseball. Defensive strategy focuses on the pitcher, who is responsible for trying to strike out the team that is at bat. Offensive strategy centers on batting, and attempting to turn batters into runners.

Safety practices in softball are also similar to baseball. Enforcing discipline and maintaining student attentiveness to prevent the chance of injury is of utmost importance. Instructors must also emphasize to the students that they should not swing the bat when other students are in the area.

Equipment required for softball practice includes a softball bat and softball, fielding gloves, appropriate protective gear, and base markers of some sort.

Baseball – Skills that students studying baseball will acquire include accurate throwing and catching, and the correct way to swing and hit with a baseball bat.

Defensive strategy in baseball focuses on the actions of the pitcher, who is responsible for trying to strike out the team that is at bat. Offensive strategy in baseball centers on batting, and attempting to turn batters into runners.

Safety practices in baseball include maintaining discipline among the students, as horseplay and lack of attentiveness can lead to injury (e.g. a ball could hit a student who isn't paying attention). In addition, instructors should remind students the baseball bat is not a toy, and they should handle it with care and not swing it near other students.

Equipment required for baseball practice includes baseball bats, baseballs, baseball gloves (though for some educational situations, the gloves are not necessary), base markers of some kind, and protective padding for the catcher.

Overview of Target Sports

Golf – The most fundamental skills for students to learn when studying golf include the correct way to execute a golf swing with proper posture and how to judge distance for shot selection correctly. Further, students should learn specific shots and their names (e.g. tee shot, fairway shot, bunker shot, putt).

Strategy in golf centers on properly gauging distances and required force to control the ball to the best extent possible.

Safety practices in golf, especially with students, involve ensuring that the course is clear and there are no students nearby when players are swinging. Instructors should also remind students that golf clubs are not toys, and that misuse can result in injury.

Equipment necessary for a golf class includes a proper set of clubs and golf balls (a golf course or open area for hitting balls is also necessary).

Archery – Skills that students study in archery classes include proper care for their equipment, properly stringing the bow, drawing, and shooting with accuracy (including compensating for distance, angle, and wind).

Safety practices in archery include respectful handling of the equipment (which is potentially dangerous) and ensuring that students only draw bows when pointed at a (non-living) target. Finally, instructors should keep students away from the path between firing students and their targets at all times.

Proper equipment for archery classes include a bow and arrows, which can vary greatly in technical complexity and cost, and a target.

Bowling – Skills that students will learn in bowling classes include learning to select a ball of comfortable weight and appropriate for the shot they need to make, properly controlling the ball so it hits the pins they are aiming for, and learning the dynamics of pin interaction to plan the proper angle of entry for the ball.

Safety practices in bowling include wearing proper footwear, handling the balls cautiously, and preventing horseplay (to avoid situations where a heavy bowling ball may drop inopportunely and cause injury).

Equipment needed for a bowling class include proper footwear, a bowling ball, pins, and a lane.

Nontraditional, Global and Cooperative Games and Activities

Pickle-Ball – When playing Pickle-Ball the serve must be hit underhand and each team must play the first shot off the bounce. After the ball has bounced once on each side, both teams can either volley the ball in the air or play it off the bounce. No volleying is permitted within the seven-foot non-volley zone. A game is played to eleven points and a team must win by at least two points. Points are lost by hitting the ball out of bounds, hitting the net, volleying the ball from the non-volley zone, or volleying the ball before it has bounced on both sides of the net.

Bocce ball – Requires a flat, level playing surface (packed dirt, gravel or grass are ideal). The instructor divides students into two teams of one, two, or four players each. Each team gets four balls, divided equally among the players. A player from the starting team stands behind the foul line (10 feet from the throwing end of the court) and throws the small ball ("pallina") toward the opposite end of the playing surface. The player then throws one of the larger balls ("boccia"), trying to get it as close to the pallina as possible without touching it. Players from the opposing team take turns throwing their balls until one of the balls stops closer to the pallina than the starting player's ball. If they fail to do so, the starting team tries to outdo its first attempt. Teams continue to take turns in this manner until they have thrown all the balls. The team with closest ball gets a point. This game emphasizes throwing skills (coordination, gross and fine motor skills).

Unicycling – Good activity for training coordination, gross motor skills, and balance. Safety precautions include practice on a padded surface if possible (gym mats or grass) and safety gear (helmets, elbow, and kneepads). As with most activities, horseplay is prohibited, and no one should interfere with a practicing unicyclist – the practice area should be kept free of obstruction and the unicyclist has the "right-of-way". Unicyclists should have a spotter at all times.

Juggling and Team Juggling – develops psychomotor skills (timing, hand-eye coordination, throwing, and catching – both gross and fine motor skills), cognitive skills (recognizing rise and fall patterns of the juggled objects and comprehending cyclic rhythm), affective skills (goal setting, tracking improvement, perseverance, and delay of gratification), and teamwork in the case of Team Juggling.

Dance Concepts and Forms

Students of dance acquire many skills during their course of study. The student identifies and demonstrates movement elements in dance performance and uses correct body alignment, strength, flexibility, and stamina (for more demanding performances). Crucial to any form of dance is the concept of coordination in the performance of technical movements. Technical movements must look as though they are easy to perform. The dancer must perform technical dance skills with artistic expression including musicality and rhythm. As the student progresses, he or she will perform more extended movement sequences and rhythmic patterns. The student will then have enough experience to introduce his or her own stylistic nuance into the performance. The student will also be able to use improvisation to solve movement problems and adjust choices based on the movement responses of other dancers in the ensemble. Through continued experience, he or she will become a skillful, seasoned dancer whose technique and ability will transcend any form of dance.

Instructors can create rhythmic activities by putting on music with a strong beat and asking students to dance to the beat. Tell the students to listen to the beat and move accordingly (e.g. stomping their feet or clapping their hands in time with the beat). It's important for children to learn to move to various sounds and use their bodies to mimic the beat. Another idea is to have the students take turns beating on a coffee can while trying to keep movements in sync with the rhythm. In more structured dance forms, technique or skill comes into play.

For instance, in ballet, dancers must have good flexibility, body control, and coordination. Ballet dancers must also have a sense of rhythm, an understanding of music, good turnout and alignment, and a sense of balance and counterbalance. These skills take many years to acquire and, once acquired, take many more years to master and maintain. Ballet dancing may express a mood, tell a story, or simply reflect a piece of music and is the most classical of all dance forms. Other types of music may have similar requirements in terms of a sense of musicality and rhythm. For example, tap dance requires a greater degree of footwork and modern is comparable to ballet, but more flowing and less rigid.

Skill 50.2   Recognize basic rules and social etiquette for physical activities.

Apply Rules to Various Games

ARCHERY:
- Arrows that bounce off the target or go through the target count as 7 points.
- Arrows landing on lines between two rings receive the higher score of the two rings.
- Arrows hitting the petticoat receive no score.

BADMINTON:
- Intentionally balking opponent or making preliminary feints results in a fault (side in = loss of serve; side out = point awarded to side in).
- When a shuttlecock falls on a line, it is in play (i.e. a fair play).
- If the striking team hits shuttlecock before it crosses net it is a fault.
- Touching the net when the shuttlecock is in play is a fault.
- The same player hitting the shuttlecock twice is a fault.
- The shuttlecock going through the net is a fault.

BOWLING:
- No score for a pin knocked down by a pinsetter (human or mechanical).
- There is no score for the pins when any part of the foot, hand, or arm extends or crosses over the foul line (even after ball leaves the hand) or if any part of the body contacts division boards, walls, or uprights that are beyond the foul line.
- There is no count for pins displaced or knocked down by a ball leaving the lane before it reaches the pins.
- There is no count when balls rebound from the rear cushion.

RACQUETBALL/HANDBALL:
- A server stepping outside service area when serving faults.
- The server is out (relinquishes serve) if he/she steps outside of serving zone twice in succession while serving.
- Server is out if he/she fails to hit the ball rebounding off the floor during the serve.
- The opponent must have a chance to take a position or the referee must call for play before the server can serve the ball.
- The server re-serves the ball if the receiver is not behind the short line at the time of the serve.
- A served ball that hits the front line and does not land back of the short line is "short"; therefore, it is a fault. The ball is also short when it hits the front wall and two sidewalls before it lands on the floor back of the short line.
- A serve is a fault when the ball touches the ceiling from rebounding off the front wall.

- A fault occurs when any part of the foot steps over the outer edges of the service or the short line while serving.
- A hinder (dead ball) is called when a returned ball hits an opponent on its way to the front wall - even if the ball continues to the front wall.
- A hinder is any intentional or unintentional interference of an opponent's opportunity to return the ball.

TENNIS:
A player loses a point when:
- The ball bounces twice on her side of the net.
- The player returns the ball to any place outside of designated areas.
- The player stops or touches the ball in the air before it lands out-of-bounds.
- The player intentionally strikes the ball twice with the racket.
- The ball strikes any part of a player or racket after initial attempt to hit the ball.
- A player reaches over the net to hit the ball.
- A player throws his racket at the ball.
- The ball strikes any permanent fixture that is out-of-bounds (other than the net).
    - a ball touching the net and landing inside the boundary lines is in play (except on the serve, where a ball contacting the net results in a "let" – replay of the point)
- A player fails, on two consecutive attempts, to serve the ball into the designated area (i.e. double fault).

Appropriate Behavior in Physical Education Activities

Appropriate Student Etiquette/Behaviors include: following the rules and accepting the consequences of unfair action, good sportsmanship, respecting the rights of other students, reporting own accidents and mishaps, not engaging in inappropriate behavior under peer pressure encouragement, cooperation, paying attention to instructions and demonstrations, moving to assigned places and remaining in own space, complying with directions, practicing as instructed to do so, properly using equipment, and not interfering with the practice of others.
Appropriate Content Etiquette/Behaviors include the teacher describing the performance of tasks and students engaging in the task, the teacher assisting students with task performance, and the teacher modifying and developing tasks.
Appropriate Management Etiquette/Behaviors include the teacher directing the management of equipment, students, and space prior to practicing tasks; students getting equipment and partners; the teacher requesting that students stop "fooling around."

Rules of Team Sports
BASKETBALL:
- A player touching the floor on or outside the boundary line is out-of-bounds.
- The ball is out of bounds if it touches anything (a player, the floor, an object, or any person) that is on or outside the boundary line.
- An offensive player remaining in the three-second zone of the free-throw lane for more than three seconds is a violation.
- A ball firmly held by two opposing players results in a jump ball.
- A throw-in is awarded to the opposing team of the last player touching a ball that goes out-of-bounds.

SOCCER:
The following are direct free-kick offenses:
- Hand or arm contact with the ball
- Using hands to hold an opponent
- Pushing an opponent
- Striking/kicking/tripping or attempting to strike/kick/trip an opponent
- Goalie using the ball to strike an opponent
- Jumping at or charging an opponent
- Kneeing an opponent
- Any contact fouls

The following are indirect free-kick offenses:
- Same player playing the ball twice at the kickoff, on a throw-in, on a goal kick, on a free kick, or on a corner kick.
- The goalie delaying the game by holding the ball or carrying the ball more than four steps.
- Failure to notify the referee of substitutions/re-substitutions and that player then handling the ball in the penalty area.
- Any person, who is not a player, entering playing field without a referee's permission.
- Unsportsmanlike actions or words in reference to a referee's decision.
- Dangerously lowering the head or raising the foot too high to make a play.
- A player resuming play after being ordered off the field.
- Offsides – an offensive player must have two defenders between him and the goal when a teammate passes the ball to him or else he is offsides.
- Attempting to kick the ball when the goalkeeper has possession or interference with the goalkeeper to hinder him/her from releasing the ball.
- Illegal charging.
- Leaving the playing field without referee's permission while the ball is in play.

SOFTBALL:
- Each team plays nine players in the field (sometimes 10 for slow pitch).
- Field positions are one pitcher, one catcher, four infielders, and three outfielders (four outfielders in ten player formats).
- The four bases are 60 feet apart.

- Any ball hit outside of the first or third base line is a foul ball (i.e. runners cannot advance and the pitch counts as a strike against the batter)
- If a batter receives three strikes (i.e. failed attempts at hitting the ball) in a single at bat he/she strikes out.
- The pitcher must start with both feet on the pitcher's rubber and can only take one step forward when delivering the underhand pitch.
- A base runner is out if:
  - A. The opposition tags him with the ball before he reaches a base.
  - B. The ball reaches first base before he does.
  - C. He runs outside of the base path to avoid a tag.
  - D. A batted ball strikes him in fair territory.
- A team must maintain the same batting order throughout the game.
- Runners cannot lead off and base stealing is illegal.
- Runners may overrun first base, but can be tagged out if off any other base.

VOLLEYBALL:

The following infractions by the receiving team result in a point awarded to the serving side and an infraction by serving team results in side-out:

- Illegal serves or serving out of turn.
- Illegal returns or catching or holding the ball.
- Dribbling or a player touching the ball twice in succession.
- Contact with the net (two opposing players making contact with the net at the same time results in a replay of the point).
- Touching the ball after it has been played three times without passing over the net.
- A player's foot completely touching the floor over the centerline.
- Reaching under the net and touching a player or the ball while the ball is in play.
- The players changing positions prior to the serve.

Skill 50.3   Select activities for their potential to include all students regardless of gender, race, culture, religion, abilities, or disabilities.

Inclusion and Mainstreaming

A major goal of contemporary physical education is inclusion and mainstreaming of all types of students. Instructors must modify activities to include students with disabilities and students of all ability levels. In addition, the physical education program should embrace the cultural, linguistic, and familial differences of all students. Inclusion and mainstreaming shifts the focus of physical education from competitive, athletic activities to cooperative, skill-building activities that benefit all children and promote inclusion. Thus, the primary goal and focus of physical education is promotion of physical activity, motor-skill development, and socialization.

Appropriate Activities and Adaptations for Students with Limitations
Appropriate activities are those activities in which handicapped students can successfully participate.

Adaptations include individualized instruction and modified rules, modified environments, and modified tasks. As needs warrant, instructors can move participants to less restrictive environments. Instructors can also initiate periodic assessments to advance a student's placement, review progress, and determine what the least restrictive environment is for each participant (including changing services to produce future optimum progress). However, the most appropriate placement depends on meeting the physical education needs, both educational and social, of the handicapped student.

Functional Adaptations
Instructors can provide blind students with auditory or tactile clues to help them find objects or to position their bodies in the activity area. Blind students also can learn the patterns of movement by manually mimicking the correct patterns or by verbal instructions.

Deaf students can read lips or learn signing to communicate and understand instructions.

Physically challenged students may have to use crutches to enable them to move.

Asthmatics can play goalie or similar positions requiring less cardio-respiratory demands.

Simplifying rules can accommodate a retarded participant's limited comprehension.

Adapting Selected Activities
Walking: adapt distance, distance over time, and number of steps in specified distance; provide handrails for support; change slope for incline walking; and change width of walking pathway.
Stair climbing: change pathway, pace of climbing, and number and height of steps.
Running: change distance over time, use an incline-changing slope (distance over time), and form a maze (distance over time).
Jumping: change distance and height of jump, change distance in a series and from a platform, change participants' arm positions.
Hopping: change distance for one and two hops (using preferred and non-preferred leg) and distance through obstacle course.
Galloping: change number of gallops over distance, change distance covered in number of gallops, and widen pathway.
Skipping: change number of errorless skips, change distance covered in number of skips, change number of skips in distance, and add music for skipping in rhythm.
Leaping: change distance and height of leaps.

Bouncing balls: change size of ball (larger), have participant use two hands, reduce number of dribbles, bounce ball higher, have participant stand stationary and perform bounces one at a time.

Catching: use larger balls and have participant catch balls thrown at chest level from a lower height of release, shorten catching distance, have participant stop and then catch ball (easier than moving and catching).

Adapting for Problems with Strength, Endurance, and Power Activities
1. Lower basketball goals or nets; increase size of target.
2. Decrease throwing distance between partners, serving distance, and distance between bases.
3. Reduce size or weight of projectiles or balls.
4. Shorten length and/or reduce weight of bat or other striking apparatus.
5. Play games in lying or sitting positions to lower center of gravity.
6. Select a "slow ball" (one that will not get away too fast), deflate ball in case it gets away, or attach a string to the ball for recovery.
7. Reduce playing time and lower number of points to win.
8. Use more frequent rest periods.
9. Rotate often or use frequent substitution when needed.
10. Use mobilization alternatives, such as using scooter boards one inning/period and feet for one inning/period.

Adapting for Balance and Agility Problems
1. Verify if balance problem is due to medication (you may have to consult physician).
2. Use chairs, tables, or bars to help with stability.
3. Have participants learn to utilize eyes optimally for balance skills.
4. Teach various ways to fall and incorporate dramatics into fall activities.
5. Use carpeted surfaces.
6. Lower center of gravity.
7. Have participant extend arms or provide a lightweight pole.
8. Have participant keep as much of his/her body in contact with the surface.
9. Widen base of support (distance between feet).
10. Increase width of walking parameters.

Adapting for Coordination and Accuracy
Throwing Activities: use beanbags, yarn or nerf balls, and/or smaller-sized balls.
Catching and Striking Activities: use larger, softer, and lighter balls; throw balls to mid-line; shorten distance; and reduce speed of balls.
Striking/Kicking Activities: enlarge striking surface, choke up on bats, begin with participant successfully striking stationary objects and then progress to striking with movement, and increase target size.

Skill 50.4   Integrate activities with other content areas, such as math and science.

Physical education is a key component of an interdisciplinary learning approach because it draws from many other curriculum areas. Instructors can relate concepts from the physical sciences, mathematics, natural sciences, social sciences, and kinesiology to physical education activities.

Physical science is a term for the branches of science that study non-living systems. However, the term "physical" creates an unintended, arbitrary distinction, since many branches of physical science also study biological phenomena. Topics in physical science such as movement of an object through space and the effect of gravity on moving objects are of great relevance to physical education. Physical sciences allow us to determine the limits of physical activities.

Mathematics is the search for fundamental truths in pattern, quantity, and change. Examples of mathematical applications in sport include measuring speed, momentum, and height of objects; measuring distances and weights; scorekeeping; and statistical computations.

Natural science is the study of living things. Content areas in the natural sciences of great importance to physical education include physiology, nutrition, anatomy, and biochemistry. For example, a key component of physical education is an understanding of proper nutrition and the affect of food on the body.

The social sciences are a group of academic disciplines that study the human aspects of the world. Social scientists engage in research and theorize about both aggregate and individual behaviors. For example, a basic understanding of psychology is essential to the discussion of human patterns of nutrition and attitudes toward exercise and fitness. In addition, sport psychology is a specialized social science that explores the mental aspects of athletic performance.

Finally, kinesiology encompasses human anatomy, physiology, neuroscience, biochemistry, biomechanics, exercise psychology, and sociology of sport. Kinesiologists also study the relationship between the quality of movement and overall human health. Kinesiology is an important part of physical therapy, occupational therapy, chiropractics, osteopathy, exercise physiology, kinesiotherapy, massage therapy, ergonomics, physical education, and athletic coaching. The purpose of these applications may be therapeutic, preventive, or high-performance. The application of kinesiology can also incorporate knowledge from other academic disciplines such as psychology, sociology, cultural studies, ecology, evolutionary biology, and anthropology. The study of kinesiology is often part of the physical education curriculum and illustrates the truly interdisciplinary nature of physical education.

DOMAIN II – SELF-IMAGE AND PERSONAL DEVELOPMENT

COMPETENCY 51.0 PHYSICAL GROWTH AND DEVELOPMENT

Skill 51.1   Identify the sequential development of fine and gross motor skills in children and young adolescents.

The development of motor skills in children is a sequential process. We can classify motor skill competency into stages of development by observing children practicing physical skills. The sequence of development begins with simple reflexes and progresses to the learning of postural elements, locomotor skills, and, finally, fine motor skills. The stages of development consider both innate and learned behaviors.

Stages of Motor Learning

Stage 1 – Children progress from simple reflexes to basic movements such as sitting, crawling, creeping, standing, and walking.

Stage 2 – Children learn more complex motor patterns including running, climbing, jumping, balancing, catching, and throwing.

Stage 3 – During late childhood, children learn more specific movement skills. In addition, the basic motor patterns learned in stage 2 become more fluid and automatic.

Stage 4 – During adolescence, children continue to develop general and specific motor skills and master specialized movements. At this point, factors including practice, motivation, and talent begin to affect the level of further development.

Sequential Development for Locomotor Skills Acquisition

Sequential Development = crawl, creep, walk, run, jump, hop, gallop, slide, leap, skip, step-hop.

Sequential Development for Nonlocomotor Skills Acquisition

Sequential Development = stretch, bend, sit, shake, turn, rock and sway, swing, twist, dodge, and fall.
Sequential Development for Manipulative Skills Acquisition

Sequential Development = striking, throwing, kicking, ball rolling, volleying, bouncing, catching, and trapping.

Skill 51.2   Describe the influence of growth spurts and body type on movement and coordination.

Recognizing individual students' physical changes helps with understanding how their physiques affect motor performance. The child's physique has a definite affect on their motor performance. Somatype, another term for body type, deals with how fat, muscular, and linear your body is. The three body types are endomorph, mesomorph, and ectomorph. Everyone is some combination of the three types, with one classification usually prevailing over the others. You cannot change your body type but you can modify it through your eating habits and level of physical exercise, which in turn affects your body-fat percentage. Certain body types are more suited for certain sports, but it doesn't mean you won't be successful if your somatype is different from what's mentioned. Somatype classification is important because it shows how children differ in body physique and how vital it is that instruction accommodates individual differences.

Endomorphs are naturally "large" or "big boned" with a pear-shaped bodies and a slow metabolism. Endomorphs are often very strong, but have little speed. They experience difficulty at most sports, including both aerobic and anaerobic activities. Individual sports such as shot or discus throwing in track, wrestling, and judo are activities well suited for endomorphs.

Mesomorphs are "muscular" with an hourglass figure, broad shoulders, small waist, strong thighs, fast metabolism, and little body fat. Often called "natural athletes," they participate with ease and look forward to physical competition of any sort. These children perform best in team sports that require strength, speed, and agility such as football and baseball, or individual sports such as swimming. Ectomorphs, often called "skinny," are extremely thin, with very little body fat, little or no muscle development, and an ultra fast metabolism. Ectomorphs have difficulty gaining weight or muscle mass. Because they lack power and strength, they are better suited for aerobic endurance activities such as cross-country running, many track and field events such as the high or long jump, sprints, relays, and middle-distance running.

Developmental Issues During Human Growth
Understanding the rate of the developmental growth process that occurs during adolescence will help educators understand growth and development norms and identify early or late maturing students. The age when the puberty growth spurt occurs and the speed with which adolescents experience puberty vary greatly within each gender and may affect participation in physical activity and sports. If the instructor pays attention to the varying body sizes and maturity stages, forming teams in co-educational classes can easily accommodate the needs of both genders' changing maturities.

Starting in middle school and continuing into high school, it is perfectly acceptable for boys and girls to participate in non-contact physical activities together that rely on lower-body strength and agility (e.g. capture the flag, ultimate Frisbee, running). In more physical activities that require upper body strength, coaches should form teams based on individual skill levels to prevent injury. Matching teams evenly based on skill and maturity is important so that individual skill level deficiencies are not as apparent and the activity remains fun for all participants. Teachers need to monitor and adjust physical activities as needed to ensure a positive, competitive experience. Appropriate activities would include individual or partner badminton or tennis matches and team competitions in flag football.

Skill 51.3 Recognize the impact of factors such as exercise, relaxation, nutrition, stress, and substance abuse on physical health and general well-being.

The effect of factors such as gender, age, environment, nutrition, heredity and substance abuse is also crucial in understanding adolescent fitness performance. Girls mature earlier than boys do, but boys quickly catch up and grow larger and stronger. Age, combined with maturity level, influences a child's physical strength, flexibility, and coordination. Good nutrition positively influences the quality of a child's physical activity level, while poor nutrition has the opposite effect. Adverse environmental conditions such as high heat or poor air quality strongly affect activity level. Students that inherit favorable physical characteristics will perform better and with more ease than those who aren't so fortunate. Substance abuse of any sort – alcohol, tobacco, or drugs – is a detriment to physical performance.

Dealing with factors that are out of the teacher's control requires both structure and flexibility. When necessary, make adjustments amongst the students and/or the activity. For example, when teaching how to throw a softball, don't hesitate to pair girls with boys if their maturity and strength levels are similar. If the distance is too far for some pairs, move them closer. If some pairs are more advanced, challenge them by increasing the partner's distance while continuing to work on accuracy and speed. Add a personal challenge to see how many times they can toss without dropping the ball. Finally, having more advanced students teach their peers that aren't as competent will benefit all students. A variety of influences affects a student's motor development, growth, and fitness level:

Psychological – Psychological influences on motor development and fitness include a student's mental well-being, perceptions of fitness activities, and level of comfort in a fitness-training environment (both alone and within a group). Students experiencing psychological difficulties, such as depression, will tend to be apathetic and lack both the energy and inclination to participate in fitness activities. As a result, their motor development and fitness levels will suffer. Factors like the student's confidence level and comfort within a group environment, related to both the student's level of popularity within the group and the student's own personal insecurities, are also significant. It is noteworthy, though, that in the case of psychological influences on motor development and fitness levels, there is a more reciprocal relationship than with other influences. While a student's psychology may negatively affect their fitness levels, proper fitness training has the potential to positively affect the student psychologically, thereby reversing a negative cycle.

Cultural – Culture is a significant and sometimes overlooked influence on a student's motor development and fitness, especially in the case of students belonging to minority groups. Students may not feel motivated to participate in certain physical activities, either because they are not associated with the student's sense of identity or because the student's culture discourages these activities. For example, students from cultures with strict dress codes may not be comfortable with swimming activities. On the same note, students (especially older children) may be uncomfortable with physical activities in inter-gender situations. Educators must keep such cultural considerations in mind when planning physical education curricula.

Economic – The economic situation of students can affect their motor development and fitness because lack of resources can detract from the ability of parents to provide access to extra-curricular activities that promote development, proper fitness training equipment (ranging from complex exercise machines to team sport uniforms to something as simple as a basketball hoop), and even adequate nutrition.

Familial – Familial factors that can influence motor development and fitness relate to the student's home climate concerning physical activity. A student's own feelings toward physical activity often reflect the degree to which caregivers and role models (like older siblings) are athletically inclined and have a positive attitude towards physical activity. It isn't necessary for the parents to be athletically inclined, so much as it is important for them to encourage their child to explore fitness activities that could suit them.

Environmental and Health – Genetic make-up (i.e. age, gender, ethnicity) has a big influence on growth and development. Various physical and environmental factors directly affect one's personal health and fitness. Poor habits, living conditions, and afflictions such as disease or disability can impact a person in a negative manner. A healthy lifestyle with adequate conditions and minimal physical or mental stresses will enable a person to develop towards a positive, healthy existence. A highly agreed upon motor development theory is the relationship between one's own heredity and environmental factors.

Instructors should place students in rich learning situations, regardless of previous experience or personal factors, which provide plenty of positive opportunities to participate in physical activity. For example, prior to playing a game of softball, have students practice throwing by tossing the ball to themselves, progress to the underhand toss, and later to the overhand toss.

Identify Common Signs of Stress

Emotional signs of stress include: depression, lethargy, aggressiveness, irritability, anxiety, edginess, fearfulness, impulsiveness, chronic fatigue hyper excitability, inability to concentrate, frequent feelings of boredom, feeling overwhelmed, apathy, impatience, pessimism, sarcasm, humorlessness, confusion, helplessness, melancholy, alienation, isolation, numbness, purposelessness, isolation, numbness, self-consciousness; inability to maintain an intimate relationship.

Behavioral signs of stress include: elevated use of substances (alcohol, drugs; tobacco), crying, yelling, insomnia or excessive sleep, excessive TV watching, school/job burnout, panic attacks, poor problems solving capability, avoidance of people, aberrant behavior, procrastination, accident proneness, restlessness, loss of memory, indecisiveness, aggressiveness, inflexibility, phobic responses, tardiness, disorganization; sexual problems.

Physical signs of stress: pounding heart, stuttering, trembling/nervous tics, excessive perspiration, teeth grinding, gastrointestinal problems (constipation, indigestion, diarrhea, queasy stomach), dry mouth, aching lower back, migraine/tension headaches, stiff neck, asthma attacks, allergy attacks, skin problems, frequent colds or low grade fevers, muscle tension, hyperventilation, high blood pressure, amenorrhea, nightmares; cold intolerance.

Identify Both Positive and Negative Coping Strategies for Individuals Under Stress

Positive coping strategies to cope with stress include using one's social support system, spiritual support, managing time, initiating direct action, re-examining priorities, active thinking, acceptance, meditation, imagery, biofeedback, progressive relaxation, deep breathing, massage, sauna, Jacuzzi, humor, recreation and diversions, and exercise.

Negative coping strategies to cope with stress include: using alcohol or other mind altering substances, smoking, excessive caffeine intake, poor eating habits, negative "self-talk;" expressing feelings of distress, anger, and other feelings in a destructive manner.

COMPETENCY 52.0 SELF-IMAGE

Skill 52.1   **Describe the role of physical activity in the development of a positive self-image, and how psychological skills such as goal setting are selected to promote lifelong participation in physical activity.**

For most people, the development of social roles and appropriate social behaviors occurs during childhood. Physical play between parents and children, as well as between siblings and peers, serves as a strong regulator in the developmental process. Chasing games, roughhousing, wrestling, or practicing sport skills such as jumping, throwing, catching, and striking, are some examples of childhood play. These activities may be competitive or non-competitive and are important for promoting social and moral development of both boys and girls. Unfortunately, fathers will often engage in this sort of activity more with their sons than their daughters. Regardless of the sex of the child, both boys and girls enjoy these types of activities.

Physical play during infancy and early childhood is central to the development of social and emotional competence. Research shows that children who engage in play that is more physical with their parents, particularly with parents who are sensitive and responsive to the child, exhibited greater enjoyment during the play sessions and were more popular with their peers. Likewise, these early interactions with parents, siblings, and peers are important in helping children become more aware of their emotions and to learn to monitor and regulate their own emotional responses. Children learn quickly through watching the responses of their parents which behaviors make their parents smile and laugh and which behaviors cause their parents to frown and disengage from the activity.

If children want the fun to continue, they engage in the behaviors that please others. As children near adolescence, they learn through rough-and-tumble play that there are limits to how far they can go before hurting someone (physically or emotionally), which results in termination of the activity or later rejection of the child by peers. These early interactions with parents and siblings are important in helping children learn appropriate behavior in the social situations of sport and physical activity.

Children learn to assess their social competence (i.e., ability to get along with and acceptance by peers, family members, teachers and coaches) in sport through the feedback received from parents and coaches. Initially, authority figures teach children, "You can't do that because I said so." As children approach school age, parents begin the process of explaining why a behavior is right or wrong because children continuously ask, "why?"

Similarly, when children engage in sports, they learn about taking turns with their teammates, sharing playing time, and valuing rules. They understand that rules are important for everyone and without these regulations, the game would become unfair. The learning of social competence is continuous as we expand our social arena and learn about different cultures. A constant in the learning process is the role of feedback as we assess the responses of others to our behaviors and comments.

In addition to the development of social competence, sport participation can help youth develop other forms of self-competence. Most important among these self-competencies is self-esteem. Self-esteem is how we judge our worth and indicates the extent to which an individual believes he is capable, significant, successful and worthy. Educators have suggested that one of the biggest barriers to success in the classroom today is low self-esteem.

Children develop self-esteem by evaluating abilities and by evaluating the responses of others. Children actively observe the responses of parents and coaches to their performances, looking for signs of approval or disapproval of their behavior. Children often interpret feedback and criticism as either a negative or a positive response to the behavior. In sports, research shows that the coach is a critical source of information that influences the self-esteem of children.

Little League baseball players whose coaches use a "positive approach" to coaching (e.g. more frequent encouragement, positive reinforcement for effort and corrective, instructional feedback), had significantly higher self-esteem ratings over the course of a season than children whose coaches used these techniques less frequently. The most compelling evidence supporting the importance of coaches' feedback was found for those children who started the season with the lowest self-esteem ratings and increased considerably their self-assessment and self-worth. In addition to evaluating themselves more positively, low self-esteem children evaluated their coaches more positively than did children with higher self-esteem who played for coaches who used the "positive approach." Moreover, studies show that 95 percent of children who played for coaches trained to use the positive approach signed up to play baseball the next year, compared with 75 percent of the youth who played for untrained adult coaches.

We cannot overlook the importance of enhanced self-esteem on future participation. A major part of the development of high self-esteem is the pride and joy that children experience as their physical skills improve. Children will feel good about themselves as long as their skills are improving. If children feel that their performance during a game or practice is not as good as that of others, or as good as they think mom and dad would want, they often experience shame and disappointment.

Some children will view mistakes made during a game as a failure and will look for ways to avoid participating in the task if they receive no encouragement to continue. At this point, it is critical that adults (e.g., parents and coaches) intervene to help children to interpret the mistake or "failure." We must teach children that a mistake is not synonymous with failure. Rather, a mistake shows us that we need a new strategy, more practice, and/or greater effort to succeed at the task.

Goal Setting

Goal setting is an effective way of achieving progress. In order to preserve and/or increase self-confidence, you and your students must set goals that are frequently reachable. One such way of achieving this is to set several small, short-term goals to attain one long-term goal. Be realistic in goal setting to increase fitness levels gradually. As students reach their goals, set more in order to continue performance improvement. Keep in mind that maintaining a current fitness level is an adequate goal provided the individual is in a healthy state. Reward your students when they reach goals. Rewards serve as motivation to reach the next goal. Also, be sure to prepare for lapses. Try to get back on track as soon as possible.

DOMAIN III – SOCIAL DEVELOPMENT

COMPETENCY 53.0 SOCIAL ASPECTS OF PHYSICAL EDUCATION

Skill 53.1 **Recognize individual differences such as gender, race, culture, ability, or disability.**

Biological and Environmental Influence on Gender Differences in Motor Performances

The differences between males and females in motor performance result from certain biological and environmental influences. Generally, people perceive the males as stronger, faster, and more active than females. This higher activity level can stem from childhood behaviors influenced by certain environmental factors and superior motor performance results largely from the biological make up of males versus females.

In most cases, the male body contains less fat mass and more muscle mass than the female body. In addition, the type of muscle differs between males and females. Males have more fast-twitch muscle fibers allowing for more short duration, high intensity movements such as jumping and sprinting. In addition, males generally, but not always, display better coordination. Females have proved their superiority at certain activities, such as skipping, and tend to display better fine movements, such as neater handwriting.

Certain environmental factors also contribute to the gender differences in motor performance. As children, boys tend to be more physically active. Society expects boys to participate in sports and play games that involve running around, such as tag and foot races. On the other hand, society expects girls to be more social and less active. They participate in activities such as playing with dolls. In addition, parents rarely ask girls to perform tasks involving manual labor.

Skill Level
Expectations relating to skill level influence the development of self-concept by setting the baseline for the performance that students will expect to deliver, both when attempting tasks that they are familiar with and new tasks (students with a high skill level will expect to do well, and students who are good at several things will expect to be good at other, new things).

Culture
Cultural expectations influence the development of self-concept by suggesting to the child traits they should include in their personal self-assessment. For example, students from a very warm and energetic cultural background, where there is a strong emphasis on family life, may develop self-concepts that incorporate those traits into their personal self-description. Cultural gender roles may also express themselves in this way.

Disability

In general, teachers may need to modify instructional methods to accommodate students with disabilities participating in physical education class. The physical educator should ensure that students with disabilities understand the purpose of the lesson before the activity begins. The teacher should design lesson plans that include alternate activities in the event that the originally planned activity does not work well for the student(s) with disabilities. Teachers should not place students with disabilities in activities where they have no chance of success. Thus, teachers should avoid elimination games. The physical educator should praise even minor displays of progress and achievement. The teacher should work with the student(s) with disabilities to set achievable goals, as goal attainment is a wonderful motivator.

Physical educators must have a strong, working knowledge of specific disabilities and how they affect a student's ability to learn. When working with students mentally retarded students, instructors should emphasize progressive gross motor movement. Teacher instruction should focus on demonstration rather than oral explanation. Instructors should reward effort displayed by students. Additionally, the practice periods for students with mental retardation should be short to alleviate boredom and aggravation. Instructors should also make modifications for the visually impaired student. Lesson planning for the visually impaired student should focus on individual movement activities. The physical educator should use a whistle or loud verbal cues in class. If the visually impaired student has some residual eyesight, the teacher might have the student utilize a brightly colored ball against a contrasting backdrop. When working with a student with a hearing impairment, the physical education teacher should use visual cues. The instructor or other students must read all written instructions aloud. During all stages of instruction, the hearing-impaired student should be close to the teacher. If a student with an orthopedic disability is present in class, lesson plans should focus on individual and dual sports to maximize the student's chance of success. Lastly, instructors may need to make modifications for students with emotional disabilities. Students with emotional disabilities can succeed in a stable, organized setting. The teacher should praise individual accomplishments. In order to avoid or minimize behavior disruptions, the instructor should clearly identify and consistently enforce rules and expectations. Finally, when working with a student with any given disability, it is crucial that the physical education teacher follows the physician instructions exactly.

Skill 53.2   Describe the developmental appropriateness of cooperation, competition, and responsible social behavior for children of different ages.

Cooperative and Competitive Games

Cooperative games are a class of games that promote teamwork and social interaction. The emphasis is on activity, fitness, skill development, and cooperation, rather than competition. There are many cooperative games available to the physical education instructor that helps develop various coordination skills and teamwork. Examples of cooperative games include throwing and catching, freeze tag, and parachute.

Competitive games are a class of games that emphasize score, winning, and beating an opponent. Physical education instructors should integrate competitive games into the curriculum to generate student interest and teach concepts of fair play and sportsmanship. Competitive games are most suitable for students that are more mature and possess more developed skills. All of the traditional sporting events are competitive games.

Instructors can organize games by grade levels, homerooms, clubs, societies, physical education classes, study groups, age, height, weight, residential districts, or by arbitrary assignment.

SKILL 53.3   List activities to provide opportunities for enjoyment, self-expression, and communication.

Enjoyment and Personal Expression

In addition to the previously discussed achievement benefits of physical activity, physical activity also provides many people with pure enjoyment and the opportunity for personal expression. Exercise promotes a sense of well-being and usually improves a person's mood. Sports also provide a venue for social interaction and enjoyment of nature. Finally, many sports and activities, especially freestyle activities like skateboarding, figure skating, dance, and surfing, allow for a high level of personal expression.

Communication

By participating in physical activities, students develop various aspects of the self that are easily applicable to other settings (e.g., the workplace). Communication is one skill that improves enormously through participation in sports and games. Students will come to understand that skillful communication can contribute to a better all-around outcome, whether it be winning the game or successfully completing a team project. They will see that effective communication helps to develop and maintain healthy personal relationships, organize and convey information, and reduce or avoid conflict.

COMPETENCY 54.0 CULTURAL AND HISTORIC ASPECTS OF PHYSICAL MOVEMENT FORMS

Skill 54.1   **Understand the significance of cultural and historical influences on games, sports, dance, and other physical activities.**

Contributions of Early Societies to the Profession

Games often had a practical, educational aim like playing house. In addition, games such as gladiatorial games had political aims. Economic games included fishing and hunting. Families played board games. There were ceremonial reasons for games found in dances. Finally, ball games provided an opportunity for socialization.

Early society - The common activities performed in early societies included war-like games, chariot racing, boating and fishing, equestrian, hunting, music and dancing, boxing and wrestling, bow and arrow activities, dice, and knucklebones.

Egyptian - The common activities performed in Egypt were acrobatics, gymnastics, tug of war, hoop and kick games, ball and stick games, juggling, knife-throwing games of chance, board games, and guessing games (e.g. how many fingers are concealed).

Bronze Age - The activities performed during the Bronze Age (3000 to 1000 BC) were bullfights, dancing, boxing, hunting, archery, running, and board games.

Greek Age - The Greeks are best known for the Olympic Games, but their other contributions were the pentathlon, which included the jump, the discus, and the javelin. The Pankration was a combination of boxing and wrestling. The Greeks also played on seesaws, enjoyed swinging, hand guessing games, blind man's bluff, dice games (losers had to carry their partner's pick-a-back), and hoop and board games. There also were funeral games in The Iliad.

Romans - The Romans kept slaves and were advocates of "blood sports." Their philosophy was to die well. There were unemployment games. Roman baths were popular, as were ball games, stuffed feathers, pila trigonalis, follis, and balloon or bladder ball. The Capitoline games were held in 86 AD. These union guild athletes were paid for their activities, which included artificial fly-fishing. The games that were popular during this period were top spinning, odds and evens, riding a long stick, knucklebones, and hide and seek.

Chinese - The Chinese contributed the following: jujitsu, fighting cocks, dog racing, and football. In Korea, Japan, and China, children played with toys and lanterns. Common activities included building snowmen, playing with dolls, making/playing with shadows, flying kites, and fighting kites. Children enjoyed ropewalker toys, windmills, turnip lanterns, ring puzzles, and playing horse.

Noblemen engaged in hopping, jumping, leapfrog, jump rope, seesaw, and drawing.

Major Events in the History of Physical Education

Egypt - Sport dancing among the nobility, physical skills among the masses, and physical training for wars.

Cretans - learned to swim.

Spartan and Greeks - emphasized severe physical training and NOT competitive sport.

Athenians - believed in the harmonious development of the body, mind and spirit.

Romans – The Romans established the **worth of physical education**. During the dark ages, children learned fitness and horsemanship. The squires learned how to become knights by boxing and fencing. Swimming was also popular. During the Renaissance, people developed the body for health reasons. The Romans **combined the physical and mental** aspects of exercise in their daily routines.

1349-1428 - Physical education was necessary for a person's total education and also a means of recreation.

In **1546,** Martin Luther saw PE as a substitute for vice and evil.

Sweden - Ling in 1839 strove to make PE a **science.**

Colonial period - Religions denounced play. Pleasures were either banned or frowned upon.

The **National Period** began in 1823. Games and sports were available as after school activities. There was an introduction of **gymnastics and calisthenics.**

Civil War (1860) - Gymnastics and non-military use of PE. Physical Education became **organized.** PE became part of the school curriculum and held a respectable status among other subjects. **YMCA's** were founded. Gulick was the Director of PE at NYC and Dudley Allen Sargent was teaching physical education at Harvard.

Great Depression of the 1930s - Physical fitness movement. Bowling was the number one activity. Dance, gymnastics and sports were popular. The Heisman Trophy was awarded in 1935. After WWII, outdoor pools were common for the average American.

COMPETENCY 55.0 SKILLS AND ABILITIES

Skill 55.1   Understand the key factors in the development, analysis, and assessment of basic motor skills.

Development

Physical education helps individuals attain a healthy level of fitness and renders significant experiences in movement. It provides an opportunity to refine and develop motor skills, stamina, strategies and the pure pleasure of physical activity and participation. Children, infants, and the disabled are all entitled to benefit from physical education. Physical activities can be adapted by recognizing the individual's abilities, learning skills, needs, etc. This requires knowledge about the science of movement, the process of skill development, social and psychological components, physical fitness, assessment of the practices of physical activities, and development and implementation of proper and appropriate activities.

Children are at a developmental stage where their physical, emotional, motor, and social skills are not fully constructed. Children in different age groups have distinct and urgent developmental needs. A developmental need varies from child to child. Instructors should respect a child's developmental needs and pace of learning. The child should be put in an environment that stimulates him and offers challenges that are appropriate to his age, developmental needs, and ability. A child should not be forced to take up an activity. Coercion discourages the child and he/she resists learning. However, motivation and stimulants can be put within the activity to encourage the child without direct intervention of an adult. Self-motivation is the best tool for learning. Children need to challenge themselves through constant exploration and experimentation. The activity should suit the developmental age of the child so that he/she can perform it with minimal outside assistance. An adult should act as an assistant who provides help only when it is required.

The physical education program for children should be geared to suit their developmental needs (i.e., constructing their motor skills, concept of movement). Physical activity should be fun, pleasurable and aimed at developing and maintaining health. Motor skills are comprised of locomotor skills, non-locomotor skills and manipulative and coordination skills. Games like Bean Bag, parachute, hula hoop, gymnastics and ball activities that instructors can modify and adapt to suit the particular needs of children, are particularly helpful. Physical activity should have the scope to adapt itself to suit an individual child's needs and goals. For an individual incapable of using his/her legs, an instructor can incorporate wheelchair races or activities that require the use of hands. For children in the grades 1 – 3, instructors should incorporate the concepts of movement and motor skills, allowing the child to perfect them.

Concepts of movements like spatial consciousness regarding location, level or height and direction, body awareness and recognition of how the body can be manipulated to perform an activity, effort required regarding time, flow and force, relationship to the various objects and to others, are developed through various activities.

Instructors should also emphasize the significance of personal hygiene. With greater development of motor skills and concepts about movement, instructors can integrate more energetic and vigorous physical activities like volleyball, gymnastics, football, and hockey, into the physical education program. Along with these skills, instructors should select activities that develop group participation skills. It is essential to instill the values of physical education and its connection to general well-being and health. Apart from this, physical education for middle grade children should help develop a good body image and enhance their social skills. Activities like advanced volleyball, dance, and gymnastics can help to develop these areas.

A normal three-year-old should be able to walk up and down the stairs, jump from the lowest step, and land on both the feet without falling. They should also be capable of standing on one foot and balancing and kicking a large ball (though not with a lot of force). A three-year-old can jump on the same spot, ride on a small tricycle, and throw a ball (although not very straight and with limited distance). The large motor skills are more or less developed, but fine motor skills and hand-eye coordination need refining. For example, a three-year-old may not be able to dodge a ball or play games like badminton, which require greater hand-eye coordination, speed, and balance, but a three-year-old can catch a big ball thrown to him/her from a short distance.

A four-year-old is capable of walking on a straight line, hopping using one foot, and pedaling a tricycle with confidence. A four-year-old can climb ladders and trees with relative ease. A four-year-old child can run around obstacles, maneuver, and stop when necessary. A four-year-old can throw a ball a greater distance and is capable of running around in circles.

A five-year-old is capable of walking backwards, using the heel and then the toe, and is able to easily climb up and down steps by alternating feet without any outside help. Five-year-olds can touch their toes without bending at the knee and balance on a beam. They may be able to do somersaults provided it is taught in a proper and safe manner. A five-year-old can ride a tricycle with speed and dexterity, make almost ten jumps or hops without losing balance and falling, and stand on one foot for about ten seconds.

Early elementary school children have already acquired many large motor and fine motor skills. Their movement is more accurate and with purpose, though some clumsiness may persist. An elementary student is always on the run and restless. A child older than five finds pleasure in more energetic and vigorous activities. He/she can jump, hop, and throw with relative accuracy and concentrate on an activity which sustains his/her interest. However, concentration on a single activity usually does not last long. Early elementary students enjoy challenges and can benefit greatly from them.

When proper and appropriate physical education is available, by the time a child finishes the fourth grade he is able to demonstrate well-developed locomotor movements. He is also capable of manipulative and nonlocomotor movement skills like kicking and catching. He is capable of living up to challenges like balancing a number of objects or controlling a variety of things simultaneously. Children at this developmental age begin to acquire specialized movement skills like dribbling. When a child has finished eighth grade, he is able to exhibit expertise in a variety of fine and modified movements (e.g. dance steps). Children begin to develop the necessary skills for competitive and strategic games. Despite a lack of competency in a game, they learn to enjoy the pleasure of physical activity. By the time the children finish the twelfth grade they can demonstrate competency of a number of complex and modified movements with relative ease (e.g. gymnastics, dual sports, dance). Students at this age display their interest in gaining a greater degree of competency at their favorite game or activity.

Motor Skill Assessment

Teachers should divide assessments in the psychomotor domain into two groups: skill-related fitness and sport-specific skills. The physical education teacher can objectively measure skill-related fitness utilizing assessments specifically designed to evaluate each component. Speed, agility, coordination, balance, and reaction time are the components of skill-related fitness. Teachers may choose to use standardized tests developed to assess each of these components. Most of these tests also include normative data. Similarly, many standardized tests are also available as an objective assessment of sport-specific skills. Many of these tests also include normative data.

Teachers should thoroughly evaluate an assessment before choosing to utilize it, as some of the existing tests are quite complicated and burdensome to implement. If a teacher chooses not to use an existing assessment, adaptation of an existing assessment is always an option. To adapt an existing assessment, the physical educator can evaluate the assessment and determine which components of the assessment are reasonable to implement and provide a valid assessment of the specified skill. The teacher would delete the remaining components from the assessment prior to implementation. In addition to the option of deleting segments of the existing assessment, the teacher might choose to make general modifications to the overall assessment.

The physical educator can measure both skill-related fitness and sport-specific skills subjectively through informal assessments. Examples of informal assessments include student interviews, student self-evaluation, and checklists.

Skill 55.2 **Understand how to structure lessons to promote maximum participation, inclusion, and engagement in a variety of traditional and nontraditional games, sports, dance, and other physical activities.**

There are three options for maximizing participation: activity modification, multi-activity designs, and homogeneous or heterogeneous grouping.

Activity modification is the first option to achieve maximum participation by simply modifying the type of equipment used or the activity rules. However, keep activity as close to the original as possible (i.e. substitute a yarn ball for a birdie for badminton).

Multi-activity designs permit greater diversification of equipment and more efficient use of available facilities (keeps all students involved).

Homogeneous and heterogeneous grouping for the purpose of individualized instruction, enhancing self-concepts, equalizing competition, and promoting cooperation among classmates.

Furthermore, plan activities that encourage the greatest amount of participation by utilizing all available facilities and equipment, involving students in planning class work/activities, and being flexible. Instructors can also use tangible rewards and praise.

Skill 55.3 **Select lessons and activities based on factors such as the developmental levels of students and individual differences.**

Aerobic Activities
Aerobics are a fundamental component of every physical education or training program. Aerobic activities are necessary for all because they are central to weight reduction, cardiovascular fitness, muscular strength development, and performance in all sports events.

Appropriate aerobic activities for various developmental levels vary from low and moderate intensity exercises to high intensity ones. Low and moderate intensity activities include doing household work, walking, playing with children, and working on the lawn. High-intensity aerobic activities include jogging, cycling, participating in sports like ice or roller-skating, downhill skiing, and swimming. Treadmills and other equipment help create strenuous aerobic exercises.

Instructors and students must take care while undertaking such high-intensity aerobic exercises, because they can be highly strenuous and taxing on muscles, especially during the initial stages. At this beginning stage, the exercise intensity must be low. With passage of time and development towards higher stages, the student can increase the level and intensity of aerobic exercises.

Muscular Strength and Endurance

Whether the goal is to develop the body's ability to undergo high levels of muscular activity or just to remain fit, there are aerobic activities suited to every developmental stage and for every person.

Possessing the strength and ability to overcome any resistance in one single effort or in repeated efforts over a period of time is muscular strength and endurance. It represents the ability to complete a heavy task in a single effort. Muscular strength and endurance not only helps in keeping body ailments in check, but also in enabling better performance in any sporting event.

Health experts usually regard calisthenics as the best form of exercises in order to increase muscular development and strength. Although calisthenics are good beginning exercises, later on participants should complement them with progressive resistance training so that there will be an increase in bone mass and connective tissue strength. Such a combination would also help in minimizing any damages or injuries that are apt to occur at the beginning or initial training stages.

Besides calisthenics and progressive resistance training, aerobics can also help in maintaining muscular strength and endurance.

Muscular strength is the maximum amount of force that one can generate in an isolated movement. Muscular endurance is the ability of the muscles to perform a sub-maximal task repeatedly or to maintain a sub-maximal muscle contraction for extended periods of time. Body-support activities (e.g. push-ups and sit-ups) and callisthenic activities (e.g. rope jumping) are good exercises for young students or beginners of all ages. Such exercises use multiple muscle groups and have minimal risk of injury. At more advanced levels of development and for those students interested in developing higher levels of strength and muscle mass, weight lifting is the optimal activity.

To improve muscular strength and endurance a student can:

- Train with free weights
- Perform exercised that use an individual's body weight for resistance (e.g., push-ups, sit-ups, dips, etc.)
- Do strength training exercises two times per week that incorporate all major muscle groups

Balance and Body Control
Beginners:

- Helping the children to keep still allows them to explore their balance and body control abilities. Appropriate activities include simple balance activities and making of body shapes.

- Next, beginners must learn to maintain body control while moving. An appropriate activity to develop this skill is asking the child to point his/her toes while holding a balance position.

- In order to introduce apparatus work, help the children to find a safe way to interact with the equipment as well as the floor space. For example, the instructor can have all the students roll and jump on mats and slide through apparatuses.

Intermediate:

- At this stage, children should work on improving the quality of their movements. The instructor should ask the children to balance, transfer weight, roll, turn, etc. while concentrating on the precision of their movements.

- Middle-aged children should learn how to link phases of movement. They can do this by moving in and out of positions of stillness (e.g. balance on hands, knees, and elbows and move smoothly into a balanced position on one foot).

- Children of this age should develop a range of actions, body shapes, and balances. Physical education instructors should help their students practice agility activities and actions. They should also have the children perform these movements with a change of speed, level, or direction.

Advanced:

- Advanced students should be able to move from the floor to apparatus, to change levels on the apparatus, and to move safely from the apparatus to the floor. This will help the students perform actions, shapes, and balances consistently and fluently.

- Teachers should talk to their students about the need for accuracy, consistency, and clarity of movement. The students should then share their feedback about successful combinations of actions, shapes, and balances.

- In order to become more fluent and refined, instructors should teach students how to adapt their actions from apparatus to floor.

Skill 55.4   Design appropriate exercise programs and activities based on physical fitness concepts and applications that encourage physically active lifestyles.

Individual Fitness Plan Adaptation

After assessing an individual's fitness level, a personal fitness trainer or instructor can prescribe a training program. Prescription of a fitness program begins with:
1. Identifying the components of fitness that need changing (via assessment)
2. Establishing short-term goals
3. Developing a plan to meet the established goals
4. Keeping records to record progress
5. Evaluating progress of goals and making changes based on success or failure

For successful programs, the instructor and student should formulate new goals and change the personal fitness program to accomplish the new goals.

For unsuccessful programs, changing the goals, particularly if the goals were too unrealistic, is an appropriate response. Adjusting goals allows individuals to make progress and succeed. In addition, analyzing positive and negative results may identify barriers preventing an individual's success in her personal fitness program. Incorporating periodic, positive rewards for advancing can provide positive reinforcement and encouragement.

Skill 55.5   Analyze the impact of factors such as exercise, relaxation, nutrition, stress, and substance abuse on physical health and well being, and can design activities to provide opportunities for enjoyment, self-expression, and communication.

See Skill 51.3

Skill 55.6 Create cooperative and competitive movement activities that require personal and social responsibility.

See Skills 52.1 and 53.2

Skill 55.7 Understand the significance of cultural and historical influences on games, sports, dance, and other physical activities.

See Skill 54.1

CONTENT AREA – HUMAN DEVELOPMENT

DOMAIN I – COGNITIVE DEVELOPMENT FROM BIRTH THROUGH ADOLESCENCE

COMPETENCY 56.0 COGNITIVE DEVELOPMENT

Skill 56.1   Define basic concepts of cognitive and moral development.

Children go through patterns of learning beginning with pre-operational thought processes and move to concrete operational thoughts. Eventually they begin to acquire the mental ability to think about and solve problems in their head because they can manipulate objects symbolically. Children of most ages can use symbols such as words and numbers to represent objects and relations, but they need concrete reference points. It is essential children be encouraged to use and develop the thinking skills that they possess in solving problems that interest them. The content of the curriculum must be relevant, engaging, and meaningful to the students.

Skill 56.2   Identify stages in cognitive and language development and use them to describe the development of individuals, including persons with special needs

It is important for teachers to consider students' development and readiness when deciding instructional decisions. If an educational program is child-centered, then it will surely address the developmental abilities and needs of the students because it will take its cues from students' interests, concerns, and questions. Making an educational program child-centered involves building on the natural curiosity children bring to school, and asking children what they want to learn.

Teachers help students to identify their own questions, puzzles, and goals, and then structure for them widening circles of experience and investigation of those topics. Teachers manage to infuse all the skills, knowledge, and concepts that society mandates into a child-driven curriculum. This does not mean passive teachers who respond only to students' explicit cues. Teachers also draw on their understanding of children's developmentally characteristic needs and enthusiasms to design experiences that lead children into areas they might not choose, but that they do enjoy and that engage them. Teachers also bring their own interests and enthusiasms into the classroom to share and to act as a motivational means of guiding children.

Implementing such a child-centered curriculum is the result of very careful and deliberate planning. Planning serves as a means of organizing instruction and influences classroom teaching. Well thought-out planning includes specifying behavioral objectives, specifying students' entry behavior (knowledge and skills), selecting and sequencing learning activities so as to move students from entry behavior to objective, and evaluating the outcomes of instruction in order to improve planning.

Factors that Affect Student Learning

There are many factors that affect student learning including how students learn and how learning is presented and/or based on background knowledge or experiences. There are several educational learning theories that can be applied to classroom practices. One classic learning theory is Piaget's stages of development which consist of four learning stages: sensory motor stage (from birth to age 2); pre-operation stages (ages 2 to 7 or early elementary); concrete operational (ages 7 to 11 or upper elementary); and formal operational (ages 7-15 or late elementary/high school). Piaget believed children passed through this series of stages to develop from the most basic forms of concrete thinking to sophisticated levels of abstract thinking.

Some of the most prominent learning theories in education today include brain-based learning and the Multiple Intelligence Theory. Supported by recent brain research, brain-based learning suggests that knowledge about the way the brain retains information enables educators to design the most effective learning environments. As a result, researchers have developed twelve principles that relate knowledge about the brain to teaching practices. These twelve principles are:

- The brain is a complex adaptive system
- The brain is social
- The search for meaning is innate
- We use patterns to learn more effectively
- Emotions are crucial to developing patterns
- Each brain perceives and creates parts and whole simultaneously
- Learning involves focused and peripheral attention
- Learning involves conscious and unconscious processes
- We have at least two ways of organizing memory
- Learning is developmental
- Complex learning is enhanced by challenged (and inhibited by threat)
- Every brain is unique (Caine & Caine, 1994, Mind/Brain Learning Principles)

Educators can use these principles to help design methods and environments in their classrooms to maximize student learning.

The Multiple Intelligent Theory, developed by Howard Gardner, suggests that students learn in (at least) seven different ways. These include visually/spatially, musically, verbally, logically/mathematically, interpersonally, intrapersonally, and bodily/kinesthetically.

The most current learning theory of constructivist learning allows students to construct learning opportunities. For constructivist teachers, the belief is that students create their own reality of knowledge and how to process and observe the world around them. Students are constantly constructing new ideas, which serve as frameworks for learning and teaching. Researchers have shown that the constructivist model is comprised of the four components:

1. Learner creates knowledge
2. Learner constructs and makes meaningful new knowledge to existing knowledge
3. Learner shapes and constructs knowledge by life experiences and social interactions
4. In constructivist learning communities, the student, teacher and classmates establish knowledge cooperatively on a daily basis.

Kelly (1969) states "human beings construct knowledge systems based on their observations parallels Piaget's theory that individuals construct knowledge systems as they work with others who share a common background of thought and processes." Constructivist learning for students is dynamic and ongoing. For constructivist teachers, the classroom becomes a place where students are encouraged to interact with the instructional process by asking questions and posing new ideas to old theories. The use of cooperative learning that encourages students to work in supportive learning environments using their own ideas to stimulate questions and propose outcomes is a major aspect of a constructivist classroom.

The metacognition learning theory deals with "the study of how to help the learner gain understanding about how knowledge is constructed and about the conscious tools for constructing that knowledge" (Joyce and Weil 1996). The cognitive approach to learning involves the teacher's understanding that teaching the student to process his/her own learning and mastery of skill provides the greatest learning and retention opportunities in the classroom. Students are taught to develop concepts and teach themselves skills in problem solving and critical thinking. The student becomes an active participant in the learning process and the teacher facilitates that conceptual and cognitive learning process.

Social and behavioral theories look at the social interactions of students in the classroom that instruct or impact learning opportunities in the classroom. The psychological approaches behind both theories are subject to individual variables that are learned and applied either proactively or negatively in the classroom.

The stimulus of the classroom can promote conducive learning or evoke behavior that is counterproductive for both students and teachers. Students are social beings that normally gravitate to action in the classroom, so teachers must be cognizant in planning classroom environments that are provide both focus and engagement in maximizing learning opportunities.

Role of Oral Development
In 2000, the National Reading Panel released its now well-known report on teaching children to read. In a way, this report slightly put to rest the debate between phonics and whole-language. It argued, essentially, that word-letter recognition was important, as was understanding what the text means. The report's "big 5" critical areas of reading instruction are as follows:

- Phonemic Awareness: The acknowledgement of sounds and words. For example, a child's realization that some words rhyme. Onset and rhyme, for example, are skills that might help students learn that the sound of the first letter "b" in the word "bad" can be changed with the sound "d" to make it "dad." The key in phonemic awareness is that when you teach it to children, it can be taught with the students' eyes closed. In other words, it's all about sounds, not about ascribing written letters to sounds.

- Phonics: As opposed to phonemic awareness, the study of phonics must be done with the eyes open. It's the connection between the sounds and letters on a page. In other words, students learning phonics might see the word "bad" and sound each letter out slowly until they recognize that they just said the word.

- Fluency: When students practice fluency, they practice reading connected pieces of text. In other words, instead of looking at a word as just a word, they might read a sentence straight through. The point of this is that in order for the student to comprehend what she is reading, she would need to be able to "fluently" piece words in a sentence together quickly. If a student is NOT fluent in reading, he or she would sound each letter or word out slowly and pay more attention to the phonics of each word. A fluent reader, on the other hand, might read a sentence out loud using appropriate intonations. The best way to test for fluency, in fact, is to have a student read something out loud, preferably a few sentences in a row—or more. Sure, most students just learning to read will probably not be very fluent right away; but with practice, they will increase their fluency. Even though fluency is not the same as comprehension, it is said that fluency is a good predictor of comprehension. Think about it: If you're focusing too much on sounding out each word, you're not going to be paying attention to the meaning.

- Comprehension: Comprehension simply means that the reader can ascribe meaning to text. Even though students may be good with phonics and even know what many words on a page mean, some of them are not good with comprehension because they do not know the strategies that would help them to comprehend. For example, students should know that stories often have structures (beginning, middle, and end). They should also know that when they are reading something and it does not make sense, they will need to employ "fix-up" strategies where they go back into the text they just read and look for clues. Teachers can use many strategies to teach comprehension, including questioning, asking students to paraphrase or summarize, utilizing graphic organizers, and focusing on mental images.
- Vocabulary: Students will be better at comprehension if they have a stronger working vocabulary. Research has shown that students learn more vocabulary when it is presented in context, rather than in vocabulary lists, for example. Furthermore, the more students get to use particular words in context, the more they will (a) remember each word, and (b) utilize it in the comprehension of sentences that contain the words.

Methods used to teach these skills are often featured in a "balanced literacy" curriculum that focuses on the use of skills in various instructional contexts. For example, with independent reading, students independently choose and books that are at their reading levels; with guided reading, teachers work with small groups of students to help them with their particular reading problems; with whole group reading, the entire class will read the same text, and the teacher will incorporate activities to help students learn phonics, comprehension, fluency, and vocabulary. In addition to these components of balanced literacy, teachers incorporate writing so that students can learn the structures of communicating through text.

Content area vocabulary is the specific vocabulary related to the particular concepts of various academic disciplines (social science, science, math, art, etc.). While teachers tend to think of content area vocabulary as something that should just be focused on at the secondary level (middle and high school), even elementary school-aged students studying various subjects will understand concepts better when the vocabulary used to describe them is explicitly explained. But it is true that in the secondary level, where students go to teachers for the various subjects, content area vocabulary becomes more important. Often, educators believe that vocabulary should just be taught in the Language Arts class, not realizing that (a) there is not enough time for students to learn the enormous vocabulary in order to be successful with a standards-based education, and (b) that the teaching of vocabulary, related to a particular subject, is a very good way to help students understand the subject better.

Now, how do content area teachers teach vocabulary? First and foremost, teachers should help students learn strategies to figure out the meanings for difficulty vocabulary when they encounter it on their own. Teachers can do this by teaching students how to identify the meanings of words in context (usually through activities where the word is taken out, and the students have to figure out a way to make sense of the sentence). In addition, dictionary skills must be taught in all subject areas. Teachers should also consider that teaching vocabulary is not just the teaching of words: rather, it is the teaching of complex concepts, each with histories and connotations.

When teachers explicitly teach vocabulary, it is best when they connect new words to words, ideas, and experiences that students are already familiar with. This will help to reduce the strangeness of the new words. Furthermore, the more concrete the examples are, the more likely students will know how to use the word in context.

Finally, students need plenty of exposure to the new words. They need to be able to hear and use the new words in many naturally-produced sentences. The more one hears and uses a sentence in context, the more the word is solidified in the person's long-term vocabulary.

All this being said, what can teachers expect to find in their students' literacy development? Are there benchmarks that can be expected by age?

The answer to these questions is fuzzy. While we can anticipate that certain skills CAN BE mastered by certain ages, all children are different. But when development is too far off the general target, then intervention may be necessary. By their first year, babies can identify words and notice the social and directive impacts of language. By their second year, children have decent vocabularies, make-believe that they are reading books (especially if their role models read), and they can follow simple oral stories. By their third year, children have more advanced skills in listening and speaking. Within the next few years, children are capable of using longer sentences, retelling parts of stories, counting, and "scribbling" messages. They are capable of learning the basics of phonemic awareness. (See http://www.learningpt.org/pdfs/literacy/readingbirthtofive.pdf for more detailed information.)

At about five years old, children are really ready to start in on phonics. Many teachers mistake phonics as being just a step in the process toward comprehension, when in fact, children are fully capable of learning how to comprehend and make meaning at the same age. Phonics, though, ideally will be mastered by second to third grade.

Skill 56.3   Identify characteristics of play and their influence on cognitive development

Too often, recess and play is considered peripheral or unimportant to a child's development. It's sometimes seen as a way to allow kids to just get physical energy out or a "tradition" of childhood. The truth is, though, that play is very important to human development. First, an obvious point, in this country, even though we are very industrious, we believe strongly that all individuals deserve time to relax and enjoy the "fruits of our labors."

But even more importantly, for the full development of children (who will soon be active citizens of our democracy, parents, spouses, friends, colleagues, and neighbors), play is an activity that helps teach basic values such as sharing and cooperation. It also teaches that taking care of oneself (as opposed to constantly working) is good for human beings and further creates a more enjoyable society.

The stages of play development do indeed move from solitary (particularly in infancy stages) to cooperative (in early childhood), but even in early childhood, children should be able to play on their own and entertain themselves from time to time. Children who do not know what to do with themselves when they are bored should be encouraged to think about particular activities that might be of interest.

But it is also extremely important that children play with peers. While the emerging stages of cooperative play may be awkward (as children will at first not want to share toys, for example), with some guidance and experience, children will learn how to be good peers and friends.

Play—both cooperative and solitary—helps to develop very important attributes in children. For example, children learn and develop personal interests and practice particular skills. The play that children engage in may even develop future professional interests.

Finally, playing with objects helps to develop motor skills. The objects that children play with should be varied and age appropriate. For example, playing with a doll can actually help to develop hand-eye coordination. Sports, for both boys and girls, can be equally valuable. Parents and teachers, though, need to remember that sports at young ages should only be for the purpose of development of interests and motor skills—not competition. Many children will learn that they do not enjoy sports, and parents and teachers should be respectful of these decisions.

In general, play is an appropriate place of children to learn many things about themselves, their world, and their interests. Children should be encouraged to participate in different types of play, and they should be watched over as they encounter new types of play.

Skill 56.4 **Recognize different perspectives on intelligence and their implications for identifying and describing individual differences in cognitive development.**

Generally speaking, concepts can be taught in two manners: deductively or inductively. In a deductive manner, the teacher gives a definition along with one or two examples and one or two non-examples. As a means of checking understanding, the teacher will ask the students to give additional examples or non-examples and perhaps to repeat the definition. In an inductive manner, the students will derive the definition from examples and non-examples provided by the teacher. The students will test these examples and non-examples to ascertain if they possess the attributes that meet the criteria of the definition.

Research indicates that when students gain knowledge through instruction that includes a combination of giving definitions, examples, non-examples, and by identifying attributes, they are more likely to grasp complicated concepts than by other instructional methods. Several studies have been carried out to determine the effectiveness of giving examples as well as the difference in effectiveness of various types of examples. It was found conclusively that the most effective method of concept presentation included giving a definition along with examples and non-examples and also providing an explanation of the examples and non-examples. These same studies indicate that boring examples were just as effective as interesting examples in promoting learning.

Learning is further enhanced when critical attributes are listed along with a definition, examples, and non-examples. Classifying attributes is an effective strategy for both very young students and older students. According to Piaget's pre-operational phase of development, children learn concepts informally through experiences with objects just as they naturally acquire language. One of the most effective learning experiences with objects is learning to classify objects by a single obvious feature or attribute. Children classify objects typically, often without any prompting or directions. This natural inclination to classify objects carries over to classifying attributes of a particular concept and contributes to the student's understanding of concepts.

It is not always guaranteed that once a teacher instructs a concept, that students have automatically retained the information. It is often the case that students may need to see or hear information in more than one manner (kinesthetically, spatially, and visually) before it is truly internalized. Teachers can accomplish this by presented information to benefit various learning styles (or multiple intelligences), as well as utilizing technologies (i.e., overhead projectors, related video clips, music, Power Point presentations, etc) or other additional resources to supplement student learning and retention.

DOMAIN II – SOCIAL AND PHYSICAL DEVELOPMENT FROM BIRTH THROUGH ADOLESCENCE

COMPETENCY 57.0 SOCIAL DEVELOPMENT

Skill 57.1 Define concepts related to the development of personality and temperament.

The development of children's personalities and temperaments is part biological and part environmental. Development is biological when it is based on genetics and pre-disposed features. This can be both basic and fairly intense. Basic biological personality traits are noticeable within a family, yet it is also hard to tell whether it is imitation of older family members that is driving similarities in personality and temperament. Intense biological personality traits might be based—at least in part—on a predisposition to depression, for example.

Most personality traits develop over time and are a combination of biology and environment. While some children are predisposed to being responsive, for example, they will fully display such characteristics if give the opportunities to demonstrate them early on. Environmental factors in personality development occur based on many of the emotions children go through as they experience the world through their mental and physical developmental stages.

Attachment is the theory that explains why children feel the need to be close with other individuals, particularly their parents. Generally, children have a desire to be close with certain individuals, and when those individuals are present, they will feel secure.

As children develop, they will slowly gain a self-concept that is separate from those individuals they are attached to. Generally, self-concept is theory that individuals will develop and hold specific beliefs and opinions about themselves based on the perceptions that they develop about themselves, as well as the perceptions they notice others have about themselves. As children develop a self-concept, they start to remove themselves from the individuals they were once very attached to. This is where they start to see themselves as individuals.

Autonomy is a stage of development in childhood that is rooted within the idea of self-concept. After the child has begun to see him or herself as a unique individual, apart from the parent, for example, the child will want to start controlling more of his or her life.

Finally, identity is developed as children move beyond simple self-concept. They are ready to be independent, they have developed basic concepts of themselves, and they understand perceptions others have of themselves. They finally develop a true identity by being self-aware of all these components in life. They see themselves more and more as responsible for their actions and behaviors.

Personality and temperament develop as children go through these stages. They develop based in large part on each of the different facets of each stage: those who they are attached to, the concepts they develop about themselves, the concepts others perceive of themselves, the ways in which they become autonomous and independent, and the identity they construct for themselves.

Skill 57.2   Describe the social development of children and young adolescents, including persons with special needs

Children progress through a variety of social stages beginning with an awareness of peers but a lack of concern for their presence. Young children engage in "parallel" activities playing alongside their peers without directly interacting with one another. During the primary years, children develop an intense interest in peers. They establish productive, positive social, and working relationships with one another. This stage of social growth continues to increase in importance throughout the child's school years including intermediate, middle school, and high school years. It is necessary for the teacher to recognize the importance of developing positive peer group relationships and to provide opportunities and support for cooperative small group projects that not only develop cognitive ability but promote peer interaction. The ability to work and relate effectively with peers is of major importance and contributes greatly to the child's sense of competence. In order to develop this sense of competence, children need to be successful in acquiring the knowledge and skills recognized by our culture as important, especially those skills which promote academic achievement.

Developing a Good Self Image

Helping students to develop healthy self-images and self-worth are integral to the learning and development experiences. Learning for students who are experiencing negative self-image and peer isolation is not necessarily the top priority, when students are feeling bullied or negated in the school community. When a student is attending school from a homeless shelter or is lost in the middle of a parent's divorce or feeling a need to conform to fit into a certain student group, the student is being compromised and may be unable to effectively navigate the educational process or engage in the required academic expectations towards graduation or promotion to the next grade level or subject core level.

Most schools will offer health classes that address teen issues around sexuality, self-image, peer pressure, nutrition, wellness, gang activity, drug engagement and a variety of other relevant teen experiences. Students are required to take a health class as a core class requirement and graduation requirement, so the incentive from the District and school's standpoint is that students are exposed to issues that directly affect them. The fact that one health class is not enough to effectively appreciate the multiplicity of issues that could create a psychological or physiological trauma for a teenager is lost in today's era of school budgets and financial issues that provide the minimum educational experience for students, but loses the student in the process.

Some schools have contracted with outside agencies to develop collaborative partnerships to bring in after school tutorial classes; gender and cultural specific groupings where students can deal authentically with integration of cultural and ethic experiences and lifestyles. Drug intervention programs and speakers on gang issues have created dynamic opportunities for school communities to bring the "undiscussable" issues to the forefront and alleviate fears that are rampant in schools that are afraid to say "No to Drugs and Gangs." Both students and teachers must be taught about the world of teenagers and understand the social, psychological and learning implications that underscore the process of academic acquisition for societies most vulnerable citizens.

Socialization

Teaching social skills can be rather difficult because social competence requires a repertoire of skills in a number of areas. The socially competent person must be able to get along with family and friends, function in a work environment, take care of personal needs, solve problems in daily living, and identify sources of help. A class of emotionally handicapped students may present several deficits in a few areas or a few deficits in many areas. Therefore, the teacher must begin with an assessment of the skill deficits and prioritize the ones to teach first.

Type of Assessment	Description
Direct Observation	Observe student in various settings with a checklist
Role Play	Teacher observes students in structured scenarios
Teacher Ratings	Teacher rates student with a checklist or formal assessment instrument

Socio-metric Measures: Peer Nomination	Student names specific classmates who meet a stated criterion (i.e., playmate). Score is the number of times a child is nominated.
Peer Rating	Students rank all their classmates on a Likert-type scale (e.g., 1-3 or 1-5 scale) on stated criterion. Individual score is the average of the total ratings of their classmates.
Paired-Comparison	Student is presented with paired classmate combinations and asked to choose who is most or least liked in the pair.
Context Observation	Student is observed to determine if the skill deficit is present in one setting, but not others
Comparison with other student	Student's social skill behavior is compared to two other students in the same situation to determine if there is a deficit, or if the behavior is not really a problem.

Social skills instruction can include teaching for conversation skills, assertiveness, play and peer interaction, problem solving and coping skills, self-help, task-related behaviors, self-concept related skills (i.e., expressing feelings, accepting consequences), and job related skills.

One advantage of schooling organizations for students is to facilitate social skills and social development. While teachers cannot take the largest role for developing such traits as honesty, fairness, and concern for others, they are extremely important in the process. The first recommendation is to be a very good role model. As we all know, actions do indeed speak louder than words. Second, teachers need to communicate expectations and be firm about them. When teachers ignore certain "infractions" and make a big deal about others, they demonstrate to students that it isn't about manners and social skills, but rather discipline and favoritism. All students need to feel safe, cared about, and secure with their classmates. Teachers are the best
people to ensure that students understand how to be generous, caring, considerate, and sociable individuals.

Skill 57.3 **Identify characteristics of play and their impact on social development, and they describe influences on the development of prosocial behavior.**

Too often, recess and play is considered peripheral or unimportant to a child's development. It is sometimes seen as a way to allow kids to just get physical energy out or a "tradition" of childhood. The truth is, though, that play is very important to human development. First, an obvious point, in this country, even though we are very industrious, we believe strongly that all individuals deserve time to relax and enjoy the "fruits of our labors."

But even more importantly, for the full development of children (who will soon be active citizens of our democracy, parents, spouses, friends, colleagues, and neighbors), play is an activity that helps teach basic values such as sharing and cooperation. It also teaches that taking care of oneself (as opposed to constantly working) is good for human beings and further creates a more enjoyable society.

The stages of play development move from solitary (particularly in infancy stages) to cooperative (in early childhood), but even in early childhood, children should be able to play on their own and entertain themselves from time to time. Children who do not know what to do with themselves when they are bored should be encouraged to think about particular activities that might be of interest.

But it is also extremely important that children play with peers. While the emerging stages of cooperative play may be awkward (as children will at first not want to share toys, for example), with some guidance and experience, children will learn how to be good peers and friends.

Play—both cooperative and solitary—helps to develop very important attributes in children. For example, children learn and develop personal interests and practice particular skills. The play that children engage in may even develop future professional interests.

Finally, playing with objects helps to develop motor skills. The objects that children play with should be varied and age appropriate. For example, playing with a doll can actually help to develop hand-eye coordination. Sports, for both boys and girls, can be equally valuable. Parents and teachers, though, need to remember that sports at young ages should only be for the purpose of development of interests and motor skills—not competition. Many children will learn that they do not enjoy sports, and parents and teachers should be respectful of these decisions.

In general, play is an appropriate place of children to learn many things about themselves, their world, and their interests. Children should be encouraged to participate in different types of play, and they should be watched over as they encounter new types of play.

COMPETENCY 58.0 PHYSICAL DEVELOPMENT

Skill 58.1   Describe the scope of physical development at different ages

The teacher has a broad knowledge and thorough understanding of the development that typically occurs during the students' current period of life. More importantly, the teacher understands how children learn best during each period of development. The most important premise of child development is that all domains of development (physical, social, and academic) are integrated. Development in each dimension is influenced by the other dimensions. Moreover, today's educator must also have knowledge of exceptionalities and how these exceptionalities affect all domains of a child's development.

It is important for the teacher to be aware of the physical stage of development and how the child's physical growth and development affect the child's learning. Factors determined by the physical stage of development include: ability to sit and attend, the need for activity, the relationship between physical skills and self-esteem, and the degree to which physical involvement in an activity (as opposed to being able to understand an abstract concept) affects learning.

Skill 58.2   Identify individual differences in physical development, including the development of persons with special needs.

The types of disabilities in children and adults are very numerous. Some disabilities are entirely physical, while others are entirely related to learning and the mind. Some involve a combination of both. While it would be a disservice to say that all kids should display the same types of characteristics to be considered "normal," when abnormalities are noticed, such as a student's incredible ability to solve a math problem without working it out (a potential attribute of giftedness) or another student's extreme trouble with spelling (a potential attribute of dyslexia), a teacher may assume that a disability or exceptional ability is present.

Children of all ages develop physically at different rates and in different ways. Most significantly, boys and girls have many differences in physical development at each stage. But even among boys and among girls, significant differences exist. Some can be causes for concern; others are a result of the normal diversity of human life.

While basic individual differences include height, weight, and coordination, many physical differences occur due to developmental delays. Many physical delays are evidenced through body coordination (trouble with running, trouble with simple sports, inability to do simple games like "hopscotch"), hand-eye coordination, and basic visual problems. Sometimes, bone density is a factor in physical delays. Many children who have physical disabilities can do certain activities, but they may have reduced stamina compared to other students. Students with certain disabilities, including Cerebral Palsy and Spina Bifida, will most likely not be able to participate in general physical education activities. Other disabilities, including ADHD, may simply require that the teacher provides more guidance and differentiation.

The trouble with identifying an abnormality in physical development is that it could be a result of many different things. For example, a middle-grade student who has trouble playing simple sports like basketball may have minor motor skill impairments, may not have significant strength for his or her age and height, or may simply be going through a "growth spurt" where awkwardness may be typical. Generally, from childhood to adolescence, boys' bodies will increase in muscle content and girls' bodies will increase in body fat content. In either case, students' physical compositions will change, and their bodies will react differently than they did as children. This will most likely be frustrating to students, and particularly in physical education environments, sensitivity and differentiation is extremely important. Sensitivity is particularly important as students who do not develop physically until older (which is normal) will still appear child-like well into adolescence (or they will appear adolescent well into the middle teenage years). Not only will this affect these students' self-concepts, it will reduce their ability to perform physically in sports compared to their more rapidly-developing peers.

DOMAIN III – INFLUENCE ON DEVELOPMENT FROM BIRTH THROUGH ADOLESCENCE

COMPETENCY 59.0 INFLUENCES ON DEVELOPMENT

Skill 59.1 Identify potential impacts on the development of children and young adolescents from genetic or organic causes, socio-cultural factors, socioeconomic factors, and sex and gender.

Oftentimes, students absorb the culture and social environment around them without deciphering contextual meaning of the experiences. When provided with a diversity of cultural contexts, students are able to adapt and incorporate multiple meanings from cultural cues vastly different from their own socioeconomic backgrounds. Socio-cultural factors provide a definitive impact on a students' psychological, emotional, affective, and physiological development, along with a students' academic learning and future opportunities.

The educational experience for most students is a complicated and complex experience with a diversity of interlocking meanings and inferences. If one aspect of the complexity is altered, it affects other aspects, which may impact how a student or teacher views an instructional or learning experience. With the current demographic profile of today's school communities, the complexity of understanding, interpreting, synthesizing the nuances from the diversity of cultural lineages can provide many communication and learning blockages that could impede the acquisition of learning for students.

Teachers must create personalized learning communities where every student is a valued member and contributor of the classroom experiences. In classrooms where socio-cultural attributes of the student population are incorporated into the fabric of the learning process, dynamic interrelationships are created that enhance the learning experience and the personalization of learning. When students are provided with numerous academic and social opportunities to share cultural incorporations into the learning, everyone in the classroom benefits from bonding through shared experiences and having an expanded viewpoint of a world experience and culture that vastly differs from their own.

Researchers continue to show that personalized learning environments increase the learning affect for students; decrease drop-out rates among marginalized students; and decrease unproductive student behavior which can result from constant cultural misunderstandings or miscues between students. Promoting diversity of learning and cultural competency in the classroom for students and teachers creates a world of multicultural opportunities and learning.

When students are able to step outside their comfort zones and share the world of a homeless student or empathize with an English Language Learner (ELL) student who has just immigrated to the United States and is learning English for the first time and is still trying to keep up with the academic learning in an unfamiliar language; then students grow exponentially in social understanding and cultural connectedness.

Personalized learning communities provide supportive learning environments that address the academic and emotional needs of students. As socio-cultural knowledge is conveyed continuously in the interrelated experiences shared cooperatively and collaboratively in student groupings and individualized learning, the current and future benefits will continue to present the case and importance of understanding the "whole" child, inclusive of the social and the cultural context.

Skill 59.2 Identify sources of possible abuse and neglect and describe their impact on development.

Helping students to develop healthy self-images and self-worth are integral to the learning and development experiences. Learning for students who are experiencing negative self-image and peer isolation is not necessarily the top priority, when students are feeling bullied or negated in the school community. When a student is attending school from a homeless shelter or is lost in the middle of a parent's divorce or feeling a need to conform to fit into a certain student group, the student is being compromised and may be unable to effectively navigate the educational process or engage in the required academic expectations towards graduation or promotion to the next grade level or subject core level.

Most schools will offer health classes that address teen issues around sexuality, self-image, peer pressure, nutrition, wellness, gang activity, drug engagement and a variety of other relevant teen experiences. Students are required to take a health class as a core class requirement and graduation requirement, so the incentive from the district and school's standpoint is that students are exposed to issues that directly affect them. The fact that one health class is not enough to effectively appreciate the multiplicity of issues that could create a psychological or physiological trauma for a teenager is lost in today's era of school budgets and financial issues that provide the minimum educational experience for students, but loses the student in the process.

Some schools have contracted with outside agencies to develop collaborative partnerships to bring in after school tutorial classes; gender and cultural specific groupings where students can deal authentically with integration of cultural and ethic experiences and lifestyles. Drug intervention programs and speakers on gang issues have created dynamic opportunities for school communities to bring the "undiscussable" issues to the forefront and alleviate fears that are rampant in schools that are afraid to say "No to Drugs and Gangs." Both students and teachers must be taught about the world of teenagers and understand the social, psychological and learning implications that underscore the process of academic acquisition for societies most vulnerable citizens.

Unfortunately, many students come from past or previous exposure to dangerous situations. Child abuse may perpetuate itself in a phenomenon known as chronic shock. The system becomes geared up to handle the extra flow of hormones and electrical impulses accompanying the "fight or flight" syndrome each time the abuse happens, creating a shift in the biology of the brain and allied systems. Essentially, the victim becomes allergic (hyper-sensitized) to stress of the kind that prevailed during the period of abuse. Recent research indicates such a shift is reflected in brain chemistry and structural changes and may last a lifetime.

The abused child differs from the neglected one. While the neglected child suffers from under-stimulation, the abused one suffers from over-stimulation. The neglected child will be withdrawn, quiet, unanticipating, sedate almost, while the abused child may be angry, energetic, rebellious, aggressive, and hard to control. In each case, the environment of abuse or neglect shapes the behavior of the child away from home. Often, out of reflex, the child will flinch when seeming to anticipate a blow, or be unable to accept or understand healthy attention directed to him. The teacher merely needs to watch the child's reaction to a sudden loud noise, another child's aggression, or the response when offered some companionship by another child, or test their own feelings to sense what the child's feelings and experiences may be.

The affective range of the abused and/or neglected child varies from very limited and expressionless to angry, to a distracted effect that is characterized by inattentiveness and poor concentration. Some are tearful, some angry and hitting, and some are just sedentary. In most cases, the effect displayed will not be appropriate to the situation at hand. They have just too much to think about in their mind, their sense of powerlessness is too strong and unable to tell the terrible tale, and they may block it out or become obsessed by it.

The obvious thing the teacher sees are marks from the hand, fist, belt, coat hangers, kitchen utensils, extension cord, and any other imaginable implement for striking and inflicting pain on a child. Now, the suspicion has to be backed up with hard evidence. Unusual marks in geometric shapes may indicate the presence of an implement for spanking such as a spoon, home-made paddle, extension cord, or coat hanger. Marks on the arms and legs may indicate being whipped there. Always be suspicious about bruising. Bruises on the neck and face are usually not the result of a trip and fall, but have a lot to do with intentional hitting, and even choking. Noting the size and shapes of bruises and using some simple imagination may reveal the source of the injury. Notice whether the bruise has reddened areas, indicating ruptured capillaries, or is uniformly colored but shaded toward the perimeter. The rupture of capillaries indicates a strong hit while the shaded bruise indicates a softer compression. The job of the educator who discovers this is just to have a reasonable suspicion that abuse is going on, but it helps to have some specific indicators and firm evidence, not only for the sake of the child, but also in the rare event that your report is questioned. Take note of the size of the injury. Compare it to something such as a quarter or an orange, etc.

The neglected child may appear malnourished, may gorge at lunch, yet still be thin and underweight. Quiet and shy, he's typically shabby looking, and doesn't seem to care about his appearance. Poor nutrition at home may result in him having more than his share of colds and it is of utmost importance to guarantee that his immunizations are current, as they probably have been overlooked. He is not usually a very social child, may isolate, and not respond to invitations to join in. Many children display this trait, but a persistence in social anxiety with a sad effect will indicate that something is happening at home to be concerned about.

In cases of sexual abuse the most blatant warning sign is the sexualization of the child. They become interested in matters of sexuality way before their development stage would predict. They are sexual. They may be seen to quietly masturbate in school at pre-pubertal ages, and may even act out sexually with other children of their own age. The child who suddenly begins to engage in promiscuous sexual behavior is likely to have been molested. Sexual abuse of children is widespread and takes many forms. Kissing episodes by a parent, when out of normal context, are just as damaging as more overt forms of contact, as is the sexualized leer or stare by a perverted parent or elder. Because of the complexity of dealing with sexual abuse, situations must be dealt with extreme care. Never attempt an exhaustive interview of a student who admits to being sexually abused or abused in any way, but wait for the trained professional who knows the methodology to help out. The outcome of an interview can make or break a prosecution.

Significance of Family

The student's capacity and potential for academic success within the overall educational experience are products of her or his total environment: classroom and school system; home and family; neighborhood and community in general. All of these segments are interrelated and can be supportive, one of the other, or divisive, one against the other. As a matter of course, the teacher will become familiar with all aspects of the system, the school and the classroom pertinent to the students' educational experience. This would include not only process and protocols but also the availability of resources provided to meet the academic, health and welfare needs of students. But it is incumbent upon the teacher to look beyond the boundaries of the school system to identify additional resources as well as issues and situations which will effect (directly or indirectly) a student's ability to succeed in the classroom.

Examples of Resources

- Libraries, museums, zoos, planetariums, etc.
- Clubs, societies and civic organizations, community outreach programs of private businesses and corporations and of government agencies

These can provide a variety of materials and media as well as possible speakers and presenters

    9) Departments of social services operating within the local community

These can provide background and program information relevant to social issues which may be impacting individual students. And this can be a resource for classroom instruction regarding life skills, at-risk behaviors, etc.

Initial contacts for resources outside of the school system will usually come from within the system itself: from administration; teacher organizations; department heads; and other colleagues.

Examples of Issues/Situations

a. Students from multicultural backgrounds:

Curriculum objectives and instructional strategies may be inappropriate and unsuccessful when presented in a single format which relies on the student's understanding and acceptance of the values and common attributes of a specific culture which is not his or her own.

b. Parental/family influences: Attitude, resources and encouragement available in the home environment may be attributes for success or failure.

Families with higher incomes are able to provide increased opportunities for students. Students from lower income families will need to depend on the resources available from the school system and the community. This should be orchestrated by the classroom teacher in cooperation with school administrators and educational advocates in the community.

Family members with higher levels of education often serve as models for students, and have high expectations for academic success. And families with specific aspirations for children (often, regardless of their own educational background) encourage students to achieve academic success, and are most often active participants in the process.

A family in crisis (caused by economic difficulties, divorce, substance abuse, physical abuse, etc.) creates a negative environment which may profoundly impact all aspects of a student's life, and particularly his or her ability to function academically. The situation may require professional intervention. It is often the classroom teacher who will recognize a family in crisis situation and instigate an intervention by reporting on this to school or civil authorities.

Regardless of the positive or negative impacts on the students' education from outside sources, it is the teacher's responsibility to ensure that all students in the classroom have an equal opportunity for academic success. This begins with the teacher's statement of high expectations for every student, and develops through planning, delivery and evaluation of instruction which provides for inclusion and ensures that all students have equal access to the resources necessary for successful acquisition of the academic skills being taught and measured in the classroom.

COMPETENCY 60.0 SKILLS AND ABILITIES

Skill 60.1 **Apply knowledge of cognitive, social and physical development to understanding differences between individual children.**

Knowledge of age-appropriate expectations is fundamental to the teacher's positive relationship with students and effective instructional strategies. Equally important is the knowledge of what is individually appropriate for the specific children in a classroom. Developmentally oriented teachers approach classroom groups and individual students with a respect for their emerging capabilities. Developmentalists recognize that kids grow in common patterns, but at different rates which usually cannot be accelerated by adult pressure or input. Developmentally oriented teachers know that variance in the school performance of different children often results from differences in their general growth. With the establishment of inclusion classes throughout the schools, it is vital for all teachers to know the characteristics of students' exceptionalities and their implications on learning.

The effective teacher selects learning activities based on specific learning objectives. Ideally, teachers should not plan activities that fail to augment the specific objectives of the lesson. Learning activities should be planned with a learning objective in mind. Objective driven learning activities tend to serve as a tool to reinforce the teacher's lesson presentation. Additionally, selected learning objectives should be consistent with state and district educational goals that focus on National educational goals (Goals 2000) and the specific strengths and weaknesses of individual students assigned to the teacher's class.

The effective teacher is cognizant of students' individual learning styles and human growth and development theory and applies these principles in the selection and implementation of appropriate instructional activities. In regards to the identification and implementation of appropriate learning activities, effective teachers select and implement instructional activities consistent with principles of human growth and development theory.

Learning activities selected for younger students (below age eight) should focus on short time frames in highly simplified form. The nature of the activity and the content in which the activity is presented affects the approach that the students will take in processing the information. Younger children tend to process information at a slower rate than children age eight and older. On the other hand, when selecting and implementing learning activities for older children, teachers should focus on more complex ideas as older students are capable of understanding more complex instructional activities. Moreover, effective teachers maintain a clear understanding of the developmental appropriateness of activities selected for providing educational instructions to students and select and present these activities in a manner consistent with the level of readiness of his/her students.

Skill 60.2   **Interpret similarities and differences in children's behavior with reference to concepts of human development. They use developmental concepts and principles to explain children's behavior.**

As children develop, various individualistic personality and physical traits will start to become more and more apparent. While many behavioral differences are merely the result of a developing individual identity, some behaviors are a result of the changes themselves. Others are a result of deviancy (which occurs in many different forms).

When behaviors are a result of a developing individual identity, they will develop as a result of children wanting to show independence from their parents in particular. Specific behaviors might include showing greater interests in particular things or subjects, changing patterns of communication with adults and peers, and changes in methods of play and cooperation. Generally, children will become more cooperative as they develop, but specific behaviors, such as competition, may evidence themselves as ways of trying to demonstrate superiority, for example.

When experts say that some behaviors are the result of human development changes themselves, what they are saying is that some behaviors occur due to confusion about or frustration with body or cognitive changes. For example, many children who are transitioning into adolescence are confused and embarrassed by their bodily changes; often, they will act out in rather unconventional ways as a result of this. Particularly when such changes are highlighted by adults, adolescents will waver between wanting to continue acting childish or move toward acting older.

Finally, many behaviors are considered deviant when they are abnormal. Occasionally, such behaviors are destructive. Most, however, appear by most professionals as needing intervention of some sort. There are many theories as to why children display deviant behaviors. For example, the typical Freudian theory is that deviant behaviors are related to under- or over-development of certain sexual components of one's human growth. Or, some professionals argue that deviant behavior is caused by the lack of strong and active parenting. Whatever the reason, most professionals would agree that deviant behaviors impair normal human development and turn into sometimes unwanted classroom and school behaviors.

The bottom line is that children develop at different rates and behaviors are not consistent from one child to the next. Teachers must consult with a variety of professionals on their campuses to determine if certain behaviors warrant concern.

Skill 60.3   Use developmental concepts and principles to explain children's behavior.

Many behaviors exhibited in children are the result of regular human development. Some, however, are caused (or instigated) by environmental sources (including parenting, older siblings, friends, etc.).

Often, aggressive behavior first demonstrates itself as a tool for getting what one wants. This is normal. While teachers and parents must help children learn how to channel desires into appropriate behavior (either suppressing the desire or finding a better way to get it), it is nothing to be worried about. However, aggressiveness can easily turn into bullying, particularly when children feel a need to express superiority over other children. Such a desire can be the result of not getting the kind of acceptance they feel they need at home, for example.

Defiant behavior shows up in many children with Attention Deficit Hyperactivity Disorder. Defiance is identified by a child who blames others for everything, throws things, yells often, never follows directions, and constantly wanting to seek revenge. Although not all traits of defiance are evidenced in every defiant child, generally, defiant children want to demonstrate extreme autonomy, even though, at their developmental stages, they are not successfully able to do so. While defiance can result from parenting that does not seek to help children learn socially-acceptable responses, there is a theory that defiance is a result of a disorder called Oppositional Defiant Disorder. In either case, such children need strong mentoring and occasionally professional intervention.

Some children demonstrate extreme shyness. Such a trait can be a result of traumatic events at home, but generally, it is a normal human trait occasionally will go away with time. Teachers can certainly work to help socialize shy children by placing them with friendly peers for class projects and encouraging them to partake in various activities of interest.

There are many behaviors that children exhibit as they develop. Most often, such behaviors are simply a part of the development of identity. However, some behaviors certainly do need intervention. Seek help from resource specialists and school psychologists when concerns arise.

SAMPLE TEST

The California Subject Examinations for Teachers Multiple Subject tests consists of 143 Multiple Choice questions.

Reading, Language & Literature

1. **To understand the origins of a word, one must study the:**

   A. synonyms.

   B. inflections.

   C. phonetics.

   D. etymology.

2. **Which of the following is not a characteristic of a fable?**

   A. animals that feel and talk like humans.

   B. happy solutions to human dilemmas.

   C. teaches a moral or standard for behavior.

   D. illustrates specific people or groups without directly naming them.

3. **All of the following are true about phonological awareness EXCEPT:**

   A. It may involve print.

   B. It is a prerequisite for spelling and phonics.

   C. Activities can be done by the children with their eyes closed.

   D. Starts before letter recognition is taught.

4. **If a student has a poor vocabulary the teacher should recommend that:**

   A. the student read newspapers, magazines and books on a regular basis.

   B. the student enroll in a Latin class.

   C. the student writes the words repetitively after looking them up in the dictionary.

   D. the student use a thesaurus to locate synonyms and incorporate them into his/her vocabulary.

5. **Which definition below is the best for defining diction?**

A. The specific word choices of an author to create a particular mood or feeling in the reader.

B. Writing which explains something thoroughly.

C. The background, or exposition, for a short story or drama.

D. Word choices which help teach a truth or moral.

6. **Which is an untrue statement about a theme in literature?**

A. The theme is always stated directly somewhere in the text.

B. The theme is the central idea in a literary work.

C. All parts of the work (plot, setting, mood. should contribute to the theme in some way.

D. By analyzing the various elements of the work, the reader should be able to arrive at an indirectly stated theme.

7. **Which is not a true statement concerning an author's literary tone?**

A. Tone is partly revealed through the selection of details.

B. Tone is the expression of the author's attitude toward his/her subject.

C. Tone in literature is usually satiric or angry.

D. Tone in literature corresponds to the tone of voice a speaker uses.

8. **The arrangement and relationship of words in sentences or sentence structure best describes:**

A. style.

B. discourse.

C. thesis.

D. syntax.

9. **Which of the following is a complex sentence?**

A. Anna and Margaret read a total of fifty-four books during summer vacation.

B. The youngest boy on the team had the best earned run average, which mystifies the coaching staff.

C. Earl decided to attend Princeton; his twin brother Roy, who aced the ASVAB test, will be going to Annapolis.

D. "Easy come, easy go," Marcia moaned.

10. **Followers of Piaget's learning theory believe that adolescents in the formal operations period:**

A. behave properly from fear of punishment rather than from a conscious decision to take a certain action.

B. see the past more realistically and can relate to people from the past more than preadolescents.

C. are less self-conscious and thus more willing to project their own identities into those of fictional characters.

D. have not yet developed a symbolic imagination.

11. **Which of the following is a formal reading level assessment?**

A. a standardized reading test

B. a teacher-made reading test

C. an interview

D. a reading diary.

12. **Middle and high school students are more receptive to studying grammar and syntax:**

A. through worksheets and end-of-lesson practices in textbooks.

B. through independent, homework assignments.

C. through analytical examination of the writings of famous authors.

D. though application to their own writing.

13. **Which of the following is not a technique of prewriting?**

A. Clustering

B. Listing

C. Brainstorming

D. Proofreading

14. **Which of the following is not an approach to keep students ever conscious of the need to write for audience appeal?**

    A. Pairing students during the writing process

    B. Reading all rough drafts before the students write the final copies

    C. Having students compose stories or articles for publication in school literary magazines or newspapers

    D. Writing letters to friends or relatives

15. **The children's literature genre came into its own in the:**

    A. seventeenth century.

    B. eighteenth century.

    C. nineteenth century.

    D. twentieth century.

16. **Which of the following should not be included in the opening paragraph of an informative essay?**

    A. Thesis sentence

    B. Details and examples supporting the main idea

    C. A broad general introduction to the topic

    D. A style and tone that grabs the reader's attention

17. **Which aspect of language is innate?**

    A. Biological capability to articulate sounds understood by other humans

    B. Cognitive ability to create syntactical structures

    C. Capacity for using semantics to convey meaning in a social environment

    D. Ability to vary inflections and accents

18. **Which of the following contains an error in possessive inflection?**

    A. Doris's shawl

    B. mother's-in-law frown

    C. children's lunches

    D. ambassador's briefcase

19. **To decode is to:**

    A. Construct meaning.

    B. Sound out a printed sequence of letters.

    C. Use a special code to decipher a message.

    D. None of the above.

20. **To encode means that you:**

    A. Decode a second time.

    B. Construct meaning from a code.

    C. Tell someone a message.

    D. None of the above.

21. **A teacher has taught his students several strategies to monitor their reading comprehension. These strategies include identifying where in the passage they are having difficulty, identifying what the difficulty is, and restating the difficult sentence or passage in their own words. These strategies are examples of:**

    A. graphic and semantic organizers

    B. metacognition

    C. recognizing story structure

    D. summarizing

22. **All of the following are examples of ongoing informal assessment techniques used to observe student progress EXCEPT:**

    A. analyses of student work product

    B. collection of data from assessment tests

    C. effective questioning

    D. observation of students

23. **A student has written a paper with the following characteristics: written in first person; characters, setting, and plot; some dialogue; events organized in chronological sequence with some flashbacks. In what genre has the student written?**

    A. expository writing

    B. narrative writing

    C. persuasive writing

    D. technical writing

24. **Which of the following indicates that a student is a fluent reader?**

    A. reads texts with expression or prosody.

    B. reads word-to-word and haltingly.

    C. must intentionally decode a majority of the words.

    D. in a writing assignment, sentences are poorly-organized structurally.

25. **Which of the following is an essential characteristic of effective assessment?**

    A. Students are the ones being tested; they are not involved in the assessment process.

    B. Testing activities are kept separate from the teaching activities.

    C. Assessment should reflect the actual reading the classroom instruction has prepared the student for.

    D. Tests should use entirely different materials than those used in teaching so the result will be reliable.

26. **Which of the following is an essential characteristic of effective assessment?**

    A. When it comes to assessment, age and culture are irrelevant.

    B. Teaching should be aimed at a student's weaknesses.

    C. Assessment focuses only on the students' reading skills.

    D. Assessment should be a natural part of the instruction and not intrusive.

History & Social Science

27. **Which two Native American nations or tribes inhabited the Mid-Atlantic and Northeastern regions at the time of the first European contact?**

    A. Pueblo and Inuit

    B. Algonquian and Cherokee

    C. Seminoles and Sioux

    D. Algonquian and Iroquois

28. **Which of the following were results of the Age of Exploration?**

    A. More complete and accurate maps and charts

    B. New and more accurate navigational instruments

    C. Proof that the earth is round

    D. All of the above

29. **What was the long-term importance of the Mayflower Compact?**

    A. It established the foundation of all later agreements with the Native Peoples

    B. It established freedom of religion in the original English colonies

    C. It ended the war in Europe between Spain, France and England

    D. It established a model of small, town-based government that was adopted throughout the New England colonies

30. **What was "triangular trade"?**

    A. It was regulated trade between the colonies, England and France.

    B. It was an approach to trade that transported finished goods from the mother country to the African colonies, slaves and goods from Africa to the North American Colonies, and raw materials and tobacco or rum back to the mother country.

    C. It was an approach to trade that resulted in colonists obtaining crops and goods from the Native tribes in exchange for finished goods from England

    D. It was trade between the colonists of the three regions (Southern, mid Atlantic, and New England).

31. What intellectual movement during the period of North American colonization contributed to the development of public education and the founding of the first colleges and universities?

    A. Enlightenment

    B. Great Awakening

    C. Libertarianism

    D. The Scientific Revolution

32. Which of the following contributed to the severity of the Great Depression in California?

    A. An influx of Chinese immigrants.

    B. The dust bowl drove people out of the cities.

    C. An influx of Mexican immigrants.

    D. An influx of Oakies.

33. During the period of Spanish colonialism, which of the following was not a key to the goal of exploiting, transforming and including the native people?

    A. Missions

    B. Ranchos

    C. Presidios

    D. Pueblos

34. Native communities in early California are commonly divided into several cultural areas. How many cultural areas?

    A. 4

    B. 5

    C. 6

    D. 7

35. What event sparked a great migration of people from all over the world to California?

    A. The birth of Labor Unions

    B. California statehood

    C. The invention of the automobile

    D. The Gold Rush

36. **Which of the following does not differentiate provisions of the California constitution from the U.S. Constitution?**

    A. The governor of California has the pocket veto

    B. In California representation in both houses of the legislature is based on population

    C. The Governor and Lt. Governor are elected separately

    D. The equivalent of cabinet positions are elected rather than appointed.

37. **The first European to see Florida and sail along its coast was:**

    A. Cabot

    B. Columbus

    C. Ponce de Leon

    D. Narvaez

38. **How did the United States gain Florida from Spain?**

    A. It was captured from Spain after the Spanish-American War

    B. It was given to the British and became part of the original thirteen colonies

    C. America bought it from Spain

    D. America acquired it after the First World War

39. **What is the form of local government that acts as an intermediary between the state and the city?**

    A. Metropolitan government

    B. Limited government

    C. The Mayor-Council system

    D. County Commission system

40. **New York was initially inhabited by what two native peoples?**

    A. Sioux and Pawnee

    B. Micmac and Wampanoag

    C. Iroquois and Algonquin

    D. Nez Perce and Cherokee

41. **What was the name of the cultural revival after the Civil War that took place in New York?**

    A. The Revolutionary War
    B. The Second Great Awakening
    C. The Harlem Renaissance
    D. The Gilded Age

42. **Which one of the following is not a reason why Europeans came to the New World?**

    A. To find resources in order to increase wealth

    B. To establish trade

    C. To increase a ruler's power and importance

    D. To spread Christianity

43. **Which of the following contributed to the severity of the Great Depression in California?**

    A. An influx of Chinese immigrants.

    B. The dust bowl drove people out of the cities.

    C. An influx of Mexican immigrants.

    D. An influx of Oakies.

44. **The year 1619 was a memorable for the colony of Virginia. Three important events occurred resulting in lasting effects on US history. Which one of the following is not one of the events?**

    A. Twenty African slaves arrived.

    B. The London Company granted the colony a charter making it independent.

    C. The colonists were given the right by the London Company to govern themselves through representative government in the Virginia House of Burgesses

    D. The London Company sent to the colony 60 women who were quickly married, establishing families and stability in the colony.

45. **The "divine right" of kings was the key political characteristic of:**

    A. The Age of Absolutism

    B. The Age of Reason

    C. The Age of Feudalism

    D. The Age of Despotism

46. **During the 1920s, the United States almost completely stopped all immigration. One of the reasons was:**

   A. Plentiful cheap unskilled labor was no longer needed by industrialists

   B. War debts from World War I made it difficult to render financial assistance

   C. European nations were reluctant to allow people to leave since there was a need to rebuild populations and economic stability

   D. The United States did not become a member of the League of Nations

47. **Which one of the following would not be considered a result of World War II?**

   A. Economic depressions and slow resumption of trade and financial aid

   B. Western Europe was no longer the center of world power

   C. The beginnings of new power struggles not only in Europe but in Asia as well

   D. Territorial and boundary changes for many nations, especially in Europe

48. **The belief that the United States should control all of North America was called:**

   A. Westward Expansion

   B. Pan Americanism

   C. Manifest Destiny

   D. Nationalism

49. **Capitalism and communism are alike in that they are both:**

   A. Organic systems

   B. Political systems

   C. Centrally planned systems

   D. Economic systems

50. **An economist might engage in which of the following activities?**

   A. An observation of the historical effects of a nation's banking practices.

   B. The application of a statistical test to a series of data.

   C. Introduction of an experimental factor into a specified population to measure the effect of the factor.

   D. An economist might engage in all of these.

51. The advancement of understanding in dealing with human beings has led to a number of interdisciplinary areas. Which of the following interdisciplinary studies would NOT be considered under the social sciences?

A. Molecular biophysics

B. Peace studies

C. African-American studies

D. Cartographic information systems

52. For the historian studying ancient Egypt, which of the following would be least useful?

A. The record of an ancient Greek historian on Greek-Egyptian interaction

B. Letters from an Egyptian ruler to his/her regional governors

C. Inscriptions on stele of the Fourteenth Egyptian Dynasty

D. Letters from a nineteenth century Egyptologist to his wife

53. $\left(\dfrac{^-4}{9}\right) + \left(\dfrac{^-7}{10}\right) =$

A. $\dfrac{23}{90}$

B. $\dfrac{^-23}{90}$

C. $\dfrac{103}{90}$

D. $\dfrac{^-103}{90}$

54. $(5.6) \times (^-0.11) =$

A. $^-0.616$

B. 0.616

C. $^-6.110$

D. 6.110

55. An item that sells for $375 is put on sale at $120. What is the percent of decrease?

A. 25%

B. 28%

C. 68%

D. 34%

56. Two mathematics classes have a total of 410 students. The 8:00 am class has 40 more than the 10:00 am class. How many students are in the 10:00 am class?

   A.   123.3

   B.   370

   C.   185

   D.   330

57. What measure could be used to report the distance traveled in walking around a track?

   A.   degrees

   B.   square meters

   C.   kilometers

   D.   cubic feet

58. What is the area of a square whose side is 13 feet?

   A.   169 feet

   B.   169 square feet

   C.   52 feet

   D.   52 square feet

59. What is the greatest common factor of 16, 28, and 36?

   A.   2

   B.   4

   C.   8

   D.   16

60. If $4x - (3 - x) = 7(x - 3) + 10$, then

   A. $x = 8$

   B. $x = -8$

   C. $x = 4$

   D. $x = -4$

61. Given the formula $d = rt$, (where d = distance, r = rate, and t = time), calculate the time required for a vehicle to travel 585 miles at a rate of 65 miles per hour.

   A.   8.5 hours

   B.   6.5 hours

   C.   9.5 hours

   D.   9 hours

62. The following chart shows the yearly average number of international tourists visiting Palm Beach for 1990-1994. How may more international tourists visited Palm Beach in 1994 than in 1991?

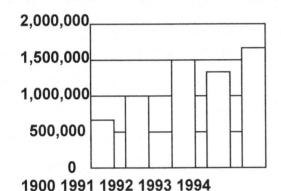

1900 1991 1992 1993 1994

    A.   100,000

    B.   600,000

    C.   1,600,000

    D.   8,000,000

63. What is the probability of drawing 2 consecutive aces from a standard deck of cards?

    A. $\dfrac{3}{51}$

    B. $\dfrac{1}{221}$

    C. $\dfrac{2}{104}$

    D. $\dfrac{2}{52}$

64. A sofa sells for $520. If the retailer makes a 30% profit, what was the wholesale price?

    A. $400

    B. $676

    C. $490

    D. $364

65. Which of the following is an irrational number?

    A.   .362626262...

    B. $4\frac{1}{3}$

    C. $\sqrt{5}$

    D. $-\sqrt{16}$

66. Corporate salaries are listed for several employees. Which would be the best measure of central tendency?

| $24,000 | $24,000 | $26,000 |
| $28,000 | $30,000 | $120,000 |

    A. Mean

    B. median

    C. mode

    D. no difference

67. Which statement is true about George's budget?

A. George spends the greatest portion of his income on food.

B. George spends twice as much on utilities as he does on his mortgage.

C. George spends twice as much on utilities as he does on food.

D. George spends the same amount on food and utilities as he does on mortgage.

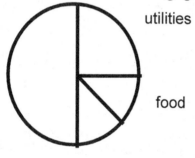

68. Given a drawer with 5 black socks, 3 blue socks, and 2 red socks, what is the probability that you will draw two black socks in two draws in a dark room?

A. 2/9
B. 1/4
C. 17/18
D. 1/18

69. Solve for x: $|2x + 3| > 4$

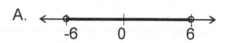
A. $-\frac{7}{2} > x > \frac{1}{2}$

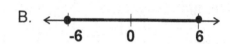
B. $-\frac{1}{2} > x > \frac{7}{2}$

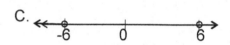
C. $x < \frac{7}{2}$ or $x < -\frac{1}{2}$

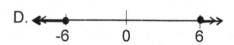
D. $x < -\frac{7}{2}$ or $x > \frac{1}{2}$

70. Graph the solution:
$|x| + 7 < 13$

A.

B.

C.

D.

71. A boat travels 30 miles upstream in three hours. It makes the return trip in one and a half hours. What is the speed of the boat in still water?

A. 10 mph
B. 15 mph
C. 20 mph
D. 30 mph

72. Given segment AC with B as its midpoint find the coordinates of C if A = (5,7) and B = (3, 6.5).

A. (4, 6.5)
B. (1, 6)
C. (2, 0.5)
D. (16, 1)

73. 3 km is equivalent to

   A. 300 cm
   B. 300 m
   C. 3000 cm
   D. 3000 m

74. The mass of a cookie is closest to:

   A. 0.5 kg
   B. 0.5 grams
   C. 15 grams
   D. 1.5 grams

75. If the radius of a right circular cylinder is doubled, how does its volume change?

   A. no change
   B. also is doubled
   C. four times the original
   D. pi times the original

76. In similar polygons, if the perimeters are in a ratio of x:y, the sides are in a ratio of

   A. $x : y$
   B. $x^2 : y^2$
   C. $2x : y$
   D. $1/2 \, x : y$

77. Find the midpoint of (2,5) and (7,-4).

   A. (9,-1)
   B. (5,9)
   C. (9/2 , -1/2)
   D. (9/2, 1/2)

78. $3x + 2y = 12$
     $12x + 8y = 15$

   A. all real numbers
   B. x = 4, y = 4
   C. x = 2, y = -1
   D. $\varnothing$

Science

79. Carbon bonds with hydrogen by _____

   A. ionic bonding.
   B. non-polar covalent bonding.
   C. polar covalent bonding.
   A. strong nuclear force

80. Which of the following is a misconception about the task of teaching science in elementary school?

   A. Teach facts as a priority over teaching how to solve problems.
   B. Involve as many senses as possible in the learning experience.
   C. Accommodate individual differences in pupils' learning styles.
   D. Consider the effect of technology on people rather than on material things.

81. Which skill refers to quantifying data, performing graphic analysis, making charts, and writing summaries?

   A. Recording
   B. Data gathering
   C. Data processing
   D. Evaluating

82. When several computers are connected together by a modem or telephone it is a:

   A. Processor
   B. Network
   C. Online
   D. Hard drive

83. Computer simulations are most appropriate for:

   A. replicating dangerous experiments.
   B. mastering basic facts.
   C. emphasizing competition and entertainment.
   D. providing motivational feedback.

84. The Doppler Effect is associated most closely with which property of waves?

   A. Amplitude.
   B. Wavelength.
   C. Frequency.
   D. Intensity.

85. Accepted procedures for preparing solutions should be made with _____ .

   A. alcohol.
   B. hydrochloric acid.
   C. distilled water.
   D. tap water.

86. Enzymes speed up reactions by _____ .

   A. utilizing ATP.
   B. lowering pH, allowing reaction speed to increase.
   C. increasing volume of substrate.
   D. lowering energy of activation.

87. The transfer of heat by electromagnetic waves is called _____ .

   A. conduction.
   B. convection.
   C. phase change.
   D. radiation.

88. Which of the following is *not* considered ethical behavior for a scientist?

   A. Using unpublished data and citing the source.

   B. Publishing data before other scientists have had a chance to replicate results.

   C. Collaborating with other scientists from different laboratories.

   D. Publishing work with an incomplete list of citations.

89. Sound waves are produced by _____ .

   A. pitch.
   B. noise.
   C. vibrations.
   D. sonar.

90. Chemicals should be stored:

   A. in the principal's office.
   B. in a dark room.
   C. according to their reactivity with other substances.
   D. in a double locked room

91. In an experiment measuring the growth of bacteria at different temperatures, what is the independent variable?

   A. Number of bacteria.
   B. Growth rate of bacteria.
   C. Temperature.
   D. Size of bacteria.

92. Which is the correct order of methodology?

   1. collecting data
   2. planning a controlled experiment
   3. drawing a conclusion
   4. hypothesizing a result
   5. re-visiting a hypothesis to answer a question

   A. 1,2,3,4,5
   B. 4,2,1,3,5
   C. 4,5,1,3,2
   D. 1,3,4,5,2

93. What cell organelle contains the cell's stored food?

   A. Vacuoles
   B. Golgi Apparatus
   C. Ribosomes
   D. Lysosomes

94. Identify the correct sequence of organization of living things from lower to higher order:

   A. Cell, Organelle, Organ, Tissue, System, Organism.
   B. Cell, Tissue, Organ, Organelle, System, Organism.
   C. Organelle, Cell, Tissue, Organ, System, Organism.
   D. Organelle, Tissue, Cell, Organ, System, Organism.

95. Which of the following is a correct explanation for scientific 'evolution'?

A. Giraffes need to reach higher for leaves to eat, so their necks stretch. The giraffe babies are then born with longer necks. Eventually, there are more long-necked giraffes in the population

B. Giraffes with longer necks are able to reach more leaves, so they eat more and have more babies than other giraffes. Eventually, there are more long-necked giraffes in the population.

C. Giraffes want to reach higher for leaves to eat, so they release enzymes into their bloodstream, which in turn causes fetal development of longer-necked giraffes. Eventually, there are more long-necked giraffes in the population.

D. Giraffes with long necks are more attractive to other giraffes, so they get the best mating partners and have more babies. Eventually, there are more long-necked giraffes in the population.

96. Which of the following is the most accurate definition of a non-renewable resource?

A. A nonrenewable resource is never replaced once used.

B. A nonrenewable resource is replaced on a timescale that is very long relative to human life spans.

C. A nonrenewable resource is a resource that can only be manufactured by humans.

D. A nonrenewable resource is a species that has already become extinct.

97. Which kingdom is comprised of organisms made of one cell with no nuclear membrane?

A. Monera.
B. Protista.
C. Fungi.
D. Algae.

98. What are the most significant and prevalent elements in the biosphere?

A. Carbon, Hydrogen, Oxygen, Nitrogen, Phosphorus.

B. Carbon, Hydrogen, Sodium, Iron, Calcium.

C. Carbon, Oxygen, Sulfur, Manganese, Iron.

D. Carbon, Hydrogen, Oxygen, Nickel, Sodium, Nitrogen.

99. Which of the following types of rock are made from magma?

A. Fossils
B. Sedimentary
C. Metamorphic
D. Igneous

100. What is the most accurate description of the Water Cycle?

A. Rain comes from clouds, filling the ocean. The water then evaporates and becomes clouds again.
B. Water circulates from rivers into groundwater and back, while water vapor circulates in the atmosphere.
C. Water is conserved except for chemical or nuclear reactions, and any drop of water could circulate through clouds, rain, ground water, and surface-water.
D. Weather systems cause chemical reactions to break water into its atoms.

101. The theory of 'sea floor spreading' explains _____

A. the shapes of the continents.
B. how continents collide.
C. how continents move apart.
D. how continents sink to become part of the ocean floor.

102. Which of the following is the best definition for 'meteorite'?

A. A meteorite is a mineral composed of mica and feldspar.
B. A meteorite is material from outer space that has struck the earth's surface.
C. A meteorite is an element that has properties of both metals and nonmetals.
D. A meteorite is a very small unit of length measurement.

103. The measure of the pull of the earth's gravity on an object is called _____

A. mass number.
B. atomic number.
C. mass.
D. weight

104. Which parts of an atom are located inside the nucleus?

A. Electrons and neutrons.
B. Protons and neutrons.
C. Protons only.
D. Neutrons only.

Physical Education & Health

105. The physical education philosophy based on experience is:

A. Naturalism

B. Pragmatism

C. Idealism

D. Existentialism

TEACHER CERTIFICATION STUDY GUIDE

106. The modern physical education philosophy that combines beliefs from different philosophies is:

A. Eclectic

B. Humanistic

C. Individualism

D. Realism

107. A physical education teacher emphasizes healthy attitudes and habits. She conducts her classes so that students acquire and interpret knowledge and learn to think/analyze, which is necessary for physical activities. The goals and values utilized and the philosophy applied by this instructor is:

A. Physical Development Goals and Realism Philosophy

B. Affective Development Goals and Existentialism

C. Motor Development Goals and Realism Philosophy

D. Cognitive Development Goals and Idealism Philosophy

108. Social skills and values developed by activity include all of the following except:

A. Winning at all costs

B. Making judgments in groups

C. Communicating and cooperating

D. Respecting rules and property

109. Activities that enhance team socialization include all of the following except:

A. Basketball

B. Soccer

C. Golf

D. Volleyball

110. Through physical activities, John has developed self-discipline, fairness, respect for others, and new friends. John has experienced which of the following?

A. Positive cooperation psycho-social influences

B. Positive group psycho-social influences

C. Positive individual psycho-social influences

D. Positive accomplishment psycho-social influences

111. **Which of the following psycho-social influences is not negative?**

A. Avoidance of problems

B. Adherence to exercise

C. Ego-centeredness

D. Role conflict

112. **Which professional organization protects amateur sports from corruption?**

A. AIWA

B. AAHPERD

C. NCAA

D. AAU

113. **Which professional organization works with legislatures?**

A. AIWA

B. AAHPERD

C. ACSM

D. AAU

114. **Research in physical education is published in all of the following periodicals except the:**

A. School PE Update

B. Research Quarterly

C. Journal of Physical Education

D. YMCA Magazine

115. **The most effective way to promote the physical education curriculum is to:**

A. Relate physical education to higher thought processes

B. Relate physical education to humanitarianism

C. Relate physical education to the total educational process

D. Relate physical education to skills necessary to preserve the natural environment

116. **The affective domain of physical education contributes to all of the following except:**

A. Knowledge of exercise, health, and disease

B. Self-actualization

C. An appreciation of beauty

D. Good sportsmanship

117. A physical education instructor anticipates and prevents potential injuries, watches for hidden injuries, and takes an injury evaluation of the entire class. Which of the following strategies to prevent injuries is the teacher demonstrating?

A. Maintaining hiring standards

B. Proper use of equipment

C. Proper procedures for emergencies

D. Participant screening

Visual Art

118. Engravings and oil painting originated in this country.

A. Italy
B. Japan
C. Germany
D. Flanders

119. A combination of three or more tones sounded at the same time is called a

A. Harmony
B. Consonance
C. A chord
D. Dissonance

120. A series of single tones which add up to a recognizable sound is called a:

A. Cadence
B. Rhythm
C. Melody
D. Sequence

121. Which is a true statement about crafts?

A. Students experiment with their own creativity.
B. Products are unique and different.
C. Self-expression is encouraged.
D. Outcome is predetermined.

122. The following is not a good activity to encourage fifth graders' artistic creativity:

A. Ask them to make a decorative card for a family member.
B. Have them work as a team to decorate a large wall display.
C. Ask them to copy a drawing from a book, with the higher grades being awarded to those students who come closest to the model.
D. Have each student try to create an outdoor scene with crayons, giving them a choice of scenery.

123. An approach to musical instruction for young children that "combines learning music, movement, singing, and exploration" is:

    A. Dalcroze Eurhythmics
    B. The Kodaly Method
    C. The Orff Approach
    D. Education Through Music (ETM)

124. During the early childhood years (ages 3-5), drama and theatre experiences are especially beneficial to children because they provide the opportunity for students to:

    A. apply the concept of turn-taking.
    B. learn the importance of listening skills.
    C. acquire the skills needed to become a proficient reader.
    D. learn early drama skills using their five senses.

125. In the area of Performing Arts, specifically dance, primary grades are expected to have a gross understanding of their motor movements. Which of the following movements would not be age-appropriate?

    A. basic rhythm
    B. early body awareness
    C. imagery
    D. listening skills

126. The history of theatre is important at an early age to describe how theatre has evolved over time. Which of the following is not a vital part of the many time periods of theatre history?

    A. Roman theatre
    B. American theatre
    C. Medieval drama
    D. Renaissance theatre

127. Creating movements in response to music helps students to connect music and dance in which of the following ways?

    A. rhythm
    B. costuming
    C. speed
    D. vocabulary skills

128. Often local elected officials and guest or residents artist are brought into the classroom to:

    A. explain their jobs or trades
    B. observe teaching skills
    C. enrich and extend arts curriculum
    D. entertain students and teachers

129. Early childhood students are expected to be able to complete tasks using basic loco-motor skills. Which of the following would not be included?

    A. walking
    B. galloping
    C. balancing
    D. jogging

130. In visual art studies students are expected to be able to interact in all of the following exercises except one.

   A. Clap out rhythmic patterns found in music lyrics.
   B. Compare and contrast various art pieces.
   C. Recognize related dance vocabulary.
   D. Identify and sort pictures organized by shape, size, and color.

Human Development

131. A six year old student in Mrs. Brack's first grade class has exhibited a noticeable change in behavior over the last month. The child was usually outgoing, alert, but she has become quiet and withdrawn, and appears to be unable to concentrate on her work. Yesterday, bruises were evident n the child's arm and right eye. Mrs. Brack should:

   A. ignore the situation.
   B. provide remedial work.
   C. Immediately report the suspected abuse to the authorities.
   D. call the girl's parents

132. Cognitive, developmental, and behavioral are three types of:
   A. economists
   B. political scientists
   C. psychologists
   D. historians

133. When are students more likely to understand complex ideas?

   A. If they do outside research before coming to class
   B. Later when they write out the definitions of complex words
   C. When they attend a lecture on the subject
   D. When they are clearly defined by the teacher and are given examples and non-examples of the concept

134. What should a teacher do when students have not responded well to an instructional activity?

   A. Reevaluate learner needs
   B. Request administrative help
   C. Continue with the activity another day
   D. Assign homework on the concept

135. What developmental patterns should a professional teacher assess to meet the needs of the student?

   A. Academic, regional, and family background
   B. Social, physical, academic
   C. Academic, physical, and family background
   D. Physical, family, ethnic background

136. At approximately what age is the average child able to define abstract terms such as honesty and justice?

    A. 10-12 years old
    B. 4-6 years old
    C. 14-16 years old
    D. 6-8 years old

137. Johnny, a middle-schooler, comes to class, uncharacteristically tired, distracted, withdrawn, sullen, and cries easily. What would be the teacher's first response?

    A. Send him to the office to sit
    B. Call his parents
    C. Ask him what is wrong
    D. Ignore his behavior

138. Marcus is a first grade boy of good developmental attainment. His learning progress is good the first half of the year. He shows no indicators of emotional distress. After the holiday break, he returns much changed. He is quieter, sullen even, tending to play alone. He has moments of tearfulness, sometimes almost without cause. He avoids contact with adults as often as he can. Even play with his friends has become limited. He has episodes of wetting not seen before, and often wants to sleep in school. What approach is appropriate for this sudden change in behavior?

    A. Give him some time to adjust. The holiday break was probably too much fun to come back to school from
    B. Report this change immediately to administration. Do not call the parents until administration decides a course of action
    C. Document his daily behavior carefully as soon as you notice such a change, report to administration the next month or so in a meeting
    D. Make a courtesy call to the parents to let them know he is not acting like himself, being sure to tell them he is not making trouble for others

139. Which statement is an example of specific praise?

A. "John, you are the only person in class not paying attention"
B. "William, I thought we agreed that you would turn in all of your homework"
C. "Robert, you did a good job staying in line. See how it helped us get to music class on time"
D. "Class, you did a great job cleaning up the art room"

140. Using pro-active expressions and repetition has what effect on students?

A. Helps student become aware of important elements of content
B. Helps students develop positive self-esteem
C. Helps students tolerate the lecture format of instruction
D. Helps students to complete homework correctly

141. How can the teacher establish a positive climate in the classroom?

A. Help students see the unique contributions of individual differences
B. Use whole group instruction for all content areas
C. Help students divide into cooperative groups based on ability
D. Eliminate teaching strategies that allow students to make choices

142. What is a good strategy for teaching ethnically diverse students?

A. Don't focus on the students' culture
B. Expect them to assimilate easily into your classroom
C. Imitate their speech patterns
D. Include ethnic studies in the curriculum

143. Who developed the theory of multiple intelligences?

A. Bruner
B. Gardner
C. Kagan
D. Cooper

Answer Key

1.	D	41.	C	81.	C	121.	D
2.	D	42.	B	82.	B	122.	C
3.	A	43.	D	83.	A	123.	D
4.	A	44.	B	84.	C	124.	D
5.	A	45.	A	85.	C	125.	C
6.	A	46.	A	86.	D	126.	B
7.	C	47.	A	87.	D	127.	A
8.	D	48.	C	88.	D	128.	C
9.	B	49.	D	89.	C	129.	D
10.	B	50.	B	90.	C	130.	C
11.	A	51.	A	91.	C	131.	C
12.	D	52.	D	92.	B	132.	C
13.	D	53.	D	93.	A	133.	D
14.	D	54.	A	94.	C	134.	A
15.	A	55.	C	95.	B	135.	B
16.	B	56.	C	96.	B	136.	A
17.	A	57.	C	97.	A	137.	C
18.	B	58.	B	98.	A	138.	B
19.	B	59.	B	99.	D	139.	C
20.	B	60.	C	100.	C	140.	A
21.	B	61.	D	101.	C	141.	A
22.	B	62.	B	102.	B	142.	D
23.	B	63.	B	103.	D	143.	B
24.	A	64.	A	104.	B		
25.	C	65.	C	105.	B		
26.	D	66.	B	106.	A		
27.	A	67.	C	107.	D		
28.	D	68.	A	108	A		
29.	D	69.	D	109.	C		
30.	B	70.	A	110.	B		
31.	A	71.	B	111.	B		
32.	D	72.	B	112.	D		
33.	B	73.	D	113.	B		
34.	C	74.	C	114.	A		
35.	D	75.	C	115.	C		
36.	A	76.	A	116.	A		
37.	A	77.	D	117.	D		
38.	C	78.	D	118.	D		
39.	A	79.	C	119.	C		
40.	C	80.	D	120.	C		

Answers with Rationale

1. D. etymology.

A synonym is an equivalent of another word and can substitute for it in certain contexts. Inflection is a modification of words according to their grammatical functions, usually by employing variant word-endings to indicate such qualities as tense, gender, case, and number. Phonetics are the science devoted to the physical analysis of the sounds of human speech, including their production, transmission, and perception.

2. D. illustrates specific people or groups without directly naming them.

A fable is a short tale with animals, humans, gods, or even inanimate objects as characters. Fables often conclude with a moral, delivered in the form of an epigram (a short, witty, and ingenious statement in verse). Fables are among the oldest forms of writing in human history: it appears in Egyptian papyri of c1,500 BC. The most famous fables are those of Aesop, a Greek slave living in about 600 BC. In India, the Pantchatantra appeared in the third century. The most famous modern fables are those of seventeenth century French poet Jean de La Fontaine.

3. A, because phonological awareness DOES NOT involve print.

The key word here is EXCEPT which will be highlighted in upper case on the test as well. All of the options are correct aspects of phonological awareness except the first one,

4. A. The student read newspapers, magazines and books on a regular basis.

It is up to the teacher to help the student choose reading material, but the student must be able to choose where s/he will search for the reading pleasure indispensable for enriching vocabulary.

5. A. The specific word choices of an author to create a particular mood or feeling in the reader.

Diction refers to an author's choice of words, expressions and style to convey his/her meaning.

6. A. The theme is always stated directly somewhere in the text.

The theme may be stated directly, but it can also be implicit in various aspects of the work, such as the interaction between characters, symbolism, or description.

7. C. Tone in literature is usually satiric or angry.

Tone in literature conveys a mood and can be as varied as the tone of voice of a speaker (see D., e.g. sad, nostalgic, whimsical, angry, formal, intimate, satirical, sentimental, etc.

8. D. Syntax.

Syntax is the grammatical structure of sentences.

9. B. The youngest boy on the team had the best earned run average which mystifies the coaching staff.

Here, the use of the relative pronoun "which", whose antecedent is "the best run average, introduces a clause that is dependent on the independent clause "The youngest boy on the team had the best run average". The idea expressed in the subordinate clause is subordinate to the one expressed in the independent clause.

10. B. See the past more realistically and can relate to people from the past more than preadolescents.

Since according to Piaget, adolescents 12-15 years old begin thinking beyond the immediate and obvious, and theorize. Their assessment of events shifts from considering an action as "right" or "wrong" to considering the intent and behavior in which the action was performed. Fairy tale or other kinds of unreal characters have ceased to satisfy them and they are able to recognize the difference between pure history and historical fiction.

11. A. a standardized reading test

If assessment is standardized, it has to be objective, whereas B, C and D are all subjective assessments.

12. D. through application to their own writing.

The answer is D. At this age, students learn grammatical concepts best through practical application in their own writing

13. D. Proofreading.

Proofreading cannot be a method of prewriting, since it is done on already written texts only.

14. D. Writing letters to friends or relatives

The answer is D. Reading all rough drafts will not encourage the students to take control of their text and might even inhibit their creativity. On the contrary, pairing students will foster their sense of responsibility, and having them compose stories for literary magazines will boost their self esteem as well as their organization skills. As far as writing letters is concerned, the work of authors such as Madame de Sevigne in the seventeenth century is a good example of epistolary literary work.

15. A. seventeenth century

In the seventeenth Century, authors such as Jean de La Fontaine and his *Fables*, Pierre Perreault's *Tales*, Mme d'Aulnoye's Novels based on old folktales and Mme de Beaumont's *Beauty and the Beast* all created a children's literature genre. In England, Perreault was translated and a work allegedly written by Oliver Smith, *The renowned History of Little Goody Two Shoes*, also helped to establish children's literature in England.

16. B. Details and examples supporting the main idea

The introductory paragraph should introduce the topic, capture the reader's interest, state the thesis and prepare the reader for the main points in the essay. Details and examples, however, should be given in the second part of the essay, so as to help develop the thesis presented at the end of the introductory paragraph, following the inverted triangle method consisting of a broad general statement followed by some information, and then the thesis at the end of the paragraph.

17. A. Biological capability to articulate sounds understood by other humans

Language ability is innate and the biological capability to produce sounds lets children learn semantics and syntactical structures through trial and error. Linguists agree that language is first a vocal system of word symbols that enable a human to communicate his/her feelings, thoughts, and desires to other human beings.

18. B. mother's-in-law frown

Mother-in-Law is a compound common noun and the inflection should be at the end of the word, according to the rule.

19. The answer is "**B**" and again the definition of this word in reading is what you have to know from your coursework.

20. The answer is "**B**" You need to memorize these special definitions.

21. B. Metacognition

Metacognition may be defined as "thinking about thinking." Good readers use metacognitive strategies to think about and have control over their reading. Before reading, they might clarify their purpose for reading and preview the text. During reading, they might monitor their understanding, adjusting their reading speed to fit the difficulty of the text and fixing any comprehension problems they have. After reading, they check their understanding of what they read.

22. B. collection of data from assessment tests

Assessment tests are formal progress-monitoring measures.

23. B. narrative writing

These are all characteristics of narrative writing. Expository writing is intended to give information such as an explanation or directions, and the information is logically organized. Persuasive writing gives an opinion in an attempt to convince the reader that this point of view is valid or tries to persuade the reader to take a specific action. The goal of technical writing is to clearly communicate a select piece of information to a targeted reader or group of readers for a particular purpose in such a way that the subject can readily be understood. It is persuasive writing that anticipates a response from the reader.

24. A. reads texts with expression or prosody.

The teacher should listen to the children read aloud, but there are also clues to reading levels in their writing.

25. C. Assessment should reflect the actual reading the classroom instruction has prepared the student for.

The only reliable measure of the success of a unit will be based on the reading the instruction has focused on.

26. D. Assessment should be a natural part of the instruction and not intrusive.

If assessment is to be effective, it must be ongoing and must not interfere with instruction and practice.

27. D. Algonquian and Iroquois

The Algonquian and Iroquois nations inhabited the Mid-Atlantic and Northeastern regions of the U.S. These Native Americans are classified among the Woods Peoples. Some of the most famous of these nations are Squanto, Pocahontas, Chief Powhatan, Tecumseh, and Black Hawk. These two nations were frequently at odds over territory. The people of these nations taught early settlers about the land and survival in the new world. They introduced the settlers to maize and tobacco. The settlers and the Native Americans gradually developed respect and opened trade and cultural sharing.

28. D. All of the above

The importance of the Age of Exploration was not only the discovery and colonization of the New World, but also better maps and charts; new accurate navigational instruments; increased knowledge; great wealth; new and different foods and items not known in Europe; a new hemisphere as a refuge from poverty, persecution, a place to start a new and better life; and proof that Asia could be reached by sea and that the earth was round; ships and sailors would not sail off the edge of a flat earth and disappear forever into nothingness.

29. D. Established a model of small, town-based government

Before setting foot on land in 1620, the **Pilgrims** aboard the Mayflower agreed to a form of self-government by signing the Mayflower Compact. The Compact served as the basis for governing the Plymouth colony for many years and set an example of small, town-based government that would proliferate throughout New England. The present day New England town meeting is an extension of this tradition. This republican ideal was later to clash with the policies of British colonial government

30. B. It was an approach to trade that transported finished goods from the mother country to the African colonies, slaves and goods from Africa to the North American colonies, and raw materials and tobacco or rum back to the mother country.

The New England and Middle Atlantic colonies at first felt threatened by these laws as they had started producing many of the same products being produced in Britain. But they soon found new markets for their goods and began what was known as a **"triangular trade**." Colonial vessels started the first part of the triangle by sailing for Africa loaded with kegs of rum from colonial distilleries. On Africa's West Coast, the rum was traded for either gold or slaves. The second part of the triangle was from Africa to the West Indies where slaves were traded for molasses, sugar, or money. The third part of the triangle was home, bringing sugar or molasses (to make more rum), gold, and silver.

31. A. Enlightenment

Enlightenment thinking quickly made the voyage across the Atlantic Ocean. Enlightenment thinking valued human reason and the importance of education, knowledge, and scholarly research. Education in the middle colonies was influenced largely by the Enlightenment movement, which emphasized scholarly research and public service. Benjamin Franklin embodied these principles in Philadelphia, which became a center of learning and culture, owing largely to its economic success and ease of access to European books and tracts.

32. D. An influx of Oakies

The Dust Bowl of the Great Plains destroyed agriculture in the area. People living in the plains areas lost their livelihood and many lost their homes and possessions in the great dust storms that resulted from a period of extended drought. People from all of the states affected by the Dust Bowl made their way to California in search of a better life. Because the majority of the people were from Oklahoma, they were all referred to as "Oakies." These migrants brought with them their distinctive plains culture. The great influx of people seeking jobs exacerbated the effects of the Great Depression in California.

33. B. Ranchos

The goal of Spanish colonialism was to exploit, transform and include the native people of California. The Spanish empire sought to do this first by gathering the native people into communities where they could both be taught Spanish culture and be converted to Roman Catholicism and its value system. The social institutions by which this was accomplished was the encouragement of the Mission System, which established a number of Catholic missions a day's journey apart. Once the native people were brought to the missions, they were incorporated into a mission society and indoctrinated in the teachings of Catholicism. The Presidios were fortresses that were constructed to protect Spanish interests and the communities from invaders. The Pueblos were small civilian communities that attracted settlers with the gift of land, seed, and farming equipment. The function of the Pueblos was to produce food for the missions and for the presidios.

34. C. 6

Due to the great diversity of the native communities, the state is generally divided into six "culture areas." The culture areas are: (1) the Southern Culture Area, (2) the Central Culture Area, (3) the Northwestern Culture Area, (4) the Northeastern Culture Area, (5) the Great Basin Culture Area, and (6) the Colorado River Culture Area. These areas are geographically distinct and supported different sorts of cultures depending upon the availability of an adequate water supply, the ability to cultivate the land, and the availability of game.

35. D. The Gold Rush

The discovery of gold in California created a lust for gold that quickly brought immigrants from the eastern United States and many parts of the world. To be sure, there were struggles and conflicts, as well as the rise of nativism. Yet this vast migration of people from all parts of the world began the process that has created California's uniquely diverse culture.

36. A. The governor of California has the pocket veto.

The answer is (A) "The governor of California has the pocket veto." One of the differences between the California constitution and the U.S. Constitution concerns the executive power to veto and nullify legislation enacted by the legislature. The pocket veto, a policy that permits the President of the United States to nullify an act of Congress by simply withholding signature on a bill, is not shared by the Governor of California. Although the Governor of California does not have this particular power, the Governor holds a power that has not been extended to the President of the United States. This is the "Line-Item Veto" which permits the Governor to veto individual items that are part of a piece of legislation without nullifying the entire piece of legislation.

37. A. Cabot

John Cabot (1450-1498) was the English explorer who gave England claim to North American and the first European to see Florida and sail along its coast. (B) Columbus (1451-1506) was sent by the Spanish to the New World and has received false credit for "discovering America" in 1492, although he did open up the New World to European expansion, exploitation, and Christianity. (C) Ponce de Leon (1460-1521), the Spanish explorer, was the first European to actually land on Florida. (D) Panfilo de Narvaez (1470-1528) was also a Spanish conquistador, but he was sent to Mexico to force Cortes into submission. He failed and was captured.

38. C. America bought it from Spain

Spain received $5 million dollars for Florida, mostly to pay for damages incurred during the war. Following the War of 1812, Spain actually ceded Florida to the United States as part of the treaty. Florida, while under Spanish control, had been a difficult issue for the United States. Runaway slaves would often seek refuge there and the Seminole Indians of Florida would attack Georgia from the South. Therefore, in 1819, the Spanish agreed to put Florida into US hands as part of a treaty to stop the fighting between the two nations. Andrew Jackson, the hero of the War of 1812 became the first governor of Florida.

39. A. Metropolitan Government

Metropolitan Government was the form of local government that acts as an intermediary between the state and the city and comes from the idea of municipal home rule first enacted by Missouri in 1875. As suburbs grew and cities declined a bit, it became more important to have an intermediary between the city and state governments.

40. C. Iroquois and Algonquin

The area now known as the State of New York was initially inhabited by several tribes that were part of one of two major Native American Nations. These were the Iroquois Nation and the Algonquian Nation. (A) Sioux and Pawnee tribal lands were found primarily in Minnesota and Nebraska respectively. (B) Micmac and Wampanoag are tribes primarily found in New England and Canada. (D) Nez Perce and Cherokee were found in the Pacific Northwest and the Eastern parts of the United States respectively.

41. C. The Harlem Renaissance

As African Americans left the rural South and migrated to the North in search of opportunity, many settled in Harlem in New York City. By the 1920s Harlem had become a center of life and activity for persons of color. The music, art, and literature of this community gave birth to a cultural movement known as the Harlem Renaissance. (A) The Revolution War (1776) occurred prior to the Civil War. (B) The Second Great Awakening occurred in the 1920s but like the (D) Gilded Age (1878 – 1889) affected the entire United States.

42. B. To establish trade

The Europeans came to the New World for a number of reasons; often they came to find new natural resources to extract for manufacturing. The Portuguese, Spanish and English were sent over to increase the monarch's power and spread influences such as religion (Christianity) and culture. Therefore, the only reason given that Europeans didn't come to the New World was to establish trade.

43. D. An influx of Oakies

The answer is "An influx of Oakies" (D). The Dust Bowl of the Great Plains destroyed agriculture in the area. People living in the plains areas lost their livelihood and many lost their homes and possessions in the great dust storms that resulted from a period of extended drought. People from all of the states affected by the Dust Bowl made their way to California in search of a better life. Because the majority of the people were from Oklahoma, they were all referred to as "Oakies." These migrants brought with them their distinctive plains culture. The great influx of people seeking jobs exacerbated the effects of the Great Depression in California.

44. B. The London Company granted the colony a charter making it independent.

In the year 1619, the Southern colony of Virginia had an eventful year including the first arrival of twenty African slaves, the right to self-governance through representative government in the Virginia House of Burgesses (their own legislative body), and the arrival of sixty women sent to marry and establish families in the colony. The London Company did not, however, grant the colony a charter in 1619.

45. A. The Age of Absolutism

The "divine right" of kings was the key political characteristic of The Age of Absolutism and was most visible in the reign of King Louis XIV of France, as well as during the times of King James I and his son, Charles I. The divine right doctrine claims that kings and absolute leaders derive their right to rule by virtue of their birth alone. They see this both as a law of God and of nature.

46. A. Plentiful cheap, unskilled labor was no longer needed by industrialists

The primary reason that the United States almost completely stopped all immigration during the 1920s was because their once, much needed, cheap, unskilled labor jobs, made available by the once booming industrial economy, were no longer needed. This has much to do with the increased use of machines to do the work once done by cheap, unskilled laborers.

47. A. Economic depressions and slow resumption of trade and financial aid

Following World War II, the economy was vibrant and flourished from the stimulant of war and an increased dependence of the world on United States industries. Therefore, World War II didn't result in economic depressions and slow resumption of trade and financial aid. Western Europe was no longer the center of world power. New power struggles arose in Europe and Asia and many European nations underwent changing territories and boundaries.

48. C. Manifest Destiny

The belief that the United States should control all of North America was called (B) Manifest Destiny. This idea fueled much of the violence and aggression towards those already occupying the lands such as the Native Americans. Manifest Destiny was certainly driven by sentiments of (D) nationalism and gave rise to (A) westward expansion.

49. C. Utility

As used in the social science of economics, (C) utility is the measurement of happiness or satisfaction a person receives from consuming a good or service. The decision of the student to increase his satisfaction by buying a second candy bar relates to this concept because he is spending money to increase his happiness.

50. B. Historiography

Historiography is a term used to refer to the actual writing of history as well as the study of this type of writing. (A) Public policy analysis is part of political science. (B) Historical perspective refers to the prevailing viewpoint of a historical time, and (D) historical analysis concerns the interpretation of historical events.

51. A. Molecular biophysics

Molecular biophysics is an interdisciplinary field combining the fields of biology, chemistry and physics. These are all natural sciences, and not social sciences

52. D. Letters from a nineteenth century Egyptologist to his wife

Historians use primary sources from the actual time they are studying whenever possible. (A) Ancient Greek records of interaction with Egypt, (B) letters from an Egyptian ruler to regional governors, and (C) inscriptions from the Fourteenth Egyptian Dynasty are all primary sources created at or near the actual time being studied. (D) Letters from a nineteenth century Egyptologist would not be considered primary sources, as they were created thousands of years after the fact and may not actually be about the subject being studied.

Mathematics

53. Find the LCD of $\dfrac{^-4}{9}$ and $\dfrac{^-7}{10}$. The LCD is 90, so you get

$\dfrac{^-40}{90} + \dfrac{^-63}{90} = \dfrac{^-103}{90}$, which is answer **D**.

54. Simple multiplication. The answer will be negative because a positive times a negative is a negative number. $5.6 \times ^- 0.11 = ^- 0.616$, which is answer **A**.

55. Use $(1 - x)$ as the discount. $375x = 120$.
$375(1 - x) = 120 \rightarrow 375 - 375x = 120 \rightarrow 375x = 255 \rightarrow x = 0.68 = 68\%$
which is answer **C**.

56. Let x = # of students in the 8 am class and $x - 40$ = # of student in the 10 am class. $x + (x - 40) = 410 \rightarrow 2x - 40 = 410 \rightarrow 2x = 450 \rightarrow x = 225$. So there are 225 students in the 8 am class, and $225 - 40 = 185$ in the 10 am class, which is answer **C**.

57. Degrees measures angles, square meters measures area, cubic feet measure volume, and kilometers measures length. Kilometers is the only reasonable answer, which is **C**.

58. Area = length times width (*lw*).
Length = 13 feet
Width = 13 feet (square, so length and width are the same).
Area = $13 \times 13 = 169$ square feet.
Area is measured in square feet. So the answer is **B.**

59. The smallest number in this set is 16; its factors are 1, 2, 4, 8 and 16. 16 in the largest factor, but it does not divide into 28 or 36. Neither does 8. 4 does factor into both 28 and 36. The answer is **B.**

60. Solve for *x*.

$$4x - (3 - x) = 7(x - 3) + 10$$

$$4x - 3 + x = 7x - 21 + 10$$

$$5x - 3 = 7x - 11$$

$$5x = 7x - 11 + 3 \qquad \text{The answer is } \mathbf{C.}$$

$$5x - 7x = {}^{-}8$$

$${}^{-}2x = {}^{-}8$$

$$x = 4$$

61. We are given *d* = 585 miles and *r* = 65 miles per hour and *d =rt*. Solve for *t*. $585 = 65t \rightarrow t = 9$ hours, which is answer **D.**

62. The number of tourists in 1991 was 1,000,000 and the number in 1994 was 1,600,000. Subtract to get a difference of 600,000, which is answer **B.**

63. **There are 4 aces in the 52 card deck.**

P(first ace) = $\dfrac{4}{52}$. P(second ace) = $\dfrac{3}{51}$.
P(first ace and second ace) = P(one ace)xP(second ace|first ace)
$= \dfrac{4}{52} \times \dfrac{3}{51} = \dfrac{1}{221}$. This is answer **B.**

64. A. $400

Let x be the wholesale price, then x + .30x = 520, 1.30x = 520. divide both sides by 1.30.

65. A. $500

12(40) = 480 which is closest to $500.

66. B. median

The median provides the best measure of central tendency in this case where the mode is the lowest number and the mean would be disproportionately skewed by the outlier $120,000.

67. C. George spends twice as much on utilities as he does on food

George spends twice as much on utilities as on food.

68. A. 2/9

In this example of conditional probability, the probability of drawing a black sock on the first draw is 5/10. It is implied in the problem that there is no replacement, therefore the probability of obtaining a black sock in the second draw is 4/9. Multiply the two probabilities and reduce to lowest terms.

69. D. $x < -\frac{7}{2}$ or $x > \frac{1}{2}$

The quantity within the absolute value symbols must be either > 4 or < -4. Solve he two inequalities $2x + 3 > 4$ or $2x + 3 < -4$.

70. A.

Solve by adding -7 to each side of the inequality. Since the absolute value of x is less than 6, x must be between -6 and 6. The end points are not included so the circles on the graph are hollow.

71. B. 15 mph

Let x = the speed of the boat in still water and c = the speed of the current.

	rate	time	distance
upstream	x - c	3	30
downstream	x + c	1.5	30

Solve the system:

$$3x - 3c = 30$$
$$1.5x + 1.5c = 30$$

72. B. (1, 6)

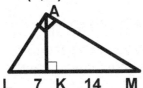

73. D. 3000 m

To change kilometers to meters, move the decimal 3 places to the right.

74. C. 15 grams a cookie is measured in grams.

75. C. four times the original

If the radius of a right circular cylinder is doubled, the volume is multiplied by four because in he formula, the radius is squared, therefore the new volume is 2 x 2 or four times the original.

76. A. x : y   The sides are in the same ratio.

77. D. (9/2, 1/2)   Using the midpoint formula

$$x = (2 + 7)/2 \quad y = (5 + -4)/2$$

78. D. $\varnothing$

Multiplying the top equation by -4 and adding results in the equation 0 = -33. Since this is a false statement, the correct choice is the null set.

79. C. Polar covalent bonding

Each carbon atom contains four valence electrons, while each hydrogen atom contains one valence electron. A carbon atom can bond with one or more hydrogen atoms, such that two electrons are shared in each bond. This is covalent bonding, because the electrons are shared. (In ionic bonding, atoms must gain or lose electrons to form ions. The ions are then electrically attracted in oppositely charged pairs.) Covalent bonds are always polar when between two non-identical atoms, so this bond must be polar. ("Polar" means that the electrons are shared unequally, forming a pair of partial charges, i.e. poles.) In any case, the strong nuclear force is not relevant to this problem. The answer to this question is therefore (C).

80. D. Strep throat.

Influenza, A.I.D.S., and the "common cold" (rhinovirus infection), are all caused by viruses. (This is the reason that doctors should not be pressured to prescribe antibiotics for colds or 'flu—i.e. they will not be effective since the infections are not bacterial.) Strep throat (properly called 'streptococcal throat' and caused by streptococcus bacteria) is not a virus, but a bacterial infection.

81. C. Mendel.

Gregor Mendel was a nineteenth-century Austrian botanist, who derived "laws" governing inherited traits. His work led to the understanding of dominant and recessive traits, carried by biological markers. Mendel cross-bred different kinds of pea plants with varying features and observed the resulting new plants. He showed that genetic characteristics are not passed identically from one generation to the next. (Pasteur, Watson, Crick, and Mendeleev were other scientists with different specialties.)

82. B. It is a known carcinogen.

Formaldehyde is a known carcinogen, so it is too dangerous for use in schools. In general, teachers should not use carcinogens in school laboratories. Although formaldehyde also smells unpleasant, a smell alone is not a definitive marker of danger. For example, many people find the smell of vinegar to be unpleasant, but vinegar is considered a very safe classroom/laboratory chemical. Furthermore, some odorless materials are toxic. Formaldehyde is neither particularly expensive nor explosive. Thus, the **answer is (B)**.

83. AA. Transfer RNA (tRNA).

The job of tRNA is to carry and position amino acids to/on the ribosomes. mRNA copies DNA code and brings it to the ribosomes; rRNA is in the ribosome itself. There is no such thing as trRNA. Thus, the **answer is (A)**.

84. C. Frequency.

The Doppler Effect accounts for an apparent increase in frequency when a wave source moves toward a wave receiver or apparent decrease in frequency when a wave source moves away from a wave receiver. (Note that the receiver could also be moving toward or away from the source.) As the wave fronts are released, motion toward the receiver mimics more frequent wave fronts, while motion away from the receiver mimics less frequent wave fronts. Meanwhile, the amplitude, wavelength, and intensity of the wave are not as relevant to this process (although moving closer to a wave source makes it seem more intense). The answer to this question is therefore(C).

85. C. Distilled water.

Alcohol and hydrochloric acid should never be used to make solutions unless instructed to do so. All solutions should be made with distilled water as tap water contains dissolved particles which may affect the results of an experiment. The correct **answer is (C).**

86. D. Lowering energy of activation.

Because enzymes are catalysts, they work the same way—they cause the formation of activated chemical complexes, which require a lower activation energy. Therefore, the **answer is (D).** ATP is an energy source for cells, and pH or volume changes may or may not affect reaction rate, so these answers can be eliminated.

87. D. Radiation

Heat transfer via electromagnetic waves (which can occur even in a vacuum) is called radiation. (Heat can also be transferred by direct contact (conduction), by fluid current (convection), and by matter changing phase, but these are not relevant here.) The answer to this question is therefore (D).

88. D. Publishing work with an incomplete list of citations.

One of the most important ethical principles for scientists is to cite all sources of data and analysis when publishing work. It is reasonable to use unpublished data (A), as long as the source is cited. Most science is published before other scientists replicate it (B), and frequently scientists collaborate with each other, in the same or different laboratories (C). These are all ethical choices. However, publishing work without the appropriate citations, is unethical. Therefore, the **answer is (D).**

89. C. Vibrations

Sound waves are produced by a vibrating body. The vibrating object moves forward and compresses the air in front of it, then reverses direction so that pressure on the air is lessened and expansion of the air molecules occurs. The vibrating air molecules move back and forth parallel to the direction of motion of the wave as they pass the energy from adjacent air molecules closer to the source to air molecules farther away from the source. Therefore, the answer is (C).

90. D. According to their reactivity with other substances.

Chemicals should be stored with other chemicals of similar properties (e.g. acids with other acids), to reduce the potential for either hazardous reactions in the storeroom, or mistakes in reagent use. Certainly, chemicals should not be stored in anyone's office, and the light intensity of the room is not very important because light-sensitive chemicals are usually stored in dark containers. In fact, good lighting is desirable in a storeroom, so that labels can be read easily. Chemicals may be stored off-site, but that makes their use inconvenient. Therefore, the best answer is (D).

91. C. Temperature

To answer this question, recall that the independent variable in an experiment is the entity that is changed by the scientist, in order to observe the effects (the dependent variable(s)). In this experiment, temperature is changed in order to measure growth of bacteria, so (C) is the answer. Note that answer (A) is the dependent variable, and neither (B) nor (D) is directly relevant to the question.

92. B. 4.2.1.3.5

The correct methodology for the scientific method is first to make a meaningful hypothesis (educated guess), then plan and execute a controlled experiment to test that hypothesis. Using the data collected in that experiment, the scientist then draws conclusions and attempts to answer the original question related to the hypothesis. This is consistent only with answer (B).

93. A. Vacuoles

In a cell, the sub-parts are called organelles. Of these, the vacuoles hold stored food (and water and pigments). The Golgi Apparatus sorts molecules from other parts of the cell; the ribosomes are sites of protein synthesis; the lysosomes contain digestive enzymes. This is consistent only with answer (A).

94. C. Organelle, Cell, Tissue, Organ, System, Organism

Organelles are parts of the cell; cells make up tissue, which makes up organs. Organs work together in systems (e.g. the respiratory system), and the organism is the living thing as a whole. Therefore, the answer must be (C).

95. B. Giraffes with longer necks are able to reach more leaves, so they eat more and have more babies than other giraffes. Eventually, there are more long-necked giraffes in the population.

Although evolution is often misunderstood, it occurs via natural selection. Organisms with a life/reproductive advantage will produce more offspring. Over many generations, this changes the proportions of the population. In any case, it is impossible for a stretched neck (A) or a fervent desire (C) to result in biologically mutated baby. Although there are traits that are naturally selected because of mate attractiveness and fitness (D), this is not the primary situation here, so answer (B) is the best choice.

96. B. A nonrenewable resource is replaced on a timescale that is very long relative to human life- spans.

Renewable resources are those that are renewed, or replaced, in time for humans to use more of them. Examples include fast-growing plants, animals, or oxygen gas. (Note that while sunlight is often considered a renewable resource, it is actually a nonrenewable but extremely abundant resource.) Nonrenewable resources are those that renew themselves only on very long timescales, usually geologic timescales. Examples include minerals, metals, or fossil fuels. Therefore, the correct answer is (B).

97. A. Monera

To answer this question, first note that algae are not a kingdom of their own. Some algae are in monera, the kingdom that consists of unicellular prokaryotes with no true nucleus. Protista and fungi are both eukaryotic, with true nuclei, and are sometimes multi-cellular. Therefore, the answer is (A).

98. A. Carbon, Hydrogen, Oxygen, Nitrogen, Phosphorus

Organic matter (and life as we know it) is based on Carbon atoms, bonded to Hydrogen and Oxygen. Nitrogen and Phosphorus are the next most significant elements, followed by Sulfur and then trace nutrients such as Iron, Sodium, Calcium, and others. Therefore, the answer is (A). If you know that the formula for any carbohydrate contains Carbon, Hydrogen, and Oxygen, that will help you narrow the choices to (A) and (D) in any case.

99. D. Igneous

Few fossils are found in metamorphic rock and virtually none found in igneous rocks. Igneous rocks are formed from magma and magma is so hot that any organisms trapped by it are destroyed. Metamorphic rocks are formed by high temperatures and great pressures. When fluid sediments are transformed into solid sedimentary rocks, the process is known as lithification. The answer is (D).

100. C. Water is conserved except for chemical or nuclear reactions, and any drop of water could circulate through clouds, rain, ground water, and surface- water.

All natural chemical cycles, including the Water Cycle, depend on the principle of Conservation of Mass. (For water, unlike for elements such as Nitrogen, chemical reactions may cause sources or sinks of water molecules.) Any drop of water may circulate through the hydrologic system, ending up in a cloud, as rain, or as surface- or ground-water. Although answers (A) and (B) describe parts of the water cycle, the most comprehensive answer is (C).

101. C. How continents move apart.

In the theory of 'sea floor spreading', the movement of the ocean floor causes continents to spread apart from one another. This occurs because crust plates split apart, and new material is added to the plate edges. This process pulls the continents apart, or may create new separations, and is believed to have caused the formation of the Atlantic Ocean. Therefore, the answer is (C).

102. B. A meteorite is material from outer space that has struck the earth's surface.

Meteoroids are pieces of matter in space, composed of particles of rock and metal. If a meteoroid travels through the earth's atmosphere, friction causes burning and a "shooting star"—i.e. a meteor. If the meteor strikes the earth's surface, it is known as a meteorite. Note that although the suffix –ite often means a mineral, answer (A) is incorrect. Answer (C) refers to a 'metalloid' rather than a 'meteorite', and answer (D) is simply a misleading pun on 'meter'. Therefore, the answer is (B).

103. D. Weight

To answer this question, recall that mass number is the total number of protons and neutrons in an atom, atomic number is the number of protons in an atom, and mass is the amount of matter in an object. The only remaining choice is (D), weight, which is correct because weight is the force of gravity on an object.

104. B. Protons and Neutrons

Protons and neutrons are located in the nucleus, while electrons move around outside the nucleus. This is consistent only with answer (B).

Physical Education

105. B. Pragmatism

As a school of philosophy, is a collection of different ways of thinking. Given the diversity of thinkers and the variety of schools of thought that have adopted this term over the years, the term pragmatism has become almost meaningless in the absence of further qualification. Most of the thinkers who describe themselves as pragmatists indicate some connection with practical consequences or real effects as vital components of both meaning and truth.

106. A. Eclectic

Are so-called philosophers who attach themselves to no system in particular. Instead, they select what, in their judgment, is true of the other philosophers. In antiquity, the Eclectic philosophy is that which sought to unite into a coherent whole, the doctrines of Pythagoras, Plato, and Aristotle. There is eclecticism in art as well as philosophy. The term was applied to an Italian school which aimed at uniting the excellence of individual intellectual masters.

107. D.

Educators use cognitive development goals to describe the act of teaching children in a manner that will help them develop as personal and social beings. Concepts that fall under this term include social and emotional learning, moral reasoning/cognitive development, life-skills education, health education, violence prevention, critical thinking, ethical reasoning, and conflict resolution and mediation. This form of education involves teaching children and teenagers such values as honesty, stewardship, kindness, generosity, courage, freedom, justice, equality, and respect. Idealism is an approach to philosophical inquiry that asserts direct and immediate knowledge can only be had as ideas or mental pictures. We can only know the objects that are the basis of these ideas indirectly.

108. A.

Winning at all costs is not a desirable social skill. Instructors and coaches should emphasize fair play and effort over winning. Answers B, C, and D are all positive skills and values developed in physical activity settings.

109. C.

Golf is mainly an individual sport. Though golf involves social interaction, it generally lacks the team element inherent in basketball, soccer, and volleyball.

110. B. Through physical activities, John developed his social interaction skills.

Social interaction is the sequence of social actions between individuals (or groups) that modify their actions and reactions due to the actions of their interaction partner(s). In other words, they are events in which people attach meaning to a situation, interpret what others mean, and respond accordingly. Through socialization with other people, John feels the influence of the people around him.

111. B.

The ability of an individual to adhere to an exercise routine due to her/his excitement, accolades, etc. is not a negative psycho-social influence. Adherence to an exercise routine is healthy and positive.

112. D. The Amateur Athletic Union (AAU) is one of the largest non-profit, volunteer sports organizations in the United States.

A multi-sport organization, the AAU dedicates itself exclusively to the promotion and development of amateur sports and physical fitness programs. Answer C may be a tempting choice, but the NCAA deals only with college athletics.

113. B. AAHPERD, or American Alliance for Health, Physical Education, Recreation and Dance, is an alliance of 6 national associations.

AAHPERD is the largest organization of professionals supporting and assisting those involved in physical education, leisure, fitness, dance, health promotion, and education, as well as all other specialties related to achieving a healthy lifestyle. AAHPERD is an alliance designed to provide members with a comprehensive and coordinated array of resources, support, and programs to help practitioners improve their skills and in turn, further the health and well-being of the American public.

114. A.

Each school has a PE Update that publishes their own periodicals about physical activities. It aims at helping the students to catch-up on what is happening around them. The school produces this update to encourage their students to become more interested in all of the physical activities that they offer. School PE Updates, however, do not include research findings.

115. C. The government treats the physical education curriculum as one of the major subjects.

Because of all of the games that we now participate in, many countries have focused their hearts and set their minds on competing with rival countries. Physical education is now one of the major, important subjects and instructors should integrate physical education into the total educational process.

116. A.

The affective domain encompasses emotions, thoughts, and feelings related to physical education. Knowledge of exercise, health, and disease is part of the cognitive domain.

117. D. In order for the instructor to know each student's physical status, she takes an injury evaluation.

Such surveys are one way to know the physical status of an individual. It chronicles past injuries, tattoos, activities, and diseases the individual may have or had. It helps the instructor to know the limitations of each individual. Participant screening covers all forms of surveying and anticipation of injuries.

Art

118. D. Based on the history and cultural aspects of artwork found in the Historical and Cultural Context 3.3

119. C. Identifying tones, music, beats etc. can be related to the Artistic Perception module 1.2

120. C. Using crafting and artistic lessons can be related to Artistic Perception 1.2

121. D. Creativity and teaching upper level thinking, reasoning, and creativity lessons can be related to Creative Expression threads 2.1-2.7

122. C. Encouraging artistic creativity can be located in the framework threads 2.2

123. D. Incorporating both musical and movement approaches related to framework of dance and music. See 2.1 and 2.4

124. D.

Students in Early Childhood ages are introduced to drama and theatre using their 5 senses. Using smell, feel, sound, touch, and taste are all senses that even at the earliest ages children know and are able to relate to.

125. C.

Early Childhood students are expected to have limited understanding of their bodies and general movement of them. However early imagery is a tool that is only developed once a student begins to mature and doesn't typically happen until late elementary or early middle school age students.

126. B.

American theatre wasn't included as a type of theatre in early age drama.

127. A.

Students should be able to understand the connections made between movement and music is related by rhythm.

128. C.

Teachers often look for outside sources to help aid in their students understanding of lessons and concepts. There are many programs utilized and the artist in residence program is an example of how artists enrich the art program of study.

129. D.

Early childhood students are only expected to complete basic motor skills at ages 3-5.

130. C.

Dance is not a related area in visual arts.

Human Development

131. C

132. C. Psychologists

Psychologists study mental processes (cognitive psychology,) the mental development of children (developmental psychology,) and observe human and animal behavior in controlled circumstances (behavioral psychology.)

133. D.When they are clearly defined by the teacher and are given examples and non-examples of the concept.

Several studies have been carried out to determine the effectiveness of giving examples as well as the difference in effectiveness of various types of examples. It was found conclusively that the most effective method of concept presentation included giving a definition along with examples and non-examples and also providing an explanation of them. These same studies indicate that boring examples were just as effective as interesting examples in promoting learning. Additional studies have been conducted to determine the most effective number of examples that will result in maximum student learning. These studies concluded that a few thoughtfully selected examples are just as effective as many examples. It was determined that the actual number of examples necessary to promote student learning was relative to the learning characteristics of the learners. It was again ascertained that learning is facilitated when examples are provided along with the definition.

134. A. Reevaluate learner needs.

The value of teacher observations cannot be underestimated. It is through the use of observations that the teacher is able to informally assess the needs of the students during instruction. These observations will drive the lesson and determine the direction that the lesson will take based on student activity and behavior. After a lesson is carefully planned, teacher observation is the single most important component of an instructional presentation. If the teacher observes that a particular student is not on-task, she will change the method of instruction accordingly. She may change from a teacher-directed approach to a more interactive approach. Questioning will increase in order to increase the participation of the students. If appropriate, the teacher will introduce manipulative materials to the lesson. In addition, teachers may switch to a cooperative group activity, thereby removing the responsibility of instruction from the teacher and putting it on the students.

135. B. Social, physical, academic.

The effective teacher applies knowledge of physical, social, and academic developmental patterns and of individual differences, to meet the instructional needs of all students in the classroom and. The most important premise of child development is that all domains of development (physical, social, and academic) are integrated. The teacher has a broad knowledge and thorough understanding of the development that typically occurs during the students' current period of life. More importantly, the teacher understands how children learn best during each period of development. An examination of the student's file coupled with ongoing evaluation assures a successful educational experience for both teacher and students.

136. A. 10-12 years old.

The usual age for the fourth stage (the formal operational stage) as described by Piaget is from 10 to 12 years old. It is in this stage that children begin to be able to define abstract terms.

137. C. Ask him what is wrong.

If a teacher has developed a trusting relationship with a child, the reasons for the child's behavior may come out. It might be that the child needs to tell someone what is going on and is seeking a confidant, and a trusted teacher can intervene. If the child is unwilling to talk to the teacher about what is going on, the next step is to contact the parents, who may or may not be willing to explain why the child is the way he/she is. If they simply do not know, then it's time to add a professional physician or counselor to the mix.

138. B. Report this change immediately to administration. Do not call the parents until administration decides a course of action.

Anytime a child's disposition, attitude, or habits change significantly, teachers and parents need to seriously consider the existence of emotional difficulties. Emotional disturbances in childhood are not uncommon and take a variety of forms. Usually these problems show up in the form of uncharacteristic behaviors. Most of the time, children respond favorably to brief treatment programs of psychotherapy. At other times, disturbances may need more intensive therapy and are harder to resolve. All stressful behaviors need to be addressed, and any type of chronic antisocial behavior needs to be examined as a possible symptom of deep-seated emotional upset. In a case where the change is sudden and dramatic, administration needs to become involved.

139. C. "Robert, you did a good job staying in line. See how it helped us get to music class on time?"

Praise is a powerful tool in obtaining and maintaining order in a classroom. In addition, it is an effective motivator. It is even more effective if the positive results of good behavior are included.

140. A. Helps student become aware of important elements of content.

Because ESL students are often grouped in classes that take a different approach to teaching English than those for native speakers, it's easy to assume that they all present with the same needs and characteristics. Nothing could be further from the truth, even in what they need when it comes to learning English. It's important that their backgrounds and personalities be observed just as with native speakers. It was very surprising several years ago when Vietnamese children began arriving in American schools with little training in English and went on to excel in their classes, often even beyond their American counterparts. In many schools, there were Vietnamese merit scholars in the graduating classes.

141. A. Help students see the unique contributions of individual differences.

In the first place, an important purpose of education is to prepare students to live successfully in the real world, and this is an important insight and understanding for them to take into that world. In the second place, the most fertile learning environment is one in which all viewpoints and backgrounds are respected and where everyone has equal respect.

142. D. Include ethnic studies in the curriculum.

Exploring a student's own cultures increases their confidence levels in the group. It is also a very useful tool when students are struggling to develop identities that they can feel comfortable with. The bonus is this is good training for living.

143. B. Gardner.

Howard Gardner's most famous work is probably Frames of Mind, which details seven dimensions of intelligence (Visual/Spatial Intelligence, Musical Intelligence, Verbal Intelligence, Logical/Mathematical Intelligence, Interpersonal Intelligence, Intrapersonal Intelligence, and Bodily/Kinesthetic Intelligence). Gardner's claim that pencil and paper IQ tests do not capture the full range of human intelligences has garnered much praise within the field of education but has also met criticism, largely from psychometricians. Since the publication of Frames of Mind, Gardner has additionally identified the 8th dimension of intelligence: Naturalist Intelligence, and is still considering a possible ninth—Existentialist Intelligence.

Sample Constructed Response Questions

Directions: In the next few pages, you will see eleven constructed response prompts. You will need to prepare a short essay for each one. Each assignment will be to write a response of about 300 words on the assigned topic. Your score will be based on these following factors:

- Purpose: You will be assessed on the extent to which you answer the question on each prompt. You must write your response so that it directly addresses what the prompt asks you to do.
- Subject-Matter Knowledge: You will be assessed on the extent to which you demonstrate content knowledge.
- Support: You will be assessed on the extent to which you provide a coherent, fully supported response. Your response should provide evidence for any assertions you make.

Even though your writing ability will not be directly assessed, please take care to write an essay that is as free of grammatical errors as possible.

Reading, Language & Literature

SAMPLE ESSAY QUESTION #1
World Literature, Important Works

Read the passage below from *The Diary of Anne Frank* (1947); then complete the exercise that follows.

Written on July 15, 1944, three weeks before the Frank family was arrested by the Nazis, Anne's diary entry explains her worldview and future hopes.

It's difficult in times like these: ideals, dreams and cherished hopes rise within us, only to be crushed by grim reality. It's a wonder I haven't abandoned all my ideals, they seem so absurd and impractical. Yet I cling to them because I still believe, in spite of everything, that people are truly good at heart.

It's utterly impossible for me to build my life on a foundation of chaos, suffering and death. I see the world being slowly transformed into a wilderness, I hear the approaching thunder that, one day, will destroy us too, I feel the suffering of millions, And yet, when I look up at the sky, I somehow feel that everything will change for the better, that this cruelty too shall end, that peace and tranquility will return once more. In the meantime, I must hold on to my ideals. Perhaps the day will come when I will be able to realize them!

Using your knowledge of literature, write a response in which you:

- Compare and contrast Anne's ideals with her awareness of the conditions in which she lives; and
- discuss how the structure of Anne's writing—her sentences and paragraphs—emphasize the above contrast.

Sample Response

This excerpt from *The Diary of Anne Frank* reveals the inner strength of a young girl who refuses, despite the wartime violence and danger surrounding her, to let her idealism be overcome by hatred and mass killing. This idealism is reflected, in part, by her emphases on universal human hopes such as peace, tranquility, and goodwill. But Anne Frank is no dreamy Pollyanna. Reflecting on her idealism in the context of the war raging around her, she matter-of-factly writes: "my dreams, they seem so absurd and impractical."

This indicates Anne Frank's awareness of not only her own predicament but of human miseries that extend beyond the immediate circumstances of her life. For elsewhere she writes in a similar vein, "In times like these... I see the world being slowly transformed into a wilderness"; despite her own suffering she can "feel the suffering of millions."

And yet Anne Frank believes, "in spite of everything, that people are truly good at heart." This statement epitomizes the stark existential contrast of her worldview with the wartime reality that ultimately claimed her life.

The statement also exemplifies how Anne's literary form—her syntax and diction—mirror thematic content and contrasts. "In spite of everything," she still believes in people. She can "hear the approaching thunder...yet, when I look up at the sky, I somehow feel that everything will change for the better." At numerous points in this diary entry, first-hand knowledge of violent tragedy stands side-by-side with belief in humanity and human progress.

"I must hold on to my ideals," Anne concludes. "Perhaps the day will come when I'll be able to realize them!" In her diary she has done so, and more.

SAMPLE QUESTION #2
The Writing Process

Using your knowledge of teaching English Composition at the middle school level, write a response in which you:

- Instruct students as to effective strategies for selecting an appropriate topic for a 400-word essay; and
- relate this to three stages of composition: pre-writing, drafting, and revision

Sample Strong Response

For this assignment my first question to students is: What is an experience, person, value or interest in your life so important to you that you want others to know about it? This question dovetails with the writer's commandment: write about what you know. Of course I will emphasize this but I will also try to inspire students by insisting that writing can be more than an academic exercise. It is also a part of self-expression.

Before choosing a topic, however, one must tailor it to the length requirement of the assignment. For a 400-word personal experience essay, the general rule is: the more narrowly focused the topic, the better. This sounds quite vague, which is why the rule will be backed up with readings of brief personal essays appearing in our course textbook. In particular, essays that cover only a very short period of time will be read. Furthermore, students will be asked to judge the likely appropriateness of sample titles that indicate how much time an essay covers: "My Year as an Exchange Student in Germany" vs. "My Most Memorable Day in Berlin" are but two possible examples intended to drive home the point: in a 400-word essay less is more.

In-class discussions and brief written assignments will follow from this, thereby giving students the opportunity to study how topics are introduced and developed by experienced writers. When techniques, structures and strategies are recognized and subsequently described, students will be encouraged to imitate them—in their own words.

Much has been made, and rightly so, about the process of writing—especially regarding the stages of pre-writing, drafting, and revision. Textbook material related to this will be introduced and thoroughly explained in class. However, I must take care to avoid making these processes seem too iron-clad or programmatic; indeed, "going too far" on this point can make writing seem terribly mechanical and boring. If a student wishes to stand on her head, speak into a tape recorder, transcribe the words, then turn them into a clear, concise, and grammatically correct essay, this would be—as far as I'm concerned—perfectly acceptable. Sometimes even revision isn't necessary, if only rarely. What counts is the final product.

History and Social Science

3. Describe the rivalry between England and France

Although geographically located on opposite sides of the English Channel, historically, France and England have been on opposite sides of conflicts for the last few centuries.

One historical event was the Hundred Years' War that lasted 116 years. The Hundred Years' War was not the beginning of this conflict; it was a continuation of one that had existed since the time of the first Norman Kings of England. Every king from Henry II to Edward II had engaged in warfare against French Kings on the continent since the English laid claim to the French throne. However, by 1214, the Kings of England had lost a substantial portion of their lands in France including Normandy.

The ongoing rivalry over the years forced the Native Americans in the New World to take sides against each other in the ensuing conflicts and battles. The French and Indian War fought in North America pitted England and the young colonists against the French explorers who were laying claim to the vast lands of the Ohio Country.

When the colonists revolted against the English King in 1776, the French were willing to help the colonists fight the English.

During the War of 1812, the Americans battled Great Britain, then the world's greatest military power, especially on the high seas, while Great Britain was fighting France during the Napoleonic Wars that ultimately brought great change to Europe.

In recent history, the two countries continue to oppose each other in the latest War in Iraq, where the United Kingdom supports the United States' efforts to fight the war on terror in the Middle East and France has provided little to no support to the United States. It would seem that if there is a conflict or global issue to be had, you will find England on one side of the table and France on the other.

4. Discuss the emergence, expansion, and evolution of Islam

Islam is a monotheistic faith that traces its traditions to Abraham and considers the Jewish patriarchs and prophets, especially Moses, King Solomon and Jesus Christ as earlier "Prophets of God".

Mohammed was born in 570 CE in a small Arabian town. Around 610, **Mohammed** came to some prominence through a new religion called **Islam** or submission to the will of God and his followers were called **Moslems.** His first converts were members of his family and his friends. As the new faith began to grow, it remained a secret society. But when they began to make their faith public, they met with opposition and persecution from the pagan Arabians who feared the loss of profitable trade with the pilgrims who came to the Kaaba every year. In 622, Mohammed and his close followers fled persecution in Mecca and found refuge in **Medina.** His flight is called the **Hegira**. Mohammed took advantage of feuds between Jews and Arabs and became the ruler, making it the capital of a rapidly growing state.

Islam changed significantly. It became a fighting religion and Mohammed became a political leader. The group survived by raiding caravans on the road to Mecca and plundering nearby Jewish tribes. It attracted many converts from Bedouin tribes. By 630, Mohammed conquered Mecca and made it the religious center of Islam, toward which all Moslems turned to pray. By taking over the sacred city, Mohammed made it easier for converts to join the religion. By the time of his death in 632, most of the people of Arabia had become adherents of Islam.

Mohammed left behind a collection of revelations (**surahs**) he believed were delivered by the angel Gabriel. The **Quran** was reputedly dictated to Muhammad as the Word of God and published in a book called the **Koran.** The revelations were never dated or kept in any kind of order. After Mohammed's death they were organized by length in diminishing order. The Koran contains Mohammed's teachings on moral and theological questions, his legislation on political matters, and his comments on current events. Five basic principles of Islam are: Allah, Pray five times a day facing Mecca, Charity, Fasting during Ramadan and Pilgrimage to Mecca.

The Islamic armies spread their faith by conquering the Arabian Peninsula, Mesopotamia, Egypt, Syria and Persia by 650 CE and expanding to North Africa and most of the Iberian Peninsula by 750 CE. During this period of expansion, the Muslim conquerors established great centers of learning in the Middle East.

Math

5.

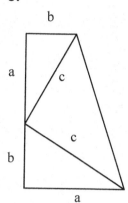

Using your knowledge of algebra and geometry:

- write an expression for the area of the trapezoid based using the formula: area = half the sum of the bases times the altitude
- write an expression for the area of the trapezoid in terms of the area of its component parts (the three triangles); and
- set these two expressions equal and show that this leads to a proof of the Pythagorean theorem.

Response:
The expression for the area of the trapezoid would be:

$$A = \frac{1}{2}(b_1 + b_2)(h) = \frac{1}{2}(a+b)(a+b) = \frac{1}{2}(a^2 + 2ab + b^2) = \frac{1}{2}a^2 + ab + \frac{1}{2}b^2$$

To determine the area of the trapezoid by adding the sum of the areas of each triangle, we use the formula $A = \frac{1}{2}bh$:

$$A = \frac{1}{2}ab + \frac{1}{2}ab + \frac{1}{2}c^2$$

By setting the two expressions equal to each other, we prove the Pythagorean Theorem:

$$\frac{1}{2}a^2 + ab + \frac{1}{2}b^2 = \frac{1}{2}ab + \frac{1}{2}ab + \frac{1}{2}c^2$$

$$\frac{1}{2}a^2 + ab + \frac{1}{2}b^2 = ab + \frac{1}{2}c^2$$

$$\frac{1}{2}a^2 + \frac{1}{2}b^2 = \frac{1}{2}c^2$$

$$a^2 + b^2 = c^2$$

Rationale

The response is considered to be good because it demonstrates the respondent's knowledge of the subject matter (algebra and geometry) and addresses the specific questions asked by the test. The thinking behind the process and the derivation of the answers are fully explained in a clear and concise manner. All areas of the calculations and proof are covered.

6. Solve the following problem using the diagram below:

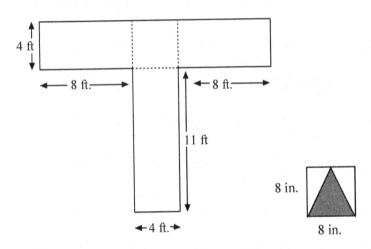

A homeowner wants to cover her foyer with 8" by 8" tiles composed of three triangular tiles of two sizes. All the tiles must be of equal size and cover the area without being cut or overlapping.

Using your knowledge of number theory and geometry:

- determine how many square tiles made up of triangles are needed to cover the area of the foyer; and
- prove that the larger, colored tiles compose exactly one-half of each square.

Sample Response

First, determine the area of each square tile. The area of a square is equal to a side squared. Since each tile is 8 inches by 8 inches, the area of the tile would be 64 square inches.

Next, determine the area of the foyer. In order to maintain the pattern, we need to determine area by section. The two ends of the top of the "T" are 8 feet by 4 feet, so each of their areas is 32 square feet. Since the tiles are measured in square inches, we need to convert the area of the foyer to square inches: 32 times 144 equals 4,608 square inches. The area of the middle section of the top of the "T" is 4 feet times 4 feet, or 16 square feet, or 2,304 square inches. The area of the stem of the "T" is 4 feet times 11 feet, or 44 square feet, or 6,336 square inches.

The total area of the foyer is the sum of the areas of each section: 4,608 + 4,608 + 2,304 + 6,336 = 17,856 square inches. To determine the number of square tiles we need, we divide the area of the foyer by the area of a tile: 17,856 ÷ 64 = 279 tiles.

To prove that the larger, colored triangle is exactly half the area of one of the square tiles, find the area of the triangle. The area of a triangle is equal to one-half the base times the height: ½(8 X 8) = ½(64) = 32 square inches. The area of the square tile is 64 square inches. Thirty-two is one-half of sixty-four. Therefore, the area of the triangle is exactly half the area of the square tile.

Rationale

The response is considered to be good because it demonstrates the respondent's knowledge of the subject matter (number sense and geometry) and addresses the specific questions asked by the test. The thinking behind the process and the derivation of the answers are fully explained in a clear and concise manner. All areas of the calculations and proof are covered.

Science

7. Using your knowledge of taxonomy and evolution, interpret the diagram below and discuss probable lineages.

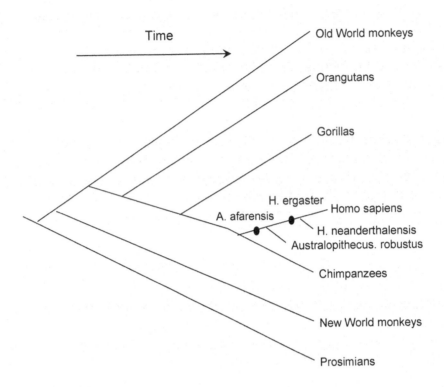

Response:
Carolus Linnaeus is termed the father of taxonomy. Taxonomy is the science of classification. Linnaeus based his system on morphology (study of structure). Later on, evolutionary relationships (phylogeny) were also used to sort and group species. The modern classification system uses binomial nomenclature. This consists of a two word name for every species. The genus is the first part of the name and the species is the second part. Notice in the levels explained below that Homo sapiens is the scientific name for humans. Starting with the kingdom, the groups get smaller and more alike as one moves down the levels in the classification of humans:

Kingdom: Animalia, Phylum: Chordata, Subphylum: Vertebrata, Class: Mammalia, Order: Primate, Family: Hominidae, Genus: Homo, Species: sapiens

The typical graphic product of a classification is a phylogenetic tree, which represents a hypothesis of the relationships based on branching of lineages through time within a group. One derives additional detail from a cladogram (such as the diagram given). Evolutionary pathways are discovered by following character states, which are categorized as plesiomorphous (ancestral features), symplesiomorphous (shared ancestral features), apomorphous (derived characteristics), and synapomorphous (shared, derived features).

Biological characteristics are also used to classify organisms. Protein comparison, DNA comparison, and analysis of fossilized DNA are powerful comparative methods used to measure evolutionary relationships between species. Taxonomists consider the organism's life history, biochemical (DNA) makeup, behavior, and how the organisms are distributed geographically. The fossil record is also used to show evolutionary relationships.

Phylogenetic trees demonstrate the evolutionary relationships between organisms. Every time you see a phylogenetic tree, you should be aware that it is making statements on the degree of similarity between organisms, or the particular pattern in which the various lineages diverged (phylogenetic history). All organisms on a branch share a common ancestor. This common ancestor is often extinct and/or unknown. Also, the length between organisms corresponds to the estimated time between their evolutionary divergences. For example, in the primate tree above, we see that while humans and New World monkeys do share a common ancestor, it was tens of millions of years ago. Humans are much more closely related to chimpanzees as can be seen by their close proximity on the phylogenetic tree. This shows that these two species more recently diverged from their common ancestor. Also notice that several ancestors of Homo sapiens are present on the tree. Two branches, those for Australopithecus robustus and H. neanderthalensis do not reach all the way to the present day, indicating that they are extinct and have no living descendents. Two additional species, A. afarensis and H. ergaster are shown as nodes as the tree, as they are extinct, but do have a living descendent in Homo sapiens. A complete phylogenetic tree would include all known primate species members, both alive and extinct.

8. Using your accumulated knowledge, discuss the components of biogeochemical cycles.

Essential elements are recycled through an ecosystem. At times, the element needs to be made available in a useable form. Cycles are dependent on plants, algae and bacteria to fix nutrients for use by animals. The four main cycles are: water, carbon, nitrogen, and phosphorous.

Two percent of all the water is fixed in ice or the bodies of organisms, rendering it unavailable. Available water includes surface water (lakes, ocean, and rivers) and ground water (aquifers, wells). The majority (96%) of all available water is from ground water. Water is recycled through the processes of evaporation and precipitation. The water present now is the water that has been here since our atmosphere was formed.

Ten percent of all available carbon in the air (in the form of carbon dioxide gas) is fixed by photosynthesis. Plants fix carbon in the form of glucose, animals eat the plants and are able to obtain the carbon necessary to sustain themselves. When animals release carbon dioxide through respiration, the cycle begins again as plants recycle the carbon through photosynthesis.

Eighty percent of the atmosphere is in the form of nitrogen gas. Nitrogen must be fixed and taken out of the gaseous form to be incorporated into an organism. Only a few genera of bacteria have the correct enzymes to break the strong triple bond between nitrogen atoms. These special bacteria live within the roots of legumes (peas, beans, alfalfa) and add bacteria to the soil so it may be taken-up by the plant. Nitrogen is necessary in the building of amino acids and the nitrogenous bases of DNA.

Phosphorus exists as a mineral and is not found in the atmosphere. Fungi and plant roots have structures called mycorrhizae that are able to fix insoluble phosphates into useable phosphorus. Urine and decayed matter returns phosphorus to the earth where it can be fixed in the plant. Phosphorus is needed for the backbone of DNA and for the manufacture of ATP.

The four biogeochemical cycles are present concurrently. Water is continually recycled, and is utilized by organisms to sustain life. Carbon is also a necessary component for life. Both water and carbon can be found in the air and on the ground. Nitrogen and phosphorous are commonly found in the ground. Special organisms, called decomposers, help to make these elements available in the environment. Plants use the recycled materials for energy and when they are consumed, the cycle begins again.

Physical Education and Health

9. Evan is a 10-year-old fifth grade student who recently completed a physical fitness evaluation in his physical education class. Evan was able to perform 6 push-ups and no pull-ups. He completed the mile run in 6:58. The evaluation also showed that Evan had below average flexibility.

Evan is a physically active child, participating in tennis and soccer outside of school. Evan is a very talented athlete looking to improve his performance in his sporting activities. Evan is also a very reserved, shy child who does not make friends easily or interact much with other children. In addition, Evan's parents feel Evan is an unusually gifted tennis player and should stop playing soccer to focus on tennis.

Based on your knowledge of physical fitness construct a written response that addresses the following:

- interpret the results of Evan's fitness evaluation; determine the components of fitness that Evan needs to address

- identify two age-appropriate fitness activities that will help Evan achieve his goals

- advise Evan's parents on their desire to have Evan focus on tennis taking into account the social and psychological aspects of participation in sports and fitness activities

Sample Response

The results of Evan's physical fitness assessment show that he has a high level of cardiovascular endurance (good mile run time), a low level of muscular endurance (poor results on push-up and pull-up test), and a low level of flexibility. Thus, a fitness program for Evan should focus on developing muscular endurance and flexibility. In addition, because Evan participates in soccer and tennis, he likely receives more than enough aerobic activity in these aerobically intensive sports.

Flexibility and muscular endurance are important, and often overlooked, aspects of tennis and soccer. Thus, developing these areas will improve Evan's athletic performance. Because Evan is only 10-years-old, I would recommend he engage in body support exercises, rather than resistance training exercises, to increase his muscular endurance. Such exercises include push-ups, pull-ups, sit-ups, lunges, and squats. I would not recommend weight training for a 10-year-old because lifting weights is dangerous and possibly detrimental for developing bodies. Evan should also engage in a regular stretching program after his tennis and soccer practices and matches. Stretching improves flexibility and stretching after physical activity is safest and most effective.

Finally, I would advise Evan's parents that he should continue to play both soccer and tennis. Sport specialization is not necessary at Evan's age to maximize performance and asking Evan to give up soccer could have other detrimental effects. Because Evan is shy and reserved, the social aspects of a team sport like soccer are important to his development. Participation in team sports promotes the development of social skills, leadership, teamwork, and interpersonal relationships. Evan will benefit from such interaction with other children and will improve his self-esteem, especially because he is a talented player. While tennis is an excellent sport, it is mainly an individual sport, and the opportunity for socialization and the development of friendships is limited.

Visual Arts

10. Using your knowledge of theatre and theatre education:

*Explain how young students should learn to describe theatrical experiences. Give specific examples.

*How does that relate to differences regarding character development.

Sample Response
Early Childhood students are the target on a broad range of new theatrical experiences. They are young and eager to learn about the world or art, artists' works, theatre, and illustration. Using a wide variety of methods a teacher should be able to teach early childhood students to describe theatrical experiences. The first method used should be exposure. The teacher should expose students to a wide variety of experiences in the arts. Beginning with theatre rich literature. Students have so much to gain from being read to. Many students first experience with literature being read aloud begins in early childhood classes. Teachers should imitate characters and voices in stories giving students examples of what a character should look, sound, and feel like in a great story. Another experience that is easily offered by teachers is the treat of puppetry. A small puppet stage in a classroom spreads excitement and allows students to watch teachers and peers model the theatre and character experiences. Students should be expected to retell stories, act out characters in stories, books, and fables. They also should being to explore early versions of character experiences like illustrating their own stories or a story for someone else. Class drama experiences should include each child having the opportunity to act out a selection of a play or story. Each child should use their five senses to explore and act out the desired effect of the story. For example, in the story of the Three Bears and Goldilocks, students should explain how he or she relates to the little pig or character he or she plays. Students should describe how small the cottage of the bears seems, how the smell of the porridge was so sweet, and how the feel of the little bed enticed Goldilocks into the bed. Using vivid descriptions involving the senses allows students to begin to truly feel the part they are portraying and also allows the audience to become engulfed in the listening experience. All of the above mentioned experiences allow early childhood students to develop not only a love for literature and drama experiences but it also guides them to discern between reality and fantasy and between real people and fictional characters.

Human Development

11. Consider the academic and the social benefits of cooperative work. Describe how children benefit cognitively, socially, and developmentally when they work with their peers on both academic assignments and in extracurricular work. Provide an example of an appropriate cooperative learning situation that would benefit a student's academic growth, as well as a student's social growth.

Sample Response

Social development cannot be explicitly taught. Rather, children need to experience different social situations and receive various opportunities to interact with one another, preferably in environments in which they can receive some adult guidance.

When children work together on academic activities, they not only enhance their learning experiences, they also get good experience in negotiating tasks, maintaining decorum, and interacting with people who have different viewpoints. Their learning experiences are enhanced for two main reasons. First, by working with students who have different beliefs, backgrounds, and opinions, they will be exposed to different ways of thinking about similar topics. Second, students with varying abilities will receive opportunities to enhance their own levels of knowledge. For example, a highly proficient student may get opportunities to teach other students in a group. Or a student who needs additional help may be able to receive it from others in the group.

From a social perspective, however, when working in groups, students must learn how to say appropriate things to one another, practice patience, respond to other group members' needs, and agree upon certain basic standards of operation. At home, most students only have to interact with their siblings, and such interaction is usually mediated by a parent. Therefore, educators are in a perfect position to help mold students' social behaviors in group learning environments.

In extracurricular environments, such as in Physical Education and Art, students get even greater opportunities to learn to work together and depend on one another. It is important for children to have structured group interaction time in a variety of capacities, including non-academic ones. In these environments, students learn how to suppress their own desires so that groups can function properly. It is extremely important, however, that students be monitored in group activities as such activities are learning experiences. All children need adults to assist them in understanding what appropriate behavior really is.

An example of a group project that would assist students in their social and cognitive development might be a group art project. For the example, let us consider using a fourth grade class. Students have been divided up into groups of four. Each group must create a diorama on a book that has just been read by the class. After modeling for the students what the teacher expects, the teacher gives students plenty of time in which to complete the work.

This project will be beneficial for students' understanding of literature in two primary ways. First, it will help students, as a group, internalize and interpret the book. Second, it will allow students the opportunity to work together in determining an appropriate way to express what it is that they know and believe about the book. In addition to literary knowledge, students will grow socially. They will be forced to work collaboratively to make decisions on how they will interpret the book. More importantly, they will have to negotiate how the work gets done, how it will be presented, and how it will demonstrate their knowledge. To do so will require that each group comes to an agreement on many elements, including opinions and understandings of the book, as well as how the book should be represented by art. Of course, it is important that students learn about literature and reading; however, this type of project is extraordinarily invaluable for the social development of children. Perhaps this is a more "real-world" experience than they would get if they were asked to do this project on their own.

XAMonline, INC. 21 Orient Ave. Melrose, MA 02176

Toll Free number 800-301-4647

TO ORDER Fax 781-662-9268 OR www.XAMonline.com

CALIFORNIA SUBJECT EXAMINATIONS   - CSET - 2007

PO#   Store/School:

Address 1:

Address 2 (Ship to other):

City, State Zip

Credit card number_____-_____-_____-_____   expiration_____

EMAIL _____

PHONE   **FAX**

ISBN #	TITLE	Qty	Retail	Total
978-1-58197-816-2	RICA Reading Instruction Competence Assessment		$34.95	
978-1-58197-800-1	CBEST CA Basic Educational Skills		$19.95	
978-1-58197-901-5	CSET French Sample Test 149, 150		$15.00	
978-1-58197-802-5	CSET Spanish 145, 146, 147		$34.95	
978-1-58197-803-2	CSET MSAT Multiple Subject 101, 102, 103		$24.95	
978-1-58197-815-5	CSET MSAT Multiple Subject 101, 102, 103 Sample Questions		$24.95	
978-1-58197-804-9	CSET English 105, 106, 107		$59.95	
978-1-58197-805-6	CSET Foundational-Level Mathematics 110, 111		$59.95	
978-1-58197-806-5	CSET Mathematics 110, 111, 112		$59.95	
978-1-58197-807-0	CSET Social Science 114, 115		$59.95	
978-1-58197-808-7	CSET General Science 118, 119		$59.95	
978-1-58197-809-4	CSET Biology-Life Science 120, 124		$59.95	
978-1-58197-395-2	CSET Chemistry 121, 125		$73.50	
978-1-58197-810-0	CSET Earth and Planetary Science 122, 126		$34.95	
978-1-58197-811-7	CSET Physics 123, 127		$15.00	
978-1-58197-812-4	CSET Physical Education, 129, 130, 131		$59.95	
978-1-58197-813-1	CSET Art Sample Subtest 140		$15.00	
978-1-58197-814-8	CSET Home Economics 181, 182, 183		$34.95	
			SUBTOTAL	
			Ship	$8.25
			TOTAL	

CPSIA information can be obtained
at www.ICGtesting.com
Printed in the USA
BVOW04s1930300617

488233BV00003B/203/P

9 781581 978032